CRIMINAL PROCEDURE

Examples and Explanations

CRIMINAL PROCEDURE

Examples and Explanations
Third Edition

Robert M. Bloom
Professor of Law
Boston College Law School

Mark S. Brodin
Professor of Law
Boston College Law School

PUBLISHERS

1185 Avenue of the Americas, New York, NY 10036
www.aspenpublishers.com

Permissions
Aspen Publishers
1185 Avenue of the Americas
New York, NY   10036

Printed in the United States of America.

ISBN 0-7355-1318-X

3 4 5 6 7 8 9 0

Library of Congress Cataloging-in-Publication Data

Bloom, Robert M., 1946–
    Criminal procedure : examples and explanations / Robert M. Bloom, Mark S. Brodin.—
3rd ed.
        p. cm.
    Includes index.
    ISBN 0-7355-1318-X
    1. Searches and seizures—United States—Problems, exercises, etc.
    2. Police questioning—United States—Problems, exercises, etc.
    3. Confession (Law)—United States—Problems, exercises, etc.
    4. Criminal procedure—United States—Problems, exercises, etc.
    I. Brodin, Mark S., 1947- II. Title.

KF9630.Z9 B58 2000
345.73′0522—dc21   00-044204

About Aspen Law & Business
Legal Education Division

With a dedication to preserving and strengthening the long-standing tradition of publishing excellence in legal education, Aspen Law & Business continues to provide the highest quality teaching and learning resources for today's law school community. Careful development, meticulous editing, and an unmatched responsiveness to the evolving needs of today's discerning educators combine in the creation of our outstanding casebooks, coursebooks, textbooks, and study aids.

ASPEN LAW & BUSINESS
A Division of Aspen Publishers, Inc.
A Wolters Kluwer Company
www.aspenpublishers.com

We specially dedicate this edition to the memory of our dear friend and colleague, Sanford J. Fox. In his extraordinarily distinguished academic career, he demonstrated great intellect, curiosity, courage, and principle. His tireless fight for the rights of children throughout the world is a constant inspiration. Sandy was an elegant and decent man who always stood up for what he believed in. He will be greatly missed.

—R.M.B.
—M.S.B.

July 2000

Summary of Contents

Contents

PART ONE
*Search and Seizure — The Framework
of the Fourth Amendment*

PART TWO
Interrogation and Confessions

Contents

PART THREE
Other Investigative Procedures

Table of Figures

Preface

No area of the law evokes more passionate debate about the balance between the prerogatives of government and the liberty of the individual than constitutional criminal procedure. The social and political history of the United States in the past four decades has been written in significant part by the opinions of the Supreme Court, adjusting and readjusting this balance. As the Court under Chief Justice Warren gave definition to the 1960s with landmark "civil liberties" decisions like *Mapp v. Ohio* and *Miranda,* so the Rehnquist Court has reflected the transformation of the political landscape in its decisions of the 1980s and 1990s, lifting many constraints on the police in their "war on crime and drugs." With the curtailment of civil liberties protections by the United States Supreme Court, state courts in recent years have turned to their own constitutions to reassert safeguards against the excesses of law enforcement.

Although there is undeniably an ideological dimension to the cases in this area, there is also a wealth of legal doctrine that must be mastered by student and practitioner. It is the purpose of this book to facilitate this mastery, while at the same time keeping the reader focused on the overarching policy issues raised in the cases.

The format of this book is a combination of text, examples, and explanations. Each chapter begins with an accessible summary of the controlling law. That summary is followed by a set of examples of increasing difficulty that explore the basic concepts, and then challenge the reader to apply them to hypothetical situations (frequently derived from reported cases) in the ever-present gray areas. The explanations permit students to both check their own work and provide additional insights not developed in the text. The goal is to convey the richness of the evolving case law while at the same time helping to demystify this highly complex domain of law. We aim, in short, to stimulate the Socratic classroom at its best.

The book's organization is designed to assist the student in the critical task of problem solving. This is accomplished by breaking down the constitutional analysis of police conduct into component issues. The "search and seizure" chapters of the book, for example, are organized to first pose the threshold issue of applicability, and then deal with the discrete questions of justification and the warrant requirement. Similarly, the chapters on "interrogation and confessions" sequentially follow the questions that must be resolved to determine the admissibility of a statement obtained by the police.

The ***Third Edition*** takes account of the significant judicial developments and trends since 1995 by way of new text, examples, and explanations. It also adds a new chapter concerning emerging issues raised by sophisticated law enforcement technology at the start of the new millennium.

Mark Brodin wishes to gratefully acknowledge three mentors who kindled his interest in and shaped his thoughts about the criminal law: Joseph L. Tauro, Moe Tandler, and the late Reuben Goodman. He dedicates this edition affectionately to Andrea, Rachel, Laura, Shirley, Susie, and to the memory of his late father, Hy.

Bob Bloom wishes to recognize two colleagues and mentors, Dean Richard G. Huber and the late Professor James Houghteling, who have been supportive throughout his career. He dedicates this edition to his wife Christina Jameson, his children, David and Martha, and to the memory of his uncle Victor Katz and his father-in-law Paul Jameson.

Mark Brodin
Robert Bloom

May 2000

1

Overview of Constitutional Criminal Procedure

Consider the following situation: One afternoon two city police officers, while patrolling in a marked cruiser, observe a car pull up to a street corner. A man emerges from the car and begins talking with an individual whom the officers recognize as Michael Chestnut, identified by an informant as the main narcotics dealer in that neighborhood. The first man hands Chestnut a large leather pouch and promptly departs. Chestnut, observing the police cruiser, begins running in the opposite direction. The officers follow Chestnut and overtake him. They inform him that he is under arrest, handcuff him, and take the pouch, which they open to find several plastic bags filled with a white powder. Chestnut is brought to the station house and booked for unlawful possession of narcotics. He is then taken into an interrogation room where he is questioned by a detective, and he makes several incriminating statements. The substance seized from Chestnut is sent to the police lab and is determined to be cocaine. Chestnut is charged with narcotic offenses in violation of state law.

Before the 1960s Chestnut's encounter with the police would represent the first step in a criminal justice process that in many states focused exclusively on the question of Chestnut's guilt or innocence. The way in which the police conducted the arrest, search, and interrogation of Chestnut would not be pertinent to the proceedings, unless made so by local law. Given the circumstances described above,

1

either a guilty plea or a verdict of guilt after trial would be the likely conclusion of the process.

The criminal justice system in the United States underwent a transformation in the 1960s, a "revolution from above" initiated by the U.S. Supreme Court. By the end of a decade of ground-breaking precedent, the question of an accused's guilt or innocence came to share the judicial spotlight with questions concerning the legality of the police conduct. Was the arrest of Chestnut and the seizure of his possessions lawful? Was the interrogation properly conducted? These questions were to be answered not under local law, but according to the U.S. Constitution as interpreted by the Supreme Court. The answers would determine whether the prosecutor could use at trial the evidence seized and the statements obtained against Chestnut, or whether they would be kept from the jury by operation of the exclusionary rule. As some commentators have put it, criminal procedure had been federalized and constitutionalized.

How did this transformation come about?

The Constitution adopted in 1787 divided sovereign power between the states on the one hand and the newly formed federal government on the other. Each had the power to prosecute offenders of its criminal laws in its own courts. Those prosecuted in the federal system were beneficiaries of the considerable procedural protections established by the Bill of Rights (the original ten amendments to the Constitution), most notably the rights to be free from unreasonable search and seizure and from compelled self-incrimination. Those prosecuted in state court (which group has always constituted the majority of criminal defendants), however, were afforded only those protections created by state constitution or other local law, which usually were significantly less protective than their federal counterparts.

The seeds of change were sown with the adoption after the Civil War of the Fourteenth Amendment, which provides that the states may not "deprive any person of life, liberty, or property without due process of law." This limit on state power raised the possibility that defendants in state prosecutions might be able to claim the same procedural protections afforded federal defendants. The "incorporation" of such rights against the states, however, was a long time coming. At first the Supreme Court applied the due process clause to state trials by employing an amorphous standard of "fundamental fairness," which did not encompass all the specific protections of the Bill of Rights. In the few cases in which the clause was successfully invoked to reverse state criminal convictions, such as *Rochin v. California*, 342 U.S. 165

(1952)[1] the Court refused to define the mandate of due process more precisely than requiring that state law enforcement officers not engage in conduct that "offends a traditional sense of justice" or "shocks the conscience."

Throughout the first half of the twentieth century, state criminal defendants were without the constitutional protections provided in the Bill of Rights, which were available to those facing federal charges. The difference in treatment was magnified when, in 1914, the federal courts adopted an exclusionary remedy requiring suppression of evidence obtained in violation of the Fourth Amendment. See *Weeks v. United States*, 232 U.S. 383 (1914). A search that would be deemed illegal under federal standards and consequently result in suppression of the evidence (and perhaps the dismissal of charges) in federal court might nonetheless be considered lawful in a state prosecution under the less stringent due process measure, opening the way to the introduction of the evidence (and possible conviction). Even after the Court imposed the same federal constitutional standards on searches conducted by state (and local) police in 1949, the exclusionary remedy was not mandated in state prosecutions.[2] As a result, dramatically inconsistent results could follow depending upon which court system the accused happened to be prosecuted in.

In the early 1960s the Court, under the leadership of Chief Justice Earl Warren, set out on a new path of uniform application of both constitutional standards and remedies in which specific provisions of the Bill of Rights were "incorporated" through the due process clause and applied to the conduct of state and local law enforcement officers. In the seminal case of *Mapp v. Ohio*, 367 U.S. 643 (1961),[3] the Court

---

1. Los Angeles deputy sheriffs entered Rochin's home without a warrant to search for narcotics. When they forced open the door to his bedroom and discovered him, he shoved two capsules into his mouth. The deputies seized Rochin and attempted to recover the capsules, but he swallowed them. They then took him to a doctor who pumped his stomach with a chemical solution, and he vomited the capsules. The Court ruled that the prosecution could not use the capsules as evidence at trial. See §11.2.

2. See *Wolf v. Colorado*, 338 U.S. 25 (1949). It should be noted that by 1961, several of the states had adopted the exclusionary rule through their own legislature or courts.

3. Cleveland police officers forced their way into Mrs. Mapp's house without a warrant to seek information regarding a person wanted in connection with a recent bombing. They handcuffed Mapp after a struggle and then engaged in an intensive search in which they seized allegedly obscene materials. The Court ruled that the prosecution could not use the materials as evidence at trial.

held that the violation of a state defendant's right against unreasonable search required precisely the same remedy as was mandated in federal prosecutions, namely suppression of the evidence obtained from the search. Five years later in *Miranda v. Arizona*, 384 U.S. 436 (1966), the Court imposed on both state and federal authorities a comprehensive set of rules (and corresponding exclusionary remedy) designed to protect the accused's Fifth Amendment right against compelled self-incrimination. Before the decade was out, the Sixth Amendment rights to counsel[4] and to a jury trial[5] and the Eighth Amendment protection against cruel and unusual punishment[6] were also applied to the states.

In sum, an accused's fate in the criminal justice process would no longer depend fortuitously upon whether he was prosecuted by the state or the federal government. A uniform body of constitutional principles now applied to both sovereigns. The Warren Court also expanded the scope of habeas corpus, thus providing state prisoners with access to federal court to enforce their newly found rights. See *Fay v. Noia*, 372 U.S. 391 (1963).

Not surprisingly, these developments generated considerable controversy in both legal and political arenas. Some argued that the "preservation of a proper balance between state and federal responsibility in the administration of criminal justice" had been upset by the adoption of nationwide standards and that the fundamental concept of "federalism" had thus been wrongly ignored. *Mapp v. Ohio*, supra, 367 U.S. at 680 (Harlan, J., dissenting). Others complained that the Warren Court decisions would tie the hands of local law enforcement officers and make the world safe for criminal offenders.[7] Criticism was levelled at the use of the criminal trial as a vehicle for enforcing norms of police conduct rather than solely as a means for determining the guilt or innocence of the accused.

The lightning rod of the controversy was (and remains) the exclusionary rule itself. As Cardozo posed the question: Should the criminal go free because the constable has blundered? *People v. Defore*, 150 N.E. 585 (N.Y. 1926). Justice Clark explained for the *Mapp* Court that other remedies such as civil actions for monetary relief and criminal prosecutions against the offending officers had proven worthless, and thus sup-

---

4. *Gideon v. Wainwright*, 372 U.S. 335 (1963).

5. *Duncan v. Louisiana*, 391 U.S. 145 (1968).

6. *Robinson v. California*, 370 U.S. 660 (1962).

7. Beginning with Richard Nixon's successful presidential campaign in 1968, this has become a major theme in American politics.

pression of evidence unlawfully seized was the only means to enforce the Fourth Amendment. Police officers and prosecutors would abide by the constraints of the Fourth Amendment, it was asserted, if they knew that evidence obtained unlawfully could not be used against the accused in court. To this deterrence rationale the *Mapp* Court added "the imperative of judicial integrity": "The criminal goes free, if he must, but it is the law that sets him free. Nothing can destroy a government more quickly than its failure to observe its own law, or worse, its disregard of the charter of its own existence." 367 U.S. at 659.

Yet discontent with the exclusionary remedy has persisted. Chief Justice Burger, in one of his early dissents on the Court, bitterly criticized the doctrine that hides probative evidence from the fact finder. See *Bivens v. Six Unknown Named Agents of the Federal Bureau of Narcotics*, 403 U.S. 388 (1971) (Burger, C.J., dissenting). Heralding a change in the Court's course that would come some years later, the Chief Justice disputed both the efficacy and necessity of the exclusionary remedy and argued for the substitution of other means (such as civil actions) to enforce constitutional dictates. He characterized the deterrence rationale as nothing more than "a wistful dream" with no empirical support, and he emphasized "the high price" it extracts from society—"the release of countless guilty criminals."[8] In explaining what he characterized as the failure of the suppression remedy to deter unlawful police conduct, Burger observed that: the rule provides no direct sanction against the offending officer; that the prosecutor who may lose the case because of the suppression generally has no official authority over the offending officer; that the time lapse between the police action and the final ruling excluding the evidence is often so long that whatever educational effect it might have had is lost; and that much police action is not directed at ultimate prosecution of the subject and therefore is not conducted in anticipation of a trial requiring proof. Moreover, he complained that the exclusionary remedy allows for no proportionality—that is, regardless of the magnitude of the police misconduct or the nature of the crime involved, the remedy is always the same. 403 U.S. at 416–418.

---

8. 403 U.S. at 416. The actual number of persons released by operation of the exclusionary rule has been a source of much disagreement. See, e.g., Oaks, Studying the Exclusionary Rule in Search and Seizure, 37 U. Chi. L. Rev. 665 (1970); Spiotto, Search and Seizure: An Empirical Study of the Exclusionary Rule and Its Alternatives, 2 J. Legal Studies 243 (1973); Impact of the Exclusionary Rule on Federal Criminal Prosecutions, U.S. Gen. Acctg. Office (GGD-79-45), 1979.

Since the 1970s the Court, apparently influenced by this critique, has significantly chipped away at the scope and applicability of the exclusionary rule in both the Fourth and Fifth Amendment contexts. Limitations have been imposed on those deemed to have "standing" to raise Fourth Amendment objections, as well as on the types of proceedings in which the suppression remedy applies (it has been held inapplicable, for example, in grand jury proceedings). A "good faith" exception now largely removes from the reach of the remedy police action that, although unlawful in retrospect, was committed in the reasonable belief that the action did not violate the Fourth Amendment. In addition, concerned with the societal costs of the exclusionary rule, the Court has modified substantive constitutional doctrine (such as the standard for probable cause) in a manner that maximizes deference to police judgment and minimizes the constraint on police conduct. Without completely abandoning *Mapp* or *Miranda* the Court has nonetheless been able to curtail their impact dramatically.

In response to these developments in federal decisional law, some states have developed their own enforceable rights for persons accused of crimes. Ironically, given the beginning of our story, state law now often provides defendants with greater protections than their federal counterparts have. See Utter, State Constitutional Law, the United States Supreme Court, and Democratic Accountability, 64 Wash. L. Rev. 19, 27 (1989) (reporting more than 450 published state court opinions interpreting state constitutions as providing more rights than the federal constitution).

This emergence of state constitutional protections, a development urged by Justice Brennan (a frequent dissenter in the Burger/Rehnquist Court's criminal procedure decisions) in an influential law review article published in 1977,[9] has itself raised a number of issues regarding the relationship between the federal and state sovereigns, that is, fed-

---

9. William J. Brennan, Jr., State Constitutions and the Protection of Individual Rights, 90 Harv. L. Rev. 489, 491 (1977) ("[S]tate courts cannot rest when they have afforded their citizens the full protections of the federal constitution. State constitutions, too, are a font of individual liberties, their protections often extending beyond those required by the Supreme Court's interpretation of federal law. The legal revolution which has brought federal law to the fore must not be allowed to inhibit the independent protective force of state law—for without it, the full realization of our liberties cannot be guaranteed.")

eralism concerns. Although it has long been established that the ultimate authority on federal law is the Supreme Court, see *Martin v. Hunter's Lessee*, 14 U.S. (1 Wheat.) 304 (1816), the Court has no authority to review a state court decision based on independent and adequate state law grounds. *Abie State Bank v. Bryan*, 282 U.S. 765, 773 (1931); see also *Herb v. Pitcairn*, 324 U.S. 117, 125–126 (1945) (Supreme Court's "only power over state judgments is to correct them to the extent that they incorrectly adjudge federal rights").

In 1983 the Court purported to reaffirm the principle that "respect for the independence of state courts, as well as avoidance of rendering advisory opinions, have been the cornerstones of refusal to decide cases where there is an adequate and independent state ground." *Michigan v. Long*, 463 U.S. 1032, 1040 (1983). The Court nonetheless expanded the authority to review state court judgments when it held in *Long* that there must be a clear indication from the state court opinion that it was relying on independent, adequate state grounds for the federal court to refuse jurisdiction. In his dissent Justice Stevens characterized the majority's approach as a reversal of the traditional presumption of the adequacy of state grounds. Id. at 1066 (Stevens, J., dissenting). Some commentators have suggested that the Supreme Court's new willingness to review state court decisions is a reaction to the expansion of state constitutional protections.[10]

Although state courts must follow the U.S. Supreme Court in matters of federal constitutional law, they are free to interpret their own law so as to provide greater protection for individual rights than that which the U.S. Constitution minimally mandates. *PruneYard Shopping Center v. Robins*, 447 U.S. 74, 81 (1980). "The federal constitution sets the floor for individual rights; state constitutions establish the ceiling." *LeCroy v. Hanlon*, 713 S.W.2d 335, 338 (Tex. 1986). Many states have interpreted their constitutional provisions with regard to individual rights in a more expansive way than the Supreme Court even when the wording of the state provision is identical to the federal Constitution.[11] On the other hand, some states have chosen through judicial decisions to link their interpretation of their own law

---

10. See, e.g., Eric B. Schnurer, The Inadequate and Dependent "Adequate and Independent State Grounds" Doctrine, 18 Hastings Const. L.Q. 371 (1991).

11. See Utter, State Constitutional Law, supra.

to that of the federal Constitution, while still other states have been directed by the electorate to follow federal law.[12]

EXAMPLES

Assume that a warrant is obtained to search Michael Chestnut's home, the search is conducted, and a large quantity of cocaine is found. The affidavit reviewed by the magistrate who issued the warrant, however, failed to demonstrate sufficient probable cause, thus making the search unlawful under the Fourth Amendment (as discussed in Chapter 4). Chestnut is charged with unlawful possession of cocaine in state court. Would the cocaine seized be admissible at Chestnut's trial:

a) before the decision in *Mapp v. Ohio?*
b) immediately after the decision in *Mapp v. Ohio?*
c) today?

EXPLANATIONS

a) Because the exclusionary remedy had not yet been imposed on the states through the Fourth Amendment, the answer would depend on whether the particular state had adopted such a rule of its own. If Chestnut were prosecuted in a state that had not done so, the illegality of the search would not be a factor in his prosecution.

b) *Mapp* mandated an exclusionary remedy, applicable in all state (as well as federal) prosecutions, for violation of the Fourth Amendment. Given the lack of probable cause, therefore, the cocaine would not be admissible in evidence, and (in the absence of other probative evidence) Chestnut would go free.

c) One of the major cutbacks in the exclusionary remedy in recent years has been the Supreme Court's adoption of a "good faith" exception. See §7.3.3. By obtaining a warrant, the officers have ensured against suppression of the cocaine under the Fourth Amendment as long as their reliance upon the warrant and their

---

12. The Florida constitution, for example, was amended by general election in 1982 so that the provision relating to search and seizure would be construed in conformity with the Fourth Amendment of the U.S. Constitution as interpreted by the U.S. Supreme Court. Similarly, by an initiative petition California requires that all relevant evidence be admissible, thus limiting the exclusionary remedy there to only that provided by federal law.

belief that probable cause existed is deemed in retrospect to have been reasonable. If Chestnut is prosecuted in a state whose own law rejects the good faith exception, however, he will be able to keep the evidence from the jury. Chestnut's fate, in short, is once again dependent on the locus of his prosecution.

PART ONE

Search and Seizure—The Framework of the Fourth Amendment

2

Introduction to the Fourth Amendment

The right of the people to be secure in their persons, houses, papers, and effects, against unreasonable searches and seizures, shall not be violated, and no Warrants shall issue, but upon probable cause, supported by Oath or affirmation, and particularly describing the place to be searched, and the persons or things to be seized.

U.S. Const. amend. IV

The Fourth Amendment reflects one of the fundamental grievances that the colonists had against the English Crown. Parliament, intent upon reducing the smuggling activity taking place in the American colonies, instituted writs of assistance, which were issued without judicial supervision or any demonstration of justification and permitted searches unlimited in scope. Officers armed with such writs had virtually unconstrained discretion to search whenever, wherever, and whomever they chose.[1] In adopting the Fourth Amendment as part of the Bill of Rights, the framers of the Republic sought to avoid the abuses of these open-ended licenses to search. This purpose is reflected in the clause requiring the demonstration of probable cause before a warrant may be issued and further limiting the reach of officers armed with a warrant to particularly described places, persons, and things.

---

1. The writs authorized officials to "go into any House, Shop, Cellar, Warehouse or Room . . . and in case of resistance, to break open Doors, Chests, Trunks and other Packages, there to seize and from thence to bring any Kind of Goods or Merchandise whatsoever, prohibited and uncustomed." Navigation Act of 1662, 13 & 14 Car. II, Ch. 11, §5 (1662).

In addition to the provision concerning warrants, the Fourth Amendment (in its first clause) prohibits "unreasonable searches and seizures." A fundamental question regarding the interpretation of the amendment has been the relationship between the two separate clauses, which are joined by the conjunction "and." Some have argued that the second clause gives meaning to the prohibition in the first, so that a search is presumptively unreasonable when it is conducted without a properly issued warrant. As Justice Frankfurter stated it in *United States v. Rabinowitz*: "What is the test of reason which makes a search reasonable? . . . There must be a warrant to permit search, barring only inherent limitations upon that requirement when there is a good excuse for not getting a search warrant. . . ." 339 U.S. 56, 83 (1950) (dissenting). For those espousing this "warrant preference" school of interpretation, the prophylactic interposition of a neutral magistrate between the officer and the citizen to be searched *prior to* the police action is the main protection afforded by the Fourth Amendment. See *Chimel v. California*, 395 U.S. 752, 766 n.12 (1969) (the Fourth Amendment is "designed to prevent, not simply redress, unlawful police action" by way of the warrant process).

The warrant preference view was at one time espoused as the prevailing doctrine. A unanimous Court stated in *Mincey v. Arizona*, 437 U.S. 385, 390 (1978): "The Fourth Amendment proscribes all unreasonable searches and seizures and it is a cardinal principle that searches conducted outside the judicial process, without prior approval by judge or magistrate, are per se unreasonable under the Fourth Amendment, subject to a few specifically established and well delineated exceptions." In recent years, however, this rhetoric has been all but abandoned. As Justice Stevens has observed, while the Court has not expressly disavowed the warrant presumption, its decisions suggest that "the exceptions have all but swallowed the general rule." *Florida v. White*, 526 U.S. 559, 569 (1999) (dissenting). See also *Wyoming v. Houghton*, 526 U.S. 295 (1999).

The opposing view is that the clauses should be read separately, and thus the reasonableness of a search does not turn on whether a warrant was obtained or whether there was an adequate excuse for not seeking one.[2] Rather, the focus is on the factual circumstances justi-

---

2. "A rule of thumb requiring that a search warrant always be procured whenever practicable may be appealing from the vantage point of easy administration. But we cannot agree that this requirement should be crystallized into a *sine qua non* to the reasonableness of a search. . . . The relevant test is not whether it is reasonable to procure a warrant, but whether the search is reasonable." *United States v. Rabinowitz*, 339 U.S. at 65–66 (1950).

fying the search and the manner in which it was conducted. The main protection afforded by the Fourth Amendment in this view lies not in prior judicial screening, but rather in the after-the-fact review of police conduct to ensure that it was reasonable given the circumstances at the time.

This focus on reasonableness has dominated the Court's jurisprudence in recent years. Indeed, it has gone beyond the question of when a warrant is required and has become the general standard for measuring the legality of police conduct, as discussed throughout this book.

The fundamental concepts arising out of the Fourth Amendment (which will be discussed in later chapters) are:

1) *Prior justification for police action*—The police must possess information sufficient to constitute probable cause (or an alternative standard of justification) in order to lawfully conduct a search or seizure. Justification in general, and probable cause in particular, are (as we shall see in Chapter 4) very fluid concepts.

2) *Limited scope of police action*—Even when justified by probable cause or otherwise, searches and seizures are confined by limitations of space and time. The scope of the permissible search is generally defined by the original justification that authorized it. (See Chapter 6.)

3) *Requirement for a warrant*—The warrant process, by which the police seek from a neutral magistrate prior approval of their request to search or arrest, is mandatory in certain situations. In others, the police may act without obtaining such prior approval. In Chapter 5 we will discuss the evolving line drawn by the courts in this regard, as well as the requirements for a valid warrant.

4) *Reasonableness clause analysis*—As noted above, the Court has increasingly relied upon the reasonableness clause to define the requirements of the Fourth Amendment. The standard of probable cause articulated in earlier cases has been significantly diluted and, in some areas, replaced by a balancing test that weighs the governmental necessity for the search against the magnitude of the privacy intrusion involved. Illustrative are the so-called administrative search cases discussed in Chapter 4, which substitute the general societal interest in conducting the search for the requirement that there be specific justification.

Before exploring these basic issues of Fourth Amendment law, we must first ask: In what situations is the Fourth Amendment applicable? After discussing this threshold issue in the next chapter, we will turn our attention to the substantive requirements of the amendment. Lastly we will consider the manner in which the Fourth Amendment is enforced, namely the operation of the exclusionary rule.

EXAMPLES

Pamela Principal at Oakdale High School received an anonymous telephone call informing her that Steve Student was selling illegal drugs and was storing his inventory in his girlfriend Sally Snook's locker. Principal checked Steve's file and discovered that he had been absent on numerous occasions during the school year and had frequently been disruptive in the classroom. Upon learning this, Principal obtained the master key from the janitor and opened both Steve's and Sally's lockers. In Steve's locker, Principal found a notebook listing the names of several students, dates, quantities, and moneys received. In Sally's locker, Principal found a large quantity of marijuana. Principal turned over both the notebook and the marijuana to the police. A school disciplinary hearing is scheduled to determine whether Steve should be suspended or expelled. In addition, Steve has been charged in juvenile court with possession of marijuana with intent to distribute.

What legal issues must be resolved regarding the searches and seizures described here?

EXPLANATIONS

At the outset, we need to determine whether the Fourth Amendment is applicable in these circumstances. This question, as we will see, involves two subquestions: First, is Pamela Principal a government official whose conduct is limited by constitutional constraints, or is she acting in a private capacity? Second, does Steve Student have the right to expect that his own locker (and his girlfriend's locker) will be free from such intrusion (does he, in other words, have a reasonable expectation of privacy in these areas)?

If we determine that the Fourth Amendment is implicated because a governmental actor has intruded into a protected area, then we need to address the justification issue: Did Pamela Principal have sufficient information to justify search of the lockers? Was her reliance on an anonymous informant proper? Should she have sought prior authorization (a warrant) from a judicial officer before opening the lockers?

If we conclude that there was not sufficient justification, or that a warrant was required, then there has been a violation of the Fourth Amendment and the attention turns to remedy. Will Steve be able to exclude the evidence seized by Principal at the disciplinary hearing? At the juvenile court hearing? Does Steve have the right to exclude the evidence taken from Sally's locker as well as that taken from his own (does he, in other words, have standing to complain)?

These questions, and more, will be addressed in later chapters.

3

When Does the Fourth Amendment Apply?

There are two threshold requirements that must be met before the Fourth Amendment will be held applicable in a particular situation. The first, which applies to all the provisions of the Bill of Rights, is that the conduct in question must be governmental. Second, the action challenged must constitute a "search," defined with reference to the concept of "reasonable expectation of privacy." Thus the Fourth Amendment is implicated only when *the government* intrudes into an area that is deemed to be one in which the citizen may *reasonably expect privacy.*

§3.1 Governmental Action—Public versus Private Search

The Fourth Amendment applies only to action by the government, not to private conduct. As the Court observed in 1921, the "origin and history [of the amendment] clearly show that it was intended as a restraint upon the activities of sovereign authority [only]." *Burdeau v. McDowell*, 256 U.S 465, 475 (1921).[1] Where the actor is a federal,

---

1. Private persons illegally entered and searched McDowell's office, seized certain papers, and then turned them over to a government prosecutor who intended to use them in a criminal case against McDowell. He unsuccessfully sought a court order for return of the papers on the theory that their seizure violated the Fourth Amendment. The Court held that because the government had played no role in the search, the papers could be used in evidence against McDowell at trial.

state, or local government agent, this requirement is met.[2] Where, however, a private party acting on his own acquires evidence that the government later seeks to introduce in a criminal case, neither the Fourth Amendment nor its exclusionary remedy is implicated.

When a private individual acts at the direction of a government agent or pursuant to an official policy, the search will be deemed public and consequently within the coverage of the amendment. Thus where a police officer requests that an airline employee open a traveler's suitcase, the Fourth Amendment is applicable. Similarly, private railroads that comply with federal regulations mandating drug screening of employees act under the constraints of the Fourth Amendment. See *Skinner v. Railway Labor Executives' Association*, 489 U.S. 602 (1989).

The issue becomes substantially more difficult in the gray area where there is no direct governmental command or policy, but merely acquiescence in the private individual's action. Suppose, for example, that police officers are summoned to a scene by persons who proceed, in the presence of the officers, to conduct an illegal search. Is that a "public" search subject to Fourth Amendment constraints? Several courts have concluded that it is.[3] Factors considered in determining whether the private party is acting as "an instrument of the state" are: 1) the degree of government encouragement, knowledge, and/or acquiescence with regard to the private actor's actions; and 2) the purpose underlying the private party's action, that is, was he pursuing a governmental interest (such as the discovery of criminal activity or evidence thereof), which points toward the conclusion that the search

---

2. The Fourth Amendment has been applied to the actions of civil authorities as well as law enforcement authorities. See, e.g., *O'Connor v. Ortega*, 480 U.S. 709 (1987) (state hospital supervisor); *New Jersey v. TLO*, 469 U.S. 325 (1985) (public school principal).

3. See *United States v. Newton*, F.2d 1149 (7th Cir. 1975) (search of luggage by an airline employee in the presence of federal agents, who were summoned when the employee became suspicious about the appearance of the luggage, constituted a public search within the scope of the Fourth Amendment); *Stapleton v. Superior Court*, 447 P.2d 967 (Cal. 1968) ("the police need not have requested or directed the search in order to be guilty of 'standing idly by'; knowledge of the illegal search coupled with a failure to protect the petitioner's rights against such a search suffices."). But see *Gundlach v. Janing*, 401 F. Supp. 1089 (D. Neb. 1975), aff'd, 536 F.2d 754 (8th Cir. 1976) (mere knowledge by police that a private person might conduct an illegal search is insufficient to transform the search into a governmental act); *Pleasant v. Lovell*, 654 F. Supp. 1082 (D. Colo. 1987) (mere acceptance by federal agents of information from a private, unpaid informant is insufficient to make the search "public").

was public, or did he act to promote his own business objectives (such as protecting against accidents, false claims, or potential liability), which makes the action private in nature. See *United States v. Walther*, 652 F.2d 788 (9th Cir. 1981); *United States v. Feffer*, 831 F.2d 734 (7th Cir. 1987). Thus when an airline employee opened a suspicious package and turned the white powder inside over to agents of the Drug Enforcement Agency (DEA), the court held that the search was not private in nature because: 1) the employee had previously reported information or turned over packages to the DEA on 11 occasions, sometimes receiving a small payment, and thus acted with the government's acquiescence; and 2) he testified that he opened the package to discover evidence of crime, with the expectation of a reward from the DEA, and not for any purpose of his employer. *Walther*, supra, 652 F.2d at 792. The Fourth Amendment was therefore applicable.

An otherwise purely private search may be transformed into one that is subject to constitutional constraints if the governmental recipient of the items seized by the private party subjects them to additional examination. In *Walter v. United States*, 447 U.S. 649 (1980), for example, sealed film cannisters were mistakenly delivered to a company whose employees, noting the suggestive labels, opened the cannisters and tried unsuccessfully to make out the images on the films. Suspecting that they were pornographic, the employees turned the films over to FBI agents, who viewed them on a projector. The Court ruled that because this viewing constituted an additional search beyond that conducted by the private parties, the Fourth Amendment came into play.

When a public official exceeds the scope of a private search, therefore, the Fourth Amendment applies to the additional intrusion. In *United States v. Jacobsen*, 466 U.S. 109 (1984) (also discussed in §3.2), however, the Court emphasized that the further examination must be substantial in order to trigger the constitutional protection. In *Jacobsen*, Federal Express employees opened a damaged package and found several plastic bags containing a suspicious white powder. They repacked the parcel and summoned federal drug agents. When they arrived, the agents reopened the package and subjected the powder to a field test designed to reveal the presence of cocaine. The powder tested positive. The Court held that although the agents went a step beyond the examination conducted by the Federal Express employees, the on-the-scene test did not constitute an additional search triggering the Fourth Amendment: "The agent's viewing of what a private party had freely made available for his inspection did not violate the Fourth Amendment," 466 U.S. at 119, and the field test constituted only a "de minimus impact on any protected property interest." Id. at 125. The latter conclusion was premised on the fact that the test could determine only the presence or absence of contraband cocaine and no other information regarding the suspect.

EXAMPLES

1. Upon leaving the Friendly Department Store, Alva Alpha was stopped by a store security guard who suspected her of shoplifting. The guard seized Alpha's shopping bag, opened it, and discovered several items of clothing that had been taken from the store's shelves but had not been paid for. The incident was reported to the police and the items were turned over to them. May Alva Alpha mount a Fourth Amendment challenge to the introduction of the items into evidence at her trial for shoplifting?

2. Curious Jack, an employee of Consolidated Utility Company, was in Sam Clay's basement to read his gas meter. Spotting a large parcel enclosed in brown paper, he proceeded to unwrap what turned out to be a painting. Jack, an amateur art expert, recognized it as a priceless work that had been stolen a month before from the Metropolitan Gallery. Jack took the painting and turned it over to the local police. May Clay invoke the Fourth Amendment to seek suppression of the painting at trial?

3. Claude von Wealthy stands accused of having murdered his wife by injecting her with a lethal dose of insulin. The prosecution intends to introduce into evidence a black bag containing a hypodermic needle, which von Wealthy's stepson found while he and a private investigator were looking for incriminating evidence in the defendant's bedroom closet shortly after the murder. Upon discovery the bag was turned over to the police, who subjected the hypodermic needle to a complete chemical analysis at the police laboratory, revealing traces of insulin. Von Wealthy moves to suppress the evidence on Fourth Amendment grounds, but the prosecution maintains that the amendment is not applicable. Is the prosecution correct?

4. Betty Bookkeeper became concerned that her employers at Flexible Plastics Company were cheating the government out of corporate taxes owed. She made several telephone calls to the Internal Revenue Service (IRS) and spoke to Agent Clean. Based on the information she provided, the agent confirmed her fears that the tax laws were being violated. Clean advised Betty that IRS policy

prevented him from encouraging her to take any documents from her employer, but that it was IRS policy to accept documents voluntarily provided. Over the next several months, Betty provided corporate records, which established a case of major tax fraud against her employer. May Flexible Plastics raise Fourth Amendment objections to the use of these documents at trial?

EXPLANATIONS

1. Consistent with the "private search" doctrine, it has been generally held that private security guards are not subject to Fourth Amendment constraints as long as they act independent of police direction. See, e.g., *United States v. Francoeur,* 547 F.2d 891 (5th Cir. 1977) (the actions of private security personnel at an amusement park who detained several persons and required them to empty their pockets did not come within the restrictions of the Fourth Amendment or its exclusionary remedy). Some courts, however, have held that security guards should be treated as governmental actors when they go beyond the protection of their employer's interests and take on a quasi-law enforcement function. See, e.g., *People v. Zelinski,* 155 Cal. Rptr. 575, 594 P.2d 1000 (1979) (although store detectives are deemed private actors when seeking to protect their employer's interest by retrieving stolen merchandise, they become public actors subject to the constraints of the Fourth Amendment when they hold the suspect for the police and turn over evidence to be used in a criminal trial). Where the privately employed guard also happens to be a police officer (as where, for example, the officer is on a private detail), courts have imposed Fourth Amendment limitations. See *Commonwealth v. Leone,* 386 Mass. 329 (1982). For an extended discussion of the private security guard issue, see 36 A.L.R.3d 553, 567–571.

   The actions of privately employed security personnel could, of course, give rise to civil liability under tort or other theories of recovery.

2. Under prevailing doctrine the resolution of this question turns upon whether the meter reader is a public or private employee. If Consolidated is a private entity, Jack's actions are not proscribed by constitutional limitations. If, however, Consolidated is a publicly owned and operated utility, then the Fourth Amendment would apply to Jack's action. This is the case even though Jack is not a law enforcement official. *See United States v. Goldstein,* 532

F.2d 1305 (9th Cir. 1976) (evidence that Goldstein was using an illegal "blue box" to avoid being billed for calls, acquired through investigation by a special agent of the General Telephone Company, was beyond the reach of the Fourth Amendment: "Although communications carriers may sometimes give the appearance of governmental agencies, they in fact are private companies which possess none of the criteria which might make them responsible under the Fourth Amendment as government bodies.").

Any significant involvement by law enforcement personnel in the private search would convert it into a public one. Thus, for example, where police officers ask a private utility employee to search a citizen's home in the course of his other duties, the Fourth Amendment is implicated. See, e.g., *Raymond v. Superior Court*, 19 Cal. App. 3d 321, 96 Cal. Rptr. 678 (1971) (police participated in the planning and implementation of a search conducted by a private party, triggering Fourth Amendment restrictions).

One state court has rejected the conclusion that *non*-law enforcement public employees are constrained by the Fourth Amendment. See *Commonwealth v. Cote*, 15 Mass. App. Ct. 229, 234, 444 N.E.2d 1282, 1286 (1983) (holding that the Fourth Amendment did not apply to the discovery of an illegal shunt by a city gas meter reader because he was not engaged in law enforcement activities: "[M]ere employment by an arm of the government is not enough to make an actor a government agent for purposes of the Fourth Amendment. Rather, the nature of the actor's employment, his specific duties and authority to act for the State and the circumstances of the search are all taken into account in deciding whether a search was 'private' or governmental in nature.").

3. Because the bag and its contents were obtained by way of a private search with no government involvement, the Fourth Amendment would not apply to their discovery. This is the case even if the intention of the stepson and private investigator was to acquire evidence to be used at trial. When the law enforcement officials subsequently had the contents chemically tested at a laboratory, however, they exceeded the scope of the prior examination and the additional intrusion constituted a public search, implicating the amendment. See *State v. Von Bulow*, 475 A.2d 995, 1012 (R.I 1984) ("No matter how egregious actions may appear in a society whose fundamental values have historically included individual freedom and privacy, the exclusionary rule cannot be invoked by defendant to bar the introduction of evidence that was procured

by while acting as private citizens. . . . Similar principles do not, however, govern our review of the evidence-gathering techniques employed by the state [the subsequent chemical testing of the fruits of the private search]. . . . When the government significantly expands a prior private search . . . the independent governmental search is subject to the proscriptions of the Fourth Amendment.").

It should be noted that the chemical analysis performed here was substantially more intrusive than the field test in *United States v. Jacobsen*, discussed at p. 21, supra, because: 1) it was conducted in the laboratory, not on the scene; and 2) the tests were designed to disclose more than simply the presence of contraband cocaine.

4. Does this private search become subject to Fourth Amendment constraints because Betty acted as "an instrument of the state"? Although the IRS did not direct her, once the government was contacted and acquiesced in the removal of documents, it could certainly be argued that constitutional constraints should be applied.

   As noted above, courts have looked to two factors in resolving such questions. See discussion of *United States v. Walther*, 652 F.2d 788 (9th Cir. 1981), at p. 21. Because it is clear that the government acquiesced in (and indeed encouraged) Betty's conduct, the first factor is met. The second factor focuses on the private party's purpose—that is, did she act solely to assist law enforcement or to further her own ends? In the case on which this example is based, *United States v. Feffer*, 831 F.2d 734 (7th Cir. 1987), the court found that the bookkeeper's fear of being held liable for her part in the tax fraud, not her desire to assist law enforcement officers, motivated her to turn over the evidence to the IRS. The court further found that she would have likely provided the documents regardless of the agent's encouragement. It was held, therefore, that the search was a private act and not subject to the Fourth Amendment. The court conceded, however, that given the agent's involvement with Betty over a long course of time, the question was a close one.

§3.2 Reasonable Expectation of Privacy

The definition of what constitutes a "search" within the meaning of the Fourth Amendment was, until 1967, closely tied to property concepts. Thus police action would be deemed a search for Fourth Amendment purposes only if it amounted to a common law trespass. As methods of surveillance and eavesdropping became more technologically sophisticated and could be accomplished without the necessity for physical intrusion, this definition became outdated and underinclusive. *Katz v. United States*, 389 U.S. 347 (1967), brought the Fourth Amendment into the modern era. Federal agents had placed a listening device against the wall of a public phone booth that was being used by Katz. Because there was no penetration of the booth and thus no trespass, the lower court ruled that the agents did not conduct a search when they listened in on Katz's conversation. In reversing, the Supreme Court held that the amendment "protects people, not places" and therefore its reach "cannot turn upon the presence or absence of a physical intrusion into any given enclosure." 389 U.S. at 353. Rather, the amendment's applicability turns on the concept of privacy: "The Government's activities in electronically listening to and recording words violated the privacy upon which he justifiably relied while using the telephone booth and thus constituted a 'search and seizure' within the meaning of the Fourth Amendment." Id.

While *Katz* seemed at first to represent a considerable expansion of the constitutional protection against unreasonable search, decisions in recent years have construed the new test narrowly. The Court has instructed that the Fourth Amendment applies only where: 1) the citizen has manifested a subjective expectation of privacy; and 2) the expectation of privacy is one that society (through the Court) accepts as "objectively reasonable." *California v. Greenwood*, 486 U.S. 35, 39 (1988). It is not enough, in other words, for the target of the intrusion *to believe* that he is acting in private; that belief must be deemed *reasonable*. Supreme Court decisions have adopted a restrictive view of what society would consider to be justifiable privacy expectations.

One major limitation on Fourth Amendment coverage derives from the observation in *Katz* that "what a person knowingly exposes to the public, even in his own home or office, is not subject to Fourth Amendment protection." 389 U.S. at 351. Protection is afforded only for "what he seeks to preserve as private." Id. The Court extended this notion when it ruled that a person who conveys information to a third party, even in an apparently private conversation, cannot reasonably expect the information to remain secret within the context of the Fourth Amendment. See *Hoffa v. United States*, 385 U.S. 293 (1966) (informant reported the conversation to government agents); *United States v. White*, 401 U.S. 745 (1971) (government agents overheard the conversation transmitted by a radio device worn by the informant). When Hoffa and White made incriminating statements to confidants who, unbeknownst to them, were acting as government informants, they assumed the risk of betrayal and disclosure. Misplaced reliance on the loyalty of others is not, the Court held, an expectation entitled to constitutional protection. When one party to the conversation "invites" the government in, therefore, no Fourth Amendment constraints apply. (Compare *Katz*, where the government intruded as the "uninvited ear" into the telephone conversation.)

Subsequent cases have extended the assumption of risk analysis to institutional third parties. It has been held that an individual who imparts information to a bank in the usual course of business,[4] or who automatically conveys the numbers dialed (for billing purposes by means of a pen register) to the telephone company when he places a call,[5] has no reasonable expectation of privacy in such information. He runs the risk that the recipient may divulge the information to the government, and thus has forfeited Fourth Amendment protection against such an event. Similarly, where a trash collector turned over defendant's garbage to the police at their request, evidence of narcotics use found inside was held not subject to Fourth Amendment challenge. *California v. Greenwood*, 486 U.S. 35 (1988). The Court concluded:

> [R]espondents exposed their garbage to the public sufficiently to defeat their claim to Fourth Amendment protection. It is common knowledge that plastic garbage bags left on or at the side of a public street are readily accessible to animals, children, scavengers, snoops, and other members of the public. Moreover, respondents placed their refuse at the curb for the express purpose of conveying it to a third party, the trash collector, who might himself have sorted through respondents' trash or permitted others, such as the police, to do so. Accordingly, having deposited their garbage in an area particularly suited for

---

4. *United States v. Miller*, 425 U.S. 435 (1976).

5. *Smith v. Maryland*, 442 U.S. 735 (1979). See also *Commonwealth v. Cote*, 407 Mass. 827 (Sup. Jud. Ct. 1990) (a defendant who utilized a telephone message service whereby both the defendant and the caller were aware that a third party was taking messages can be said to have no reasonable expectation of privacy in the message records, and thus no "search" occurred when the prosecution subpoenaed the records).

public inspection and, in a manner of speaking, public consumption, for the express purpose of having strangers take it, respondents could have no reasonable expectation of privacy in the inculpatory items they discarded.

486 U.S. at 40–41. In short, no search had occurred. Several state courts have interpreted their own constitutional provisions more broadly.[6]

A person's external physical characteristics that are exposed to the public have been deemed outside the scope of Fourth Amendment protection. "No person can have a reasonable expectation that others will not know the sound of his voice, any more than he can reasonably expect that his face will be a mystery to the world." *United States v. Dionisio,* 410 U.S. 1, 13 (1973). Thus the government can require persons to submit exemplars of their voice,[7] handwriting,[8] or fingerprints[9] without infringing upon any interest protected by the Fourth Amendment. Physical attributes not on public display and whose examination therefore requires bodily intrusion, such as blood type, do implicate the amendment.[10]

---

6. In refusing to follow the reasoning of *United States v. White,* for example, the Supreme Judicial Court of Massachusetts concluded that society would believe it "objectively reasonable to expect that conversational interchange in a private home will not be invaded surreptitiously by warrantless electronic transmission." *Commonwealth v. Blood,* 400 Mass. 61, 70, 507 N.E.2d 1029, 1034 (1987). See also *Burrows v. Superior Court,* 13 Cal. 3d 238 (1974) (rejecting the reasoning later adopted in *United States v. Miller,* supra, regarding the disclosure of bank records); *Washington v. Boland,* 115 Wash. 2d 571, 800 P.2d 112 (Wash. Sup. Ct. 1990) (rejecting the *Greenwood* analysis and holding that the seizure and inspection of trash left at the curbside intrudes on privacy expectations and thus constitutes a search within the state constitution).

7. *United States v. Dionisio,* 410 U.S. 1, 13 (1973).

8. *United States v. Mara,* 410 U.S. 19 (1973).

9. *Davis v. Mississippi,* 394 U.S. 721 (1969).

10. See *Skinner v. Railway Labor Executives' Association,* 489 U.S. 602 (1989) (blood, urine, and breath analysis all constitute searches because "they intrude upon expectations of privacy as to medical information"); *Schmerber v. California,* 384 U.S. 757 (1966) (the extraction of a blood sample from an arrestee by a physician at police direction implicated the Fourth Amendment); *Winston v. Lee,* 470 U.S. 753 (1985) (proposed surgery on defendant to remove a bullet that police believed would link him to the crime was subject to Fourth Amendment principles); *Cupp v. Murphy,* 412 U.S. 291 (1973) (applying the Fourth Amendment to the scraping of defendant's fingernails for the purpose of obtaining blood samples linking defendant to the murder). See §11.2.

The physical setting in which the intrusion occurs is of great importance in determining whether the Fourth Amendment is implicated. "Open fields," for example, have been held to fall outside the borders of the Fourth Amendment. Unlike the home itself and its curtilage,[11] the area immediately surrounding and in close proximity to the home, unoccupied and undeveloped open areas (even if enclosed and posted with "no trespassing" signs), do not enjoy a reasonable expectation of privacy. See *Oliver v. United States*, 466 U.S. 170 (1984). As the Court explained: "Open fields do not provide the setting for those intimate activities that the amendment is intended to shelter from government interference or surveillance." 466 U.S. at 179. See Figure 3–1.

Even if an area is within the traditionally protected setting of curtilage, the Court in recent years has limited Fourth Amendment protection by allowing for aerial surveillance. In *California v. Ciraolo*, 476 U.S. 207 (1986), the Court held that the naked-eye observation of a fenced-in back yard (which was deemed within the home's curtilage) from an aircraft at 1,000 feet did not constitute a search within the meaning of the amendment because in "an age where private and commercial flight in the public airways is routine, it is unreasonable for respondent to expect that his marijuana plants were constitutionally protected" from such observation. Similarly, *Florida v. Riley*, 488 U.S. 445 (1989), held that the Fourth Amendment was not implicated when the police flew by helicopter 400 feet over defendant's partially covered greenhouse (located next to defendant's mobile home) and made naked-eye observations of marijuana plants inside. Despite the fact that the contents of the greenhouse could not be observed from ground level, the Court concluded that no search had occurred because a member of the public could have similarly positioned himself in an aircraft and made the same observations through the uncovered

---

11. In *United States v. Dunn*, 480 U.S. 294 (1987), the Court addressed the distinction between curtilage and open fields. It looked to the following factors in determining whether a particular area is curtilage (and thus within the home's umbrella of protection): 1) proximity to the home; 2) whether the area is within an enclosure surrounding the home; 3) the nature of the uses to which the area is put; and 4) the steps taken to protect the area from observation. One federal judge has referred to curtilage as "an imaginary boundary line between privacy and accessibility to the public." See *United States v. Redmon*, 138 F.3d 1109, 1112 (7th Cir. 1998).

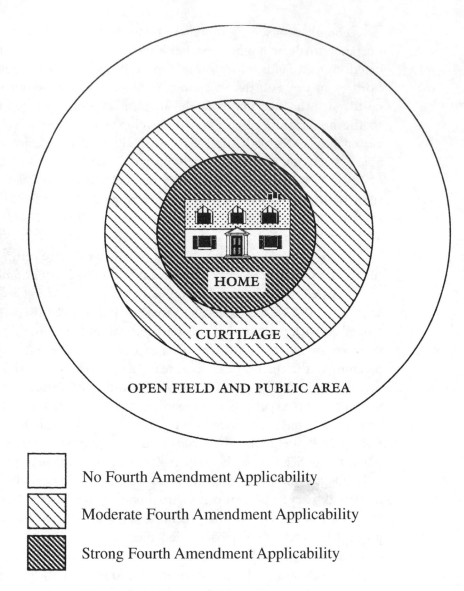

HOME

CURTILAGE

OPEN FIELD AND PUBLIC AREA

No Fourth Amendment Applicability

Moderate Fourth Amendment Applicability

Strong Fourth Amendment Applicability

Figure 3–1: Zones of Privacy Expectation

sections of the roof. Although "Riley no doubt intended and expected that his greenhouse would not be open to public inspection, and the precautions he took protected against ground-level observation," the routine nature of air travel rendered his expectation of privacy unjustified. The plurality qualified its decision by emphasizing that the flight had been within legal parameters (including Federal Aviation Administration regulations), did not interfere with the normal use of the greenhouse by way of undue noise, wind, dust, or threat of injury, and did not reveal any intimate details connected with the use of defendant's home.[12]

It is interesting to note that the Court in *Bond v. United States* 120 S.Ct. 1462 (2000) distinguishes the visual observations that existed in *Ciarolo* and *Riley* from a tactile observation. In *Bond* a customs agent boarded a bus and squeezed a carry-on canvas bag. Upon feeling a brick-like object, he asked and obtained consent to search which resulted in the finding of methamphetamine. The Court held that a physical inspection is simply more intrusive than a purely visual inspection and thus involves an expectation of privacy that society will deem to be reasonable.

As the overflight cases illustrate, the concept of expectation of privacy includes the factor of vantage point as well as setting. Where police observations are made from a location to which the public has lawful access (from air or ground), the viewing of otherwise protected areas (such as the curtilage) does not implicate the Fourth Amendment. Where, however, the police must enter the curtilage to make their observations, a "search" has taken place, triggering the amendment's protections.

A further issue arises when the police, from a lawful vantage point, employ devices that enhance the usual sensory abilities to see, hear, smell, or taste. What effect does this have on the reasonable expectation of privacy analysis? Assume, for example, that a police officer standing on a public street can observe marijuana plants growing in a bay window of Joe Bean's home. Having placed the plants in public view, Joe can have no reasonable expectation of privacy with regard to them, and the officer's observations do not constitute a search.[13] But if the plants are in a location that *cannot* be seen with the naked eye, and the officer discovers them only by use of a telescope, has a search occurred?

The Court has held that where the device employed merely facilitates surveillance that otherwise would be possible to conduct with-

---

12. One state appellate court, distinguishing *Ciraolo* and *Riley*, has held that a search occurred when a sheriff piloted a helicopter 200 feet over defendant's property and observed marijuana plants. The court found determinative the low altitude of the flight compared to *Ciraolo* (1,000 feet) and *Riley* (400 feet) and the excessive noise created by the flight, which witnesses testified disrupted the neighborhood. See *Colorado v. Pollock,* 796 P.2d 63 (Colo. Ct. App. 1990).

13. Those observations can therefore be used in establishing probable cause to obtain a warrant to search the home and seize the plants. The officer cannot, however, enter the home without a warrant. See §§5.1, 5.2.2.

out the enhancement, the Fourth Amendment is not implicated. Among the devices that have been held not to implicate the Fourth Amendment because they merely enhance sensory observation are a flashlight,[14] an aerial camera,[15] a drug-detection dog,[16] and field tests for narcotics.[17] Similarly when the police monitored an electronic tracking device attached to an automobile on public roads, no Fourth Amendment right was infringed because the movements of the car could have been observed by the naked eye. *United States v. Knotts*, 460 U.S. 276 (1983). When the police continued to monitor a beeper that had been installed in a container after it was taken into a home, however, the constraints of the amendment were held to apply because the device revealed information that could not have been obtained through unaided surveillance. *United States v. Karo*, 468 U.S. 705 (1984).

As *Karo* indicates, the physical setting in which an enhancement device is used plays a significant role in determining whether the subject's reasonable expectation of privacy has been violated. Surveillance into the home (where it has been consistently recognized the individual has a special privacy interest) is most likely to trigger the Fourth Amendment's protections. Thus the tracking of a beeper into the home was held to implicate the amendment. Similarly, while the use of a drug-detection dog to sniff luggage at an airport does not trigger the Fourth Amendment, the use of a drug-sniffing dog immediately adjacent to defendant's apartment to determine the presence of narcotics *within* has been held to trigger the amendment. See *United States v. Thomas*, 757 F.2d 1359 (2d Cir. 1985). Compare *United States v. Colyer*, 878 F.2d 469 (D.C. Cir. 1989) (holding that a dog sniff of defendant's sleeper unit on a train did not trigger the Fourth Amendment); *United States v. Lingenfelter*, 997 F.2d 632 (9th Cir. 1993) (dogs used to detect drugs by sniffing around warehouse did

---

14. *Texas v. Brown*, 460 U.S. 730 (1983); *United States v. Dunn*, 480 U.S. 294 (1987).

15. *Dow Chemical Co. v. United States*, 476 U.S. 207 (1986).

16. *United States v. Place*, 462 U.S. 696 (1983) (use of the detection dog at a public airport). But see *Commonwealth v. Johnston*, 515 Pa. 454 (1987) (holding that use of a drug-sniffing dog does constitute a search within the state constitution because "a free society will not remain free if police may use this, or any other crime detection device, at random and without reason.").

17. *United States v. Jacobsen*, 466 U.S. 109 (1984). The Court also premised its decision on the limited nature of the intrusion represented by a litmus test that can detect only the presence or absence of cocaine.

not constitute search). See also *United States v. Place*, 462 U.S. 696 (1983), discussed infra in explanation 6. As Justice Harlan observed in his concurrence in *Katz*, Fourth Amendment analysis "requires reference to a 'place.'" 389 U.S. at 361.

When police officers use a thermal imaging device to detect the levels of heat coming from within the home of a suspected drug cultivator (lights used to grow marijuana plants emit heat), is there a "search"? Not surprisingly, the courts are split on the question. Concluding that a thermal imager could reveal details such as intimate activities between two persons in a bedroom, the Ninth Circuit Court of Appeals has held that thermal scanning is definitely a search implicating the Fourth Amendment. *United States v. Kyllo*, 140 F.3d 1249 (9th Cir. 1998). "Surely a defendant, such as Kyllo, who moves his agricultural pursuits inside his house has . . . manifested a subjective expectation of privacy in those activities." Other circuits have analogized the heat detected by an imager to trash left on the curb—and under *California v. Greenwood* such "waste heat" carries no subjective expectation of privacy. See, e.g, *United States v. Robinson*, 62 F.3d 1325, 1328–1329 (11th Cir. 1995); *United States v. Myers*, 46 F.3d 668 (7th Cir. 1995). For the Tenth Circuit, these latter decisions

> misapprehended the most pernicious of the device's capabilities. The machine intrudes upon the privacy of the home not because it records white spots on a dark background but rather because the interpretation of that data allows the government to monitor those domestic activities that generate a significant amount of heat. Thus, while the imager cannot reproduce images or sounds, it nonetheless strips the sanctuary of the home of one vital dimension of its security: the "right to be let alone" from the arbitrary and discretionary monitoring of our actions by government officials.

United States v. Cusumano, 67 F.3d 1497, 1504 (10th Cir. 1995), *vacated on other grounds*, 83 F.3d 1247.

In addition to the telephone booth in *Katz*, the Court has found the Fourth Amendment applicable in several other settings outside the home. An administrator at a state hospital was held to have a reasonable expectation of privacy in his office even though "it is the nature of government offices that others—such as fellow employees, supervisors, consensual visitors, and the general public—may have frequent access to an individual's office." *O'Connor v. Ortega*, 480 U.S. 709,

717 (1987). The Court observed that as with one's home, expectation of privacy in one's place of work has "deep roots in the history of the amendment." The Court has similarly held that a student has a reasonable expectation of privacy in the public school setting. *New Jersey v. TLO*, 469 U.S. 325 (1985) (discussed in §4.5). Not surprisingly, however, a prisoner was held to have no justifiable expectation that his cell will be free from intrusion required by security concerns. *Hudson v. Palmer*, 468 U.S. 517 (1984).[18]

In analyzing the issue of whether a "search" implicating the Fourth Amendment has occurred, therefore, attention must be paid to both the setting observed and the vantage point from which the observation is made. Those factors weigh heavily in the determination of which privacy expectations are "reasonable."

It must be emphasized that we are dealing in this section solely with the threshold question of Fourth Amendment applicability: Has a "search" occurred? Or, put another way, was there a governmental intrusion that violated the citizen's reasonable expectation of privacy? If the answer is no, then the amendment does not apply. If the conduct in question does constitute a search, then the provisions of the amendment do come into play and additional questions must be answered as to the nature of the constraints on, and type of justification required for, the particular intrusion. These issues will be explored in the chapters that follow.

The Court's narrow definition of what constitutes a search in decisions such as the overflight cases, and the consequent confinement of the Fourth Amendment's reach, has met with substantial criticism. Justice Brennan has, for example, invoked the image of the Orwellian "Big Brother" to bemoan the removal of constitutional barriers from the use of technologically sophisticated surveillance. *Florida v. Riley*, 488 U.S. 445, 465 (1989) (dissenting). Undeniably, the definition of "search" is not so much a legal question as it is a basic value judgment as to what type of police conduct should be subject to constitutional scrutiny.

EXAMPLES

1. John is growing marijuana plants in a garden in his backyard immediately adjacent to the porch. The small yard is surrounded by

---

18. Where, however, the cell search is motivated not by institutional needs but by a prosecutor's desire to seize evidence, Fourth Amendment protections have been held to apply. See *United States v. Cohen*, 796 F.2d 20 (2d Cir. 1986).

an 8-foot-high stockade fence. A hot tub is located next to the garden. Has a search occurred in the following situations?

    a. Police Officer climbs over the stockade fence into the yard, enters the garden, and observes the plants.

    b. Police Officer climbs a stepladder she placed on the public sidewalk, peers over the fence, and observes the plants.

    c. Police Officer obtains the consent of John's neighbor and observes the plants from neighbor's second-story bedroom window.

    d. Assume instead that John's marijuana plants are located 75 feet from his house in a wooded area of his property (which is not encircled by a fence) and are surrounded by a dense circle of pine trees. Police Officer enters the property and observes the plants through the trees.

    e. Assume instead that John's marijuana plants are located 75 feet from his home inside a wooden shed. Police Officer enters the property and looks into the shed through an open window, thus observing the plants.

    f. Assume the same facts as in example 1e, except the officer enters the shed in order to make her observations.

2. Police officer Berkel, with the permission of the landlord, entered a crawl space under Paul Parrott's first-floor apartment. The crawl space is used when repairing pipes and wiring, but neither the tenants nor the public has regular access to it. Officer Berkel spent two hours in the space and heard Parrott engage in what appeared to be numerous sales of narcotics. Was the information obtained by Berkel accomplished through a search within the meaning of the Fourth Amendment?

3a. Drug enforcement agents stationed themselves (with the permission of the landlord) in a third-floor apartment across the street from Bad Thad's first-floor apartment. With the aid of a telescope, the agents were able to observe through the open curtains of the kitchen window Thad's activities in weighing and packaging a white powder and to read the label on a jar used by Thad, which indicated that it contained a solution known to be a diluent for cocaine. Does the agents' conduct constitute a search?

3b. Assume that instead of viewing the inside of Thad's apartment, the agents trained their telescope on a small plot of soil located behind Thad's apartment. The land is enclosed by a fence and thus not open to view from the ground. Through the telescope the agents observed marijuana seedlings. Does the agents' conduct constitute a search?

4. Acting on a hunch that narcotics activity was being conducted at 987 Fisher Road, Oakdale, the police decided to collect the garbage at that location and search it for evidence. In Oakdale, trash is not collected at curbside, but rather the municipal workers walk to the back of homes to pick up trash bags placed outside by residents. Disguised as such a municipal worker, Officer Daly walked to the back of 987 Fisher Road and found four plastic trash bags tied at the top and leaning against the wall of the home. Daly removed the bags and took them to the police station where she opened them. Inside she found a spiral notebook, which had been ripped into quarters. Daly pieced together the shredded papers, which turned out to document hundreds of narcotics sales. Has a search taken place?

5. FBI agents arrested one James Lyons on drug trafficking charges and discovered in his possession a padlock key and an Ace Storage Company rental agreement for unit #792. The agents went to the storage company, inserted the key into the lock on unit #792, and confirmed that the key turned the tumbler. They relocked the unit without opening it and reported the fact that Lyons's key opened the lock. Based on that connection, a search warrant was issued for unit #792. Defendant moves to suppress the evidence found on the grounds that the previous insertion of the key into the lock was itself a search, which was not in conformity with Fourth Amendment requirements. How should the court rule?

6. While walking through Kennedy Airport, Donald was subjected to a sniff from a drug-detection dog being used by federal agents. The dog had been trained to detect cocaine, which he indicated was present on Donald's person. Donald was arrested and searched and cocaine was found in his jacket pocket. Prior to trial he moved to suppress the cocaine on the grounds that the dog sniff constituted a search that was not conducted in conformity with Fourth Amendment requirements. How should the court rule?

7. David Copper was suspected of involvement in a bank fraud scheme. As part of their investigation the police requested and received from the Friendly Federal Bank an application he filed for a large commercial loan. The document confirmed their suspicions and David was indicted. Prior to trial he moved to suppress the application on the ground that it was obtained in violation of the Fourth Amendment. Has a search occurred within the meaning of that amendment?

8. Suspecting Carol Smooth of failure to report income, federal tax agents placed a "mail cover" on her mail. This permitted the agents to observe and record all information (name and return address of sender, place and date of postmark) located on the outside of envelopes in her incoming mail. The agents were thus able to gather evidence that Carol maintained several secret Swiss bank accounts. Carol seeks suppression of the evidence, claiming that the mail cover was an illegal search under the Fourth Amendment. Has a search occurred?

Chapter Review

9. John Sherman, the director of security operations for the Atlantic Bell Telephone Company, received a number of complaints from women alleging that Simon Sleaze (a former boyfriend of each) was making frequent obscene telephone calls to them. To verify these complaints, Sherman installed a pen register on Sleaze's residential telephone line. While such devices are routinely used to register long distance calls for billing purposes, the device placed on Sleaze's line was set to record local numbers dialed. The pen register confirmed that he was in fact placing calls to the complainants, and pursuant to company policy this information was turned over to the district attorney's office. Criminal charges have been brought against Sleaze, and he seeks to suppress the pen register evidence on Fourth Amendment grounds. Has a search occurred?

EXPLANATIONS

1a. A search has occurred here because the officer entered the curtilage of the home in order to make her observations. Under the factors set forth in *United States v. Dunn*, 480 U.S. 294 (1987), the garden is in close proximity to the home, it is an area within an enclosure surrounding the home (the fence), it is used for intimate activities (the hot tub), and John has taken steps to protect the privacy of the area (erecting the stockade fence). Thus it is clear that the garden is an area so intimately tied to the home that it should be placed under its umbrella of protection as curtilage. Had the officer instead made her observations from a walkway that was a regular approach to the house and frequently used by visitors, there would have been no reasonable expectation of privacy and thus no search. See *Lorenzana v. Superior Court of Los Angeles County*, 108 Cal. Rptr. 585, 511 P.2d 33 (Sup. Ct. Cal. 1973).

1b. No search has taken place here. While the setting remains the same as in example 1a, the vantage point from which the officer made her observations is now one to which the public has lawful (although not usual) access. On the reasoning of the aerial surveillance cases, *California v. Ciraolo* and *Florida v. Riley,* although John has protected against observations from the ground level, his property may be subjected to an above-ground view from a publicly accessible location without implicating the Fourth Amendment. A stepladder, moreover, would not be regarded as an extraordinary enhancement device triggering the Fourth Amendment's applicability.

Thus the observations made by the officer could be lawfully used to establish probable cause for the issuance of a search warrant to enter the premises and seize the plants. See Chapter 5. It must be emphasized, however, that the observation of contraband itself does not permit warrantless police entry into the curtilage. As the Court has put it: "Incontrovertible testimony of the senses that an incriminating object is on the premises belonging to a criminal suspect may establish the fullest possible measure of probable cause. But even where the object is contraband, this Court has repeatedly stated and enforced the basic rule that the police may not enter and make a warrantless seizure." *Coolidge v. New Hampshire*, 403 U.S. 443, 468 (1971). See also *United States v. Whaley*, 781 F.2d 417 (5th Cir. 1986) (holding unlawful the sheriff's warrantless entry into the curtilage and seizure of the marijuana plants following his observation of the plants from the road). There is, in short, a material difference between *observing* contraband in the home or curtilage from a lawful vantage point (an act that is not a search) and *entering* those areas to seize the item after observing it (an act that undeniably constitutes a search and seizure).

1c. The officer's vantage point, although lawful, is one to which the public does not have general access. The question posed is whether John has a reasonable expectation that his marijuana plants will be free from police observation when in fact his neighbor can view them from a bedroom window? While the Supreme Court does not appear to have ruled directly on this question, its assumption of risk decisions, as well as lower court authority, would seem to place the officer's observations outside the scope of Fourth Amendment coverage. See, e.g, *United States v. Taborda*, 635 F.2d 131 (2d Cir. 1980) (holding that unenhanced visual observations made by police from an apartment across the street from defendant's apartment was not a search). John has, in other words, assumed the risk that his neighbor would permit such an observation.

Assume the police officer trespasses on John's neighbor's property, stands on top of a stepladder, and observes the plants. Has a search occurred? Probably not. In *Sarantopoulos v. State*, 629 So. 2d 121 (Fla. 1993), involving these very circumstances, the court reasoned that a neighbor could have observed the plants from a stepladder or from the roof and this was a risk the defendant took. The court also held that the trespass did *not* make the search illegal. A similar result was reached in *United States v. Fields*, 113 F.3d 313 (2d Cir. 1997), where officers stood in the side yard of a three-family apartment house and peered into a window whose shade was partially raised. No search was deemed to have occurred despite the trespass because the officers were in a location where other tenants were free to come and go.

1d. No search has occurred. *Oliver v. United States*, 466 U.S. 170 (1984), teaches that open fields are not entitled to Fourth Amendment protection, even when efforts at concealment are made. This is true despite the fact that the officer's conduct constitutes a common law trespass onto the property. Indeed, where the police used a backhoe to dig up large areas of the defendant's farm and found the body of a murder victim, the Supreme Court of Wisconsin held that the Fourth Amendment was not implicated. *Conrad v. State*, 218 N.W.2d 252 (1974).

1e. As noted above, the police may enter the open fields surrounding John's home and make observations there without implicating the Fourth Amendment. Only if they intrude upon the curtilage of the home will the constitutional protections come into play. Given the distance between the home and the shed and the fact that the shed was not within an enclosure that surrounded the home, it is unlikely that the shed would be considered within the area so intimately tied to the home that it should be placed under the same protection. See *United States v. Dunn*, 480 U.S. 294 (1987) (area outside barn not within curtilage of the home).

1f. Yes, a search has occurred. In *United States v. Dunn* the Court assumed (without having to decide) that a barn located in an open field area and used by the property owner for business purposes was entitled to Fourth Amendment protection independent from the home and its curtilage. It would appear, then, that John's shed could not be entered without triggering the Fourth Amendment.

2. It must be determined whether Parrott had a constitutionally protected expectation that conversations within his apartment (a setting entitled to the highest degree of privacy protection) would be beyond the reach of the government's ear. His *subjective* expectation, standing alone, is not sufficient to invoke the protections of the Fourth Amendment. That expectation must be *reasonable*—that is, deemed one that society is willing to enforce. Among the considerations courts have looked to in such situations is whether the person conducting the surveillance had a lawful right to be where he was. Thus it has generally been held that an individual has no reasonable expectation of privacy in conversations that can be heard by the unaided ear of an eavesdropper who is lawfully in an adjoining apartment or hotel or motel room. See, e.g., *United States v. Hessling*, 845 F.2d 617, 619 (6th Cir. 1988); *United States v. Agapito*, 620 F.2d 324, 330–332 (2d Cir. 1980); *United States v. Jackson*, 588 F.2d 1046, 1051–1052 (5th Cir. 1979). On this reasoning Parrott has not been subjected to a search because the officer was lawfully in the crawl space by permission of the landlord.

It can be argued, however, that there is a meaningful distinction between running the risk that someone may be listening at the wall of an occupied contiguous apartment and risking that someone would be listening from a crawl space, which was closed to both the public and the tenants. The Supreme Judicial Court of Massachusetts relied on this distinction in ruling that a search had occurred under these circumstances within the meaning of the state constitution. *Commonwealth v. Panetti*, 406 Mass. 230 (1989). The court relied on a noted treatise, which asserted that "resort to the extraordinary step of positioning themselves where neither neighbors nor the general public would ordinarily be expected to be" implicated the Fourth Amendment. 1 W. LaFave, Search and Seizure §2.3(l) at 392 (2d ed. 1987).

Another issue raised by this problem is the authority of the landlord to agree to a search of a tenant's property. Third-party consent is discussed in §6.7.

3a. The place observed here is the interior of a residence, a setting embodying the highest degree of justifiable privacy expectations. If, however, Thad (who failed to close his curtains) conducted his activities in a manner that could be seen by the unaided viewing of persons lawfully placed outside (including from the building across the street), then he is entitled to no Fourth Amendment protection. Because the agents had to resort to enhancement by way of telescope in order to observe intimate details of Thad's conduct within his home, the Fourth Amendment is most likely implicated. The Second Circuit held in a case on these facts that any enhanced viewing of the interior of a home impairs a legitimate expectation of privacy, and that citizens need not protect against such enhanced surveillance (for example, by closing all curtains) in order to preserve that expectation. *United States v. Taborda*, 635 F.2d 131 (2d Cir. 1980).

3b. The setting for the observation has now changed from the interior of the home to curtilage, an area afforded somewhat less protection against intrusion. Although *Riley* and *Ciraolo* permit naked-eye observation of curtilage areas (even if enclosed) from lawful aerial vantage points, the agents here used an enhancement device to obtain their view. Thad would thus argue that the Fourth Amendment should be applicable here.

Where a surveillance camera was used to observe the open areas of an industrial complex, the Court concluded that no search had occurred. See *Dow Chemical v. United States*, 476 U.S. 227 (1986). Thad would attempt to distinguish *Dow Chemical* on the ground that the setting there was considered open fields, an area not entitled to Fourth Amendment protection. Given that the matter observed by the agents here—the growing of contraband—is not the kind of intimate activity usually associated with the home, *Riley* suggests that Thad may meet with little success. In *Kitzmiller v. State*, 548 A.2d 140 (Md. Ct. Spec. App. 1988), the court concluded that no search had occurred where an officer, with the aid of binoculars, observed marijuana plants within the curtilage of defendant's home from a vantage point in a tree 40 feet above the ground.

4. The Supreme Court has held that the Fourth Amendment does not protect against the seizure and examination of the contents of trash bags left at the curb. This is so because 1) public exposure of the trash forfeits any reasonable expectation of privacy in the bags; and 2) once the trash is conveyed to third-party collectors, the homeowner assumes the risk that they will turn the bags over to the police. See *California v. Greenwood*, 486 U.S. 35 (1988).

In this example, however, the closed bags were left within the curtilage of the home, an area that has been afforded greater protection than areas such as the curbside, which are not immediately adjacent to the home. Several courts have found this distinction to be determinative. See *United States v. Certain Real Property Located at 987 Fisher Road*, 719 F. Supp. 1396 (E.D. Mich. 1989) (and cases cited) (holding that the Fourth Amendment is implicated by the seizure of trash within the curtilage because of occupants' heightened expectation of privacy as long as the bags remain in that area). But compare *United States v. Redmon*, 138 F.3d 1109, 1112 (7th Cir. 1998) (no expectation of privacy with regard to trash left in curtilage where it is publicly accessible and left for collection). Because the seizure here involved a physical intrusion *into* the curtilage and not merely an observation from a point *outside*, the Fourth Amendment may be implicated.

Another distinction between this problem and *Greenwood* is that the police here reconstructed documents that had been shredded by the homeowner. United States District Judge Joseph Tauro concluded that use of a shredding machine manifests an expectation of privacy, which overrides the presumption in *Greenwood* and which was violated by the police action. See *United States v. Alan N. Scott*, 776 F.Supp. 629 (D. Mass 1991):

> Here, defendant had taken steps to protect his privacy rights by shredding his trash. In *Greenwood* the Court stated that it was "common knowledge" that trash left on the curb is accessible to snoops and scavengers. But, it is not "common knowledge" that snoops and scavengers may retrieve shredded materials and then painstakingly reconstruct them to learn the contents. Society would accept as reasonable, therefore, defendant's belief that once he shredded his documents, they would be shielded from public examination.

On appeal the First Circuit rejected this reasoning, holding that the garbage was placed in the public domain and the defendant assumed the risk that through human ingenuity or scientific advances someone could "break the code." 975 F.2d 927 (1st Cir. 1992). See also *United States v. Hall*, 47 F.3d 1091 (11th Cir. 1995) (no reasonable expectation of privacy in shredded documents placed in garbage bag in closed dumpster).

5. Lyons clearly had a reasonable expectation of privacy in *the contents* of the locked locker. The question raised here, however, is whether that expectation extends to the lock itself. Several courts have concluded that the insertion of a key into a lock for the lim-

ited purpose of identifying the lock's owner does not constitute a search. See *United States v. Lyons*, 898 F.2d 210, 213 (1st Cir. 1990) ("[W]e hold that the insertion of a key into a lock, followed by the turning of its tumbler in order to determine the fit, is so minimally intrusive that it does not implicate a reasonable expectation of privacy."); *United States v. DeBardeleben*, 740 F.2d 440 (6th Cir. 1984); *People v. Carroll*, 12 Ill. App. 3d 869, 299 N.E.2d 134 (1973). At least one court has concluded otherwise. See *United States v. Portillo-Reyes*, 529 F.2d 844 (9th Cir. 1975) (insertion of key into car door for purpose of ascertaining ownership constitutes a search).

United States District Judge Woodlock, in a dissenting opinion in *United States v. Lyons*, analogized the key-insertion situation to *Arizona v. Hicks*, 480 U.S. 321 (1987) (discussed in §6.8), which held that a search occurred when officers lifted stereo components to reveal the serial numbers imprinted on the bottom. He concluded that the insertion of the key, like the lifting of the equipment, exposed enough information about the object to trigger the protections of the Fourth Amendment.

6. *United States v. Place*, 462 U.S. 696 (1983), held that the use of a drug-detection dog at a public airport to determine the presence of a contraband substance did not trigger the protections of the Fourth Amendment. *Place*, however, involved a sniff of defendant's luggage. The dog in this example was used on defendant's own *person*, in which case the nature of the intrusion was, therefore, arguably greater. In the case upon which this example is based, the Ninth Circuit Court of Appeals found this distinction determinative and concluded that a search occurred when the detection dog sniffed the defendant himself. See *United States v. Beale*, 736 F.2d 1289 (9th Cir. 1984). Physically touching of luggage however does implicate the Fourth Amendment see *Bond v. United States* 592 U.S.____ (2000).

7. This question translates into whether David had an expectation of privacy that society recognizes as reasonable with regard to his loan application. Because he had voluntarily submitted the application to the bank, the case appears to fall within the assumption of risk doctrine. In *United States v. Miller*, 425 U.S. 435 (1976), an account depositor was held to have incurred the risk that information concerning his financial transactions would be revealed by his bank to the government. David in effect forfeited his expectation of privacy in the application when he submitted it to the

bank and thus has no Fourth Amendment protection. See *United States v. Grubb*, 469 F. Supp. 991 (E.D. Pa. 1979).

Recognizing the central role that banks play in our society today and the consequent fact that a customer's disclosure of information to a bank is not entirely volitional, several state courts have found a legitimate expectation of privacy in bank records under their own constitutions. See *Charnes v. DiGiacomo*, 612 P.2d 1117 (Colo. 1980); *Commonwealth v. DeJohn*, 403 A.2d 1283 (Pa. 1979) (*Miller* "opens the door to a vast and unlimited range of very real abuses of police power."); *Burrows v. Superior Court*, 118 Cal. Rptr. 166, 169, 529 P.2d 590, 593 (1974) ("It cannot be gainsaid that the customer of a bank expects that the documents, such as checks, which he transmits to the bank in the course of his business operations, will remain private, and that such an expectation is reasonable."). See also *People v. Blair*, 159 Cal. Rptr. 818, 825, 602 P.2d 738, 745 (Cal. Sup. Ct. 1979) (holding that a credit card company's disclosure of defendant's account statement to the prosecutor constituted a search under California law: " [A] person who uses a credit card may reveal his habits, his opinions, his tastes, and political views, as well as his movements and financial affairs. No less than a bank statement, the charges made on a credit card may provide a virtual current biography of an individual.").

David will, therefore, have to look to state law rather than to the Fourth Amendment in order to keep this evidence out of the trial.

8. Because the information placed on the outside of envelopes is voluntarily exposed by the sender to postal workers (and others) in the ordinary course of business, the investigative mail cover has been placed in the assumption of risk category and held not to constitute a search for Fourth Amendment purposes. See *United States v. Choate*, 576 F.2d 165 (9th Cir. 1978); *United States v. Leonard*, 524 F.2d 1076 (2d Cir. 1975). Like the pen register in *Smith v. Maryland*, 442 U.S. 735 (1979), the mail cover records information disclosed to the carrier and thus invades no reasonable expectation of privacy.

    Interception of *the contents* of mail or telephone conversations would of course be beyond the scope of the public exposure doctrine and thus constitute a search. If, however, a participant in the conversation discloses it to the government, under the "misplaced reliance" cases (*Hoffa v. United States* and *United States v. White,*) the Fourth Amendment is not implicated.

Chapter Review

9. This problem raises both types of issues regarding Fourth Amendment applicability: Has a search occurred? And, if so, was it governmental or private in nature? Regarding the latter, it must be determined whether Atlantic Bell is a private or public company. If Sherman is employed by a private utility company and acted without any request or encouragement from a governmental actor, then the placement of the pen register is a purely private action outside the scope of the Fourth Amendment. If, on the other hand, the district attorney had requested that the dialing information be gathered by the company, either in this particular case or generally whenever a complaint is made, that would constitute sufficient governmental involvement to trigger the Fourth Amendment. Something in between, such as the district attorney's long-standing policy of accepting pen register information from the phone company, may constitute acquiescence in the private search and thus convert it into governmental conduct. In this latter situation, the court would look to the company's motivation in collecting the information as well. If it were determined that the phone company had been motivated primarily by a desire to investigate criminal law violations in aid of the police, and not by an independent business purpose (such as protecting its customers), that would point to a conclusion that the conduct implicated the Fourth Amendment. See *United States v. Feffer*, 831 F.2d 734 (7th Cir. 1987); *United States v. Koenig*, 856 F.2d 843 (7th Cir. 1988); *United States v. Walther*, 652 F.2d 788 (9th Cir. 1981).

   Assuming that there is state action, the second question is whether a search has occurred, which translates into whether Sleaze had a reasonable expectation of privacy in the numbers dialed from his residential telephone. Because using the telephone automatically discloses to the telephone company the numbers dialed, under *Smith v. Maryland* the pen register has been held outside the scope of the Fourth Amendment. The Court has consistently held that the Fourth Amendment does not apply to information conveyed by *A* to *B* when *B* reveals it to the government, even if the information is conveyed by *A* on the assumption that it will remain private. *A* assumes the risk that *B* will spill the beans.

   A number of state courts have disagreed and held that use of the pen register in the manner set out in this problem does constitute a search within their own constitutions. The New Jersey Supreme Court, for example, has reasoned that the telephone user's disclosure to the company of numbers dialed "has been necessitated because of the nature of the instrumentality, but more significantly the disclosure has been made for a limited business purpose and not for release to other persons for other reasons." *State v. Hunt*, 450 A.2d 952, 956 (N.J. Super. 1982). See also *People v. Sponleder*, 666 P.2d 135 (Colo. Sup. Ct. 1983); *Commonwealth v. Melilli*, 555 A.2d 1254 (Pa. 1989). If Sleaze is prosecuted in one of these states, he has a basis to seek suppression of the evidence.

It must be remembered that applicability of the Fourth Amendment is just the threshold stage of the legal analysis of any search and seizure problem. The fact that a search has occurred means simply that the Fourth Amendment applies. Whether the amendment's provisions have been violated is an entirely different question, to which we turn our attention in the chapters that follow.

4

What Does the Fourth Amendment Require?—The Doctrine of Justification

Once it is determined that the Fourth Amendment applies in a particular situation (see Chapter 3), the question arises as to what the amendment requires. The fundamental premise underlying the Fourth Amendment is that the police must have justification (or cause) *before* they may conduct a search or seizure. The fact that they find contraband or evidence of crime is not sufficient to justify a search *after the fact*. Determination of the requisite level of cause necessary to justify a search or seizure represents an effort to balance the interest of effective law enforcement on the one hand and individual liberty on the other. The nature of the constraint placed upon the police by the Fourth Amendment will depend in large part on how much (or how little) information they are required to possess about the suspect before they may engage in intrusive action.

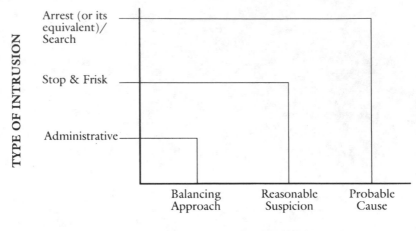

JUSTIFICATION

Figure 4–1:   Standards of Justification—Summary

Although probable cause is the only standard of justification explicitly set out in the Fourth Amendment itself,[1] the courts have invoked the reasonableness clause to craft modifications of that concept to fit different types of police action. As we will see, the justification required has generally been tied to the scope and degree of intrusion: the greater the invasion of privacy, the more cause that must be demonstrated. On the sliding scale that has resulted, probable cause and reasonable suspicion represent the two benchmarks (see Figure 4–1). Another form of justification has evolved in the so-called administrative search area where a balancing test is used to weigh the importance of the societal-governmental interest served against the interference with individual privacy to determine the appropriate level of justification for the particular intrusion.

§4.1   Probable Cause—The Standard for Search and Arrest

Probable cause is the measure of justification that applies to full-scale intrusions—that is, searches, seizures, and arrests. When the police act

---

1. While the only textual reference to probable cause appears in the warrant clause of the amendment, that standard has been held to apply to warrantless searches and seizures as well. In establishing a uniform standard of probable cause, the Supreme Court has recognized that the setting of a lower standard for warrantless searches and arrests would create an incentive for the police to avoid the warrant process, a result the Court has sought to avoid. See *Wong Sun v. United States*, 371 U.S. 471, 479–480 (1963).

by way of a warrant, the determination of whether probable cause exists is made by a magistrate prior to the proposed action (see Chapter 5). When the police act without a warrant (as they are permitted to do in certain situations, see Chapter 6), they themselves make the initial evaluation of probable cause. But that police evaluation is reviewable in court after the search, on a motion to suppress the evidence discovered.

Probable cause has been defined as the amount of facts and circumstances within the police officer's knowledge that would warrant a reasonable person to conclude that the particular individual has committed a crime (in the case of an arrest) or that specific items related to criminal activity will be found at the particular place (in the case of a search). The information may include reasonably trustworthy hearsay that has been conveyed to the officer, as well as the officer's own personal observations. An adequate showing of probable cause requires specific facts, not simply conclusory assertions. On a scale of probability, probable cause is something more than mere hunch or suspicion, but considerably less than proof beyond a reasonable doubt. As Justice Black once put it: "Of course it would strengthen the probable-cause presentation if eyewitnesses could testify that they saw the defendant commit the crime . . . [but] [n]othing in our Constitution . . . requires that the facts be established with that degree of certainty." *Spinelli v. United States*, 393 U.S. 410, 429 (1969) (Black, J., dissenting).

As stated above, somewhat different conclusions are required for arrest and search situations. The implications of this difference can be seen in the so-called staleness problem with regard to search warrants. Because items relating to crime are often transportable, establishment of probable cause to search requires a showing that the items sought are presently at the place to be searched. Thus timeliness of the information becomes more important in the context of a search than an arrest, where there is no analogous temporal limitation.

The Supreme Court has emphasized that "the central teaching of our decisions bearing on the probable cause standard is that it is a practical, nontechnical conception. In dealing with probable cause, as the very name implies, we deal with probabilities. These are not technical; they are the factual and practical considerations of everyday life on which reasonable and prudent men, not legal technicians, act." *Illinois v. Gates*, 462 U.S. 213, 231 (1983) (citations and internal quotations omitted). As a "fluid concept—turning on the assessment of probabilities in particular factual contexts— [probable cause is] not readily, or even usefully, reduced to a neat set of legal rules." Id. (citation omitted).

When weighing the adequacy of cause in a given case, courts focus on the source of the information in the possession of the police as well as the conclusions that may be reasonably drawn from it. If the information is based on the police officer's own observations, the credibility of those observations is uniformly presumed by the courts. If, however, the officer has obtained the information from a third party, the reliability of that source must be weighed together with the likely accuracy of the inferences drawn. While the courts tend to credit information conveyed by named victims or witnesses, the credibility of unnamed informants (a frequent source of probable cause) cannot be presumed, but must instead be demonstrated.

In *Aguilar v. Texas*, 378 U.S. 108 (1964) and *Spinelli v. United States*, 393 U.S. 410 (1969), the Supreme Court established a structure for evaluating probable cause based on information supplied to the police by confidential informants. The two-pronged test focuses separately on the credibility of the informant (Why should the police believe this person?) and the basis of her knowledge (How does the informant know what she claims to know?). The information supporting each prong must be specific so that the conclusions reached can be tested against the known facts. Thus a mere conclusory assertion by the officer that "the informant is credible" will not satisfy the credibility prong; rather the basis for that conclusion must be set out (for example, "This informant has provided me information on previous occasions, which led to the arrest and conviction of John Doe and Richard Roe."). Similarly, the statement that "the informant has advised me that narcotics are being sold at this address" will not satisfy the knowledge prong. The facts underlying the informant's assertion must be articulated (for example, "The informant states that she purchased narcotics at this address earlier today."). Where the informant speaks from her own personal knowledge, the courts have generally credited the information. See *United States v. Freitas*, 716 F.2d 1216 (9th Cir. 1983).

Case law has developed a variety of alternative methods to fulfill the two-pronged test. The knowledge prong, for example, may be satisfied by setting out very detailed information supplied by the informant from which it may reasonably be inferred that she is speaking from personal knowledge and not mere rumor or conjecture. See *Draper v. United States*, 358 U.S. 307 (1959). The credibility prong may be met where the informant implicates herself in criminal activity, on the premise that such admission against self-interest carries some assurance of reliability.[2] Independent corroboration by the police of specific facts asserted by the informant can be a factor in satisfying either prong (although verification of innocent details is obviously less significant than details involving criminal activity). See *Draper*, supra. The corroboration must be such to "permit the suspicions engendered by the informer's tip to ripen into a judgment that a crime was probably being committed." *Spinelli*, supra, 393 U.S. at 410.

The traditional analysis of probable cause based on informant information was modified somewhat by the Supreme Court in *Illinois v. Gates*, 462 U.S. 213 (1983). While reaffirming the importance of evaluating both the informant's credibility and the basis of her knowledge, the Court abandoned the requirement that these prongs be considered as distinct elements. It adopted instead a "totality-of-the-circumstances" approach in which the two prongs are treated as interrelated, and "a deficiency in one may be compensated for, in determining the overall reliability of a tip, by a strong showing as to the other, or by some other indicia of reliability." Thus the Court suggested that if "a particular informant is known for the unusual reliability of his predictions of certain types of criminal activities in a locality, his failure, in a particular case, to thoroughly set forth the basis of his knowledge surely should not serve as an absolute bar to a finding of probable cause based on his tip." 462 U.S. at 233. A tip from an informant whose past reliability could not be determined, might similarly be deemed adequate if the information was sufficiently detailed to justify the inference that she was speaking from personal knowledge of the circumstances. The *Gates* Court replaced an approach to probable cause that it considered "an excessively technical dissection of informants' tips" with an analysis that "permits a balanced assessment of the relative weights of all the various indicia of reliability (and unreliability) attending an informant's tip." Id. at 234. The revised standard to be met is whether there is a "fair probability that contraband or evidence of a crime will be found in a particular place." Id. at 238.

---

2. *United States v. Harris*, 403 U.S. 573, 583 (1971) ("Common sense in the important daily affairs of life would induce a prudent and disinterested observer to credit these statements. People do not lightly admit a crime and place critical evidence in the hands of the police in the form of their own admissions. Admissions of crime . . . carry their own indicia of credibility. . . ."). Where it appears, however, that the informer is implicating herself to curry favor with the police to work out a deal, courts have discounted the weight of self-implication. See, e.g., *United States v. Jackson*, 818 F.2d 345, 349 (5th Cir. 1987).

This change in probable cause analysis was prompted in part by the *Gates* Court's concern that rigorous application of the *Aguilar-Spinelli* approach would prevent the police from relying on anonymous tips. "Such tips, particularly when supplemented by independent police investigation, frequently contribute to the solution of otherwise 'perfect crimes.'" Id. at 237–238.

Despite *Gates*, the *Aguilar-Spinelli* test retains some importance. First, it delineates the two fundamental factors to be considered in weighing informant information. The *Gates* Court reiterated that "reliability" and "basis of knowledge" remain the key issues to examine. Although they are no longer entirely separate requirements for probable cause, they remain the core of the new totality of the circumstances analysis. Second, several states have adhered to the traditional two-pronged test in interpreting their own constitutional provisions regarding search and seizure. See, e.g., *Commonwealth v. Upton*, 394 Mass. 363, 476 N.E.2d 548 (1985).

It should be noted that where an officer has probable cause justifying a particular intrusion, the fact that the officer may have acted for ulterior reasons is irrelevant. Where, for example, a narcotics detective stops a car for a traffic violation but his actual motivation is to search for drugs, the legality of the search is determined solely by the existence of probable cause for the stop. See *Whren v. United States*, 517 U.S. 806 (1996), discussed in 6.9

EXAMPLES
The Basics

1. Officer Peters has concluded, based on his intuition developed over 30 years of experience, that cocaine is being sold out of Apt. 3 at 10 Main Street. Does he have probable cause to search?

2. Officer Peters, while undercover, observed a white powdery substance on the kitchen table in Apt. 3 at 10 Main Street. He further observed several persons sniffing this powder and appearing to get high. They paid large amounts of cash to the tenant in return for plastic bags of the powder. Based on his first-hand observations, as well as his long experience with narcotics, Officer Peters has concluded that the substance is cocaine. Does he have probable cause to seize the powder and arrest the participants?

3. The police assert that they have "received reliable information from a credible person and believe that narcotics are being stored" at a particular location. Do they have probable cause to search?

4. An informant reported to the police that one Fraper, traveling from Chicago, would arrive at the Denver train station on either September 8 or 9 carrying a tan zipper bag that would contain heroin. The informant, who had previously provided "accurate and reliable" information to the police regarding narcotics violations, presented a detailed physical description of Fraper and the clothing he would be wearing and reported that he would be walking very fast. Police officers staked out the train station, and on September 9 they observed a man precisely fitting that description disembark a Chicago train and proceed to walk quickly toward an exit. Is there probable cause to arrest?

5. FBI agents have observed one Pinelli, who "is known to law enforcement officers as a bookmaker," entering and leaving a particular apartment over the course of five days. A "reliable" informant told the agents that Pinelli is operating a bookmaking business at the apartment by use of two telephones inside. A check with the telephone company revealed that the apartment does have two telephones installed. Do the police have probable cause to search the apartment?

6. The Chicago Police Department received an anonymous, handwritten letter stating that Sue and Lance Bates, who live in the Greenway condominiums, were making their living selling narcotics. The letter detailed the usual manner in which this operation was carried out. Lance would typically fly to Miami, where he would purchase the drugs. Sue would drive their Volvo down and meet him. Lance would then drive the car home, with the narcotics in the trunk, and Sue would return home by plane. The letter asserted that Sue would be driving to Miami again on May 3, that Lance would fly down some days later, and that he would promptly return by car with over $100,000 worth of drugs. The writer also stated that there were drugs worth a similar amount in the Bateses' basement.

    Subsequent police investigation confirmed the Bateses' address and revealed that Lance Bates had a reservation to fly to Miami on May 5. Arrangements were made for surveillance, and he was observed boarding the flight, arriving in Florida, proceeding to a hotel, and departing the following morning in the Volvo traveling north.

    Do the police have probable cause to search the Bateses' car? Their condominium? Do the police have probable cause to arrest Lance?

The Plot Thickens

7. Officers of the Yarmouth Police Department executed a search warrant for a motel room reserved by one Kevin Kape and discovered several items belonging to persons whose homes had recently been burglarized. Later that day one of the officers received a call from an anonymous female who told him there was a motor home "full of stolen stuff" parked in front of George Grape's house. The caller described items she had seen that matched some of those taken in the prior burglaries. She added that Grape was about to move the motor home because he said "the police were getting much too close," and referred to the raid on Kape's motel room.

    The informant refused to identify herself because she said she feared Grape would kill her, but she finally admitted in response to the officer's guess that she was Grape's former girlfriend, Lynn Lotus. She told the officer that they had recently broken up and that she wanted to "really burn him bad."

    The officer, after verifying that a motor home was parked at the address stated by the caller, applied for a warrant to search it for items stolen during the burglaries. Is there probable cause to search the motor home?

8. Police received a tip from a confidential source who had provided information in the past that resulted in several indictments. The informant stated that Raymond Frank and a person named Mike were importing narcotics using a furniture company as a cover. The source indicated that Mike lived in Concord, California. Using telephone toll records the police determined that Frank spoke frequently with Michael Best, who resided in a town near Concord. A second, unrelated snitch was asked what she knew about Michael Best. She advised the police that Best and a partner were dealing narcotics "in a big way." She further stated that the narcotics were shipped to Port of San Francisco. Checking cargo records, the police discovered that two shipments of furniture from Colombia had arrived at the port within the past six weeks and that Ray Frank had signed for the shipments and trucked them away.

    Police learned that another shipment of furniture from Colombia was due on June 1. Surveillance was established at the docks. When the shipment arrived, it passed through a routine customs inspection. Ray Frank was later observed loading the shipment into his truck and departing. Frank drove to a warehouse in

Concord, where he met with two other persons unknown to the police.

Do the police have probable cause to search the truck for narcotics?

The Ingredients in the Probable Cause Recipe

9. Detective Casey received an anonymous telephone call asserting that Sammy Shay was dealing narcotics to students at the local high school. Casey made several observations of Shay on school grounds, but was unable to confirm that he was involved in illegal activity. The detective decided to check whether Shay had any prior criminal record and learned that he had four convictions for narcotics offenses within the past eight years. Does Casey now have probable cause to arrest Shay when she observes him at the school?

10. While on routine patrol two plainclothes officers observed several men standing on a street corner. On a hunch that a narcotics transaction was taking place, the officers approached the men and yelled at them to freeze. The men immediately fled, and the officers gave chase. Is there probable cause to arrest once the men seek to escape?

11. Janice Dow was standing on a street corner in Manhattan that was known to police as "drug alley." Police officers observed her from their cruiser at 12:30 A.M. In the next 50 minutes they observed her conversing separately with six persons in very short conversations. Based on their long experience in the narcotics bureau and their knowledge of this area of the city, the officers concluded that Dow was dealing drugs. Does their conclusion constitute probable cause to arrest?

12. A clerk at a convenience store telephoned police and reported that a man with a small handgun protruding from his rear pocket had just left the store and departed in a gray pickup truck with license plate 32HIN. The clerk did not indicate that the man had engaged in any criminal or suspicious conduct. Officers have spotted the vehicle. Do they have probable cause to arrest for illegal possession of a handgun or to search the vehicle for the weapon?

Here Today, Gone Tomorrow/Here Tomorrow, But Not Today

13. On June 13, Detective Holmes received information from a source who had provided reliable information on three prior occasions

that Alfred Red had just hijacked a shipment of VCRs. The informant indicated that he observed the loot being stored in Red's Plymouth Voyager van, awaiting transfer to a "fence." Holmes confirmed that such a hijacking had taken place and learned further that Red had been suspected in several other hijackings. The police proceeded to Red's residence but were unable to find him or his Voyager. Two weeks later Red's Voyager is observed parked outside his home. Do the police have probable cause to search the van?

14. Federal agents received reliable information that Richard Shale was engaged in the unlawful sale of child pornography. They were further told that a shipment of obscene photographs had been mailed to Shale's residence from a distributor in Canada. Postal authorities confirmed that a package from Canada addressed to Shale was en route to him and would be delivered in the normal course in two days. The agents, fearful that if they wait until delivery of the package to seek a warrant the materials will be moved by the time they obtain one, have applied now for a warrant to search Shale's home in two days. May such warrant be issued?

EXPLANATIONS
The Basics

1. The answer, of course, is no. The most basic rule regarding probable cause is that there must be specific facts and circumstances known to the officer that can be articulated (either to a magistrate in an application for a warrant prior to search or arrest, as discussed in Chapter 5, or to a judge reviewing the search or arrest after it occurs) and measured against an objective standard: Would a reasonable person knowing those facts reach the same conclusion? Unless the specific facts are there, probable cause is absent. Police action grounded in unarticulated hunch or suspicion is precisely what the Fourth Amendment forbids. As Chief Justice Warren put it: "[The] demand for specificity in the information upon which police action is predicated is the central teaching of this Court's Fourth Amendment jurisprudence." *Terry v. Ohio*, 392 U.S. 1, 21 n.18 (1968).

2. Unlike example 1, the facts and circumstances leading to the officer's conclusion are set out and thus subject to meaningful review. Moreover, because the source of information is the officer

himself, no problem of credibility is raised (as there is whenever an unnamed informant is used). Additionally, in the assessment of probable cause the courts grant some deference to the police officer's experience and expertise. As Chief Justice Burger wrote: "A trained officer draws inferences and makes deductions—inferences and deductions that might well elude an untrained person. . . . [Thus] when used by trained law enforcement officers, objective facts, meaningless to the untrained, can be combined with permissible deductions from such facts to form a legitimate basis for suspicion of a particular person and for action on that suspicion." *United States v. Cortez*, 449 U.S. 411, 412 (1981).

In all probability a court would find that Officer Peters's conclusion was reasonable and that he has demonstrated probable cause to seize the powder and arrest.

3. Unlike example 2, the source of the information here is not a police officer, but an unnamed third party. While probable cause may properly be based on such hearsay information, the showing here falls short on two counts. There are no facts set out to support the assertion that the informant is reliable and credible. Similarly absent are underlying facts or circumstances to support the conclusion that narcotics arc on the premises. We are given no information concerning the source of the informant's knowledge, and thus we do not know whether she has seen the narcotics or is merely repeating rumors or other secondhand information. Thus there is no concrete basis upon which a reasonable person would conclude that narcotics were on the premises to be searched. See *Aguilar v. Texas*, 378 U.S. 108 (1964); *Spinelli v. United States*, 393 U.S. 410 (1969).

4. Probable cause to arrest exists where the facts and circumstances within the officer's knowledge and of which she had fairly trustworthy information are sufficient to warrant a person of reasonable caution to believe that an offense has been or is being committed. The problem in this example is that while there is a basis (although somewhat conclusive) set out for believing in the honesty of the informant (that is, his previous accurate information), there is no factual basis for evaluating the accuracy of his conclusion that Fraper would be carrying heroin.

Nonetheless the Supreme Court ruled on similar facts in *Draper v. United States*, 358 U.S. 307 (1959), that probable cause to arrest existed because the deficiencies in the information known to the police were overcome by the detailed nature of the informant's report, as well as the verification of those details by police observations at the train station. The Court reasoned that "with every other bit of information being thus personally verified, had reasonable grounds to believe that the remaining, unverified bit of information—that Draper would have heroin with him—was likewise true." The *Draper* view that independent police verification of facts supplied by the informant can salvage an otherwise inadequate showing of cause has become an important component of contemporary probable cause analysis. As we will see, however, where the corroboration is of innocent, nonsuspicious details, courts are less likely to credit the informant's conclusions.

In a similar case, *Commonwealth v. Mebane*, 602 N.E.2d 223 (Mass. App. Ct. 1992), a confidential informant who had previously provided the police with reliable information told police that a black man named Charlie, five feet six inches tall, with facial hair and a limp, would be arriving in Boston from New Haven by train at a certain specified time carrying drugs and firearms. The police went to the station and saw a man fitting the description emerge carrying a large, gift-wrapped box. The man was approached and asked for identification. He identified himself as Charles Mebane and gave an address where he was headed. Police recognized it as the site of a raid a few days earlier that yielded drugs and weapons. Do the police have probable cause to search the box? The court held that they did. Following the *Aguilar-Spinelli* test, the credibility prong was satisfied because the informant had proven reliable in the past. Although the police did not know the basis of the informant's knowledge, the court held that the independent police corroboration of details overcame this deficiency. The corroboration of the detailed physical description along with the suspect's admitted destination, the scene of a recent drugs and weapons raid, was adequate to provide probable cause.

5. The bald conclusory assertion that Pinelli is "known" as a bookmaker is entitled to little weight without facts to support it. The reputation of the subject among law enforcement persons may be weighed in the probable cause determination, but only where specific facts are set out to support it. See *United States v. Harris*, 403 U.S. 573, 581–582 (1971) (plurality opinion) (explaining that while evidence of reputation is not admissible at trial, there are fundamental differences between the function of trials and of preliminary determinations of probable cause). Moreover, the fact

that Pinelli has been observed by police frequenting a particular apartment that contains two telephones is as consistent with innocent behavior as it is with criminal behavior and therefore is insufficient to justify a reasonable person concluding that evidence of a crime will be found on the premises.

If probable cause were to exist in this instance, it must be premised on the informant's tip. Measured against the two-pronged test, that tip is insufficient on both counts. First, there is no underlying factual support for the assertion that the informant is reliable. Second, there is no indication of how the informant knew that Pinelli was running a bookmaking operation. Did the informant herself place a bet with Pinelli (as the informant in *Harris* purchased liquor from the defendant) or is she relying on third-party sources? The tip does not describe the subject's activity in sufficient detail so that it may reasonably be inferred that the informant is speaking from firsthand knowledge, as was the case in *Draper*.

Finally, while the police investigation corroborated the informant's tip regarding Pinelli's connection to the apartment, as well as the presence of two telephones there, verification of those two innocent facts falls short of the considerable detail confirmed by the police in *Draper*. The Court so held in *Spinelli v. United States*, 393 U.S. 410 (1969), the case on which this example is based.

A post-*Gates* decision on facts quite similar to *Spinelli* comes out the same way. In *United States v. Turner*, 713 F. Supp. 714 (D. Vt. 1989), the informant (described by the officer as having provided reliable information in the past) asserted to police that Turner was conducting gambling operations at his residence. The informant described the procedure for placing bets over the telephone and provided Turner's unlisted telephone number. Police investigation corroborated that the telephone number was Turner's and also revealed that the telephone bill for the preceding month was $1,400. United States District Judge Coffrin ruled that even under the *Gates* standard, probable cause was lacking. The conclusory assertion of past reliability, without noting specific instances, was deemed insufficient to warrant reliance on the informant's credibility. Further, the basis of the informant's knowledge of the defendant's activities was deemed unclear. Finally, the corroboration of the innocent facts that the defendant had an unlisted number and that his phone bill was extremely high was held insufficient to bolster the informant's credibility or suggest criminal activity.

6. Application of the traditional two-pronged test to measure probable cause based on the informant's tip would probably require a negative answer to each question. Under that analysis we start with the tip itself; if deficiencies are found we then look to whether the results of the police investigation "would permit the suspicions engendered by the informant's report to ripen into a judgment that a crime was probably being committed." *Spinelli*, supra, 393 U.S. at 418. The letter here fails to meet the requirements that 1) there is a factual basis for believing that the informer is credible and reliable; and 2) there is a factual basis for crediting the informant's conclusion that the subjects are dealing narcotics. It can be argued that the detailed nature of the tip, together with the police corroboration of those details, satisfies the second prong. The problem is that, given the anonymous nature of the letter, there remains no basis for satisfying the credibility prong. There is simply no indication (such as the provision of accurate information on prior occasions, as in *Draper*) as to why the police should believe that the informant was speaking honestly.

With the abandonment of strict adherence to the two-pronged analysis and substitution of a totality-of-circumstances approach, a different result is reached. *Illinois v. Gates*, 462 U.S. 213 (1983), reasoned on facts similar to those set out in this example that the detailed nature of the letter to the Bloomingdale police, together with their independent verification of much of the information, constituted probable cause to search the Gateses' home and car.

> The anonymous letter contained a range of details relating not just to easily obtained facts and conditions existing at the time of the tip, but to future actions of third parties ordinarily not easily predicted. The letter writer's accurate information as to the travel plans of each of the Gateses was of a character likely obtained only from the Gateses themselves, or from someone familiar with their not entirely ordinary travel plans. If the informant has access to accurate information of this type a magistrate could properly conclude that it was not unlikely that he also had access to reliable information of the Gateses' alleged illegal activities.

462 U.S. at 245. As Justice White noted in his concurrence, while it is *possible* that a vindictive travel agent could have provided the

detailed information on the Gateses' activities, probable cause is a matter of *probabilities* and not certainties.[3]

The *Gates* approach (unlike *Aguilar-Spinelli*) permits reliance on anonymous tips by allowing a strong showing that the informant's conclusions are accurate (the basis of knowledge prong) to remedy a weak (or nonexistent) showing as to her credibility. Given the overlap in possession cases between probable cause to arrest and to search, there would seem to be sufficient cause to arrest Lance for possession of unlawful drugs and to search the car and the condominium.

It should be added that while *Gates* clearly permits police corroboration to redeem an anonymous tipster's unknown reliability or to make up for a weak showing on the basis for her knowledge, some courts have read *Gates* to require that the corroboration be more than merely innocent details. In *United States v. Solomon*, 728 F. Supp. 1544 (S.D. Fla. 1990), for example, the sheriff received an anonymous message on the telephone tips line asserting that one George Solomon, of a stated description and address, was transporting cocaine from Fort Lauderdale, Florida, to North Carolina. The message relayed that on the following day, Solomon would leave his residence at approximately 6 A.M., would travel north on Interstate 95 in his maroon Chevrolet Camino, and would be traveling with a white female of a particular description. The caller stated that Solomon would have cocaine in his car. Police staked out Solomon's home the next day and corroborated all that the caller had said with regard to the subject's description and his early morning departure with the described female. The officers stopped Solomon, placed him under arrest, and searched his car.

The U.S. District Court granted Solomon's motion to suppress the evidence seized on the grounds that the police acted without probable cause. The court ruled that corroboration of the innocent and nonsuspicious details of the tip, such as the description of the suspect and his companion as well as the time and route

---

3. 462 U.S. at 271. Justice White, concurring in the majority's conclusion that the police did have probable cause, reached that conclusion through the *Aguilar-Spinelli* framework. He reasoned that the police corroboration of the predictions set out in the anonymous letter gave rise to the inference that the informant was credible and that he had obtained his information in a reliable manner, thus satisfying both prongs of the existing analysis. 462 U.S. at 267–272.

of their travels, could not suffice (even under a totality-of-the-circumstances analysis) to establish a fair probability that contraband would be found on Solomon. The court distinguished *Gates* as a case where the corroborated details were *suspicious*—the police tracked the subjects from Illinois to Florida, a known source of drugs, and Lance spent a very short period of time there before returning north. In contrast, Solomon lived in Florida and was apprehended near his home merely because the police corroborated that he was taking a trip north on the interstate. Whether *Solomon*'s reading of *Gates* is persuasive for other courts remains to be seen.

The Plot Thickens

7. The weakness in the probable cause showing here, as in *Gates*, is the anonymous nature of the tip: If the police do not know who is providing the information, they obviously cannot check the informant's prior track record for accuracy or evaluate the basis of her knowledge. Unlike *Gates*, however, this informant finally acknowledged her identity. If she truly was the suspect's former girlfriend, then she had a close vantage point from which to observe his activities. Moreover, she asserted that she had personally seen the stolen goods on the premises and was able to give a description of them, which was consistent with the description of the items taken in the prior burglaries. In addition she knew of the search that had just been conducted in the motel room. In short, the informant seems to have had a solid basis of knowledge concerning the defendant's activities.

    Although there is no indication that the caller had previously supplied accurate information, the officers were able to corroborate the presence of the motor home in the location she had stated. At this point they had more than a mere hunch that seizable items were present in the trailer. Under the *Gates* totality-of-the-circumstances standard, they had established probable cause for the issuance of a warrant to search. See *Massachusetts v. Upton*, 466 U.S. 727, 731 (1984): "The informant's story and the surrounding facts possessed an internal coherence that gave weight to the whole."

    Crucial to the Court's determination in *Upton* that probable cause had been established was the identification of the caller as someone in a position to know about the suspect's activities. The Massachusetts Supreme Judicial Court, whose decision holding that the warrant had been issued without adequate cause was reversed by the Supreme Court, had viewed the question of the caller's identity with considerably more skepticism. The court described the officer's identification of the informer as a mere "unconfirmed guess" and noted that the caller may have merely been adopting "a convenient cover for her true identity." *Commonwealth v. Upton*, 390 Mass. 562, 570, 458 N.E.2d 717, 722 (1983). The Massachusetts court accordingly treated her as an anonymous informant, and thus the basis for crediting her statements (that is, her close relationship to the suspect) disappeared. The U.S. Supreme Court, on the other hand, concluded that the inference that the caller was Upton's girlfriend was a reasonable one for the officer and the magistrate to have drawn. Thus while "no single piece of evidence [by itself] was conclusive, . . . the pieces fit neatly together and, so viewed, support the magistrate's determination that there was 'a fair probability that contraband or evidence of crime' would be found in Upton's motor home."[4]

An interesting issue is raised by the informant's statement that she wanted "to burn" Grape. Should a court assessing probable cause discount a source's information because of a possible motivation to falsely accuse the suspect? The few courts that have explicitly dealt with such situations have not been moved by that factor. In *United States v. Copeland*, 538 F.2d 639, 642 (5th Cir. 1976), the source, who was the father-in-law of the suspect, admitted that he had "an axe to grind" with him. The court dismissed this with the observation that this "antagonism may explain Westmoreland's motivation in providing the government with the tip, but it does not necessarily lessen his credibility." See also *United States v. Hodges*, 705 F.2d 106 (4th Cir. 1983) (the district court's suppression of evidence, based on its conclusion that the informant's relationship with the suspect "reasonably provides a strong motive to speak falsely," was reversed with the observation that while such motivation was relevant to the question of veracity, it was not conclusive); *United States v. Hunley*, 567 F.2d 822 (8th

---

4. Upon remand, the Massachusetts Supreme Judicial Court again concluded that probable cause to search the motor home was lacking. See *Commonwealth v. Upton*, 394 Mass. 363, 476 N.E.2d 548 (1985). Describing the *Gates* totality-of-the-circumstances standard as "unacceptably shapeless and permissive," the Supreme Judicial Court chose to apply state constitutional provisions regarding search and seizure and continued to apply the *Aguilar-Spinelli* analysis to its own constitution.

Cir. 1977) (the fact that the source of the probable cause information had been promised a break if he cooperated with the police in their investigation of defendant does not necessarily lessen his credibility). But see *United States v. Jackson,* 818 F.2d 345, 349 (5th Cir. 1987) (where the informant's accusation shifted the blame from him to the defendant, the reliability of that accusation must be questioned).

8. We must determine whether the facts and circumstances within the knowledge of the police and of which they had reasonably trustworthy information were sufficient to warrant a person of reasonable caution to believe that contraband would be found in the truck. The primary indication of criminal activity here comes from the two informants. The observations made by the officers themselves, as well as the information they discovered, were innocuous and would not constitute adequate cause to believe criminal activity was occurring. The police investigation is important, however, insofar as it tended to corroborate certain aspects of the informants' reports.

Using the traditional *Aguilar-Spinelli* analysis, the credibility prong of the analysis seems to be satisfied for one of the informants by the assertion of past reliability. When we turn to the other prong and focus on the basis for the informants' conclusions— how did they obtain their information?—the picture becomes more problematic. There is no indication that the tips were based on their own personal knowledge, as opposed to information obtained from others, rumor, or speculation. Further, there is no alternative indicia of reliability, such as the self-implication of the informant in the criminal activity, the indication of a close relationship to the subject, or the supplying of great detail as to the subject's activities (leading to the inference of a close relationship). There is an absence, therefore, of a solid basis for crediting the informants' conclusions.

The question then becomes whether the corroboration of certain innocent details by the police, or the mutual corroboration of the two tips, can make up for the deficiencies regarding the conclusion prong. Police investigation and surveillance confirmed that Raymond Frank spoke frequently to Michael Best on the telephone, but the conclusion that he is the "Mike" referred to by the first informant was speculative. The police further confirmed that Raymond Frank had picked up two shipments of furniture from a country that is a major source of narcotics, and that he picked up the shipment now in question. The confirmation here appears to fall far short of that in *Draper*, where numerous parts of the informant's tale were confirmed. The police have not confirmed a relationship between Frank and Best beyond telephone calls. Moreover, the fact that the cargo passed a routine customs inspection, while certainly not conclusive (we would want more information about how thorough an inspection it was), is certainly cause for some skepticism regarding the presence of narcotics. It is doubtful therefore whether the police investigation provided sufficient corroboration to bring the informants' assertions up to the standard of probable cause. But see *United States v. Talley*, 108 F.3d 277 (11th Cir. 1997) (police corroboration of informant's description of suspects' car and residence where it was parked sufficient to establish probable cause to search car).

In this problem we have the additional fact that the tips, from independent informants, seem to corroborate each other. Courts have been impressed with this kind of mutual reinforcement. See, e.g., *United States v. Laws*, 808 F.2d 92, 103 (D.C. Cir. 1986) ("[T]he mutually-supporting nature of the two tips is an important ingredient in the probable-cause mix. There is no indication that the informants were acting cooperatively. The fact that two apparently unassociated persons make the same assertion increases the probability that it is true."); *United States v. Hyde*, 574 F.2d 856, 863 (5th Cir. 1978) ("When three unreliable but unconnected persons all report the same fact, it is probable that the fact is true.").

In this example, however, the tips are only partially supportive of one another. Informant 1 fingered Raymond Frank and "Mike," while Informant 2 fingered Michael Best and an unidentified partner. On close examination, the information is not completely congruent.

Whether the information constitutes probable cause under the relaxed standard of *Illinois v. Gates* is a close question. The tips lack the level of detail found so compelling in *Gates*, and the corroboration by way of police investigation is not as strong as it was in that case. On similar facts, the Ninth Circuit concluded that probable cause was lacking. See *United States v. Freitas*, 716 F.2d 1216 (9th Cir. 1983).

The Ingredients in the Probable Cause Analysis

9. The anonymous tip, even when supplemented by the officer's confirmation that Shay hangs around the school, is insufficient to establish probable cause as there is no basis to credit the information

and no corroboration of illegal conduct. May the police officer consider the suspect's past criminal record in the probable cause determination? There are obvious concerns about the use of such information to establish cause, given the prospect that anyone with a criminal record would thus be subject to arrest and/or search at any time.

Certainly the mere existence of a criminal record could not, of itself, constitute probable cause to believe the person is presently involved in criminal activity. The Supreme Court has held, however, that knowledge of the suspect's prior criminal activity may be used as confirmation of an informant's tip, as long as the officer is acting on hard information and not just rumor. See *United States v. Harris*, 403 U.S. 573 (1971). As the Court put it in *Jones v. United States*, 362 U.S. 257, 271 (1960), "that the [suspect] was a known user of narcotics made the [informant's] charge against him much less subject to skepticism than would be such a charge against one without such a history . . . [and] reduced the chances of a reckless or prevaricating tale." One court has described the element of prior convictions as bearing "weightily on the issue of probable cause." See *United States v. Laws*, 808 F.2d 92, 103 (D.C. Cir. 1986). See also *United States v. Berry*, 463 F.2d 1278, 1284 (D.C. Cir. 1972).

Is the additional knowledge in our example of Shay's prior convictions enough to push the showing up to the probable cause threshold? In light of the anonymous nature of the tip and the officer's inability to confirm any illegal activity in the school yard, it would appear unlikely that the sum total adds up to probable cause.

10. Plainly, a mere hunch is inadequate to establish probable cause. There must be specific facts to support a reasonable conclusion that a crime has been committed and that the defendant committed it. May the officers base their action on the fact that the suspects fled when they were approached?

The courts have held long that flight from a law officer can be counted as a factor in the establishment of probable cause. As noted in *Sibron v. New York*, 392 U.S. 40, 66–67 (1968), "deliberately furtive actions and flight at the approach of strangers or law officers are strong indicia of *mens rea*, and when coupled with specific knowledge on the part of the officer relating the suspect to the evidence of crime, they are proper factors to be considered in the decision to make an arrest." Thus "[i]f a police officer identifies himself while approaching a suspect and the suspect flees, the suspect's conduct suggests that he knowingly seeks to evade questioning or capture. Such conduct ordinarily supplies another element to the [probable cause] calculus." *United States v. Amuny*, 767 F.2d 1113, 1124 (5th Cir. 1985).

Flight alone has generally not been held sufficient to establish probable cause; the officer must be able to point to other specific information. *Unprovoked* flight from police in an area known for heavy narcotics trafficking may, however, be sufficient to establish reasonable suspicion for a stop. See *Illinois v. Wardlow*, 120 S. Ct. 673 (2000), discussed in §4.2. On the other hand, police should not be able to transform a hunch into probable cause by reason of conduct that they themselves have provoked. "That," the Supreme Court has warned, "would have the same essential vice as a proposition we have consistently rejected—that a search unlawful at its inception may be validated by what it turns up." *Wong Sun v. United States*, 371 U.S. 471, 484 (1963).

Thus in our example there would probably not be adequate cause to arrest the men because all the officers had was a hunch, together with the subjects' flight. Moreover, because the officers were in plain clothes, it is unclear what significance the flight had in any event. "[W]hen an officer insufficiently or unclearly identifies his office or mission, the [subject's flight] must be regarded as ambiguous conduct." *Wong Sun*, supra, 371 U.S. at 482. As the Fifth Circuit has put it, "evasive actions and flight from two strange men riding in an unmarked car and exhibiting no indicia of lawful authority were only natural reactions to the circumstance." *United States v. Jones*, 619 F.2d 494, 498 (5th Cir. 1980). Thus the flight here was "as much reasonable as it was suspicious" and "added nothing to the officers' determination of probable cause." *United States v. Amuny*, supra, 767 F.2d at 1125 (six unmarked cars surrounded a plane and the officers failed to identify themselves). Compare *United States v. Gentry*, 839 F.2d 1065, 1070 (5th Cir. 1988) (fact that subject sought to flee in his vehicle from scene of a large drug transaction, combined with information that more purchasers would be arriving at the scene, gave troopers probable cause to arrest); *United States v. Martinez-Gonzalez*, 686 F.2d 93, 99–100 (2d Cir. 1982) (where subject looked frightened and ran back into his apartment in response to the agents walking toward him at a normal pace, displaying their badges, and identifying themselves as police officers, their reasonable suspicion grew into probable cause to arrest); *United States v. Dawdy*, 46 F.3d 1427 (8th Cir. 1995) (arrestee's response to an invalid arrest or stop may provide independent probable cause for the arrest where arrestee resisted police officer's attempt to handcuff him).

11. To what extent may Dow's presence in a high-crime area count toward probable cause? Like past criminal record and flight, such presence can be used as a factor but may not, of itself, justify arrest or search. As the Supreme Court ruled in *Brown v. Texas*, 443 U.S. 47, 52 (1979), the "fact that appellant was in a neighborhood frequented by drug dealers, standing alone, is not a basis for concluding that appellant himself was engaged in criminal conduct." Weighing presence in a high-crime area too heavily in the probable cause equation would subject all residents and passersby to unjustified search on sight.

Nonetheless the courts have generally concluded that location in a high-crime area is a relevant factor in determining whether probable cause exists. "[I]f an officer observes a street corner exchange of some substance for money, such an event takes on a special meaning if it happens in a part of the community where drug traffic is intensive." Id. See also *Adams v. Williams*, 407 U.S. 143, 147–148 (1972) (fact that subject was in a high-crime area contributed to the reasonableness of the search for weapons under the *Terry* standard, discussed in §4.2). Thus as one court has put it: "[A]lthough no presumption of guilt arises from the activities of inhabitants of an area in which the police know that narcotics offenses frequently occur, the syndrome of criminality in those areas cannot realistically go unnoticed by the judiciary. It too is a valid consideration when coupled with other reliable indicia or suspicious circumstances. We make this statement warily, for it is all too clear that few live in these areas by choice." *United States v. Davis*, 458 F.2d 819, 822 (D.C. Cir. 1972).

In our example, there was not much more than the character of the area for the police to go on. They merely observed conversations occurring, not furtive conduct or objects changing hands. Compare *United States v. White*, 655 F.2d 1302 (D.C. Cir. 1981) (probable cause existed where officers recognized automobile in high-crime area as one frequently visited by known drug addicts and observed money and objects changing hands); *United States v. Green*, 670 F.2d 1148 (D.C. Cir. 1981) (probable cause existed where officer with aid of binoculars observed currency and objects being exchanged in neighborhood notorious for narcotics trafficking). Thus there would appear to be insufficient cause to arrest Dow.

This example also raises the troublesome question of how much deference the courts should grant to police expertise. The whole point of having a legal standard of probable cause requiring specific information and not mere hunch, and of placing ultimate review in the courts and not the police, is to subject the police conduct to independent judicial scrutiny. Yet the courts have properly recognized that police officers do develop expertise that is extremely useful in ferreting out crime. Thus while probable cause was originally defined from the vantage point of the reasonably prudent *person*, it has come to be viewed from the perspective of a reasonable *police officer in light of her training and experience.* See, e.g., *United States v. Green*, 670 F.2d 1148, 1152 (D.C. Cir. 1981). As one court put it, "law-enforcement officers may draw upon their expertise in translating activity that appears innocuous to the untrained mind into [probable cause]." *United States v. Laws*, 808 F.2d 92, 103 (D.C. Cir. 1986). In *Laws* the investigating officer had more than a decade of experience in narcotics investigations, and his "experience in covering the machinations of drug dealers enabled him to fit the informants' descriptions of the suspects' behavior into a pattern familiar to drug-law officers." Id. In assessing probable cause, therefore, the Supreme Court has emphasized that information "must be seen and weighed not in terms of analysis by scholars, but as understood by those versed in the field of law enforcement." *Illinois v. Gates*, 462 U.S. 213, 232 (1983). For the opposite view, see *United States v. 1964 Ford Thunderbird*, 445 F.2d 1064 (3d Cir. 1971) (the standard of probable cause is measured not by what a trained police officer would conclude, but what a *reasonable person* would conclude).

Deference to police experience does not mean deference to a hunch. The officer must still be able to articulate the specific information upon which the expert conclusion was based. There remains the risk, nonetheless, that deference becomes delegation and that courts abdicate their independent role in the probable cause review. Illustration of the problem may be found in those cases where the officer's past success rate seems to substitute for hard information in the eyes of the court. See, e.g., *United States v. White*, 655 F.2d 1302, 1304 (D.C. Cir. 1981) ("The two officers who had observed the sale had previously demonstrated their ability to recognize narcotics transactions; ninety-five to ninety-six percent of their prior, similar observations had led to the arrest of persons possessing drugs.").

12. Probable cause exists only if there are specific facts pointing toward criminal activity on the part of the subject. If possession of a hand-gun is a violation of law in the jurisdiction, the information in our example (reported by a named source through his firsthand observations) would seem to constitute such cause. If, however, possession is a crime only in the absence of a permit to carry the weapon and, further, if the officer has no knowledge whether the subject lacks a permit, then the information known to the officer is insufficient to constitute probable cause. See *Commonwealth v. Couture*, 407 Mass. 178 (1990). The Supreme Judicial Court reasoned: "[T]he police only knew that a man had been seen in public with a handgun. This unadorned fact, without any additional information suggesting criminal activity, does not give rise to probable cause. The police in this case had no reason to believe, before conducting the search of the vehicle, that the defendant lacked a license to carry the firearm. A police officer's knowledge that an individual is carrying a handgun, in and of itself, does not furnish probable cause to believe that the individual is illegally carrying that gun." 407 Mass. at 181.

One might ask how the police are to investigate *possible* illegal possession in this situation. The obvious answer would be that they may effect a brief investigative "stop" (see §4.2) and ask the subject to produce a permit. The Massachusetts court, however, foreclosed that option as well by holding that there was no "reasonable suspicion" of criminal activity that would justify such a detention. Given these rulings, enforcement of the gun law in Massachusetts is going to be problematic at best.

Here Today, Gone Tomorrow/Here Tomorrow, But Not Today

13. Probable cause to search a location is defined with reference to a particular point in time. The information known to the police must permit the reasonable conclusion that items related to crime are *presently* at the place to be searched. Probable cause to search does not last indefinitely—like bread, it gets stale over time.

In our problem, it would probably not be reasonable to believe that the hijacked VCRs will remain in Red's van for an extended period of time. Given the nature of this type of crime, the likelihood is that Red will transfer the loot as quickly as possible, and probably before the end of two weeks. By the time the police found Red's van, probable cause has likely dissipated.

The staleness issue varies with the particular situation and the crime involved. Where the criminal activity is of a continuing nature or the items to be seized are unlikely to be moved, a time gap between the receipt of the information and the time of the proposed search may not be fatal. Thus a search of a residence based on reliable information that the homeowner was in the business of growing marijuana was upheld despite the delay of five months between the receipt of the information and the search. See *United States v. Dozier*, 844 F.2d 701 (9th Cir. 1988). The court explained: "The mere lapse of substantial amounts of time is not controlling in a question of staleness. Another important factor is the ongoing nature of a crime that might lead to the maintenance of tools of the trade. In this case, marijuana cultivation is a long-term crime and the affidavit includes an experienced DEA agent's opinion that cultivators often keep the equipment at their residences between growing seasons." See also *Andresen v. Maryland*, 427 U.S. 463, 478 n.9 (1976) (petitioner's staleness argument was rejected despite the three-month delay between the completion of the allegedly fraudulent real estate transactions and the search and seizure of the incriminating documents; the Court noted that there was probable cause to believe the documents were still at his office because "it is eminently reasonable to expect that [the ordinary business] records would be maintained in those offices for a period of time and surely as long as the three months."); *United States v. McCall*, 740 F.2d 1331 (4th Cir. 1984) (probable cause to search for a stolen police revolver existed despite the delay of seven months between the receipt of the information implicating defendant and the search of his residence because it was apparent that the gun was readily identifiable as a police weapon and thus difficult to pawn or sell).

In sum, "the vitality of probable cause cannot be quantified by simply counting the number of days between the occurrence of the facts supplied and the issuance of the affidavit." *United States v. Johnson*, 461 F.2d 285, 287 (10th Cir. 1972).

Moreover, current information may be used to revive stale information. In *United States v. Viegas*, 639 F.2d 42 (1st Cir. 1981), for example, the police sought to justify their search of defendant's luggage by relying in part on an informant's tip received a year before that the defendant was dealing cocaine. While recognizing that the year-old information could not by itself establish probable cause, the court nevertheless ruled that it served to corroborate the suspicions of the officers based on their current observations of the defendant at Logan Airport, and thus probable cause was established. See also *United States v. Pene-Rodriguez*, 110 F.3d 1120, 1131 (5th Cir. 1997).

In contrast to probable cause *to search*, information establishing probable cause *to arrest* generally does not become stale over time. If there is reason to believe that Alfred Red has committed larceny, that information will keep indefinitely (or at least until further information is discovered indicating that he is not the culprit). Probable cause to arrest is not time-specific because it does not depend on the presence of specified items at a particular location.

14. To justify a search, there must be probable cause to believe that items related to crime are *presently* in the place to be searched. Because in this case there is no reason to believe that the items are presently in the place to be searched, probable cause as traditionally understood does not exist. Recent years, however, have witnessed the evolution of the anticipatory warrant. A majority of the circuits have authorized their use. See, e.g., *United States v. Hugoboom*, 112 F.3d 1081 (10th Cir. 1997). The validity of anticipatory warrants is contingent upon triggering events and the likelihood that after those events the contraband will be at the designated place to be searched. The warrant should express those events, and would then be valid only if those events occur. See *United States v. Rowland*, 145 F.3d 1194 (10th Cir. 1998); *United States v. Garcia*, 882 F.2d 699 (2d Cir. 1989) (co-conspirators cooperating with drug enforcement agents had arranged to deliver cocaine to defendant at a designated time); *United States v. Dornhofer*, 859 F.2d 1195 (4th Cir. 1988) (pornography mailed to defendant as part of sting operation); *United States v. Hale*, 784 F.2d 1465, 1469 (9th Cir. 1986) (item was in the mail); *People v. Martini*, 638 N.E.2d 397 (Ill. App. Ct.), *appeal denied*, 645 N.E.2d 1364 (Ill. 1994). Compare *United States v. Hendricks*, 743 F.2d 653, 654 (9th Cir. 1984) (warrant could not be properly issued for search of defendant's home where the contraband was presently in the possession of the police, who were attempting to get defendant to pick it up because "there was no certainty that it would ever be brought there"). Where an anticipatory warrant is sought, the magistrate

must require (in addition to the usual probable cause) additional information giving rise to probable cause to believe that the item will be in the location by the time of the search. See *United States v. Garcia*, supra, 882 F.2d at 703. Anticipatory warrants sometimes include a condition that the warrant not be executed unless the police can reasonably confirm delivery of the item to the place to be searched. Id.

For more on the use of anticipatory warrants, see §5.4.

§4.2 Reasonable Suspicion—The Standard for "Stop and Frisk"

As we have seen, the amount of justification required in order to search or arrest is probable cause. Much routine police activity does not reach the level of these full-scale intrusions. Police, for instance, routinely stop citizens on the street or pull them over in their automobiles in order to question them briefly or to enforce the traffic laws. If probable cause were required in these situations, such investigative stops would be impermissible in most cases.

Recognizing the importance of these lesser intrusions in the scheme of effective law enforcement, the Supreme Court in *Terry v. Ohio*, 392 U.S. 1 (1968), established for them a different level of justification—"reasonable suspicion"—which falls below probable cause but above a mere unparticularized hunch. *Terry* concerned the common police practice of "stop and frisk" in which an officer confronts a citizen whom she suspects may be involved in criminal activity. In addition to briefly detaining and questioning the individual, the officer also frisks her for weapons.

In *Terry*, Officer McFadden's attention was drawn to two men on a Cleveland street corner who appeared to the experienced officer to be "casing" a store for a robbery. They walked back and forth roughly 24 times, pausing to stare in the store window and confer with each other. Acting on his suspicions, McFadden approached the men and asked them to identify themselves. When they mumbled something in response, McFadden patted the men down, felt a pistol on each, and removed the guns. The men were then placed under arrest for possession of a concealed weapon. Prior to trial on that charge they moved unsuccessfully to suppress the guns.

On review, the Supreme Court rejected Ohio's argument that the stop and frisk practice does not implicate the Fourth Amendment at all because it falls short of a full-blown search and arrest. The Court also rejected the defendant's position that the police must possess probable cause before they can lawfully stop or frisk. Deferring to the interest of "effective crime prevention and detection," the Court held that in appropriate circumstances and in an appropriate manner police officers may briefly detain a person for purposes of investigating possible criminal activity, even though there is no probable cause to make an arrest.

Observing that "street encounters between citizens and police officers are incredibly rich in diversity," ranging from exchanges of information to hostile confrontations, the Court invoked the Fourth Amendment's reasonableness clause to fashion a flexible standard for measuring the lawfulness of such encounters. Under this approach (which set the tone for subsequent Fourth Amendment jurisprudence) the Court weighed the governmental interest in conducting stops and frisks against the resulting interference with individual liberty. Balancing an intrusion that is less than arrest and search against the societal interest in preventing crime through such procedures, the Court concluded that a standard of justification below probable cause was called for. Thus when an officer by means of physical force or show of authority stops and detains an individual, the officer need not have probable cause but must nonetheless be able to articulate the specific facts that gave rise to reasonable suspicion that criminal activity may have been afoot.

Because the additional step of patting down or frisking the individual is a further intrusion, it requires additional justification: reasonable suspicion that the suspect may be armed and dangerous.[5] The scope of this protective search is limited by the exigencies that justify its initiation[6] and is therefore restricted to that which is necessary to discover weapons—usually an initial pat-down of the suspect's clothing to determine whether she is carrying a weapon, followed by a reach into pockets or other hidden areas if (and only if) the pat-down reveals the likely presence of a weapon.

---

5. The *Terry* Court rejected Justice Harlan's view (set out in his concurrence) that the right to frisk follows automatically from the right to stop. Courts have not, however, been rigorous in enforcing this requirement for separate justification. Where there is reasonable suspicion to believe the person stopped is involved in a serious crime (particularly one of violence), a frisk is generally deemed reasonable.

6. The Court observed: "The Fourth Amendment proceeds as much by limitations upon the scope of governmental action as by imposing preconditions upon its initiation." 392 U.S. at 28–29.

Measured against these standards the Court ruled that Officer McFadden had lawfully stopped and frisked Terry and his companions to investigate a possible crime, and the evidence the officer seized could thus be admitted at trial. As *Terry* illustrates, the officer conducting an investigative stop and frisk need not (as with probable cause to arrest) have reason to believe that a crime *has been* committed; it will suffice if the officer has reason to believe a crime is *about to be* committed.

Like probable cause, the definition of "reasonable suspicion" is of necessity a flexible one.

> Courts have used a variety of terms to capture the elusive concept of what cause is sufficient to authorize police to stop a person. Terms like "articulable reasons" and "founded suspicion" are not self-defining; they fall short of providing clear guidance dispositive of the myriad factual situations that arise. But the essence of all that has been written is that the totality of the circumstances—the whole picture—must be taken into account. Based upon that whole picture the detaining officers must have a particularized and objective basis for suspecting the particular person stopped of criminal activity.

United States v. Cortez, 449 U.S. 411, 417 (1981). As a level of suspicion below probable cause, reasonable suspicion is "considerably less than proof of wrongdoing by a preponderance of the evidence," but more than an inchoate and unparticularized suspicion or hunch. *United States v. Sokolow*, 490 U.S. 1 (1989).

Again, like probable cause, reasonable suspicion may be based upon information received from an informant, but that information need not carry as much indicia of reliability as required in probable cause analysis. *Adams v. Williams*, 407 U.S. 143 (1972). The Court has held that reasonable suspicion may even be based upon an anonymous telephone tip as long as the police are able to corroborate certain of its details. In *Alabama v. White*, 496 U.S. 325 (1990), the police received an anonymous tip that one Vanessa White would be leaving a particular apartment at a particular time in a particular vehicle, that she would be going to a particular motel, and that she would be in possession of cocaine. They proceeded to the apartment building, observed a woman leave the building and enter the car described, and followed her along the route toward the motel. Having thus corroborated some of the predictions of the caller, the Court held that the police were justified in stopping and detaining White just short of the motel. Adopting a totality-of-the-circumstances approach reminiscent of *Illinois v. Gates* (see §4.1), the Court concluded that while the tip itself was inadequate to justify police action (because there was no basis for crediting either the caller's veracity or the accuracy of his predictions), police corroboration established sufficient indicia of reliability to establish reasonable suspicion and thus permit an investigative stop. The Court invoked the proposition that when an informant is shown to be right about some things, that increases the probability that she is right about the other facts asserted. In addition, the caller was able to predict White's future actions, thus demonstrating "inside information—a special familiarity with respondent's affairs." 496 U.S. at 330.[7]

In *Florida v. J.L.* 120 S.Ct. 254 (2000), the Court refused to allow a *Terry* stop based exclusively on an anonymous tip. Unlike *Alabama v. White*, there was no way to test the credibility of the tip.

The *Alabama v. White* Court summed up the relation between the two standards of justification: "Reasonable suspicion is a less demanding standard than probable cause not only in the sense that reasonable suspicion can be established with information that is different in quantity or content than that required to establish probable cause, but also in the sense that reasonable suspicion can arise from information that is less reliable than that required to show probable cause." 496 U.S. at 330.

Many of the cases interpreting the reasonable suspicion standard have arisen in the context of stops in airport terminals of persons suspected of involvement in narcotics trafficking. The following are among the "red flags" (often referred to as a "drug courier profile") relied upon by the courts in determining whether these detentions were justified: 1) the subject paid cash for the airline ticket; 2) she traveled under an assumed name; 3) she did not check her luggage; 4) she traveled to or from a narcotics source city; 5) she stayed only a

---

7. The dissenters, emphasizing that the tipster had predicted that White would be carrying a brown attache case containing the cocaine but that the woman observed by the police was empty-handed, observed: "Millions of people leave their apartments at about the same time every day carrying an attache case and heading for a destination known to their neighbors. . . . An anonymous neighbor's prediction about somebody's time of departure and probable destination is anything but a reliable basis for assuming that the commuter is in possession of an illegal substance—particularly when the person is not even carrying the attache case described by the tipster." 496 U.S. at 330 (Stevens, J., joined by Brennan and Marshall, JJ., dissenting).

brief time in the destination city; and 6) she appeared nervous during the trip. As the Supreme Court held in *United States v. Sokolow*, 490 U.S. 1 (1989), although none of these factors alone is itself proof of illegal conduct, a combination of them may amount to an objectively reasonable suspicion that criminal activity is afoot.[8]

A question that has arisen frequently is the role of flight in the determination of reasonable suspicion. In Illinois, state courts had ruled that defendant's flight upon the mere approach of a police vehicle patrolling in a high-crime area was *not* itself sufficient to justify an investigatory stop. The U.S. Supreme Court disagreed and reversed, holding that unprovoked flight from police in an area known for heavy narcotics trafficking is sufficient to establish reasonable suspicion for a stop. *Illinois v. Wardlow*, 120 S. Ct. 673 (2000).

§4.3   What Constitutes a "Stop"?

"Obviously," as the Court observed in *Terry*, "not all personal intercourse between policemen and citizens involves seizures of persons." The Fourth Amendment is implicated only "when the officer, by means of physical force or show of authority, has in some way restrained the liberty of [a] citizen." *Terry v. Ohio*, 392 U.S. 1 20 n.16 (1968). The demarcation between a forcible seizure or stop and something less intrusive (as where, for example, the officer merely addresses questions to a citizen who is free to ignore them and leave) will separate those situations in which the officer can act only with reasonable suspicion from those in which *no* justification is required because the Fourth Amendment does not come into play.

In defining what constitutes a "stop," or seizure of the person, the Court has adopted an objective test:

> [A] person has been "seized" within the meaning of the Fourth Amendment only if, in view of all the circumstances surrounding the incident, a reasonable person would have believed that

---

8. The dissenters bemoaned the profile's "chameleon-like way of adapting to any particular set of observations." 490 U.S. at 13 (Marshall, J., dissenting). Justice Marshall cited cases in which contradictory characteristics were considered suspicious, including being the first passenger to deplane, the last to deplane, and deplaning in the middle of the crowd; holding a round-trip ticket and holding a one-way ticket; traveling nonstop and changing planes; carrying no luggage and carrying luggage; traveling alone and traveling with companions; acting too nervously and acting too calmly.

he was not free to leave. Examples of circumstances that might indicate a seizure, even where the person did not actually attempt to leave, would be the threatening presence of several officers, the display of a weapon by an officer, some physical touching of the person of the citizen, or the use of language or tone of voice indicating that compliance with the officer's request might be compelled.

United States v. Mendenhall, 446 U.S. 544, 554 (1980).

California v. Hodari D., 499 U.S. 621 (1991), involved an individual who was chased by police on foot. The Court held that Hodari had not been seized at the time he tossed away a rock of cocaine because the police had not yet caught him or placed any physical restraint upon him. Rejecting Hodari's argument that mere pursuit by the police was sufficient to create a reasonable belief on his part that he was not free to leave, the Court held that a seizure of the person occurs in the context of a pursuit only where there is either an actual application of force on the subject or a submission to police authority.

In a similar vein the Court has held that a bus passenger is not necessarily seized when confronted by officers conducting a drug interdiction sweep. In *Florida v. Bostick*, 501 U.S. 429 (1991), armed and uniformed officers approached passenger Bostick as he sat in the cramped confines of the bus. They asked to inspect his ticket and identification, advised him they were searching for narcotics, and then requested to inspect his luggage. The Court refused to adopt the analysis of the state supreme court, which held such drug sweep encounters to be per se seizures implicating the Fourth Amendment. Emphasizing the ad hoc nature of the inquiry, the Supreme Court instructed: "In order to determine whether a particular encounter constitutes a seizure, a court must consider all the circumstances surrounding the encounter to determine whether the police conduct would have communicated to a reasonable person that the person was not free to decline the officers' requests or otherwise terminate the encounter." 501 U.S. at 439.

The Court has cautioned that the reasonable person test is "necessarily imprecise, because it is designed to assess the coercive effect of police conduct." *Michigan v. Chesternut*, 486 U.S. 567, 573 (1988). Thus "what constitutes a restraint on liberty prompting a person to conclude that he is not free to leave will vary, not only with the particular police conduct at issue, but also with the setting in which the conduct occurs." Id. The standard has been defended on the grounds that the alternative—a subjective test—would peg the applicability of the Fourth Amendment to the peculiar state of mind and eccentricities of the person confronted. Id. at 574.

When does a routine traffic stop turn into a *Terry* encounter requiring reasonable suspicion? The usual questioning accompanying such stops, together with the request for license and registration and a field computer check, are generally not deemed to be investigatory stops. See, e.g., *United States v. Galvan-Muro*, 141 F.3d 904 (8th Cir. 1998) (even though motorist detained for 15 minutes, no investigatory stop occurred). But compare *United States v. Ramos*, 42 F.3d 1160 (8th Cir. 1994) (separation of brothers stopped for not wearing seatbelts for purpose of further questioning after computer check came back clean expanded the scope of the stop and required reasonable suspicion). The threatening presence of several officers, display of a weapon by an officer, physical touching of the motorist, or the use of intimidating language or tone may convert a traffic stop into a detention requiring justification. *United States v. White*, 81 F.3d 775, 779 (8th Cir. 1996).

At the other end of the intrusion spectrum, the question arises as to when the duration of an investigative stop reaches a point where it ripens into the equivalent of a full-scale arrest, thus requiring greater justification in the form of probable cause. If, for example, the subject of the stop and frisk is brought to the station house and detained for extensive questioning, justification clearly could no longer be based merely on reasonable suspicion, but rather probable cause must be shown. *Dunaway v. New York*, 442 U.S. 200 (1979). Drawing the line between a stop and a more substantial intrusion was the subject of *Florida v. Royer*, 460 U.S. 491 (1983), which involved the detention at Miami International Airport of an individual believed to fit the "drug courier profile." Royer was approached by two detectives and at their request turned over his airline ticket and driver's license, then accompanied them to a police interrogation room. His luggage was brought in, and (again at the officers' request) Royer opened his suitcase, revealing marijuana. The entire sequence of events occupied approximately 15 minutes. In ruling that by the time the suitcase was opened the detention had become a more serious intrusion than a brief investigative stop, which is permitted on reasonable suspicion, the Court wrote:

> The predicate permitting seizures on suspicion short of probable cause is that law enforcement interests warrant a limited intrusion on the personal security of the suspect. The scope of

> the intrusion permitted will vary to some extent with the partic-
> ular facts and circumstances of each case. This much, however,
> is clear: an investigative detention must be temporary and last
> no longer than is necessary to effectuate the purpose of the
> stop. Similarly, the investigative methods employed should be
> the least intrusive means reasonably available to verify or dispel
> the officer's suspicion in a short period of time.

460 U.S. at 500. The Court concluded that Royer had been subjected
to the functional equivalent of an arrest, and, absent probable cause,
his detention was unlawful.

Together with duration, courts weigh the degree of intrusion and
the amount of force used on the subject in determining whether a stop
has crossed the boundary and become the equivalent of an arrest. The
Court has refused to establish a bright-line rule for determining when
a *Terry* stop exceeds its permissible duration. In *United States v. Sharpe*,
470 U.S. 675 (1985), the Court rejected the 20-minute limit proposed
by the Model Code of Pre-Arraignment Procedure, and (in an apparent departure from *Royer*) warned against too much judicial second-
guessing of whether the officers acted in the least intrusive and most
expeditious manner in conducting the investigative stop. "In evaluating whether an investigative detention is unreasonable," the Court
cautioned, "common sense and ordinary human experience must govern over rigid criteria." 470 U.S. at 685.

In exceptional circumstances, detentions ranging from 40 minutes to 16 hours have been held permissible as *Terry* stops because
that was the time necessary to effectuate the original purpose of the
stop—that is, to confirm or dispel the initial suspicion. In *Sharpe* the
officers were following two vehicles suspected of involvement in drug
trafficking, but initially were able to stop only one. The first driver was
detained for a period of 40 minutes, which was the time it took to
overtake and stop the second driver and return him to the location of
the first vehicle. In *United States v. Montoya De Hernandez*, 473 U.S.
531 (1985), an air traveler from Colombia was detained incommunicado by customs officials for 16 hours because she was suspected of
being a "balloon swallower," which is a smuggler who hides narcotics
in her alimentary canal. In both cases the Court treated the detentions
as stops, not arrests, because it concluded that the duration did not
exceed the time necessary to complete the preliminary field investigation. In the case of the balloon swallower, 16 hours was the time
necessary to await a bowel movement.[9]

---

9. The *Montoya De Hernandez* Court did emphasize that its decision was
rendered in the unique context of a customs inspection.

To summarize, decisional law has established gradations of justification or cause that correspond to the scope and degree of the particular intrusion. This appears consistent with the intention of the Fourth Amendment's drafters who sought to limit broad discretionary activity by law enforcement officers. If the police merely question or communicate with an individual on the street without detaining her against her will, the Fourth Amendment is not implicated and *no justification* need be shown. At the point at which a reasonable person would believe she is no longer free to leave and is being detained, a stop has occurred and the Fourth Amendment is triggered, requiring that the officer have *reasonable suspicion that criminal activity is afoot*. To support the additional intrusion of a frisk, the officer must have *reasonable suspicion that the subject is armed and dangerous*. Finally, if the nature and duration of the detention rise to the level of a full-scale arrest or its equivalent, *probable cause* must be shown. Figure 4–2 demonstrates the connection between degree of intrusion and justification required.

§4.4 The Expansion of *Terry*: Vehicle Stops, Detention of Effects, Protective Sweeps, and Plain Feel

The authority of police officers to briefly detain subjects for investigative purposes on information amounting to reasonable suspicion has been expanded beyond the street-encounter context of *Terry*. Thus an officer may stop and briefly detain a motorist in her automobile where the officer has "at least articulable and reasonable suspicion" that the motorist is violating the law, including motor vehicle infractions. *Delaware v. Prouse*, 440 U.S. 648 (1979). The stop also encompasses the authority to order the driver and passengers out of the car (based on the Supreme Court's premise that such order is a minimal intrusion beyond the stop itself, and is justified by safety concerns). *Pennsylvania v. Mimms*, 434 U.S. 106 (1977); *Maryland v. Wilson*, 519 U.S. 408 (1997).[10]

If the officer has reason to believe that the driver or an occupant is armed and dangerous, then the officer may frisk and also conduct a limited search of the interior of the car immediately within the suspect's control. Such a search is permissible even where the suspect is being held by the police outside the car, because of the possibility that

---

10. Some states have rejected these decisions and have interpreted their own constitutions to require reasonable suspicion before persons may be ordered out of a stopped vehicle. See, e.g., *Commonwealth v. Gonsalves*, 429 Mass. 658, 711 N.E.2d 108 (1999).

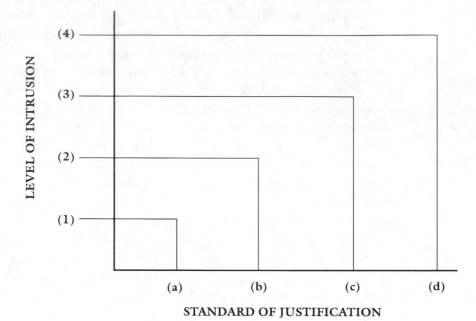

(1) Subject confronted but free to leave.
(2) Stop—subject confronted and not free to leave.
(3) Frisk—limited to pat-down search.
(4) Arrest or intrusion equivalent to arrest.

(a) No justification required.
(b) Reasonable suspicion that criminal activity is afoot. More than a hunch or unparticularized suspicion.
(c) In addition to (b), reasonable suspicion that suspect is armed and dangerous.
(d) Probable cause.

Figure 4–2: Arrest/Stop and Frisk—Justification

she may break away from the officers during the detention or have access to weapons in the car after she is released. In *Michigan v. Long*, 463 U.S. 1032 (1983), police officers saw a car swerve into a ditch and, after stopping to investigate, made observations that the driver was intoxicated and that there was a large hunting knife on the floorboard inside the vehicle. The Court held that the officers were justified in searching the passenger compartment as well as frisking the driver. The police were aware of specific facts that would "warrant reasonable officers in believing that the suspect is dangerous and the suspect may gain immediate control of weapons." Id.

Reasonable suspicion that a package or piece of luggage contains contraband or evidence of a crime has been held to justify its temporary seizure. *United States v. Place*, 462 U.S. 696 (1983); *United States v.*

Van Leeuwen, 397 U.S. 249 (1970). Applying the *Terry* balancing test, the Supreme Court has concluded that where reasonable suspicion exists, the governmental interest in briefly detaining such personal effects outweighs the minimal intrusion to the owner. As with stops of the person, these seizures must be limited in both time and scope. Thus a suitcase may be temporarily held by law enforcement agents at an airport for the purpose of subjecting it to a narcotics sniffing dog, but a detention of 90 minutes has been deemed excessive and unreasonable. *United States v. Place*, supra.

The *Terry* rationale has also been applied to permit a protective sweep of a home in which an arrest is being made. Where the officers possess "a reasonable belief based on specific and articulable facts that an area to be swept harbors an individual posing a danger to those at the arrest scene," the officers may engage in a limited search for such an individual. *Maryland v. Buie*, 494 U.S. 325 (1990). See also §6.3. The Court has emphasized that the sweep may extend only to a cursory inspection of those spaces where a person may be found and may last only as long as is required to resolve the suspicion of danger. This expansion of the stop and frisk doctrine led Justice Brennan to observe in dissent:

> *Terry* and its early progeny permitted only brief investigative stops and extremely limited searches based on reasonable suspicion . . . but this Court more recently has applied the rationale underlying *Terry* to a wide variety of more intrusive searches and seizures prompting my continued criticism of the emerging tendency on the part of the Court to convert the *Terry* decision from a narrow exception into one that swallows the general rule that [searches] are reasonable only if based on probable cause.

494 U.S. at 339.

As previously noted, when a police officer believes the subject of a stop is armed and dangerous, the officer may conduct a pat-down search. Originally, the scope of this intrusion was limited to a pat-down for weapons so as to protect the officer. But it has since been expanded to allow an officer, who during a pat-down search feels an object that is immediately recognized as contraband, to seize the object (the so-called plain feel doctrine). See *Minnesota v. Dickerson*, 508 U.S. 366 (1993).

EXAMPLES
What Constitutes a "Stop"?

1. Two federal drug agents in plain clothes approached Mindy as she proceeded through an airport terminal. They identified themselves

and requested to see her identification and ticket, which she produced. They posed several questions about her travel plans and returned her papers. At the agents' request Mindy then accompanied them to a nearby office. Was Mindy subjected to a stop during the initial encounter (before she proceeded to the office)? After she followed the agents to the office? Does it matter whether the agents intended to detain her? Does it matter whether Mindy actually believed she was not free to leave?

2. Police officers on routine patrol observed a man standing on a corner who, when he saw the cruiser, turned and ran. The officers followed the man around the corner and drove alongside him for a short distance. As they did so, the officers observed the man pull a number of packets from his pocket and discard them on the ground as he ran. The police retrieved the packets, examined them, and found pills that appeared to be contraband. The man was then stopped and placed under arrest. He was later charged with narcotics possession and moved to dismiss the charges on the ground that he had been unlawfully seized during the initial police pursuit preceding his disposal of the packets. Did this pursuit constitute a seizure within the meaning of the Fourth Amendment (thus requiring a showing of reasonable suspicion)?

3. In the course of its work, the Immigration and Naturalization Service (INS) conducts "factory surveys" to determine whether any illegal aliens are present at the worksite. Uniformed and armed officers disperse themselves throughout the building and systematically approach each employee. After identifying themselves and displaying their badges, the officers ask three questions relating to the employee's citizenship. During the survey, employees are free to continue their work and walk around the building. Does this conduct amount to a stop, implicating the Fourth Amendment requirement for justification?

4. The City of Fantasy has experienced a serious and violent crime wave. Mayor Hack responds by instructing the police patrolling in high-crime areas to be "aggressive," specifically to stop citizens and demand identification from them. As legal counsel to the mayor, how would you advise her regarding the legality of this practice?

5. An officer in a high-crime area observed a couple in a car and suspected prostitution. When asked what they were doing, they replied, "Waiting for Bill," and pointed to a man who was ap-

proaching. The officer asked, "Are you Bill?" The man's response could not be understood because he had something in his mouth. When the officer ordered him to spit it out the man spat out vials of crack. Was this a stop?

Reasonable Suspicion to Stop and Frisk

6. Two experienced officers on cruiser patrol at 4 A.M. observed a late-model Cadillac traveling along Main Street with a youthful driver and passenger, both appearing to be in their early 20s. Although the Cadillac did not commit any traffic violation, the officers' attention was drawn to it. As the cruiser approached the car from the adjoining lane, the driver raised his hand to his face, thereby obscuring his features from the officers' view. Their suspicions aroused, the officers stopped the vehicle. Was this stop justified?

7. Officer Mann, while on routine foot patrol in an area of New York City known for its brisk narcotics traffic, made observations of Sam Slam over a period of several hours. During that period he saw Sam converse with several persons known to the officer as narcotics users. Mann did not overhear any of the conversations, nor did he see anything pass between Sam and those he spoke with. The officer finally confronted Sam at a restaurant and ordered him to step outside, which he did. While questioning Sam on the street, Officer Mann reached into Sam's pocket and pulled out several packets that contained heroin. Was this seizure legally justified?

8. Officer Jones observed Felix, whom she recognized as an enforcer for a local drug gang, emerge from a notorious crack house that has been the scene of many violent encounters. When Felix spotted Jones he turned and ran in the opposite direction. Based on the evasive action and the other previously mentioned facts, Jones ordered Felix to stop and then administered a pat-down search. The search revealed no weapons, but Jones felt a lump in Felix's pocket, which she examined further with her fingers. The finger search revealed cellophane commonly used to package crack cocaine. Jones seized the small plastic bag, which contained a small amount of crack cocaine. Was this seizure lawful?

9. An officer on patrol in a high-crime area at 2:15 A.M. was informed by a person known to him (and who had provided information in the past) that an individual in a nearby car was in possession of narcotics and had a gun at his waist. The officer approached the car, tapped on the window, and asked the occupant to open the

door. Instead the occupant rolled down the window, at which point the officer reached into the car and removed a revolver from the occupant's waistband. Was this seizure legally justified?

10. While on routine patrol a police officer observed a person who was suspected of having committed a robbery the week before. In the absence of information amounting to probable cause to arrest, may the officer nevertheless briefly detain the suspect to question her concerning the robbery?

11. An experienced police officer observed three men in flashy clothes conversing on a street corner. Acting on a hunch that a drug transaction was occurring, the officer approached the men and addressed a question to them about their activities. They immediately turned away and began to quickly depart. May the officer stop and frisk them at this point?

12. At 9:15 A.M. narcotics agents at the Dallas/Ft. Worth airport observed a young woman disembark a flight from Miami, Florida. She carried a small gym bag and walked quickly to a restroom. As she walked she looked around as if she was expecting to meet someone. She left the restroom and went to a set of telephones where she made a call lasting 30 minutes. She then proceeded to the baggage claim area where she waited for several minutes but did not pick up any baggage. Finding her conduct suspicious, the agents approached the woman, displayed their identification, and asked if they could speak with her. The woman appeared extremely nervous and began to perspire; her voice cracked and her hands trembled. She agreed to speak with the agents and at their request gave them her airline ticket. When they asked for identification, she replied that she had lost her wallet. The agents asked how long she intended to stay in Dallas and she replied one week. At that point the agent noticed that her ticket indicated that she was scheduled for a return flight to Miami that afternoon. Is there justification to further detain the woman?

The Proper Scope of the Investigative Detention—When Does a "Stop" Grow into an "Arrest"?

13. Two police officers were approached by a pedestrian (previously unknown to them) who stated that a person named Leon was in Joe's Grill on Oak Street and that Leon had several bags of heroin for sale. She provided a detailed description of this individual and his clothing. The officers proceeded to Joe's Grill and found no one of that description. Immediately upon leaving the bar they

observed an individual meeting Leon's description walking quickly away along the sidewalk. The officers approached this person, blocked his movement, and asked him to identify himself. He nervously responded that he was Leon Silver. At that point one of the officers asked the subject to remove his shoes, which he did, and they continued to question him. What level of cause is required to justify this encounter, and did the police possess it?

Overview—Putting It All Together

14. On Tuesday at 2:30 P.M. Officer Harvey was on routine cruiser patrol in a suburban neighborhood that had been experiencing a spate of daytime burglaries. Harvey's attention was drawn to a car parked in a residential driveway. The car's trunk was open, exposing several large green plastic trash bags, which appeared full and of the type reportedly used to remove the loot in some of the break-ins. The uniformed officer made a U-turn and pulled into the driveway behind the car. At that moment the driver had just closed the trunk and was beginning to back out, but the police car now blocked her exit. The driver got out of the car and, appearing quite nervous, asked the officer to move the cruiser. The officer responded instead by asking the driver for identification, which she produced. The identification indicated an address on the other side of town. At that point the officer frisked the driver, took the keys to her car from her coat pocket, opened the trunk and then the trash bags inside. Finding TVs, stereo components, jewelry, and cash, the officer placed the driver under arrest. It was later determined that the items had been stolen from a nearby residence. The driver-now-defendant moved to suppress the items. Were the officer's actions justified?

15. Deputy Sheriff Boyer was on cruiser patrol when he heard a report over the police radio that a bank had just been robbed and that the four male perpetrators, who were armed with guns, had escaped in a 1975 red Ford Maverick with no license plate. Ten minutes later Boyer observed a vehicle of that description (but with a license plate) traveling in the direction away from the bank. He followed the car and signaled for it to stop, which it did. As Boyer approached the car he observed two men and a woman inside, and they appeared startled and upset. Boyer drew his revolver and ordered the occupants out. As they complied, the deputy observed a bulge in the pocket of the driver. Boyer patted the subject down, felt a hard object, and reached into the subject's

pocket, removing a small caliber pistol. What level of justification did the deputy need for each stage of this encounter, and did he have such justification?

EXPLANATIONS
What Constitutes a "Stop"?

1. A person is considered to have been seized within the meaning of the Fourth Amendment if, in view of all the circumstances surrounding the incident, a reasonable person in such situation would believe that she was not free to leave. In *United States v. Mendenhall*, 446 U.S. 544 (1980), the case upon which example 1 is based, the Supreme Court splintered as to whether under this definition a seizure had taken place during the initial encounter. Emphasizing that the encounter occurred in a public place, that the agents did not *demand* to see the subject's papers, but rather merely requested them, and that there was no display of weapons or any other force, Justice Stewart (joined only by Justice Rehnquist) concluded that no stop had occurred because "nothing in the record suggests that [Mendenhall] had any objective reason to believe that she was not free to end the conversation in the concourse and proceed on her way." Three members of the Court assumed that the confrontation amounted to a seizure, but concluded nonetheless that it was justified because there were sufficient facts to establish reasonable suspicion. 446 U.S. at 560 (Powell, J., concurring in part and concurring in the judgment). The four remaining Justices, while believing that a remand on the question was desirable, treated the encounter as a stop and concluded there was insufficient justification for it. Id. at 570–571 (White, J., dissenting).

    Obviously, the reasonable person standard leaves considerable room for differences of opinion, and the particular factual context of the encounter becomes of primary importance. In *Florida v. Royer*, 460 U.S. 491 (1983) (discussed in §4.3), for example, the Court reviewed an airport encounter that seems quite similar to that in *Mendenhall*, but somehow concluded that a stop *had* occurred, explaining:

    > Asking for and examining Royer's ticket and his driver's license were no doubt permissible in themselves, but when the officers identified themselves as narcotics agents, told Royer that he was suspected of transporting narcotics, and

asked him to accompany them to the police room, while retaining his ticket and driver's license and without indicating in any way that he was free to depart, Royer was effectively seized for the purposes of the Fourth Amendment. These circumstances surely amount to a show of official authority such that a reasonable person would have believed he was not free to leave.

460 U.S. at 501–502. The only obvious distinction between Royer's experience (held to be a seizure) and Mendenhall's (held not a seizure) seems to be that the police returned Mendenhall's papers while they retained Royer's.

While the reasonable person standard is imprecise, some things are clear concerning its operation. One is that the *actual belief* of the subject that she is (or is not) being detained is not determinative. As one court put it, "the test is an objective one, concerned with whether a reasonable person would feel he could leave, [and] it does not matter whether a particular defendant feels intimidated or at ease." *United States v. Berryman*, 717 F.2d 651, 655 (1st Cir. 1983). Similarly, because the standard focuses on the state of mind of the subject, the *actual but unstated intention* of the officers to detain is irrelevant to the inquiry. See *United States v. Hensley*, 469 U.S. 221, 235 (1985). Thus in our problem neither the agents' intent, nor Mindy's subjective perceptions, are determinative on the issue of whether a seizure occurred. As in tort law, the reasonable person reigns supreme here.

Factors that are considered by the courts in applying the *Mendenhall* test include: 1) the number and position of the officers involved; 2) the tone of voice used by the officers; 3) whether the encounter occurred in a public place; 4) whether the subject's path was blocked; 5) whether the subject was asked to accompany the police or step aside with them; and 6) whether the officers retained the subject's identification, ticket, or other possession for more than a minimal amount of time. See *United States v. Gonzales*, 842 F.2d 748 (5th Cir. 1988), *overruled on other grounds, United States v. Hurtado*, 905 F.2d 74 (5th Cir. 1990). The failure to notify the suspect that she is free to leave also weighs (but not determinatively) in favor of the conclusion that the encounter amounted to a seizure. See *United States v. Berryman*, 717 F.2d 651 (1st Cir. 1983). Compare *United States v. Ortega-Santana*, 869 F.2d 12 (1st Cir. 1989) (the fact that the subject was twice informed that he was free to leave required the conclusion that his accompanying of the agents to their office was not a seizure). Also pointing toward a conclusion that a seizure has occurred is the statement to the subject that she is suspected of criminal activity. See *United States v. White*, 890 F.2d 1413 (8th Cir. 1989) (a reasonable person would not feel that he was free to depart, despite the agents' assurances to that effect because in response to his question as to why they had stopped him, the agents told the subject that he exhibited the characteristics of a drug trafficker); *United States v. Berry*, 670 F.2d 583, 597 (5th Cir. 1982) ("Statements which intimate that an investigation has focused on a specific individual easily could induce a reasonable person to believe that failure to cooperate would lead only to formal detention."). Where the officers merely approach the individual, display their badges, and ask questions, it is unlikely that a seizure will be found. See *United States v. Hanson*, 801 F.2d 757, 761 (5th Cir. 1986).

For other cases raising the issue of whether airport encounters constitute a seizure, see *Reid v. Georgia*, 448 U.S. 438 (1980); *Florida v. Rodriquez*, 469 U.S. 1, 5 (1985) ("The initial contact between the officers and respondent, where they simply asked if he would step aside and talk with them, was clearly the sort of consensual encounter that implicates no Fourth Amendment interest.").

Remember that if we conclude the agents did not stop Mindy within the meaning of the Fourth Amendment, they need not demonstrate any level of cause to justify their action. Regardless of our conclusion as to the initial encounter, however, it would appear that a seizure did occur when Mindy was asked to accompany the agents to the office, and thus reasonable suspicion would be required at that point in the events.

2. As we have seen, there is no bright-line rule to determine what constitutes a seizure. Rather, the test is whether a reasonable person, viewing the particular conduct of the police and the surrounding circumstances, would have believed that her liberty was constrained and she was not free to leave. Under certain limited circumstances a police chase may constitute a seizure, as in *Brower v. County of Inyo*, 489 U.S. 593 (1989), where the motorist had been chased by the police for 20 miles and finally crashed into a roadblock set up by the police.

On the facts here, however, no seizure occurred during the initial pursuit. A unanimous Supreme Court held in *Michigan v. Chesternut*, 486 U.S. 567 (1988), that such a brief pursuit by the police, without more, would not have communicated to a reasonable person that they sought to capture him or otherwise restrain his freedom. Because no stop occurred, the police were not required to have a particularized objective basis for suspecting the subject of criminal activity in order to so pursue him. Two members of the *Chesternut* Court, Justices Kennedy and Scalia, proposed a change from the *Mendenhall* test that would require the officers' pursuit to actually achieve a "restraining effect" before a seizure could be said to occur. 486 U.S. at 577 (Kennedy, J., concurring). The Court appears to have adopted this position in *California v. Hodari D.*, 499 U.S. 621 (1991), which underscores the fact that the chase itself is not sufficient to constitute a seizure. Rather, there must be either an application of restraining force on the subject or the latter must yield to the officers.

3. The Supreme Court answered this question in the negative in *INS v. Delgado*, 466 U.S. 210 (1984). "Interrogation relating to one's identity or a request for identification by the police does not, by itself, constitute a Fourth Amendment seizure. . . . Unless the circumstances of the encounter are so intimidating as to demonstrate that a reasonable person would have believed he was not free to leave if he had not responded, one cannot say that the questioning resulted in a detention under the Fourth Amendment." 466 U.S. at 210. Again, however, the members of the Court disagreed on the application of the *Mendenhall* test. The dissenters found it "plain beyond cavil that the manner in which the INS conducted these surveys demonstrated a show of authority of sufficient size and force to overbear the will of any reasonable person." Id. at 229.

In another factory seizure case, *Martinez v. Nygaard*, 831 F.2d 822 (9th Cir. 1987), the court held that a worker was not seized even when he was grabbed by the shoulder by an INS officer because the action was designed only to get the worker's attention, and he was released immediately. In addition, the worker later testified that he was not put in fear. The basis for this ruling would seem questionable given the objective, not subjective, focus of the *Mendenhall* standard. A co-worker was, however, held to have been seized when she was physically prevented from leaving her work area.

4. While this sort of brief detention may appear so minimal as to require no specific justification, the Supreme Court has held in several contexts that *any* detention (within the *Mendenhall* defi-

nition) triggers the Fourth Amendment and thus must be justified by a showing of reasonable suspicion. In *Brown v. Texas*, 443 U.S. 47 (1979), officers stopped an individual in a high-crime area of El Paso because he "looked suspicious" and they wanted to ascertain his identity. The Court ruled the stop unconstitutional, explaining:

> In the absence of any basis for suspecting appellant of misconduct, the balance between the public interest and appellant's right to security and privacy tilts in favor of freedom from police interference. . . . [E]ven assuming that [a strong social] purpose is served to some degree by stopping and demanding identification from an individual without any specific basis for believing he is involved in criminal activity, the guarantees of the Fourth Amendment do not allow it. When such a stop is not based on objective criteria, the risk of arbitrary and abusive police practices exceeds tolerable limits.

443 U.S. at 52. The Court observed that while "the record suggests an understandable desire to assert a police presence . . . that purpose does not negate Fourth Amendment guarantees." Id. at 51.

The Court has similarly ruled unlawful the common police practice of stopping motorists at random to check their driver's license and registration. See *Delaware v. Prouse*, 440 U.S. 648 (1979). Although such spot checks are minimal intrusions, they are nevertheless "constitutionally cognizable" and thus may be conducted only where there is "articulable and reasonable suspicion" that the motorist is unlicensed or unregistered or is otherwise in violation of law. 440 U.S. at 661.

The determinative issue in example 4, however, is whether the proposed "aggressive" encounters on the street amount to seizures triggering the Fourth Amendment. The case of *Florida v. Bostick*, 501 U.S. 429 (1991), holding that drug sweeps of buses do not necessarily constitute seizures, might indicate that the proposed street encounters may not be within the purview of the amendment and thus can occur without any specific justification. The question is how aggressive the police officers can be: Can they forcibly restrain the individual until she identifies herself?

5. The court said it was in *Commonwealth v. Houle*, 622 N.E.2d 638 (Mass. App. Ct. 1993). A uniformed officer ordering a person in "authoritarian language" to spit out what was in her mouth is of

such a nature that it would reasonably be regarded as offensive in ordinary social intercourse. Bill could reasonably be expected to believe that he had to comply. The result of compliance was an intrusion on Bill's privacy. A stop requires a reasonable suspicion that criminal activity is afoot and the officer had no reasonable suspicion that Bill was involved in a criminal act. Presence in a high-crime area is inadequate. The court reasoned that Bill could have been chewing gum or tobacco or could have had a speech impediment and therefore the fact that there was something in his mouth was not enough to establish reasonable suspicion.

In *Clayton v. State*, 616 So. 2d 615 (Fla. Dist. Ct. App. 1993), seven officers in three vehicles acting as a narcotics task force and wearing jackets reading "Sheriff's Office Drug Task Force" observed the defendant toss a waist pouch into the back of his truck in a convenience store parking lot. Two of the police vehicles pulled up and four officers jumped out. One ran up to the defendant and asked aggressively, "What was that you threw in the truck?" The defendant replied, "That was my gun." Is this a stop or a voluntary police/citizen encounter? The court held this constituted a stop and therefore required a reasonable suspicion of criminal activity. The threatening presence of several officers as well as the officer's authoritarian tone made it reasonable for the defendant to believe the question was a command to answer, rather than a request.

Reasonable Suspicion to Stop and Frisk

6. Given the totality of circumstances, did the officers have concrete facts that would establish a reasonable suspicion that the subjects were involved in criminal activity? The answer is probably no. The fact that the youths were in an expensive automobile late at night is not sufficient in itself to give the officers anything more than a hunch that something criminal was afoot. Even if the driver's gesture obscuring his face reasonably appeared to the officers as a deliberate attempt at concealment (as opposed to an off-hand movement), there is still very serious doubt whether justification for a *Terry* stop was present. The Massachusetts Supreme Judicial Court, while refusing to rule as a matter of law that such secretive conduct could never constitute reasonable suspicion in conjunction with other circumstances, held that the circumstances in our example did not justify a stop of the Cadillac. See *Commonwealth v. Bacon*, 381 Mass. 642 (1980).

7. Sam was clearly subjected to a stop, and thus Officer Mann must be prepared to articulate the facts giving rise to a reasonable suspicion that Sam was involved in criminal activity. Given the limited information known to him, Mann is unable to do so. As the Supreme Court observed in the companion case to *Terry*, upon which this problem is based, the officer was completely ignorant regarding the content of the conversations between Sam and the narcotics users and could point to no concrete indication that criminal transactions were occurring: "So far as he knew, they might indeed have been talking about the World Series." *Sibron v. New York*, 392 U.S. 40, 47 (1968). The Court added: "The inference that persons who talk to narcotics addicts are engaged in the criminal traffic of narcotics is simply not the sort of reasonable inference required to support an intrusion by the police upon an individual's personal security." 392 U.S. at 62. Moreover, as Justice Harlan observed in his concurrence, at the time the officer confronted Sibron in the restaurant there was no apparently imminent crime about to occur, as there was in *Terry* where Officer McFadden interrupted what he reasonably believed was an unfolding robbery.

Because the stop was unlawful, the evidence seized during the subsequent search must be suppressed. (See Chapter 7.) Even if the stop had been justified, however, Officer Mann's reach into Sam's pocket was not. In order to justify a frisk, Officer Mann would have to be able to articulate facts from which it may be reasonably inferred that Sam was armed and dangerous. As the *Sibron* Court concluded, "the suspect's mere act of talking with a number of known narcotics addicts over an eight-hour period no more gives rise to reasonable fear of life or limb on the part of the police officer than it justifies [the initial stop]." Id. at 64.

In addition to the absence of adequate justification in the form of reasonable suspicion, the scope of the search conducted by Officer Mann exceeded permissible bounds:

> The search for weapons approved in *Terry* consisted solely of a limited patting of the outer clothing of the suspect for concealed objects which might be used as instruments of assault. Only when he discovered such objects did the officer in *Terry* place his hands in the pockets of the men he searched. In this case, with no attempt at an initial limited exploration for arms, [the officer] thrust his hand into Sibron's pocket and took from him envelopes of heroin. His

> testimony shows that he was looking for narcotics, and he found them. The search was not reasonably limited in scope to the accomplishment of the only goal which might conceivably have justified its inception—the protection of the officer by disarming a potentially dangerous man.

Id. at 65.

8. Given the information regarding Felix's reputation, the stakeout, and the evasive action, there appears to be enough justification for both a stop and a frisk. This is especially true in light of *Illinois v. Wardlow*, 120 S. Ct. 673 (2000), which permits consideration of evasive action. Jones, however, goes beyond a lawful frisk by fingering the lump in the pocket. The fingering occurred after Jones concluded there was no weapon, so it is beyond the scope of a lawful frisk. Thus the further invasion of fingering and resulting seizure is unlawful. If, however, as part of the frisk she immediately recognized the package as cocaine, this would fall under the plain feel doctrine established by *Minnesota v. Dickerson*, 508 U.S. 366 (1993).

9. There are several problems regarding the officer's actions here. First, unlike Officer McFadden in *Terry*, the officer in this example acted on the basis of information supplied by a third party, rather than on his own personal observations. Second, while the informant had previously supplied information, we do not know if it turned out to be accurate. Third, we do not know anything about the basis of the informant's conclusion that the subject was in possession of narcotics and a gun. Fourth, even if the officer had reasonable grounds to suspect that the subject was in violation of the law and was armed and dangerous, he did not limit his initial action to a pat-down of the clothing, but rather immediately intruded into the driver's waistband and removed the gun.

    Despite similar complications, the Court held in *Adams v. Williams*, 407 U.S. 143 (1972), that the officer's actions there were lawful. Conceding that the informant's tip would not satisfy the requirements for justification of a full-scale search or arrest (probable cause), the Court nevertheless ruled that the information "carried enough indicia of reliability" to justify a forcible stop. Further, "[w]hen Williams rolled down his window, rather than complying with the policeman's request to step out of the car so that his movements could more easily be seen, the revolver allegedly at Williams' waist became an even greater threat. Under these circumstances the policeman's action in reaching to the spot where the gun was thought to be hidden constituted a limited intrusion designed to insure his safety, and we conclude that it was reasonable." 407 U.S. at 148.

The *Adams v. Williams* Court explicitly rejected the argument that reasonable suspicion can only be based on the officer's own personal observations. As with probable cause, the source may be a third party as long as the information carries sufficient indicia of reliability. Examples of such information would be the description of an assailant by the victim herself and the warning from a credible, confidential informant that a specific crime is about to occur. *Alabama v. White*, 496 U.S. 325 (1990), added anonymous tips (with sufficient police corroboration) to the permissible sources of information leading to reasonable suspicion. Although in *Florida v. J.L.*, 2000 WL 309131 decided on March 28, 2000, the Court refused to allow a *Terry* stop based exclusively on an anonymous tip.

In upholding the police action, the *Adams v. Williams* Court explicitly referred to the fact that the stop occurred in a high-crime area. 407 U.S. at 144. See also *United States v. Brignoni-Ponce*, 422 U.S. 873, 884 (1975) ("Officers may consider the characteristics of the area in which they encounter a vehicle."); *United States v. Cortez*, 449 U.S. 411, 419 (1981) ("Of critical importance, the officers knew that the area was crossing point for illegal aliens."). Compare *United States v. Guillen-Cazares*, 989 F.2d 380 (10th Cir. 1993) (even though the area was near the border and the road was often used as a checkpoint, the court held there was no reasonable suspicion to stop two heavily loaded cars driving close together because many cars on the road might possess these characteristics). Courts have tended to weigh the location of a stop quite heavily. As one court has put it, the "reputation of an area for criminal activity is an articulable fact upon which a police officer may legitimately rely." *United States v. Rickus*, 737 F.2d 360, 365 (3d Cir. 1984). Obviously, as with probable cause, location alone is insufficient itself to justify a *Terry* stop; there must still be particular facts pointing to the suspect's involvement in criminal activity. See *United States v. Trullo*, 809 F.2d 108, 111 (1st Cir. 1987).

The courts appear to apply an objective rather than a subjective analysis to determine whether a frisk is justified. In *Commonwealth v. Johnson*, 602 N.E.2d 555 (Mass. 1992), for example, the defendant's vehicle almost hit a police car. A chase ensued and another police car headed him off. The first officer saw the defendant place something in the waistband of his pants so he drew his weapon while the other officers pulled the defendant out of the car. The defendant was subjected to a pat-down search and the officer pulled out of his waistband a bag of white powder and three bullets in a pouch. At trial, the state failed to show that the officer actually believed the bulge to be a weapon. Was there adequate justification for a frisk?

The stop was clearly reasonable because the defendant committed a traffic violation. The chase and the sight of the defendant putting something in his waistband gave the officer a reasonable suspicion that the defendant might be armed. Thus the officer was justified in conducting a frisk. The officer, however, reached into the defendant's pocket even though he did not actually believe the bulge was a weapon (at least he did not testify to as much in court). The court nonetheless found the scope of the search justified, reasoning that the subjective belief of the officer was not determinative of the issue of justification for a frisk.

Assume that a sobriety checkpoint has been established and meets constitutional muster. An officer spots a motorist turning down an unpaved, uninhabited road in the early morning to avoid the checkpoint. Would this provide the officer with reasonable suspicion to stop the defendant? In *Steinbeck v. Commonwealth*, 862 S.W.2d 912 (Ky. Ct. App. 1993), the court found that the sudden turn down such a road before the checkpoint gave the officer a reasonable suspicion that criminal activity was afoot. The officer testified that in his experience a person who acted in such a manner generally had been drinking. Similarly, in *People v. Chafee*, 590 N.Y.S.2d 625 (N.Y. App. Div. 1992), an officer was deemed to have reasonable suspicion to stop a motorist who made a very quick stop when police flares became visible, turned into a motel parking lot, and drove around the lot without parking.

10. The issue raised here is whether a stop is permissible where its purpose is not (as was Officer McFadden's) to investigate a crime that is about to occur, but rather to investigate a crime that has *already occurred*. While recognizing that *Terry* was premised on the societal interest in permitting police to intervene and *prevent* crime, the Court has nonetheless authorized the use of stop and frisk for the investigation of past felonies, finding that the interest

in solving such crimes and removing perpetrators from the streets also outweighs the individual liberty interest invaded. *United States v. Hensley*, 469 U.S. 221 (1985). It is of course still necessary for the level of justification to reach reasonable suspicion— that is, to be "grounded in specific and articulable facts that a person they encounter was involved in or is wanted in connection with a completed felony." 469 U.S. at 222.

11. A mere hunch clearly is not adequate justification to detain an individual, however briefly. The issue raised in this example is whether the refusal of the men to respond to the officer's questions gave him the reasonable suspicion required to stop them. The answer is no. "[A] person approached [by an officer] need not answer any question put to him; indeed, he may decline to listen to the questions at all and may go on his way. He may not be detained even momentarily without reasonable, objective grounds for doing so; *and his refusal to listen or to answer does not, without more, furnish those grounds.*" *Florida v. Royer*, 460 U.S. 491, 498 (1983) (emphasis added). Similarly, a subject's refusal to consent to a search of her baggage or other possessions cannot be used as the sole basis for the requisite reasonable suspicion. See *United States v. White*, 890 F.2d 1413, 1417 (8th Cir. 1989). "To suggest otherwise would mean that all innocent persons must submit to [searches] to avoid arousing the suspicion of law enforcement officers, in disregard of the underlying premises of the Fourth Amendment." *United States v. Malachi*, 728 F. Supp. 777, 781 (D.D.C. 1989). With the recent decision in *Illinois v. Wardlow*, 120 S. Ct. 673 (2000), however, unprovoked flight in a high-crime area might provide sufficient justification for a stop.

   In our example, the officer had neither reasonable suspicion that criminal activity was afoot nor reasonable suspicion that the subjects were armed and dangerous. There can thus be no lawful stop or frisk.

12. Clearly, if there is reasonable suspicion to suspect the woman of criminal activity, it must be based on something more than her conduct prior to being approached by the agents. While she might have matched some of the factors in the drug courier profile—she traveled from a known source city for narcotics, was young, appeared unusually nervous, and carried little luggage—these characteristics are shared by so many travelers that to permit stops based on them would subject large numbers of innocent persons to intrusive police activity. See *Reid v. Georgia*, 448 U.S. 438, 441

(1980). Her inability to produce identification, together with the inconsistency between her stated travel plans and those reflected on her ticket, however, do raise particular suspicion about her. On similar facts the Fifth Circuit Court of Appeals found the suspicion to be reasonable and thus sufficient to justify an investigative detention. *United States v. Gonzales*, 842 F.2d 748 (5th Cir. 1988).

The *Gonzales* court observed that "law enforcement officials are entitled to evaluate the specific and articulable facts known to them in light of their experience in narcotics enforcement, and we are inclined to give due credit to the experience and expertise of these officers." 842 F.2d at 753. The Supreme Court has underscored the proposition that the officer's experience is entitled to deference on the question of justification for stop and frisk: "Among the circumstances that can give rise to reasonable suspicion are the agent's knowledge of the methods used in recent criminal activity and the characteristics of persons engaged in such illegal practices." *United States v. Mendenhall*, 446 U.S. 544, 563 (1980). Because of their expertise, officers are "able to perceive and articulate meaning in given conduct which would be wholly innocent to the untrained observer." *Brown v. Texas*, 443 U.S. 47, 52 n.2 (1979). As with probable cause, however, deference must not become abdication of the responsibility for detached judicial review of police conduct.

The Proper Scope of the Investigative Detention—When Does a "Stop" Grow into an "Arrest"?

13. In evaluating the legality of a *Terry* stop, it must be determined 1) whether there was justification (in the form of reasonable suspicion) for the stop; and 2) whether the degree of intrusion into the suspect's liberty was reasonably related in scope to the situation at hand.

    The officers here had reasonable suspicion to believe the subject was involved in criminal activity based upon the pedestrian's information and their location of a man of Leon's description near the bar. This level of cause permitted a brief investigative detention for questioning and, if they further developed reasonable suspicion that he was armed and dangerous, they would have been justified in frisking him for weapons.

    The problem is that the officers immediately took the additional step of having the subject remove his shoes, thus raising the issue as to whether they exceeded the permissible scope of a *Terry* stop. While there is no bright-line test for determining when a stop becomes the functional equivalent of an arrest (thereby requiring probable cause), the Supreme Court has looked to the duration of the detention as well as the question of whether the police employed "the least intrusive means reasonably available to verify or dispel the officer's suspicion in a short period of time." See *Florida v. Royer*, 460 U.S. 491, 500. See also *United States v. Sharpe*, 470 U.S. 675 (1985). Even though the detention in the example did not approach the duration of the stop in *Royer* (nearly 15 minutes), the removal of Leon's shoes was an escalation of the intrusion that does not appear to have been the least restrictive investigative method. Mere questioning would have achieved the result sought—information from the subject to confirm or dispel the initial suspicion. Moreover, neither the information from the original source nor the officers' own observations gave them any reason to suspect that Leon was armed and dangerous or that he would attempt to flee, and thus the action taken cannot be justified as protective.

It appears, therefore, that the officers' conduct was not "reasonably related in scope to the circumstances which justified the interference in the first place." *Terry v. Ohio*, 392 U.S. 1, 20 (1968). The Massachusetts Supreme Judicial Court so concluded in holding that the stop had become an arrest in the case upon which this problem is based. See *Commonwealth v. Borges*, 395 Mass. 788, 482 N.E.2d 314 (1985).

Once the stop here is upgraded to the functional equivalent of an arrest, it is clear that it was without adequate justification because the requisite probable cause was lacking. Neither the knowledge nor the credibility prong of the traditional test is met with regard to the previously unknown pedestrian's information. All that the police corroborated themselves was Leon's description. Thus there was insufficient information from which the officers could reasonably conclude that Leon had committed a crime.

It should be noted that while they are certainly critical factors to weigh, "neither handcuffing nor other restraints will *automatically* convert a *Terry* stop into a de facto arrest requiring probable cause." *United States v. Kapperman*, 764 F.2d 786, 790 n.4 (11th Cir. 1985). Rather "in evaluating whether an investigative detention is unreasonable, common sense and ordinary human experience must govern over rigid criteria." *United States v. Sharpe*, 470 U.S. 675, 695 (1985). Thus where a single officer confronting three persons in a high-crime area had reasonable suspicion that the suspects were engaged in criminal activity and were armed and dangerous, the officer's demand that the driver turn off the ignition and surrender his car keys was deemed a reasonable protective measure that did not convert the stop into an arrest. See *Commonwealth v. Moses*, 408 Mass. 136 (1990) ("[I]t is common knowledge that a person who wants to avoid police questioning, very often will recklessly drive away, resulting in serious injury to the police officer and bystanders. . . . [Thus the officer's actions] were similar to and consistent with the protective measures that have been sanctioned in *Terry*. . . ." 408 Mass. at 140.). Similarly, the fact that the officer drew his gun on the suspect was held not to convert the stop into an arrest where there was reasonable suspicion of narcotics dealing, a pattern of activity generally involving deadly weapons, and the confrontation occurred in a high-crime area. See *United States v. Trullo*, 809 F.2d 108, 113 (1st Cir. 1987). See also *United States v. Hardnett*, 804 F.2d 353, 357 (6th Cir. 1986) ("We believe that the use of arms in the present case was reasonably necessary under the circumstances. The officers were acting in a situation which justified a fear for personal safety. The officers had been told by [the informant] that the occupants of the car in front of her home were armed. Therefore, when the officers approached the car, it was reasonable for them to display their weapons for their own protection. Under these circumstances, the use of arms did not convert the investigative stop into an arrest."); *United States v. Jones*, 759 F.2d 635, 640–641 (8th Cir. 1985) ("We believe that, viewed through the eyes of a cautious and experienced police officer, [the limited actions of removing their guns] from their holsters to make their weapons more accessible were reasonable precautions as they initially approached and evaluated the situation. . . . These activities did not constitute an 'arrest' of Jones."). Compare *United States v. Ceballos*, 654 F.2d 177, 184 (2d Cir. 1981) (the drawing of guns is one of the "trappings of a technical formal arrest").

Some courts have indicated that the use of force in making a stop will not convert the stop into an arrest if it is precipitated by the evasive or threatening conduct of the person being detained. See *United States v. Beck*, 598 F.2d 497, 501 (9th Cir. 1979).

One area of controversy concerning judicial review of the reasonableness of police conduct is whether the focus should be solely on the specific events in question or whether generalizations about the type of crime may be weighed. Judge Bownes, for example, criticized the majority's use of general characteristics of certain kinds of lawbreakers or "high-crime" neighborhoods in evaluating the reasonableness of a stop in *Trullo*, supra, 809 F.2d at 118 (dissenting). See also *United States v. Ceballos*, 654 F.2d 177, 182–184 (2d Cir. 1981) ("[T]he initial question before us is whether the blocking of appellant's car and the approach by the officers with guns drawn was so intrusive as to be tantamount to an arrest. This question must be resolved based on the particular facts of this case, and the degree of intrusion, the amount of force used, and the extent to which appellant's freedom of movement was curtailed. . . . [Although we agree that narcotics traffickers are often armed and violent], that generalization, without more, is insufficient to justify the extensive intrusion which occurred in this case. If it were, any narcotics suspect, even if unknown to the agents and giving no indication that force is necessary, could be faced with a 'maximal intrusion' based on mere reasonable suspicion.").

Overview—Putting It all Together

14. The threshold task is to identify each gradation of intrusion and then determine whether the requisite justification was present. The police officer was entitled to address questions to the driver without any justification at all as long as the encounter remained voluntary. Once the officer blocked the individual's path with the cruiser and refused to move, however, a forcible stop occurred (that is, a reasonable person in those circumstances would believe she was not free to leave), and the Fourth Amendment kicked in with the requirement that there be reasonable suspicion that the driver was engaged in criminal activity. See *United States v. Kerr*, 817 F.2d 1384 (9th Cir. 1987).

What specific facts were known to the officer at that point? That the driver was parked in a neighborhood where break-ins were occurring, that she had green trash bags in the trunk, and that she appeared nervous in the face of the officer and cruiser blocking her path. The officer did not then know who lived in the residence or what automobiles they owned, and thus did not know whether the driver was leaving her own home or not. These facts are inadequate to constitute reasonable suspicion, and thus the initial stop of the driver was unlawful. See *United States v. Kerr*, supra. Moreover, the detention was already in progress by the time the officer saw the driver's identification and learned she was not a resident of the home, and this after-the-fact knowledge (even assuming it would raise the level of suspicion to reasonable, which is not altogether clear) cannot be weighed in measuring the legality of the initial stop. See *United States v. Nunley*, 873 F.2d 182, 185 (8th Cir. 1989) ("The government rightly relies only on the agents' observations before the investigative stop began. It does not argue that Nunley's reactions after [the officer] explained his mission (e.g., her shaking hands or quivering voice) helped establish a reasonable suspicion.").

The subsequent frisk was also impermissible. The only additional information learned by the officer at that point—that the suspect did not reside at that address but rather on the other side of town—is not an adequate basis for suspecting that the driver was armed and dangerous, and thus there was no justification for a frisk. Such police action is premised on the need for an officer to protect herself against an attack. Moreover, the scope of the frisk is limited to a pat-down. Only if the officer feels something that she reasonably believes may be a weapon can she enter the pockets or clothing of the subject. Officer Harvey, apparently without feeling anything like a weapon, reached into the subject's pocket and removed her keys. Compounding the illegality, the officer used the keys to open the trunk and then searched the bags. This latter action requires probable cause to believe seizable items will be found (see §6.4), a standard that is clearly not met here. Lastly, there does not appear to be probable cause to arrest because the officer at that point had no basis for determining that the items were stolen.

15. When Deputy Boyer signaled the car to pull over, that clearly constituted a stop requiring reasonable suspicion that criminal activity was afoot. The only information he had linking this car to the bank robbery was a report he heard over the police radio. Can reasonable suspicion be based on such a report? The Supreme Court has answered yes. Both *United States v. Hensley*, 469 U.S. 221 (1985), and *Whiteley v. Warden*, 401 U.S. 560 (1971), stand for the proposition that an officer may rely on information received from the police radio or a police flyer, but that the information

itself must meet the standard of probable cause. The issue is "whether the officers who issued the flyer possessed probable cause to make the arrest [or reasonable suspicion to effect a stop]. It does not turn on whether those relying on the flyer were themselves aware of the specific facts which led their colleagues to seek their assistance." *Hensley*, 469 U.S. at 231. The Court explained: "In an era when criminal suspects are increasingly mobile and increasingly likely to flee across jurisdictional boundaries, this rule is a matter of common sense: it minimizes the volume of information concerning suspects that must be transmitted to other jurisdictions and enables police in one jurisdiction to act promptly in reliance on information from another jurisdiction." Id.

The focus thus shifts to the basis the officers who issued the radio report had for the description of the perpetrators. If bank employees or eyewitnesses provided the police with the description of the red Maverick, that would constitute credible and reliable information upon which either reasonable suspicion or probable cause could properly be based. If, on the other hand, the description was based solely on an anonymous tip, justification for police action would be lacking. It would therefore be necessary to find out what information the police possessed prior to their issuance of the radio report.

Assuming that the report was based on reliable information, it would appear that Deputy Boyer had reasonable suspicion to stop the Maverick. The car met the description given except for the presence of a license plate. That variance, together with the conflict between the four male occupants reported and the two male and one female occupants observed by the officer several minutes later, is probably not significant enough to undercut the reasonableness of Boyer's stop (although it may defeat the existence of probable cause). Moreover, his own observations that the occupants appeared nervous contributed to the reasonableness of his suspicion.

Deputy Boyer clearly escalated the stop when he drew his gun. This action, as noted above, does not automatically convert the stop into an arrest (which would require probable cause). Where an officer's action is justified by reasonable concerns for her safety, the courts have generally held that the drawing of guns or other protective action is within the scope of a permissible stop. The radio report indicated that the perpetrators were armed, and it would appear therefore that Boyer, who was alone and outnumbered, was justified in taking this action. Moreover, an officer is authorized to order the occupants out of a vehicle that she has lawfully stopped, *Pennsylvania v. Mimms*, 434 U.S. 106 (1977); *Maryland v. Wilson*, 519 U.S. 408 (1997). Thus Boyer's order to the occupants was also within proper bounds.

The deputy's observation of a bulge in the pocket of one of the occupants, together with the information he had received over the radio, provided him with reasonable suspicion to believe the subject was armed and dangerous. Boyer was thus justified in patting him down and, upon feeling an object that might be a weapon, reaching into the pocket and removing it.

In sum, Deputy Boyer conducted a lawful stop and frisk under these circumstances. See *United States v. Jacobs*, 715 F.2d 1343 (9th Cir. 1983).

§4.5   Administrative Searches

A third category of justification has arisen out of the Supreme Court's distinction between searches related to criminal investigations and searches conducted for a noncriminal purpose. As we have seen, the former must be supported by specific information tying the subject to a crime that has been or is about to be committed (at a level of suspicion of either probable cause or reasonable suspicion). The noncriminal searches, however, have been judged against an open-ended test of reasonableness, which has produced a form of justification not dependent on such particularistic information. In recent years the "administrative search" rationale has, in the eyes of some critics, served as the vehicle for diluting or even abandoning the requirement of prior justification.

The concept of the administrative or regulatory search was first recognized in the 1967 decision of *Camara v. Municipal Court*, 387 U.S. 523, which involved the health code inspection of residential dwelling units. Holding that such inspections were subject to Fourth Amendment constraints, the Court nonetheless rejected the conclusion that the appropriate standard of justification was "traditional criminal law probable cause." Invoking the reasonableness clause, the Court balanced the public interest in enforcing safety codes against the "relatively limited invasion of the urban citizen's privacy" (given that "the inspections are neither personal in nature nor aimed at the discovery of evidence of crime") and concluded that such searches could be conducted as long as "reasonable legislative or administrative standards for conducting an area inspection are satisfied with respect to a particular dwelling." Such standards, the Court suggested, would focus on the type of building, the condition of the surrounding area, and the time that has passed since the last inspection, rather than specific knowledge of the particular dwelling to be viewed. Unlike the justification required for criminal searches, which is designed to ensure that there is a reasonable likelihood that the subject is involved in criminal activity, the justification envisioned in *Camara* is designed simply to ensure evenhandedness and to avoid arbitrary or selective enforcement. (The issue of when a warrant is required in the context of administrative searches is discussed in §5.4 and §6.6.)

The Court has explained that the "standard of probable cause is peculiarly related to criminal investigations, not routine, noncriminal procedures. . . . The probable-cause approach is unhelpful when analysis centers upon the reasonableness of routine administrative caretaking functions, particularly when no claim is made that the protective procedures are a subterfuge for criminal investigations." *Colorado v. Bertine*, 479 U.S. 367, 371 (1987). The constraints placed upon administrative searches operate, therefore, not to ensure prior knowledge of probable wrongdoing, but to limit discretion and prevent arbitrary treatment of individuals. The courts have therefore imposed a requirement that such searches be conducted according to neutral standardized criteria and procedures, which also prevent the administrative search from being used as a pretext for an investigative foray.

As Judge Richard Posner has described it, the difference between the traditional criminal search and one characterized as "administrative" is that the constitutionality of the former is assessed at the level of the individual search, while the latter is assessed at the level of the entire program. *Edmond v. Goldsmith*, 183 F.3d 659 (7th Cir. 1999), *cert. granted*, 120 S. Ct. 3519 (Feb. 22, 2000) (discussed infra in explanation 2).

A good example of the balancing approach upon which the administrative search rationale is premised can be found in the case of *Vernonia School District v. Acton*, 515 U.S. 646 (1995). The issue before the Court was the validity of a policy that would require every student who wanted to participate in athletics to submit to a random urinalysis for drugs. In allowing this search without individualized suspicion, the Court balanced the intrusion on an individual's Fourth

Amendment interests with the government's legitimate interest. With regard to the intrusion the Court indicated that public school students—in particular, athletes—have less of a privacy expectation because they routinely submit to medical examinations such as scoliosis screening, dress together in locker rooms, and voluntarily participate in regulated sports. Further, the method by which urine was obtained was not intrusive and the test would only determine specific drugs, with the results reported only to those school personnel legitimately needing to know. On the other side of the balance, the Court noted the governmental interest in determining "drug use by our Nation's school children." Thus, through the magic of balancing, the Court once again limited the need for individualized suspicion as a justification for Fourth Amendment activity.

The administrative search rationale has been applied in a wide range of contexts to dispense with the prerequisite for individualized suspicion. These include inspections of licensed or highly regulated business establishments;[11] arson investigations of fire scenes;[12] the use of a fixed checkpoint near a border to stop vehicles and briefly question the occupants in an effort to detect illegal aliens;[13] the use of fixed sobriety checkpoints to look for signs of intoxication in motorists passing through;[14] routine inventory searches of impounded automobiles

---

11. *New York v. Burger*, 482 U.S. 691 (1987) (statutorily authorized warrantless inspection of automobile junkyard); *Donovan v. Dewey*, 452 U.S. 594 (1981) (statutorily authorized warrantless inspections of mines); *United States v. Biswell*, 406 U.S. 311 (1972) (statutorily authorized warrantless search of a federally licensed gun dealer). The Court reasoned in these cases that persons choosing to engage in such highly regulated or licensed enterprises do so with the knowledge that they will be subject to periodic inspections and thus have reduced expectations of privacy. Compare *Marshall v. Barlow's Inc.*, 436 U.S. 307 (1978) (holding unconstitutional the practice of warrantless inspections under the Occupational Safety and Health Act on the grounds that the industries covered have not traditionally been pervasively regulated; the Court imposed a requirement for a *Camara*-type warrant).

12. *Michigan v. Clifford*, 464 U.S. 287 (1984); *Michigan v. Tyler*, 436 U.S. 499 (1978).

13. *United States v. Martinez-Fuerte*, 428 U.S. 543 (1976). Search of the vehicle, a far more serious intrusion, may only be conducted if there is probable cause to believe it contains aliens. See *United States v. Ortiz*, 422 U.S. 891 (1975) (search at fixed checkpoint); *Almeida-Sanchez v. United States*, 413 U.S. 266 (1973) (search by roving patrol units). Vehicles may be stopped by roving patrols near the border and occupants briefly questioned about their immigration status only upon reasonable suspicion that the vehicle contains illegal aliens. See *United States v. Brignoni-Ponce*, 422 U.S. 873 (1975).

14. *Michigan Dept. of State Police v. Sitz*, 496 U.S. 444 (1990).

and personal effects of arrestees;[15] and mandatory drug testing of public and private employees and high school athletes.[16]

Typical of the calculus applied in the administrative search cases is the following excerpt from the decision upholding employee drug screening:

> Because the testing program adopted by the Customs Service is not designed to serve the ordinary needs of law enforcement, we have balanced the public interest in the Service's testing program against the privacy concerns implicated by the tests, without reference to our usual presumption in favor of the procedures specified in the Warrant Clause, to assess whether the tests required by Customs are reasonable. We hold that the suspicionless testing of employees [involved in] the interdiction of illegal drugs . . . is reasonable.[17]

A Georgia statute mandating drug screening for candidates for public office was, however, invalidated because of the lack of special need in that nonsafety-related context.[18]

In weighing the extent of the intrusion, these cases have recognized a reduced expectation of privacy on the part of individuals who work in a highly regulated industry or workplace (for example, Customs officials and railroad employees). Another fundamental factor is the existence of precise constraints upon the discretion of the inspector (as, for example, written guidelines for the operation of a sobriety checkpoint).[19] See Figure 4-3.

---

15. *Colorado v. Bertine*, 479 U.S. 367 (1987) (routine inventory of the contents of a van impounded after the owner was arrested for drunk driving); *Illinois v. Lafayette*, 462 U.S. 640 (1983) (routine inventory of arrestee's shoulder bag); *South Dakota v. Opperman*, 428 U.S. 364 (1976) (inventory of a car impounded for multiple parking violations).

16. See *National Treasury Employees Union v. Von Raab*, 489 U.S. 656 (1989) (urinalysis of Customs Service employees involved in drug interdiction); *Skinner v. Railway Labor Executives' Assn.*, 489 U.S. 602 (1989) (blood and urine tests of railroad employees involved in serious accidents); *Vernonia School District v. Acton*, supra (urinalysis of high school athletes as precondition for participation).

17. *Von Raab*, supra, 489 U.S. at 679.

18. *Chandler v. Miller*, 520 U.S. 305 (1997).

19. See, e.g., *Skinner*, supra, 489 U.S. at 602: "In light of the limited discretion exercised by the railroad employers under the [drug testing] regulations, the surpassing safety interests served by toxicological tests in this context, and the diminished expectation of privacy that attaches to information pertaining to the fitness of covered employees, we believe it is reasonable to conduct such tests in the absence of a warrant or reasonable suspicion that any particular employee may be impaired."

The premise that noncriminal searches should be measured by standards different from those seeking evidence for use in prosecution has been extended beyond the realm of routine inspections and applied in another category where "special needs beyond the normal need for law enforcement make the warrant and probable cause requirements impracticable." *Skinner v. Railway Labor Executives' Association*, 489 U.S. 602, 619 (1989). The Court has held that some form of individualized suspicion, but not probable cause, must be demonstrated in these cases. *New Jersey v. TLO*, 469 U.S. 325 (1985), for example, involved the search of a student's purse by an assistant principal who suspected her of violating the public high school's rule against smoking. The search turned up evidence of marijuana use. Striking the balance between "the schoolchild's legitimate expectations of privacy and the school's equally legitimate need to maintain an environment in which learning can take place," the Court dispensed with both the requirement for a warrant and for probable cause. 469 U.S. at 340. It imposed instead the less onerous standard that there be reasonable grounds for suspecting that the search will turn up evidence that the student is in violation of either school rules or the law.

Similarly, in *O'Connor v. Ortega*, 480 U.S. 709 (1987), where the search of a government employee's office was conducted by agency personnel as part of an investigation of work-related misconduct, and *Griffin v. Wisconsin*, 483 U.S. 868 (1987), where a probation officer searched the home of a probationer under his supervision, the appropriate standard of justification was held to be reasonable suspicion. As in *TLO* the primary purpose of these searches was noncriminal and the "special needs beyond normal law enforcement" (the need to maintain supervision and discipline) were found to justify the departure from the higher standard of probable cause.

The decisions in these "special needs" cases use what Justice Brennan critically characterized as a "Rohrschach-like" balancing test to sanction full-scale searches on a relaxed standard of reasonableness in sharp contrast with prior precedent. *TLO*, supra, 469 U.S. at 360 (Brennan, J., dissenting).

While the separate treatment afforded administrative searches has been premised on the fact that they are conducted for noncriminal purposes, the "special needs" cases indicate that the line between administrative and criminal searches has been significantly blurred since *Camara*. The Court has placed in the administrative search category inspections that are designed at least in part to secure evidence of crime. In *New York v. Burger*, 482 U.S. 691 (1987), for example, the Court upheld a statute authorizing police officers to make warrantless

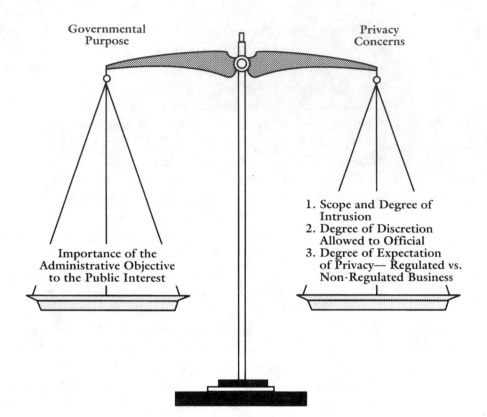

Governmental
Purpose

Privacy
Concerns

Importance of the
Administrative Objective
to the Public Interest

1. Scope and Degree of
   Intrusion
2. Degree of Discretion
   Allowed to Official
3. Degree of Expectation
   of Privacy— Regulated vs.
   Non-Regulated Business

Figure 4–3: Administrative Search Balancing Analysis

inspections of automobile junkyards despite the fact that this "administrative" scheme operated in close conjunction with the criminal justice process.[20]

Another blurring of the line occurs where the original purpose of an inspection is purely administrative, but items of contraband or incriminating evidence are discovered during its course. The courts have held such items admissible in subsequent criminal prosecutions. "The discovery of evidence of crimes in the course of an otherwise proper administrative inspection does not render that search illegal or the administrative scheme suspect." See *New York v. Burger*, supra, 482 U.S. at 716. Courts have uniformly rejected the view that, because administrative searches are permitted without individualized suspicion, their fruits should be inadmissible as evidence in a criminal trial. See, e.g.,

---

20. The New York Court of Appeals had struck down the statute because it found that the administrative label was a pretext designed in reality to permit searches for evidence of crime.

United States v. Mitchell, 458 F.2d 960 (9th Cir. 1972) (Ely, J., dissenting).

In sum, the characterization of a search as "administrative" places it outside the usual Fourth Amendment requirement for individualized justification and into an area where a more relaxed standard of reasonableness applies.

EXAMPLES

1. David Bly was ticketed on an International Airlines flight to London. As he approached the airport loading gate, he was subjected to a routine security check. This is the familiar program in force at all American airports designed to prevent hijackings or air terrorism by barring persons from taking weapons or explosives aboard. Boarding passengers and their carry-on luggage must pass through a metal detector. The detector indicated the presence of a metal object in Bly's briefcase, and a security officer took the briefcase from Bly and opened it. Inside she found a large caliber pistol. Both the gun and Bly were turned over to the police, and Bly was charged with unlawful possession of a firearm. Bly moves to suppress the gun on the grounds that the search violated the Fourth Amendment. What standards should the court use to measure the legality of this search?

2. The State of Maine is considering institution of a Stop Drunk Driving Program designed as an "aggressive" response to the problem. As part of the proposed program state police officers will be assigned to various checkpoints on the highways where they will flag down motorists and briefly converse with them in an effort to detect signs of intoxication. If an officer believes a driver may be drunk, the driver will be referred to another officer who will conduct a series of sobriety tests. As legal counsel to the state police, what would you advise them as to the constitutionality of this program?

3. Springfield State Hospital adopted a mandatory screening program for its employees who are involved in direct patient care. The program, growing out of concern for patient safety as well as efficient operation of the hospital, is designed to detect both infection by the AIDS virus and use of narcotics. A notice was posted notifying employees that random blood testing would be conducted. Elmer King, a nurse at the hospital, was tested pursuant to the program and narcotics were found in his blood. When King

refused to resign his position, the test results were turned over to the prosecutor's office. Does this procedure violate the Fourth Amendment?

4. Trooper Wyman stopped a motorist for speeding and, after determining he was under the influence of alcohol, arrested him. The driver had a briefcase next to him on the seat, which Wyman seized "for safekeeping." After transporting the driver to the police station and delivering him to the booking officer, the trooper proceeded to inventory the contents of the briefcase. While doing so she discovered several marijuana cigarettes in a paper bag. The driver was then charged with unlawful possession. Did the trooper violate the Fourth Amendment when she opened and searched the briefcase? Does it matter that the trooper admits that she was "keeping an eye out for contraband" at the same time she was conducting the inventory?

5. The Newtowne School Committee voted to institute a policy that conditioned several student actvities upon the consent of the student (together with his or her parents) to random drug testing (by way of urinalysis conducted by a reputable testing service). The activities include participation in ahtletics, student government, theater productions, and driving to and from school. Is the policy vulnerable to a Fourth Amendment challenge?

6. A teacher at the Warwick Public High School noticed a commotion around a locker outside her classroom and informed Vice Principal Skull. Skull identified the locker as belonging to Bill Kits, who had been a constant behavior problem and was suspected of selling drugs at school. Skull used the master key to open the locker, but found only three dozen boxes of Girl Scout cookies. The vice principal took these, and later, after learning that there had been a theft of such cookies from the PTA, turned the boxes over to police detective Roche. Kits is charged with the theft, and now seeks to suppress the evidence. Was the search of his locker lawful?

EXPLANATIONS

1. If the search of Bly's briefcase were to be judged by traditional Fourth Amendment standards, it would clearly be unlawful. There was no probable cause or reasonable suspicion to justify subjecting the briefcase to a metal detector scan; even after the scan indicated

the presence of a metal object, that is scant basis for concluding that Bly was involved in criminal conduct.

This search would not, however, be measured by traditional standards. The primary impetus for such airport screening is concern for the safety of passengers and crews aboard aircraft, not criminal prosecution. Thus the primary objective of these searches is to prevent passengers from taking weapons and explosives on board, not gaining evidence to be used at a criminal trial. The appropriate standards for evaluating the airport search program are found in the administrative search cases. The thrust of these decisions is that searches conducted as part of a general regulatory scheme for an administrative purpose, rather than as part of a criminal investigation designed to secure evidence for prosecution, do not require individualized cause directed at a particular person or place to be searched.

What constitutional standards do apply to an administrative search? Most fundamentally, the inspection must not be used as a subterfuge for a search seeking evidence of crime. If, for example, a building code inspector is sent into Smith's apartment at the instigation of the police to search for stolen VCRs, that action could not be properly characterized as administrative, and the traditional requirement for particularized cause would apply. See *United States v. $124,570 U.S. Currency*, 873 F.2d 1240 (9th Cir. 1989). In our example, however, there is no indication that the inspection of Bly was anything but routine.

The basic test of an administrative search scheme is derived from the Fourth Amendment standard of reasonableness. As *Camara v. Municipal Court* teaches, it must appear on balance that the governmental need to search outweighs the intrusion involved or, as the Court later put it, that "the privacy interests implicated by the search are minimal, and where an important governmental interest furthered by the intrusion would be placed in jeopardy by a requirement of individualized suspicion." *Skinner v. Railway Labor Executives' Association*, supra, 489 U.S. at 624. That seems clearly to be the case here, where the risk of air terrorism is measured against the relatively minor annoyance of the screening. Beyond that threshold, there must be an assurance of evenhandedness in the inspection process. That is, the decision as to who will be screened and the scope of the search cannot be left to the discretion of the officer. Rather, objective standardized criteria must control throughout the process. Assuming that all passengers are subjected to the airport screening, that the procedures are set out with sufficient detail and clarity so that the discretion of the officer is constrained, and that there is uniform application, the program would be considered reasonable and pass muster under the Fourth Amendment.

In one of the first decisions to review the nationwide airport safety program, the Ninth Circuit emphasized the additional factor of notice in its decision upholding the program. Would-be passengers were notified of the upcoming screening by conspicuous signs before they got into the boarding line and they had the option to avoid the screening by electing not to board the aircraft. *United States v. Davis*, 482 F.2d 893 (9th Cir. 1973). In this sense it could be said that they consented to the search. The concept of a "consent" search is discussed in §6.7.

That same court later suppressed evidence not related to air safety that was discovered during an airport screening. In *United States v. $124,570 U.S. Currency*, 873 F.2d 1240 (9th Cir. 1989), airport security officers discovered a large sum of money in a traveler's briefcase. By prior agreement with the Customs Service to aid in the enforcement of currency and narcotics law, the officers seized the money and turned it over to government agents who later linked it to narcotics trafficking. Because the security officers were not acting with the single-minded objective of air safety, but also with the purpose of discovering evidence of illegal narcotics activity, the Ninth Circuit held that the administrative search rationale did not apply. "[I]n *Davis* we recognized the danger that the screening of passengers and their carry-on luggage for weapons and explosives will be subverted into a general search for evidence of crime." 873 F.2d at 1243. In ruling the search unlawful, the court "emphasized the importance of keeping criminal investigatory motives from coloring administrative searches." Id. at 1244.

Nonetheless, as a general rule evidence inadvertently discovered during a bona fide administrative search may be used in evidence at a criminal trial. What prompted the suppression of evidence in *$124,570 U.S. Currency* was that the search was conducted *from the outset* for the dual purpose of finding evidence for prosecution as well as to achieve the administrative goal of protecting air passengers. Id. at 1244.

2. As a general rule, motorists can be stopped only if there is specific justification in the form of reasonable suspicion or probable cause

to believe the driver or occupants are in violation of the law. In *Delaware v. Prouse*, 440 U.S. 648 (1979), the Supreme Court held that suspicionless discretionary spot checks of motorists to inspect the driver's license and vehicle registration violated the Fourth Amendment. The Court emphasized, however, that it was not foreclosing other methods of spot checking in furtherance of an important governmental purpose as long as the decision as to whom to stop was not left to the unconstrained discretion of the officer. By way of example, the Court suggested a roadblock in which all cars were stopped.

The *Prouse* decision anticipated the sobriety checkpoint program upheld in *Michigan Department of State Police v. Sitz*, 496 U.S. 444 (1990). Police checkpoints were set up at which all drivers were stopped and briefly (an average of 25 seconds) observed for signs of intoxication. If such signs were found, the driver would be detained for sobriety testing and, if the indication was that the driver was intoxicated, an arrest would be made. Rejecting a constitutional challenge to the program, the Court held that the initial seizures that occurred when cars were stopped at the checkpoints were reasonable under the Fourth Amendment. Applying the balancing test that substitutes for the probable cause requirement in administrative search cases, the Court weighed the magnitude of the governmental interest in eradicating the drunk driving problem against the slight intrusion to motorists stopped briefly at the fixed checkpoints. Moreover, evenhandedness was ensured because the locations of the checkpoints were chosen pursuant to written guidelines and the police were directed to stop every approaching vehicle—the officers themselves did not decide where or whom to stop. The fact that motorists were not notified of the upcoming checkpoints or given an opportunity to make a U-turn to avoid them was not regarded by the Court as fatal to the legality of the Michigan program. Compare *United States v. Davis* discussed in example 1, supra.[21]

It should be noted, however, that several courts have concluded that drug interdiction checkpoints, unlike sobriety checkpoints, are unconstitutional because they are primarily directed at searching for evidence of drug trafficking and other contraband,

---

21. Justices Stevens, Brennan, and Marshall, however, concluded in their dissenting opinion that the lack of "fair notice" and opportunity to avoid the stop rendered it unreasonable. 496 U.S. at 460.

and the Supreme Court has agreed to decide this issue. See *Edmond v. Goldsmith*, 183 F.3d 659 (7th Cir. 1999), *cert. granted*, 120 S. Ct. 3519; *Commonwealth v. Rodriguez*, 430 Mass. 577, 722 N.E.2d 429 (2000) (drug interdiction checkpoints violate state constitution's Declaration of Rights).

The threshold issue in example 2 is whether the court will treat the program under the administrative search category (or, as Judge Posner put it in *Edmond v. Goldsmith*, supra, whether the court will assess legality at the level of the program, or of the individual search). If this is not an administrative search, then the suspicionless stopping of motorists is clearly unconstitutional. The program does appear to fit the distinguishing characteristic of the administrative search in that its primary purpose is not to uncover evidence to be used in criminal prosecution but to remove the threat to the public created by drunk drivers. The fact that the police will be gathering evidence of crime simultaneously with the achievement of this goal does not defeat the administrative nature of the program.

Measured by the *Camara* balancing test, we have the same compelling public interest in highway safety that existed in *Sitz*. On the other side of the balance, however, we have a more serious intrusion into individual liberty than in that case. Unlike the fixed checkpoints in *Sitz* or *Davis* (see example 1), the Maine program involves flagging down motorists on the road. The Court has traditionally treated roving patrol stops as significantly more intrusive than fixed checkpoint stops: "[Unlike roving patrols, at] traffic checkpoints the motorist can see that other vehicles are being stopped, he can see visible signs of the officers' authority, and he is much less likely to be frightened or annoyed by the intrusion." *United States v. Ortiz*, 422 U.S. 891, 894–895 (1975), quoted with approval in *Sitz*, 496 U.S. at 452–453. A court may therefore conclude that the surprise and unannounced nature of the intrusion in the Maine program outweighs the public interest supporting it.

Even if the program survives this initial stage of scrutiny, other problems remain. There would have to be specific guidelines determining who would be stopped and what procedures they would be subjected to. As far as we know, there are no constraints upon the officer's discretion regarding both matters. Such unbridled authority would likely result in the program's being declared violative of the Fourth Amendment. See, e.g., *United States v. Ramos*, 733 F. Supp. 260 (S.D. Tex. 1989) (holding illegal a one-man roving checkpoint in which an officer stopped drivers to check for license and registration—where there was no plan or limitations controlling location, who would be stopped, and what procedures would be followed—because it permitted "unconstrained exercise of discretion"). Compare *People v. Rister*, 803 P.2d 483 (Colo. 1990) (upholding sobriety checkpoint program where the discretion of the officers as to which vehicles could be stopped was constrained by requirement that all cars be stopped, with the only exception being that the officers could permit all cars to proceed through if traffic backed up).

Emphasizing that "[a]dherence to a neutrally devised, preplanned blueprint in order to eliminate arbitrariness and discretion has been principal prerequisite for abandoning the requirement of individualized suspicion in roadblock stops," the Massachusetts Supreme Judicial Court held that the stop of the driver some 15 minutes after the scheduled deadline for termination of a roadblock was unconstitutional. See *Commonwealth v. Anderson*, 406 Mass. 343, 349 (1989).

In *Covert v. State*, 612 N.E.2d 592 (Ind. Ct. App. 1993), a case involving safety checkpoints at which cars' lights, brakes, tires, and mufflers were inspected, the court balanced the interests and found that although the public had an interest in auto safety and proper regulation, the danger was not as grave as underage drinking and drunk driving. The court also noted that the effectiveness of such a program was unknown. Since motorists were not warned of the stop, deterrence would be minimal. The public interest and the effectiveness of the program were thus not compelling enough to justify the intrusion on the motorists' liberties.

3. The Supreme Court has upheld suspicionless mandatory drug and alcohol testing in two contexts. The U.S. Customs Service program requiring employees who apply for promotion to positions involving interdiction of illegal drugs or who are required to carry firearms to provide urine samples for analysis was upheld in *National Treasury Employees Union v. Von Raab*, 489 U.S. 656 (1989). Similarly, the federal regulations mandating blood and urine testing of railroad employees following major accidents were upheld in *Skinner v. Railway Labor Executives' Association*, supra. Both decisions applied the *Camara* balancing test rather than the requirement for particularized suspicion. This was deemed appropriate because the programs were not designed to serve the ordinary needs of law enforcement (that is, obtaining evidence of

crime and using it to prosecute), but instead were adopted to protect the public interest by ensuring a drug-free (and thus safer) workplace. The Customs Service regulations explicitly provided that the test results could not be turned over to any other agency or prosecutor.

Under the *Camara* analysis, the public interest served by the program is balanced against the intrusion on individual privacy. In both *Skinner* and *Von Raab*, the Court recognized the compelling governmental interest in preventing substance abusers from performing the safety-sensitive jobs involved and held that this outweighed the privacy interests of persons in those positions. The intrusions involved were considered relatively minor. Moreover, the employees worked in jobs that historically had been highly regulated and were specifically notified that they were subject to screening under the programs. (In *Von Raab* they were notified five days in advance of the test date.) Consequently the subjects had a reduced expectation of privacy with regard to the intrusions. Lastly, the screening procedures were set out in detail and allowed little or no discretion (in, for example, determining which employees would be tested or when) on the part of the officials implementing them.

Applying this analysis to example 3, the public interest in detecting and preventing narcotics users from working in a patient care capacity is clear and weighty. The same can be said for the interest in knowing that such an employee is infected with the AIDS virus. This legitimate concern for the safety of patients and co-workers would probably be held to outweigh the limited intrusion into the bodily integrity and privacy of those subject to the program. Further, the hospital employees would likely be deemed to have a diminished expectation of privacy given the historical regulation of their workplace and the fact that they received notice of the screening program.

More information would be required, however, regarding the degree of discretion left to the officials implementing the screening program. Unless there are neutral written guidelines delineating the manner in which the program operates to ensure evenhandedness as to who is tested, when, and how, the program is likely to be struck down as unreasonable.

Another potential problem is that the Springfield State Hospital program apparently permits officials to turn the test results over to criminal prosecutors, which they have done in King's case.

The program upheld in *Von Raab* specifically precluded this, and neither that case nor *Skinner* explicitly confronted the question of use of the results in a criminal prosecution because both cases were declaratory judgment challenges to the implementation of the programs at their outset. While as a general rule evidence discovered during a lawful administrative search *is* admissible in a subsequent criminal trial, it is conceivable that a court would not permit such use here where the program's constitutionality is founded upon its emphatically noncriminal purpose.

For civil actions raising the issue of AIDS testing in a hospital context, see *Leckelt v. Board of Commissioners of Hospital District No. 1,* 909 F.2d 820 (5th Cir. 1990) (upholding program); *Glover v. Eastern Nebraska Community Office of Retardation,* 867 F.2d 461 (8th Cir. 1989) (holding program violated the Fourth Amendment).

4. As we will see in Chapter 6, this search cannot be upheld as incident to the arrest because it is not contemporaneous with the arrest. It also cannot be upheld under the "automobile exception" because there was no probable cause to search the vehicle. The Supreme Court has held, however, that in limited circumstances a suspicionless "inventory search" may be conducted of an impounded automobile or object. See *Colorado v. Bertine,* 479 U.S. 367 (1987) (backpack in impounded vehicle); *Illinois v. Lafayette,* 462 U.S. 640 (1983) (personal effects of an arrestee); *South Dakota v. Opperman,* 428 U.S. 364 (1976) (glove compartment of impounded vehicle). The justification for such a suspicionless search is that it is being conducted not for the purpose of investigating criminal conduct, but for administrative reasons: protecting the police from danger (from, for example, a bomb inside the briefcase); protecting the owner's property while he is in police custody; and protecting the police from claims of lost, stolen, or damaged property. The search can permissibly include the opening of packages found within the object to be inventoried.

The main prerequisite for a lawful inventory is that it is conducted according to standardized procedures or established routine. The insistence on such procedures serves three purposes: 1) it ensures evenhanded treatment of all subjects; 2) it precludes the use of the inventory as a pretext for an investigatory search; and 3) it ensures that the intrusion is limited in scope to the extent necessary to carry out the caretaking function. It has been held that the standard practice must be that of the department and not simply the routine followed by the individual officer. See *United States v. Kordosky*, 909 F.2d 219 (7th Cir. 1990). In the absence of such procedures, the police may not conduct a lawful inventory. See *Florida v. Wells*, 495 U.S. at 4, 5 (1990) ("[T]he Florida Highway patrol had no policy whatever with respect to the opening of closed containers during an inventory search. We hold that absent such a policy, the instant search was not sufficiently regulated to satisfy the Fourth Amendment. . . .").

Ideally, the procedures should be set forth in writing, as for example, regulations printed in a state trooper manual. See *United States v. Wanless*, 882 F.2d 1459, 1463 (9th Cir. 1989). They should explicitly control the scope and extent of the inventory and leave no discretion to the officer conducting it. The Court has, however, upheld an inventory conducted pursuant to criteria that *did* allow the officer to choose between impounding the vehicle or parking it locked in a public place (and thus not searching it), but it emphasized that such discretion must be constrained by "standard criteria and [be exercised] on the basis of something other than suspicion of criminal activity." *Colorado v. Bertine*, 479 U.S. at 375. The officer must not be allowed so much latitude that inventory searches are turned into "a purposeful and general means of discovering evidence of crime." Id. See also *1975 Chevrolet v. State of Texas*, 801 S.W.2d 565 (Tex. 1990).

In example 4, therefore, we would have to determine whether the trooper was acting according to established inventory procedures and, if so, whether those procedures sufficiently constrained her discretion with regard to the conduct of the search. Assuming we find affirmative answers to both questions, and that we have no indication that she was engaged in a pretextual search, the inventory would be permitted by the Fourth Amendment.

The result is not changed by the trooper's admission that she kept an eye out for contraband while conducting the inventory. A "legitimate nonpretextual inventory search is not made unlawful simply because the investigating officer remains vigilant for evidence during his inventory search." *United States v. Khoury*, 901 F.2d 948, 959 (11th Cir. 1990). If, however, Trooper Wyman exceeded the scope of the standardized procedures in her hunt for contraband, then the search would be unlawful. In *Khoury*, for example, the officer flipped through the pages of an impounded notebook pursuant to procedures requiring him to determine whether there was anything of value hidden in the pages. He then proceeded to read the pages and determined that the book contained incriminating entries. This additional inspection of the notebook was held to violate the Fourth Amendment.

5. This policy obviously goes significantly further than that involved in *Vernonia School District v. Acton*, 515 U.S. 646 (1995), which was limited to participation in athletics. Suspicionless searching of students who want to take part in student government or plays is much harder to justify because the need to screen for drugs is less compelling and the expectation of privacy greater than that of student athletes, whose activities are more regulated and who engage in group showering and dressing. These distinctions did not, however, impress the Seventh Circuit in *Todd v. Rush County School*, 133 F.3d 984 (7th 1998), *rehearing en banc denied*, 139 F.3d 571, which upheld that a program under which all high school students who wished to participate in any extracurricular activities had to consent to random and suspicionless urine testing for alcohol, unlawful drug, and cigarette usage. The court emphasized that the program was designed to deter drug use and not to catch and punish users, and found that the reasoning in *Vernonia* justifying drug testing of athletes also applies to testing of students involved in other extracurricular activities that require "healthy students."

     The Supreme Court of Colorado reached the opposite result in *Trinidad School District v. Lopez*, 963 P.2d 1095 (1998), striking down mandatory drug testing of all students in grades 6 through 12 who participate in any extracurricular activity. The court relied upon *Chandler v. Miller*, 520 U.S. 305 (1997), for the proposition that simply being a role model by virtue of participation in an extracurricular activity is insufficient to support a conclusion that the drug testing program was reasonable.

6. *New Jersey v. TLO*, 469 U.S. 325 (1985), applied the Fourth Amendment to searches conducted on school property, but not the traditional requirement for probable cause. Rather, the student's privacy interest is balanced against the school's need to maintain order, in the typical "administrative search" reasonableness analysis. Although *TLO* specifically leaves the locker search question unaddressed, its analysis of school searches requires that in order to be constitutionally valid the search of Kits' locker must be justified at its inception, and the scope of the search must be reasonably related to the circumstances that necessitated it. With regard to the first issue, there is serious question in our example

as to whether Vice Principal Skull had reasonable grounds for suspecting that the search would turn up evidence that Kits had violated the law or the rules of the school. All we have here is the commotion in front of the locker and the generalized suspicion that Kits may be dealing drugs. Compare *Singleton v. Board of Education*, 894 F. Supp. 386 (D. Kan. 1995) (prior to locker search, adult had identified student as person who had stolen $150 from her car); *Greenleaf v. Cote*, 77 F. Supp. 2d 168 (D. Me. 1999) (previously reliable student-informant reported that she had heard girls discussing how they had been drinking beer in locker room with other students). If sufficient justification is found, it would appear that the scope of the locker search was permissible since drugs could be found in the place searched. Finally, the fact that the search begins as an admininstrative search but then turns up evidence of crime does not preclude admission of the evidence at Kits' criminal trial.

Another issue is whether the existence of the master key further reduces the already lowered expectation of privacy a student has at public school. At least one court has held that within the setting of a police station, an officer's locker carries a reasonable expectation of privacy even though the department retains a master key. See *United States v. Speights*, 557 F.2d 362 (3d Cir. 1977).

5

Search and Arrest Warrants

A warrant is a judicial authorization for police action, either to search a particular place (a search warrant) or to arrest a particular person (an arrest warrant). In this chapter we will explore two basic questions:

1) When is a warrant required prior to a search or an arrest?
2) What are the prerequisites for a valid warrant?

§5.1   The Search Warrant Requirement

As indicated in Chapter 2, a fundamental question running through Fourth Amendment jurisprudence has been the role of the warrant in the search and seizure process. By requiring the authorization of a neutral third party prior to a proposed search, the warrant process affords the citizen protection against the unilateral action of the overly zealous law enforcement officer. On the other hand, requiring the police to seek judicial authorization for *all* searches regardless of the urgency of the particular circumstances would impair effective law enforcement.

Thus, although the Supreme Court has frequently articulated a preference for searches conducted pursuant to a warrant (see Chapter 2), it has carved out numerous categorical exceptions premised on either the impracticality of seeking a warrant in exigent circumstances or the diminished expectation of privacy in the area searched. These exceptions will be discussed in Chapter 6. In those cases that do not fall within the established exceptions, the police are required to obtain a warrant before conducting a search. The prime example would be the search of a home.[1]

§5.2   The Components of a Valid Search Warrant

The basic purpose served by the warrant process is to interpose a neutral and disinterested person between the law enforcement authorities and the individual whose effects they seek to search. As the Supreme Court has explained: "The point of the Fourth Amendment, which often is not grasped by zealous officers, is not that it denies law enforcement the support of the usual inferences which reasonable men draw from evidence. Its protection consists in requiring that those inferences be drawn by a neutral and detached magistrate instead of being judged by the officer engaged in the often competitive enterprise of ferreting out crime." *Johnson v. United States*, 333 U.S. 10, 13–14 (1948). Once issued, the warrant also serves the additional purpose of confining the scope of the intrusion to the areas and items specified.

In order to be lawful, a warrant must meet the following requirements:

1) It must be issued by a **neutral and detached magistrate.**
2) There must be presented to the magistrate an adequate showing of **probable cause (either to search or arrest) supported by oath or affirmation**. This is usually in the form of an affidavit from police officers.
3) The warrant must **describe with particularity the place to be searched and the items or persons to be seized.**

Because warrants are of necessity issued ex parte (if the subject of the search is tipped off to the application for the warrant, the evidence sought may be removed or destroyed), challenges to the issuance of a warrant on these (or other) grounds will be heard after the search has occurred and on the defendant's motion to suppress the evidence seized.

---

1. The authority to make a warrantless search of a home under emergency circumstances is discussed in §6.2.

§5.2.1 Neutral and Detached Magistrate

While it is not constitutionally required that the person issuing the warrant be an attorney or a judge, he must be 1) "neutral and detached," and 2) "capable of determining whether probable cause exists for the requested arrest or search." *Shadwick v. City of Tampa*, 407 U.S. 345, 350 (1972). The first requirement is that the issuer be part of the judicial apparatus, such as a court clerk or magistrate, and not be associated with the prosecutor's office or the police.[2] Thus where the issuing magistrate accompanied the police as they executed a warrant for obscene materials and assisted them in determining what items to seize, this participation rendered the magistrate not sufficiently detached to satisfy the requirements of the Fourth Amendment: "He was not acting as a judicial officer, but as an adjunct law enforcement officer." *Lo-Ji Sales v. New York*, 442 U.S. 319, 327 (1979). The magistrate cannot have a financial interest in the issuance of the warrant. See *Connally v. Georgia*, 429 U.S. 245 (1977) (invalidating a scheme in which the justice of the peace was paid a fee only if he issued a warrant, and no fee if he declined to issue it).

The second requirement is that the issuer have the training and experience necessary to meaningfully assess the probable cause showing. A court clerk was held to have this capacity with regard to arrest warrants for minor municipal offenses. *Shadwick*, supra. More sophisticated determinations of probable cause to search or arrest probably demand a judge.

§5.2.2 Probable Cause Showing

The Fourth Amendment provides that a warrant may be issued only "upon probable cause, supported by oath or affirmation." The concept

---

2. The State Attorney General in charge of investigating and prosecuting a murder case, for example, was held not to be the "neutral and detached magistrate required by the Constitution" and thus could not lawfully issue a search warrant for the defendant's car. See *Coolidge v. New Hampshire*, 403 U.S. 443 (1971). But a magistrate who had formerly been an assistant U.S. Attorney and had worked on an unrelated case involving the same defendant was considered sufficiently detached to issue a warrant. See *United States v. DeLuna*, 763 F.2d 897, 908 (8th Cir. 1985); *United States v. Outler*, 659 F.2d 1306, 1312 (5th Cir. 1981), *overruled on other grounds, United States v. Steele*, 147 F.3d 1316 (11th Cir. 1998).

of probable cause is discussed in Chapter 4. The actual demonstration of probable cause usually comes in the form of a sworn affidavit prepared by the investigating officers and presented to the magistrate. Some jurisdictions permit the issuance of warrants on sworn oral testimony, even communicated by telephone, where compelling circumstances justify dispensing with the written affidavit.[3] A court subsequently reviewing the issuance of a warrant to determine whether probable cause existed will limit its focus to only the information that was presented to the magistrate at the time.[4]

Challenges to the issuing magistrate's determination that an adequate demonstration of probable cause was made may take two forms. The first is an assertion that the probable cause showing was inadequate on its face. See §4.1. As we will learn in §7.3.3, the adoption of the "good faith" exception to the exclusionary rule significantly affects such challenges. Evidence seized pursuant to a search warrant issued on an inadequate demonstration of probable cause will be suppressed only if the affidavit is "so lacking in indicia of probable cause as to render belief in its existence entirely unreasonable." *United States v. Leon*, 468 U.S. 897 (1984). If the officer acts in reasonable reliance upon the warrant, the fact that the magistrate mistakenly issued it in the absence of sufficient cause will not render the search unlawful.

The second type of challenge goes behind the affidavit and disputes the truthfulness of the facts it sets out. In order to mount such a "credibility challenge," the defendant must negotiate several difficult obstacles. See *Franks v. Delaware*, 438 U.S. 154 (1978). First, he must make a substantial preliminary showing that the affidavit contains: 1) a *false statement*; 2) made *by the affiant police officer*; 3) either *knowingly and intentionally, or with reckless disregard for the truth*. Neither inadvertent or negligent misstatements of the officer, nor false statements of informers or other sources, are sufficient to satisfy this threshold requirement. Second, it must be demonstrated that the false statement was necessary to the finding of probable cause. If there was sufficient information to establish probable cause even without the false statement, the misrepresentation is treated as a harmless error. A

---

3. See e.g., Fed. R. Crim. P.41(c). The magistrate is required to record the conversation by mechanical or stenographic means.

4. *Whiteley v. Warden*, 401 U.S. 560 (1971). Permitting the record to be expanded with information known to the police but not disclosed to the issuing magistrate would "render the warrant requirements of the Fourth Amendment meaningless." 401 U.S. at 565 n.8.

defendant who succeeds at making this showing is then entitled to a full evidentiary hearing (with witnesses and documentary evidence) in which he must prove (by a preponderance of the evidence) the allegation of knowing or reckless falsehood. If he establishes this, the judge must excise the false statements from the affidavit and determine whether the remainder makes out probable cause to search. If it does not, then the warrant and the search conducted pursuant to it are deemed unlawful.

It must be emphasized that the false statement that triggers the *Franks* remedy must be that of the officer who filed the affidavit, not that of nongovernmental sources relied upon. Showing that an informant lied to the police, for example, will not result in the suppression of the evidence seized. Where, however, the defendant can establish that the officer created a fictional informant[5] or deliberately misrepresented what an informant reported,[6] then the *Franks* remedy is available. Given that the identity of confidential informants is protected from disclosure by a generally recognized privilege,[7] making such a showing is difficult (if not impossible) for many defendants.

In sum, *Franks* recognizes that there is no constitutional requirement that "every fact recited in the warrant affidavit is necessarily correct, for probable cause may be founded upon hearsay and upon information within the affiant's own knowledge that sometimes may be garnered hastily." 438 U.S. at 165. All that is constitutionally required is that the officer filing the affidavit not deliberately or recklessly misrepresent the facts.

---

5. See *Commonwealth v. Lewin,* 405 Mass. 566 (1989). But see *United States v. Pace,* 898 F.2d 1218 (7th Cir. 1990); *Commonwealth v. Singer,* 29 Mass. App. 708, 564 N.E.2d 1037 (Mass. App. Ct. 1991) (the fact that the officers had filed numerous affidavits setting out similar stories from the same informant was not sufficient in itself to establish that the informant was fictional).

6. In *Franks,* for example, defendant submitted written statements from two sources who were named in the warrant as having described defendant's typical attire to the police, but who now asserted that they did not give such information.

7. See *McCray v. Illinois,* 386 U.S. 300 (1967) (holding that the Constitution does not compel the disclosure of the informant's identity for the purpose of challenging the probable cause showing, but only if the informant will be testifying at trial). The court may conduct an in-camera hearing on the veracity challenge in which the judge questions the officer and the informant outside the presence of counsel to ascertain the facts without disclosing the identity of the informant. See, e.g., *United States v. Barone,* 787 F.2d 811 (2d Cir. 1986).

§5.2.3   *The Particularity Requirement*

The Fourth Amendment requires that warrants "shall issue . . . particularly describing the place to be searched and the person or things to be seized." This language was inserted to avoid the general warrants (writs of assistance) of the colonial period, which allowed officers to search whenever, wherever, and whomever they chose. A valid warrant is therefore not only a document that ensures that there is *sufficient justification* for the search; it functions as well to limit the *permissible bounds* of that search.

The standard of particularity regarding the place to be searched requires that the description be sufficiently precise so that "the officer with a search warrant can with reasonable effort ascertain and identify the place intended." *Steele v. United States,* 267 U.S. 498, 503 (1925). Minor errors or inconsistencies will therefore not generally invalidate the warrant, as long as they do not present a significant risk that some other premises may be mistakenly searched.[8]

The standard of particularity regarding the items to be seized requires that the description leave nothing to the discretion of the officers executing the warrant. See *Marron v. United States,* 275 U.S. 192, 196 (1927). Thus where the description requires the executing officers to interpret a statute or legal concept to determine which items may be seized, the particularity requirement is violated.[9] Where, however, the items are readily identifiable as contraband, the courts have permitted generic descriptions. Thus warrants authorizing the seizure of all items related to illegal gambling or narcotics manufacture have generally been upheld. See *United States v. DeLuna,* 763 F.2d 897, 908 (8th Cir. 1985); *United States v. Alexander,* 761 F.2d 1294 (9th Cir.

---

8. In one case, for example, a typographical error in the address of the apartment to be searched did not invalidate the warrant because the executing officer checked with the magistrate by telephone and ascertained the correct address before searching. See *United States v. Arenal,* 768 F.2d 263 (8th Cir. 1985).

9. Thus a warrant specifying all "material evidence of violation of 21 U.S.C. §841" (which prohibits the manufacture and possession of amphetamine with intent to distribute) was held not sufficiently particularized. See *United States v. Crozier,* 674 F.2d 1293, 1299 (9th Cir. 1982). A warrant authorizing the seizure of "illegally obtained films" was invalidated because of the discretion it allowed the officers in determining which films were "illegal." See *United States v. Cook,* 657 F.2d 730 (5th Cir. 1981). A warrant for seizure of "all evidence of association" between the defendant and seven other persons was struck down as overbroad. See *United States v. Washington,* 782 F.2d 807, 819 (9th Cir. 1986).

1985). The particularity requirement is afforded its most scrupulous enforcement when the items to be seized implicate First Amendment rights, such as books or organizational membership lists. See *Zurcher v. Stanford Daily*, 436 U.S. 547, 565 (1978); *Stanford v. Texas*, 379 U.S. 476, 485 (1965).

As we have seen before, these standards have been modified by the adoption of the "good faith" exception (see §7.3.3), which limits the exclusionary remedy to situations where the search warrant is "so facially deficient—i.e., in failing to particularize the place to be searched or the things to be seized—that the executing officer cannot reasonably presume it to be valid." *United States v. Leon*, 468 U.S. 897, 923 (1984). The operation of this reasonableness standard is illustrated by *Maryland v. Garrison*, 480 U.S. 79 (1987), in which the warrant authorized a search of one McWebb and his third-floor apartment at a particular address. The officers believed at the time and represented to the magistrate that there was only one apartment on that floor. It turned out, however, that there were two separate apartments on the third floor, one occupied by McWebb and the other by Garrison. Without realizing this, the officers searched both apartments and discovered contraband in Garrison's. The Court upheld the search despite the ambiguity in the warrant and the officers' mistake on the scene. With regard to the former, the Court held that the validity of the warrant must be measured based on the information known at the time the warrant was issued, and the subsequent discovery that the third floor was divided does not retroactively invalidate the warrant. Further, the mistake made by the officers in executing the warrant was "objectively understandable and reasonable," and thus did not violate the particularity requirement of the Fourth Amendment. While observing that "the purposes justifying a police search strictly limit the permissible extent of the search," the Court nonetheless recognized "the need to allow some latitude for honest mistakes that are made by officers in the dangerous and difficult process of making arrests and executing search warrants." 480 U.S. at 86.

In another application of the good faith mistake exception in the context of the particularity requirement, the Court in *Massachusetts v. Sheppard*, 468 U.S. 981 (1984) (see also §7.3.3), upheld a search even though the warrant mistakenly described the items to be seized as controlled substances instead of evidence of a recent homicide, which was what the officers actually were looking for and seized. Because the issuing judge had assured the officers that he would correct the inaccuracy, and the officers were deemed to have reasonably relied on that representation when they executed the warrant, the search and seizure of items not described in the warrant was held constitutional. There was, the Court ruled, an "objectively reasonable basis for the officers' mistaken belief" that the warrant authorized the search for evidence linking Sheppard to the murder. 468 U.S. at 988.

In sum, the Fourth Amendment particularity requirement read together with the good faith exception mandates that either 1) the place searched and the items seized must be specifically and accurately described in the warrant; or 2) if not correctly described, the mistake is deemed to have been objectively reasonable. A failure to particularize in the warrant itself, or an unreasonable mistake in its execution, will invalidate the search.

An additional gloss on the particularity requirement is the "plain view" doctrine, discussed more fully in §6.8. The doctrine recognizes that in the course of searching for the particular items described in the warrant, police may come upon contraband or other evidence of crime not included in the warrant. Rather than require the police to ignore the discovery or to seek another warrant specifically describing the items, the police are permitted to seize them at that time, provided two conditions are met. First, the items must be in plain view while the officers are acting within the confines of the originally authorized search. Thus officers executing a lawful warrant to search for rifles would be permitted to seize marijuana they discover in a bedroom closet while looking for the rifles. They would not, however, be permitted to seize marijuana discovered when they opened a small desk drawer because that location is obviously not within the proper scope of a search for rifles. Second, the items must be immediately apparent as contraband or evidence of crime, not requiring any further search or analysis to determine that they are. Thus the officers could not seize a bottle of pills on the hunch that they might be illegal and send them off for laboratory testing. The plain view doctrine, in sum, permits the *seizure* of an item that has already come into the officer's view during the course of a lawful search; it does not authorize any *additional search* beyond that described in the warrant.

EXAMPLES

1. Consider the following documents:

State of New York
County of Westchester } Circuit Court of Westchester County

Search Warrant

On this 5th day of May, 1990, Police Officer Harvey Lance has subscribed and sworn to before me an application for search warrant and accompanying affidavit. Upon examination of the affidavit, I find that it states facts sufficient to show probable cause.

I therefore authorize a search of the home of Lester Webster, located at apartment 6 in the building at 231 Longfellow Avenue, Scarsdale, New York, and I further authorize a seizure of all electronic appliances stolen in the burglary of Joe's Appliance Store, Main Street, Scarsdale, on April 29, 1990.

Issued May 5, 1990 ss/ Judge Linda Black

State of New York } Circuit Court of Westchester County
County of Westchester

Application for Search Warrant and
Affidavit in Support of Application

Police Officer Harvey Lance now appears before the undersigned judge of the Circuit Court of Westchester County and requests the issuance of a warrant to search the home of Lester Webster, located at apartment 6 in the building at 231 Longfellow Avenue, Scarsdale, New York, and to seize the following articles and things: all items taken in the burglary of Joe's Appliance Store, Main Street, Scarsdale, on April 29, 1990, which constitute evidence of that crime.

Applicant further states that he has probable cause to believe that the above listed things to be seized are evidence of the offense of burglary and are now located upon the premises indicated above. Probable cause is based upon the following:

An informant, who has provided accurate information to me on several occasions in the past (leading to the arrest of one Raymond Rowe and one Sally Stowe) and who wishes to remain unidentified, reported to me today that on May 2, 1990, she was in the apartment of Lester Webster at the above address and observed several electronic appliances including a color TV and video camera, and that Webster stated to her that he had taken those and other items when he broke into Joe's Appliance Store on April 29. I confirmed with the store manager that a break-in did occur that day and that several items including a color TV and video camera were taken.

ss/ Harvey Lance

Subscribed and sworn to before me on the 5th day of May, 1990.

ss/ Judge Linda Black

Does this warrant comply with the requirements of the Fourth Amendment?

Some Twists and Turns

2. Assume that all deficiencies on the face of the documents in example 1 have been corrected and the warrant issued. The search of Lester Webster's apartment was conducted, and the police seized several items including some that were in fact stolen from Joe's Appliance Store. Would the lawfulness of the search be undercut by any of the following additional facts?

    a. Subsequent to the search, Police Officer Harvey Lance was overheard telling a fellow officer in the courthouse men's room that he had concocted the entire story about an informant being in Webster's place and seeing the loot because Lance had a hunch Webster was the perpetrator, but had no hard information to go by.

    b. Instead of the scenario set out in example 2a, assume that Lance is overheard telling a fellow officer that there actually was an informant who provided the information about Webster set out in the affidavit, but that the informant had been inaccurate on two of six previous occasions when she had given Lance tips.

    c. While the officers were searching Webster's apartment, they discovered an automatic assault weapon in his hall closet. As possession of this weapon is a crime, they seized it. The officers then found in the closet a small cigar box, which they opened to discover unlawful hollow-nosed bullets inside. The officers then seized the bullets.

    d. When the officers appeared at Webster's apartment to conduct the search, they found him and three other persons inside. They frisked all four men and found an unlawful pistol on one of the visitors.

    e. Instead of the scenario set out in example 2d, assume that when the officers appeared to conduct the search, Webster was leaving his apartment. After identifying themselves and showing him the warrant, the officers requested that he remain. When he refused, one officer detained Webster in the hallway while the others conducted the search.

EXPLANATIONS

1. In order to satisfy constitutional requirements, the warrant must 1) be issued by a neutral and detached magistrate; 2) be based upon a showing of probable cause supported by oath or affirmation; and 3) describe with particularity the place to be searched and the items to be seized.

    The first requirement appears to be met. The warrant is signed by a judge of the county court, a judicial officer who has (as far as we know) no association with the prosecutor or police and no personal or financial stake in the issuance.

    The probable cause showing is properly in the form of a sworn affidavit from the officer. Does the showing amount to probable cause to believe that seizable items are present at the place to be searched? As pointed out in Chapter 4, probable cause may be based upon hearsay information provided by a third party. When the source is an unnamed informant, as is the case here, there must be information in the affidavit supporting the officer's reliance on both the informant's credibility and the accuracy of his conclusion that incriminating evidence will be found (although under the *Gates* totality of the circumstances standard, a strong showing in one regard may compensate for a weak showing in the other). The informant's credibility is adequately supported in Officer Lance's affidavit by the assertion of past reliability. Further, the informant's conclusion that the loot from the burglary is present at the apartment seems well supported by her own personal observations and Webster's incriminatory statement. Moreover, the police officer's independent investigation corroborated that the burglary had occurred and that the items described by the informant had indeed been taken from Joe's Appliance.

    A question may be raised regarding the time lapse between the informant's observations and the application for the warrant. As noted in §4.1, probable cause to search must be based on information sufficiently fresh to make it likely that the items will still be at the location to be searched. The application here is filed three days after the informant asserts she saw the stolen items. Although it could be argued that it was no longer reasonable to conclude that the items would still be there on the date that the warrant is actually executed, the time lapse is probably not great enough to support this contention. It should be noted that the Fourth Amendment has been interpreted to require that a search warrant be executed within a reasonable time of its issuance to ensure that probable cause still exists at the time of the search. "If the police were allowed to execute the warrant at leisure, the safeguard of judicial control over the search which the Fourth Amendment is intended to accomplish would be eviscerated." *United States v. Bedford*, 519 F.2d 650, 655 (3d Cir. 1975). Thus Officer Lance must conduct the search promptly and without unreasonable delay.

Turning to the particularity requirement, it would appear that the place to be searched is specified sufficiently so that the officer executing the warrant can ascertain the location intended with reasonable effort. There is, however, serious question as to the particularity of the items to be seized. Given the principle that the description should leave little or nothing to the discretion of the officer executing the warrant, the authorization to seize "all electronic appliances stolen in the burglary of Joe's Appliance Store" on the specified date is probably inadequate. Because a precise description of the items stolen (including serial numbers) could apparently have been obtained from the store manager at the time of issuance, such specificity should have been provided. Unlike contraband such as narcotics, there is nothing about the characterization "stolen" property that makes it readily identifiable. See *Commonwealth v. Rutkowski*, 406 Mass. 673, 676 (1990) ("To describe general items like guns and jewelry as 'stolen' adds nothing instructive to a description in a warrant."); *Namen v. Alaska*, 665 P.2d 557 (Alaska Ct. App. 1983) (held that a search warrant for defendant's residence authorizing seizure of jewelry stolen from a certain home on a certain date did not satisfy the particularity requirement because it did not provide meaningful guidance to the officers conducting the search as to what items could be seized, especially since an inventory of the items stolen was available at the time of issuance). Compare *United States v. Strand*, 761 F.2d 449, 453 (8th Cir. 1985) (upheld a warrant that authorized a search for "stolen mail" because the court found that the generic description nevertheless permitted the officers to readily identify items of mail not addressed to or from the person being searched).

It should be noted that certain crimes, such as those involving money laundering or fraudulent activities, often require so extensive a search of records that there is no feasible way to limit the search to evidence of crime. In such cases, the courts have admonished law enforcement officials to conduct themselves in a manner that minimizes unwarranted intrusions upon privacy. *Andresen v. Maryland*, 427 U.S. 463, 482 (1976). As Circuit Judge Jon Newman has written: "It is true that a warrant authorizing seizure of records of criminal activity permits officers to examine many papers in a suspect's possession to determine if they are within the described category. But allowing some latitude in this regard simply recognizes the reality that few people keep documents of their criminal transactions in a folder marked 'drug records.' " *United States v. Riley*, 906 F.2d 841, 845 (2d Cir. 1990).

The problem of describing the items to be seized with sufficient particularity is especially challenging when the search is for documents on a computer. For more on computer searches, see Chapter 12. See also *United States v. Carey*, 172 F.3d 1268 (10th Cir. 1999); *United States v. Upham*, 168 F.3d 532 (1st Cir. 1999); *United States v. Simpson*, 152 F.3d 1241 (10th Cir. 1998); *United States v. Kow*, 58 F.3d 423 (9th Cir. 1995); *United States v. Hunter*, 13 F. Supp. 2d 574 (D. Vt. 1998); *Steve Jackson Games, Inc. v. U.S. Secret Service*, 816 F. Supp. 432 (W.D. Texas 1993), *aff'd*, 36 F.3d 457 (5th Cir. 1994).

The warrant in our example amounts to a license to seize any item that conceivably could have been taken from an appliance store. Moreover, the clear failure to particularize the actual items stolen would probably not be excused as an objectively reasonable good faith error under *Maryland v. Garrison*, 480 U.S. 79 (1987), and *Massachusetts v. Sheppard*, 468 U.S. 981 (1984). As the Court noted in *United States v. Leon*, 468 U.S. 897, 923 (1984), the good faith exception does not apply if the warrant is "so facially deficient—i.e, in failing to particularize the place to be searched or the things to be seized—that the executing officers cannot reasonably presume it to be valid." See also *United States v. Stubbs*, 873 F.2d 210, 212 (9th Cir. 1989) (executing officers could not have reasonably presumed a facially overbroad warrant authorizing seizure of all of defendant's business records to be valid).

Some Twists and Turns

2a. Defendant could pursue a challenge to the veracity of the affidavit under the terms of *Franks v. Delaware*, 438 U.S. 154 (1978). The formidable preconditions may be summarized as follows: 1) defendant must allege specifically which portions of the search warrant affidavit are claimed to be false; 2) defendant must challenge the statements as deliberate or reckless falsehoods, not simply unknowing or negligent; 3) the false statements must be those of the officer or agent filing the affidavit, not the informant or other sources; 4) a detailed offer of proof, including affidavits, must accompany the allegations; and 5) the challenged statements must be necessary to the establishment of probable cause. See also *United States v. DiCesare*, 765 F.2d 890 (9th Cir. 1985).

Assuming that the witness who overheard Officer Lance is willing to file a sworn statement to that effect, Webster has a good chance of making a successful preliminary showing of deliberate perjury on matters that go to the very heart of the probable cause set forth in the affidavit. Setting aside the informant's assertions would leave this affidavit with no other information upon which to base probable cause to search Webster's apartment.

The challenge would then proceed to an evidentiary hearing in which Webster would have to actually prove (by a preponderance of the evidence) that the police officer engaged in a deliberate or reckless falsehood. This would now require the testimony of the witness to Lance's admission. In all likelihood, the officer would deny under oath that he falsified the affidavit, and the ultimate fact question would have to be resolved by the judge. If it were determined that the officer did in fact concoct the story about the informant, then the warrant would be held unlawful as having been issued without probable cause and the items seized ruled inadmissible in evidence.

2b. Unlike example 2a, the deliberate falsehood here does not so clearly undercut the existence of probable cause in the affidavit. The omission of information concerning the informant's past unreliability on two of six occasions, even if shown to have been deliberate, may be considered harmless in the sense that the warrant would have been issued anyway had this been disclosed. Such omissions have not been the stuff of successful *Franks* challenges. See, e.g., *United States v. Hadfield*, 918 F.2d 987 (1st Cir. 1990) (officer failed to reveal that the same request for a warrant had earlier been submitted to and denied by another magistrate, and also that the source of information relied upon for the firearms seizure was uncertain about whether the particular weapon used by defendant was a lawful BB gun or an unlawful .22 caliber); *United States v. Parcels of Land*, 903 F.2d 36 (1st Cir. 1990) (omission of information showing that defendant had substantial sources of legitimate income and that several big-ticket purchases he made were financed through loans and not cash); *United States v. Rumney*, 867 F.2d 714 (1st Cir. 1989) (omission of the facts that the primary source of information had changed his story several times and had a criminal record); *United States v. DiCesare*, 765 F.2d 890 (9th Cir. 1985) (the officer failed to reveal that a previous arrest of defendant referred to in the affidavit had not resulted in prosecution).

2c. While a primary purpose of the warrant is to limit the scope of the search to the particular items described, the police are permitted to seize other articles of contraband or evidence of crime that they come upon in the ordinary course of the original search. The rationale for this plain view doctrine is that once the lawful search uncovers the article, it is obvious that no additional invasion of privacy occurs when the officers view it. Seizure of the item, which clearly does amount to an incremental intrusion, is nevertheless justified on the grounds that it would make little sense to require the officer either to ignore the item or to seek a warrant for its seizure (for which he now clearly has probable cause).

The two prerequisites for plain view seizure are that 1) the item in question was found while the officer confined his search to the original parameters authorized in the warrant; and 2) the item was immediately apparent as contraband or evidence of crime. The first requirement ensures that the officer has lawfully arrived at the place from which the plain view is made and that the scope of the authorized search is not exceeded; the second limits the additional items that can be seized to those that (without need for further examination) are obviously incriminating. Both requirements operate to prevent the plain view doctrine from becoming a license for a general search.

In example 2c, the warrant authorized a search of the apartment for electronic appliances. The officers were therefore acting within lawful confines when they opened the bedroom closet, where such items could be hidden, and discovered the assault weapon. Moreover, the gun was immediately apparent to them as an unlawful weapon; they did not need to engage in further examination to determine that. Compare *Coolidge v. New Hampshire*, 403 U.S. 443 (1971) (the probative value of the automobile seized in plain view was not clear until its interior was subjected to vacuuming and microscopic analysis); *United States v. Rutkowski*, 877 F.2d 139, 143 (1st Cir. 1989) (seizure of metal strips could not be justified under plain view doctrine because it was not immediately apparent that they were incriminating: "Possession of platinum is not itself illegal. Furthermore, when he found the metal in the envelopes, he was not able to identify it as platinum—much less to identify it as stolen platinum.").[10] The seizure of the weapon, which the officers could readily see was illegal, was therefore lawful despite the fact that it was not specified in the warrant.

The seizure of the bullets, however, cannot be justified under the plain view doctrine. The officers did not find the bullets in plain view during an appropriate search for electronic appliances. They clearly exceeded the proper scope of a search for televisions and VCRs when they opened a small cigar box. Compare *United States v. Rutkowski*, supra (officers executing a warrant to search for jewelry and coins had the right to open a coffee can and envelopes contained in it). Although the box itself was found in plain view during the authorized search, it was not immediately apparent that it was, or contained, evidence of crime.

Because the bullets were not specified in the warrant, and the plain view doctrine is inapplicable, seizure of them was unlawful.

2d. Armed with a warrant to search Webster's apartment for specified items, may the officers frisk persons found inside at the time of the search? *Ybarra v. Illinois*, 444 U.S. 85 (1979), ruled unlawful the frisk of patrons who happened to be in a tavern at the time it was searched for narcotics pursuant to a warrant. Neither the affidavit in support of the warrant nor the warrant itself made any reference to unlawful activity of customers at the tavern. A person's mere presence in a place suspected of criminal activity does not give rise to justification to search that person. In contrast, given the reduced expectation of privacy in a car as well as the greater likelihood of complicity in the driver's criminal enterprise, mere presence in an automobile being lawfully searched permits examination of a passenger's belongings. See *Wyoming v. Houghton*, 526 U.S. 295 (1999), discussed in §6.4.

If any authority to frisk exists in example 2d, therefore, it must emanate from the officer's reasonable suspicion that the occupants

---

10. Circuit Judge Selya described the principle of "immediately apparent" as "akin to that underlying the incandescent light bulb. When an officer spots an object not described in the warrant, authority to seize depends upon knowledge—the extent to which bits and bytes of accumulated information then and there fall into place. The sum total of the searchers' knowledge must be sufficient to turn on the bulb; if the light does not shine during the currency of the search, there is no 'immediate awareness' of the incriminating nature of the object." 877 F.2d at 142.

of the apartment were armed and dangerous. See §4.2. The officers must be able to point to some threatening gesture or other aggressive action on the part of the occupants, which provided a reasonable belief that danger was at hand. Otherwise, the frisk resulting in the seizure of the weapon was unlawful.

2e. Armed with a warrant to search Webster's apartment for specified items, may the officers detain him for the duration of the search? The Court has answered this affirmatively in *Michigan v. Summers*, 452 U.S. 692 (1981), in which the occupant of a home about to be searched was detained by the executing officers and later arrested when narcotics were found on the premises. The Court reasoned that the existence of probable cause to search the home provides an adequate basis for suspecting criminal activity on the part of its resident, and that justifies the detention. Moreover, detention during the search was viewed as only a slight increment above the intrusion of the search itself. And it serves the legitimate purposes of preventing flight in the event incriminating evidence is found and of facilitating the orderly completion of the search (by making the resident available, for example, to open locked doors or containers).

§5.3 Execution of a Search Warrant

Most jurisdictions have limitations on the period during which a search warrant can be executed. See, e.g, Federal Rules of Criminal Procedure 41(c) (10 days). Even without these rules a long delay could result in the dissipation of probable cause. See §4.1. In addition, rules sometimes require that the warrants be executed during the daytime hours unless otherwise authorized.

In *Wilson v. Arkansas*, 514 U.S. 927 (1995), the Court held that the Fourth Amendment incorporates the common-law requirement that police knock on a dwelling's door and announce their identity and purpose before attempting forcible entry. (18 U.S.C. §3109 requires federal law enforcement officers to give such warning). Recognizing the need for flexibility in light of countervailing law enforcement concerns, however, a unanimous Court held that no-knock entry is governed by the Fourth Amendment's reasonableness clause and left it to the lower courts to determine when an unannounced entry might be reasonable. Circumstances presenting a threat of physical violence, escape, or destruction of evidence will generally justify a no-knock entry. See, e.g., *United States v. Bates*, 84 F.3d 790 (6th Cir. 1996). Absent exigent circumstances, the failure of law enforcement officials to knock and announce their presence renders the evidence procured by forcible entry inadmissible. Many courts have concluded that an entry obtained by ruse (such as false assertion of an emergency) does not violate knock-and-announce requirements because it is not a forcible entry. See *Coleman v. United States*, 728 A.2d 1230 (D.C. Ct. App. 1999) (and citations).

The Court has refused to create a blanket exception to the knock-and-announce rule where the object of the search is drugs, rejecting the argument that such searches invariably involve exigent circumstances. *Richards v. Wisconsin*, 520 U.S. 385 (1997). The Fourth Amendment does not hold officers to a higher standard when a no-knock entry results in the destruction of property. *United States v. Ramirez*, 523 U.S. 65 (1998).

In a matter related to the execution of a warrant, the Court has refused to permit media "ride-alongs" during searches of residences, concluding that permitting reporters to observe and photograph the event violates the privacy rights of the homeowner. See *Wilson v. Layne*, 526 U.S. 603 (1999). The Court distinguished the situation where the presence of a third party directly aids in the execution of the warrant, as in the case of an owner identifying stolen property.

§5.4   Administrative Search Warrants

As discussed in §4.5, warrants have been required for certain administrative or regulatory searches. Unlike the search and arrest warrants discussed above, however, these *Camara*-type warrants are not issued on the basis of particularized probable cause. Rather, what is required is a showing that the location to be inspected was chosen according to a prescribed plan that relies on neutral criteria (as, for example, the date of last inspection). See *Marshall v. Barlow's Inc.*, 436 U.S. 307 (1978).

§5.5   Anticipatory Search Warrants

As discussed in example 14 in §4.1, the majority of the circuits have approved the use of anticipatory warrants. Anticipatory warrants differ from traditional search warrants in that at the time of issuance, they are not supported by probable cause that the item related to the crime will be at the place to be searched. Instead they are issued upon a showing of probable cause to believe that seizable items *will be present* at the place to be searched at a specified time in the very near future. Such warrants are used when the police expect delivery of contraband at a particular location and further anticipate that the contraband will be removed shortly after arrival. As Circuit Judge Pratt explained the policy reasons for issuing such warrants:

> Courts—though not yet the Supreme Court, to be sure—have upheld the anticipatory warrant, in large part, because they see it as desirable, whenever possible, for police to obtain judicial approval before searching private premises. Indeed, the Fourth Amendment mandates that, with few exceptions, a warrant be obtained before any search of a dwelling occurs. Yet one of the major practical difficulties that confronts law enforcement officials is the time required to obtain a warrant. In many instances, the speed with which government agents are required to act, especially when dealing with the furtive and transitory activities of persons who traffic in narcotics, demands that they proceed without a warrant or risk losing both criminal and contraband. . . . [T]he purposes of the Fourth Amendment are best served by permitting government agents to obtain warrants in advance if they can show probable cause to believe that the contraband will be located on the premises at the time that search takes place.

United States v. Garcia, 882 F.2d 699, 703 (2d Cir. 1989).

§5.6 The Arrest Warrant Requirement

As indicated in §5.1, a warrant is generally required to authorize the seizure of things unless the circumstances fit within an established exception to the warrant requirement (discussed in Chapter 6). With regard to seizures of *the person* (arrests), however, the reverse is true— that is, warrantless arrest is the rule and arrest by warrant is the exception. Decisional law permits the police to arrest *without* prior judicial authorization as long as the arrest occurs in a public place and provided there is probable cause to believe the subject has committed a crime (see §4.1). The warrantless arrest is permitted even if there is sufficient time to seek an arrest warrant and no practical impediment to doing so. *United States v. Watson*, 423 U.S. 411 (1976).

The one context in which the Court has imposed a warrant requirement is where the arrest occurs in a home rather than a public place. Given the sanctity of the home in Fourth Amendment jurisprudence, an arrest warrant is required to enter and effect a *nonexigent* arrest of the subject in his own home. *Payton v. New York*, 445 U.S. 573 (1980). The Fourth Amendment, the Court held, draws a firm line at the entrance to one's home, and absent exigent circumstances (discussed in Chapter 6), that line cannot be crossed without a warrant.

A valid arrest warrant implicitly carries with it the authority to enter the suspect's own dwelling (when there is probable cause to believe he is there) and to search for him anywhere in the house that he may be found. There is no necessity to have a search warrant for his home in addition to the arrest warrant; the latter has been deemed sufficient to protect the interest of the arrestee in the privacy of his own home. Where the police seek to arrest a suspect in the residence of a *third party*, however, they must (again absent exigent circumstances) obtain a search warrant to enter and search that home for the suspect. This warrant is issued on a showing of probable cause to believe that the suspect is on the premises. The search warrant is deemed necessary to protect the third party's privacy interest in his home. *Steagald v. United States*, 451 U.S. 204 (1981). Without this requirement the police would be permitted to enter and search any building in which the suspect might be, such as the homes of all his friends, relatives, and acquaintances.

In sum, while arrests on the street or in public buildings may be effected without seeking prior authorization from a magistrate, an arrest warrant is required for the arrest of a person in his own home and a search warrant is required for his arrest in the home of another. (Keep in mind that this search warrant requirement is designed to protect the interests of the third party as opposed to the arrestee. This issue will be explored in the examples that follow.) As Justice Rehnquist observed in his dissent in *Steagald*, the issue will inevitably arise as to what constitutes the suspect's *own* home. At what point in the suspect's stay with another does the third party's home (which ordinarily can be entered only by way of a search warrant issued on the basis of probable cause to believe the suspect is present) become the suspect's residence, so that it may be entered by way of an arrest warrant (issued on the basis of probable cause to believe he committed the crime)?

The importance of this distinction lies in the difference between the showing required for the two warrants.

§5.7 The Components of a Valid Arrest Warrant

Like the search warrant, an arrest warrant must be issued by a neutral and detached magistrate. The probable cause required focuses on facts and circumstances that connect the suspect to specific criminal activity (and not the presence of incriminating items at the place to be searched). See §4.1. The suspect must be particularly identified in the warrant either by name or with a sufficiently specific description so that the officers may locate him with reasonable effort.

EXAMPLES

Jack, a suspect in a bank robbery, has been a fugitive for a number of months. The police have just received a tip that he has been staying at a house (on a hill) leased to his girlfriend, Jill.

a. With regard to Jack, what "paperwork" is required to lawfully enter the house and arrest Jack?

b. With regard to Jill, what "paperwork" is required to lawfully enter and arrest Jack?

EXPLANATIONS

a. Although Jack may be lawfully arrested in a public place without a warrant as long as the police have probable cause to believe that he has committed a crime, a warrant is required if the arrest is to occur in a private home. When the police seek to cross the threshold of a residence, a magistrate must agree beforehand that the information known to the police amounts to probable cause. The type of warrant required depends on whether the home is the arrestee's or a third party's. An arrest warrant is all that the police need to enter and arrest Jack if the house is *his* residence. See *Payton v. New York*, 445 U.S. 573 (1980) (an arrest warrant implicitly authorizes entry into the suspect's own dwelling when there is probable cause to believe he is present). This is true even if he shares the house with Jill. See *United States v. Ramirez*, 770 F.2d 1458 (9th Cir. 1985). If the house is considered the sole residence of Jill, an arrest warrant is still all that is required to protect Jack's rights. An arrestee cannot claim greater Fourth Amendment protection in the home of a third party than he can in his own house. See *United States v. Kaylor*, 877 F.2d 658 (8th Cir. 1989) (a warrant for Kaylor's arrest, together with the officer's reasonable belief that he was inside, justified entry into a third party's home as far as the arrestee's rights were concerned); *United States v. Underwood*, 717 F.2d 482 (9th Cir. 1983); *United States v. Buckner*, 717 F.2d 297 (6th Cir. 1983).

Thus for Jack (assuming he has standing to complain—to be discussed in Chapter 7), all that would be required to enter and effect an arrest would be an arrest warrant.

b. With regard to Jill, the question of whether the house is exclusively hers or is also the residence of Jack becomes more important. If the house is solely her residence, then a search warrant is required to protect her privacy interest in the home. See *Steagald v. United States*, 451 U.S. 204 (1981) (a search warrant is required to arrest subject while he is in the home of a third party). Securing a search warrant would require that the police present the magistrate with probable cause to believe that Jack will be found at Jill's home. The magistrate, and not the police, would therefore weigh the reliability of the tip as to Jack's whereabouts before the search for him could occur. If, on the other hand, Jack shared the house with Jill, then an arrest warrant would be sufficient to effect the arrest. The arrest warrant would issue on probable cause to believe Jack committed the crime. Jill could not claim the additional protection of a search warrant.

For Jill, then, the determinative question is whose residence is the house. The question of how a court should decide this question has received little attention in the case law. It has been held that courts should not deem a temporary stay to constitute residence: "We would impermissibly diminish the protection offered by *Steagald* were we to hold that, for purposes of the homeowner's Fourth Amendment rights, the dwelling is the 'home' of whoever happens to be staying there. . . . The Fourth Amendment right to be secure against warrantless searches within the home is too vital to justify entry without a search warrant to execute an arrest warrant upon a guest in the home." *Perez v. Simmons*, 884 F.2d 1136, 1141–1142 (9th Cir. 1988).

6

Warrantless Searches and Seizures

§6.1 Introduction

Although the Supreme Court has frequently expressed the view that searches conducted outside the warrant process are presumptively unlawful (see Chapter 2), it has nevertheless recognized that in many situations it is impracticable (and indeed dangerous) to require the police to delay their action pending judicial authorization. The Court has therefore carved out several *categorical* exceptions to the warrant requirement. This approach establishes certain classes of cases in which it has been predetermined that a search without a warrant is reasonable and thus lawful. If the particular facts of a case fall within one of the categories, then a warrantless search is permissible. In this chapter we will explore each of these exceptions, focusing on three basic questions:

1) What are the characteristics common to cases in this category that justify circumvention of the warrant process?
2) What requirements must be met for the specific exception to apply?
3) What is the permissible scope of a search within the exception?

As we shall see, the extent of police activity covered by these "few specifically established and well-delineated exceptions," *Katz v. United States*, 389 U.S. 347, 357 (1967), has grown considerably in recent years. Moreover, while the original justification for carving out the exceptions lay in the impracticality of securing a warrant, more recent years have seen a movement toward justifying warrantless searches on other rationales, primarily reduced expectation of privacy. Indeed, the trend of the decisions has led Justice Stevens to accuse the majority of paying only "lip service" to the "cardinal principle that searches conducted outside the judicial process, without prior approval by judge or magistrate, are per se unreasonable under the Fourth Amendment." See *California v. Acevedo*, 500 U.S. 565, 585 (1991) (Stevens, J., dissenting).

In studying the exceptions to the warrant requirement, it is helpful to categorize them in terms of the justification required before the police may act. We have therefore divided them into three groups (with reference to the categories of justification discussed in Chapter 4): 1) exceptions that require *probable cause*; 2) exceptions that require *reasonable suspicion*; and 3) exceptions that require *administrative justification*. A fourth category of warrantless intrusion encompasses two doctrines, consent and plain view, which virtually circumvent the Fourth Amendment and thus require no specific justification.

§6.2   Exceptions that Require Probable Cause: The Emergency Exception ("Exigent Circumstances")

Perhaps the purest example of an exception premised on the impracticability of obtaining a warrant is the emergency exception. The basic concept is that where the exigencies of the situation compel the police to act immediately or risk either imminent danger to themselves or others, the destruction of evidence, or the escape of a suspect, it would be unreasonable to require resort to the warrant process. This exception excuses the necessity for either a search or arrest warrant, whichever is required under the circumstances. See Chapter 5.

The prerequisites for a warrantless search or arrest under the emergency exception are that: 1) the circumstances presented the police with a sufficiently *compelling urgency, making resort to the warrant process both impracticable and risky*; and 2) the police had justification amounting to *probable cause* to believe that items relating to crime would be found (in the case of a search) or that the suspect had committed a crime (in the case of an arrest).

Most of the cases under the emergency exception have involved the "hot pursuit" doctrine. When the police are in immediate pursuit of a suspect fleeing from the scene of a crime, they are permitted to chase her into a building or home without a warrant in order to arrest her. While inside, they may also conduct a warrantless search for the suspect and for any weapons to which she may have access.

In *Warden v. Hayden*, 387 U.S. 294 (1967), two cab drivers who had witnessed an armed robbery followed the perpetrator to a particular house and summoned the police. Officers arrived within minutes, entered the house, and proceeded to search it for the robber. While looking for him, the police discovered and seized evidence connected to the robbery as well as two guns. Hayden was then found and arrested, and the items seized were later offered in evidence over his objection at trial. On review, the Supreme Court held that the items were properly admissible because the entry into the home, although warrantless, was reasonable under the exigent circumstances to prevent the escape of the fleeing suspect. Once inside, the officers could lawfully search for the suspect and, in the process, seize evidence and weapons found in plain view[1] while searching those areas where the suspect or weapons might be hidden.

It must be emphasized that the exigencies of a hot pursuit are not, on their own, sufficient to fit a case within the emergency exception. The police must also have probable cause to believe the subject has just committed a crime *and* is in the particular dwelling. As *Hayden* demonstrates, the police need not *themselves* have witnessed the crime or the perpetrator's flight; the probable cause may be based on other reliable sources. The emphasis is on the *heat* of the chase. Hot pursuit requires that there be "immediate and continuous pursuit of from the scene of the crime." *Welsh v. Wisconsin*, 466 U.S. 740, 741 (1984). When the chase turns cold, the rationale for circumventing the warrant process evaporates.

The Supreme Court has indicated that warrantless entry into a dwelling may not be permissible even under exigent circumstances where the suspect is sought for a minor crime. In *Welsh v. Wisconsin*, police entered the suspect's home and arrested him for the noncriminal offense of drunk driving. The Court refused to sanction circumvention of the warrant process under those circumstances. While withholding decision on the question of "whether the Fourth Amendment may impose an absolute ban on warrantless home arrests for certain minor offenses," the Court held that the gravity of the offense for which the suspect is sought is an important factor to consider in applying the

---

1. The concept of plain view seizure is discussed in §6.8.

emergency exception. "Home entry should rarely be sanctioned when there is probable cause to believe that only a minor offense . . . has been committed." 466 U.S. at 750 n.11.

In addition to hot pursuit, the emergency exception is also applicable to other situations where the delay required to obtain a warrant would create an imminent risk of 1) destruction of evidence; 2) escape of the suspect; or 3) danger to the police or others. See *Minnesota v. Olson*, 495 U.S. 91 (1990). Application of this exception requires a fact-specific analysis to determine whether resort to the warrant process (and to the telephonic warrant, where applicable)[2] was truly impracticable. In *Olson* the prosecution sought to justify a warrantless entry and arrest of the suspect in a duplex unit that the police had surrounded. Although there was probable cause to believe that Olson had been the driver of a getaway car involved in a robbery and murder the day before, the Supreme Court held that failure to obtain a warrant could not be excused under the circumstances presented. The gravity of the crime and the likelihood that the suspect is armed must, the Court held, be considered as factors in assessing the urgency of the situation. Although a grave crime had been committed, Olson was suspected of being the driver of the getaway car, not the murderer. Further, the police had already recovered the murder weapon and there was no suggestion of danger to anyone in the building. Finally, the police had the building surrounded and Olson could not have escaped without being apprehended. The Court ruled that "these facts do not add up to exigent circumstances."

Because the emergency exception has the obvious potential to swallow the Fourth Amendment's warrant provisions, it is not surprising that the courts have been careful to contain its borders. The scope of the permissible search is strictly limited by the exigencies upon which it is based. Thus the hot pursuit intrusion into a dwelling is limited to those areas where the suspect, or weapons she may use, might be hidden. It is not a general search. In *Mincey v. Arizona*, 437 U.S. 385 (1978), the Court rejected the argument that the emergency exception justified an extensive four-day warrantless search of a homicide scene. While not questioning the right of the police to make warrantless entries and searches when they reasonably believe that a person inside is in need of immediate aid, or when they come upon a homicide scene and promptly survey the immediate area for victims or

---

2. See, e.g., Fed. R. Crim. P. 41(a)(2). See *United States v. Alverez*, 810 F.2d 879 (9th Cir. 1987).

the perpetrator, the Court concluded that the search of Mincey's apartment far exceeded the necessities of the moment: "All the persons in Mincey's apartment had been located before the investigating homicide officers arrived there and began their search. And a four-day search that included opening dresser drawers and ripping up carpets can hardly be rationalized in terms of the legitimate concerns that justify an emergency search." 437 U.S. at 393.

Under the same rationale that the scope of an emergency search must be limited by the nature of the emergency, a two-hour search of a residence that was the scene of a murder and suicide attempt was ruled unlawful because the victims had already been removed and the area secured. Moreover, the search had widened to include opening drawers and examining items in a wastebasket. See *Thompson v. Louisiana*, 469 U.S. 17 (1984). And while a warrantless entry into a burning dwelling for the purposes of determining the source of the fire and extinguishing it is permitted for obvious reasons, once the origin of the fire is discovered and it is brought under control the authorities must obtain a warrant to conduct a further investigation of the premises. See *Michigan v. Clifford*, 464 U.S. 287 (1984); *Michigan v. Tyler*, 436 U.S. 499 (1978).

Law enforcement officers have two options when faced with a situation where they anticipate that incriminating evidence at a particular location may be destroyed or removed, but the compelling justification required for a warrantless emergency search is absent. First, the Court has suggested that officers may secure the premises to prevent persons from entering while they await a warrant. See *Segura v. United States*, 468 U.S. 796 (1984). Second, the officers may seek a telephonic warrant as authorized in some jurisdictions including the federal system. See n. 2, supra.

EXAMPLES

1a. A man armed with a pistol robbed Josie's Convenience Store. Josie (the fearless proprietor) pursued the perpetrator on foot and chased him until he entered a nearby house. Josie then called the police from a telephone booth outside. Officers soon arrived, and after hearing Josie's story and getting her description of the perpetrator, they entered the house and arrested the robber inside. In the absence of either an arrest or search warrant, is this action lawful?

1b. Assume instead that the day after the robbery, the police observed a man meeting the exact description of the perpetrator standing on the sidewalk. They attempt to arrest him, but he flees inside the house. May they pursue him inside and make a warrantless arrest?

2. Unlucky Larry was observed by Police Officer Bones as he robbed the Main Street Bank with a gun and then fled into the Chesterfield Residence Hotel across the street. Bones followed Larry into the hotel, which contained 24 rooms. Not seeing which room Larry entered, Officer Bones played his lucky number and entered Room 333. He immediately observed a bundle of new large-denomination bills lying on the floor and seized the bundle. Bones then searched the room and discovered Larry hiding in the shower stall, where he was placed under arrest. Were the officer's actions lawful? Would the seizure of the bills be lawful if they had been found by Bones while searching the drawer of a night table prior to apprehending Larry?

3. Federal agents received reliable information that a purple-throated Polynesian parrot, an endangered species whose importation is a federal felony, had been delivered to the home of taxidermist Grant Greedy. Greedy had been under investigation for several months and the agents had developed probable cause to believe he was operating an illegal enterprise out of his home in which animals that were near extinction were killed, stuffed, and sold to unscrupulous wealthy collectors. After receiving the information about the Polynesian parrot, several agents proceeded to Greedy's home to wait for their supervisor, who was applying for a warrant to search the premises. Before the warrant could be issued, however, the agents observed Greedy leave the dwelling, bid farewell to his brother Lee, and depart in his car. Two agents followed Greedy, who appeared to realize they were pursuing him and began driving evasively at great speed. The agents finally overtook him and pulled him over at a gas station. Before being taken into custody, Greedy yelled to the attendant (whom he appeared to know), "Call my brother Lee and tell him to get rid of the bird quick!" Fearing destruction of the precious animal, the agents proceeded immediately back to Greedy's home and entered just as Lee was about to place the parrot into the trash compactor. They seized the bird and arrested Lee. In the absence of a warrant, was the police action lawful?

4. Informant Z told drug investigators that Maxy Mum had sold her cocaine on numerous occasions. The agents asked Informant

arrange another sale with Maxy, and it took place on Monday on the sidewalk outside Maxy's apartment. The agents witnessed the transaction from a remote location. After later confirming that the substance sold by Maxy was cocaine, the agents asked Informant to arrange another sale for the next day to occur inside Maxy's apartment. At the appointed time on Tuesday, Informant went into the apartment. She came out 15 minutes later and informed the agents that the sale had occurred and that a large quantity of cocaine remained on the premises. Fearing that the contraband might be sold off to others, the agents moved in immediately, arresting Maxy and seizing the cocaine. Was this warrantless action lawful?

5. The police were summoned by United Parcel Service (UPS) employees who had a package that had been returned by the driver as "addressee unknown." When opened, it was found to contain a large brick of a substance that the UPS testers determined was cocaine. After conducting a field test that confirmed that the substance was cocaine, the police resealed the package and placed it the "undelivered" section at UPS. They then waited for someone to pick it up. A woman appeared later in the day, claimed the package, and departed. The police followed her to a home known to them to be that of Sherman West, long suspected of being a major narcotics dealer but who had previously eluded prosecution by being particularly attentive to surveillance and disposing of the narcotics whenever the police got too close. Within minutes after the woman entered West's home with the package, the police entered, arrested both of them, and seized the cocaine. Was this warrantless action lawful?

EXPLANATIONS

1a. Yes, the warrantless entry and arrest were lawful. As discussed in §5.5, under ordinary circumstances a warrantless entry into a home to effect an arrest would violate the Fourth Amendment. An arrest warrant would normally be required to enter the suspect's own home, and a search warrant would be required to enter a third party's residence. In this example, however, the police were not engaged in a routine arrest, but were in hot pursuit of a suspect whom they had probable cause to believe (based on the victim-witness's information) had just committed an armed robbery and was in the dwelling. Because of these exigent circumstances, the absence of prior judicial authorization to enter, search for, and arrest the suspect would be excused under the emergency exception. See *Warden v. Hayden*, 387 U.S. 294 (1967).

1b. Yes, the warrantless entry and arrest were lawful. Although there is no hot pursuit from the scene of the crime, the police may chase the suspect into his home without a warrant when they attempt to effect a lawful arrest in a public place, but are unsuccessful because the suspect retreats inside. (Remember that the police may make a warrantless arrest in a public place as long as they have probable cause to believe the subject committed a felony, see §5.5.) See *United States v. Santana*, 427 U.S. 38 (1976) (suspect was observed in the doorway of her home and retreated inside before the police could apprehend her). "A suspect may not defeat an arrest which has been set in motion in a public place, and is therefore proper under *Watson*, by the expedient of escaping to a private place." 427 U.S. at 43.

2. In order to conduct a lawful hot pursuit into Room 333, Officer Bones needed probable cause to believe 1) that Larry had just committed a crime; and 2) that he had fled into the room. As an eyewitness to the robbery, Bones certainly meets the first prerequisite. Regarding the second, however, because the building contained 24 rooms and Bones did not have any information at the time indicating into which room Larry may have fled, probable cause to search Room 333 (or any other particular room at the Chesterfield) was lacking. In a case involving facts similar to those in this example, in which there was an absence of cause to enter a particular room, a divided Ninth Circuit Court of Appeals (sitting en banc) held that the hot pursuit exception did not apply and that the warrantless intrusion violated the Fourth Amendment. See *United States v. Winsor*, 846 F.2d 1569 (9th Cir. 1988). The dissenters, observing that the officer had himself pursued the fleeing felon without interruption from the scene of the crime to the hotel and that the safety of the officer and other occupants of the hotel was threatened by the presence of the armed perpetrator in an unknown room, would have permitted warrantless intrusion into each of the 24 rooms.

Assuming that the entry into the room could be justified under the emergency exception, Officer Bones would be permitted to search any portion of the room where the perpetrator might be hiding or where weapons accessible to him might be found. *Warden v. Hayden*, 387 U.S. 294 (1967). Because the bundle of bills was found in plain view upon entering, it was clearly within the permissible scope of such a search and could properly be seized. In our variation, where the officer opened a night table drawer and discovered the money, that seizure would also be lawful provided it was determined that Bones was searching for weapons accessible to the fleeing suspect and was not engaged in a general search of the room.

3.   Probable cause is a necessary, but not a sufficient, condition to conduct a lawful search of a home. Thus, although the agents have probable cause to believe that criminal activity is occurring in the house and that evidence of such activity is present inside, the Fourth Amendment generally requires that a magistrate (by way of the warrant process) weigh the justification, authorize entry, and prescribe the contours of a permissible search. To circumvent this process, the circumstances must be sufficiently compelling to fit within the emergency exception. In this context the police needed facts from which they could reasonably conclude that the evidence would be destroyed or removed before they could secure a search warrant. Because it appears that such facts existed here, and because the police had probable cause to search, the emergency exception is likely applicable. See *United States v. Rubin*, 474 F.2d 262 (3d Cir. 1973) (upholding a warrantless search on similar, although less exotic, facts).

In approaching the fact-specific determination of whether the emergency exception applies, courts have considered the following factors: 1) the degree of urgency, taking into account the amount of time necessary to obtain a warrant (the availability of telephonic warrants is also weighed in this context); 2) the reasonableness of the belief that the contraband is about to be destroyed or removed; 3) the possibility of danger to the police who are watching the location to be searched; 4) common behavioral characteristics of persons involved in the particular criminal activity (big-time narcotics dealers, for example, are generally known to be heavily armed); 5) an indication by the suspects that they are aware the police are on their trail; and 6) whether the emergency arose from the action of the police themselves. *United States v. Howard*, 106 F.3d 70, 74 (5th Cir. 1997). The presence of drugs alone does not give rise to exigent circumstances justifying a warrantless entry and search.

With regard to the last factor just mentioned, the Supreme Court refused to hold that an arrest on the street can provide its own "exigent circumstance" justifying a warrantless search of the arrestee's house. *Vale v. Louisiana*, 399 U.S. 30, 35 (1970). The officers conducted a warrantless entry and search of the suspect's home after arresting him outside, thus arguably creating a risk that persons inside would destroy narcotics believed to be there. As one circuit court has observed, "an exception to the warrant requirement that allows police fearing the destruction of evidence to enter the home of an unknown suspect should be . . . supported by clearly defined indicators of exigency *that are not subject to police manipulation or abuse*." *United States v. Aquino*, 836 F.2d 1268, 1272 (10th Cir. 1988) (emphasis added).

The exigency relied upon to excuse the failure to obtain a warrant must arise in the natural course of things and not be the result of deliberate police action. Where, for example, the police knocked on the door of a person whom they had cause to believe was an armed and dangerous narcotics dealer, then kicked his door down and entered when he retreated into another room, the court rejected the argument that the officers acted properly because they feared he might retrieve a weapon or destroy the narcotics.

> [T]he government could not justify a warrantless search on the basis of exigent circumstances of its own making. Agents Byant and Keefer knew when they knocked on the patio door that, once having made their presence known to Munoz-Guerra (and possibly to other occupants) it would be necessary to conduct a security search of the premises and to restrain the condominium's inhabitants. Warrantless entry was thus a foregone conclusion the instant the agents revealed themselves to Munoz-Guerra at the patio door.

United States v. Munoz-Guerra, 788 F.2d 295, 298 (5th Cir. 1986) (citations omitted).

It should be noted that the government has the burden of demonstrating that "exigent" circumstances existed. In making this showing, the government must present something more than an unfounded belief by law enforcement officers on the scene that the suspect was suspicious or nervous. *United States v. Anderson*, 154 F.3d 1225, 1233 (10th Cir. 1998) (neither agent's belief that Anderson's child pornography collection was being stored inside the office building, nor his concern about the presence of an incinerator in the office building, nor Anderson's failure to respond to the agents knocking on the office doors justified warrantless entry). Compare *United States v. Scroger*, 98 F.3d 1256 (10th Cir. 1996) (officers' warrantless entry into defendant's residence was justified by exigent circumstances where defendant answered door holding hot plate commonly used to manufacture methamphetamine; defendant's fingertips were stained rust-colored, which was common result from methamphetamine production, residence had odor of methamphetamine production; and it was highly likely that evidence would have been destroyed if officers waited).

Getting back to our example 3, the urgent concern about the possible destruction of the purple-throated evidence arose because of the unanticipated departure and chase of the suspect. It was not the inevitable result of action by the police themselves designed to circumvent the warrant requirement. The probability is good, therefore, that the warrantless search would be held lawful within the emergency exception.

4. The police in these circumstances would be hard pressed to claim exigency. They had probable cause to arrest (and most likely to search the apartment as well) based upon the transaction that occurred on Monday together with the arrangement for the upcoming sale. There was more than sufficient time to apply for an arrest and search warrant *before* the Tuesday transaction. Because the emergency exception applies only where the circumstances are such that resort to the warrant process is not practicable given the risks of delay, the exception would not apply in this situation. See *United States v. Beltran*, 917 F.2d 641 (1st Cir. 1990).

5. The facts that support application of the emergency exception here are that 1) the police were not aware of the destination of the package until it was actually delivered; 2) the destination was the abode of a suspected drug dealer likely to be suspicious of tampering with the package; and 3) the narcotics in the package could quickly and easily be destroyed. Together with the probable cause to believe narcotics were on the premises, the exigencies of this situation would appear to justify the warrantless entry, arrest, and seizure.

If the police had information tying the package to a particular location *prior* to delivery, the excuse for circumventing the warrant process would no longer exist. See, e.g., *United States v. Duchi*, 906 F.2d 1278 (8th Cir. 1990) (emergency exception inapplicable because officers had sufficient information and time to seek warrant for location where, based on their investigation, they expected package to be delivered).

One court has articulated the standard for application of the emergency exception as follows: The police must be faced with circumstances that would cause a reasonable person to believe that entry was necessary to prevent physical harm to the officers or other persons, the destruction of relevant evidence, the escape of the suspect, or some other consequence improperly frustrating legitimate law enforcement efforts. The exigencies must be viewed from the totality of facts known to the officers at the time of the warrantless intrusion. Moreover, because the phrase "exigent circumstances" necessarily implies insufficient time to obtain a warrant, the government has the burden of showing that a warrant could not have been secured in time. See *United States v. Lindsey*, 877 F.2d 777 (9th Cir. 1989). Exigent circumstances will normally not exist where the suspects are unaware of the police surveillance or presence. See *United States v. Tobin*, 923 F.2d 1506 (11th Cir. 1991).

Caveat: Would example 5 be an appropriate case for an anticipatory search warrant? See §5.5.

§6.3 Exceptions that Require Probable Cause: Search Incident to Arrest

Unlike the generic emergency exception just discussed, the other warrant exceptions are divided along specific categorical lines and are (or at least originally were) based on the exigencies presented by a particular type of confrontation between police officer and citizen. The two most frequently encountered categories are the search incident to an arrest (discussed in this section) and the search of a motor vehicle stopped on the road (discussed in §6.4, infra).

When a police officer places an individual under arrest, there is an obvious danger that the arrestee may violently resist and use any weapon on her person or within her reach. Recognizing this, as well as the risk that evidence within the arrestee's control may be destroyed by the arrestee, courts long ago carved out an exception to the warrant requirement that permits search of the person and the area immediately surrounding the subject of an arrest. The impracticality of obtaining a search warrant in the heat of an arrest situation justifies this limited license.

The basic prerequisite for such a search is that the underlying arrest be lawful, that is, based upon probable cause to believe the subject has committed a crime (see Chapter 4) and, in the case of an arrest in a private building, that the arrest warrant be valid (see §5.5). The general rule is that the arrest must *precede* the search because it is the former that justifies the latter, not the reverse. The Court has, however, sanctioned searches as incident to an arrest where the arrest *follows* the search, but only where the police had sufficient probable cause to arrest prior to the search and merely delayed announcement of the formal arrest. See *Rawlings v. Kentucky*, 448 U.S. 98 (1980).

Based on the fundamental tenet that license to conduct a search without prior judicial approval should be strictly circumscribed by the necessities of the moment, the scope of the search incident to an arrest is limited to the person of the arrestee (including pockets) and the "grabable space" around her from which she could reach weapons or evidence. See *Chimel v. California*, 395 U.S. 752 (1969). Similarly, the search must occur at the time of the arrest; once the subject is securely in custody and the immediate exigencies of the arrest situation disappear, so too does the excuse for circumventing the warrant process. Thus a search has been deemed incident to an arrest only if it was *substantially contemporaneous* with it and was confined to the *immediate vicinity* of the arrest.[3]

Since *Chimel*, the Court has broadened the scope of the search incident exception in significant ways. First, it has increased the license to search within the grabable space by authorizing the seizure and opening of items found within that area. In *United States v. Robinson*, 414 U.S. 218 (1973), the Court held that a cigarette package found on arrestee's person could lawfully be removed and opened by the officer at the time of the arrest. An important limitation is that this search must occur *contemporaneously* with the arrest. Where agents seized a footlocker at the time of arrest but did not open it until an hour later when back at their office, the search was held unlawful. Because the exigent circumstances created by the arrest no longer existed, a warrant was required to search the contents of the private receptacle. See *United States v. Chadwick*, 433 U.S. 1 (1977). This

---

3. In one case the Court has permitted a delayed search of an arrestee's clothing under unusual circumstances. In *United States v. Edwards*, 415 U.S. 800 (1974), the seizure and search of Edwards's clothing ten hours after his arrest and placement in a jail cell was held reasonable because the delay was necessitated by the lack of any substitute clothing until the following morning. Some courts have read *Edwards* to authorize a delayed search of the suspect's clothing (but *not* effects) on a theory of reduced expectation of privacy. See, e.g., *United States v. Monclavo-Cruz*, 662 F.2d 1285, 1289–1290 (9th Cir. 1981) (warrantless search of suspect's purse at station house was not permissible under *Edwards*). But compare *United States v. Sonntag*, 684 F.2d 781 (11th Cir. 1982) (upholding delayed search of suspect's wallet).

special protection for closed suitcases, bags, and packages, which was premised on the assumption that the owner has a high expectation of privacy in them, came to be known as the "container doctrine." (More about this in §6.4.)

Second, for arrests of persons stopped in automobiles, the Court has designated the entire interior of the passenger compartment (as well as containers found there) as within the proper scope of a contemporaneous search incident to the arrest, even if the subjects have already been removed from the vehicle and thus cannot actually reach into it. In *New York v. Belton*, 453 U.S. 454 (1981), the Court held that the pockets of a jacket found on the back seat could be opened while the arrestees stood outside and away from the car. Reasoning that "articles within the relatively narrow compass of the passenger compartment of an automobile are in fact generally, even if not inevitably, within the area into which an arrestee might reach in order to grab a weapon or evidentiary item," the Court opted for a bright-line standard to guide law enforcement personnel.

Robinson and *Belton* represent an important trend in Fourth Amendment jurisprudence—the rejection of ad hoc review in favor of a uniform, standardized approach. The suspect in *Robinson*, arrested for operating a motor vehicle after his license had been revoked, argued (and the Court of Appeals agreed) that the opening of the cigarette package could not be justified by either rationale of the search incident exception. It was highly unlikely that a weapon was hidden inside and equally unlikely that evidence of the crime for which Robinson was arrested would be found inside. The Supreme Court rejected the proposition that "there must be litigated in each case the issue of whether or not there was present one of the reasons supporting the authority for a search of the person incident to a lawful arrest." 414 U.S. at 235. Recognizing that a "police officer's determination as to how and where to search the person of a suspect whom he has arrested is necessarily a quick ad hoc judgment," the Court held that the authority to search is *automatic* and does not depend on whether *in the particular case* there actually was a need to secure weapons or evidence. Id. As long as the arrest is lawful, no additional justification is required to conduct a search incident to it.[4] The Court similarly opted for the uniform

---

4. In *Gustafson v. Florida*, 414 U.S. 260 (1973), a companion case to *Robinson*, the Court upheld a search incident to an arrest for a minor traffic offense even though the officer was not mandated to take the suspect into custody but could have proceeded by way of a summons.

approach in *Belton*, observing that a "single, familiar standard is essential to guide police officers, who have only limited time and expertise to reflect on and balance the social and individual interests involved in the specific circumstances they confront." 453 U.S. at 458 (citation omitted).

The categorical right to search is, however, premised on an arrest actually occurring. A unanimous Court (in an opinion authored by Chief Justice Rehnquist) held that an officer who opts to issue a traffic citation to a suspect in lieu of an arrest, *even though a state statute authorized an arrest in the circumstances*, may not conduct a search. *Knowles v. Iowa*, 525 U.S. 113 (1998). In the absence of an arrest, neither rationale of *Robinson*—protection of the officer and prevention of the destruction of evidence—applies.

The scope of a search incident to an arrest was further expanded in *Maryland v. Buie*, 494 U.S. 325 (1990), to permit a "protective sweep" of the premises when the police make an arrest in a home. The officers are authorized to search areas (including closets and other spaces) in the immediate vicinity of the arrest from which an attack could be launched against them. Where the police have reasonable suspicion to believe they are in danger from accomplices lurking elsewhere, they may also make a cursory inspection of those other spaces, but the sweep may last no longer than is necessary to dispel the reasonable suspicion of danger (and in any event must end by the time the arrest is complete and the suspect is removed from the premises).

In response to the Court's considerable broadening of the search permitted as incident to an arrest, many states have resorted to their own laws to constrain the police.[5]

EXAMPLES

1. In which of the following circumstances has the officer conducted a lawful search incident to an arrest?

    a. Officer Keystone, with a hunch that Patty Pedestrian is carrying narcotics in her sports bag, stops her and searches the bag. The officer finds cocaine and places Patty under arrest.

---

5. Massachusetts, for example, enacted the following statute, which reflects the original rationale behind searches incident to arrest: "A search conducted incident to an arrest may be made only for the purposes of seizing fruits, instrumentalities, contraband, and other evidence of the crime for which the arrest has been made, in order to prevent its destruction or concealment; and removing any weapon the arrestee might use to resist arrest or effect his escape." Mass. Gen. L. ch. 276, §1.

    b. Officer Keystone, with probable cause to believe that Patty Pedestrian is carrying unlawful narcotics in her sports bag, stops her and searches the bag. The officer finds cocaine and places Patty under arrest.

    c. Officer Keystone, with probable cause to believe that Patty Pedestrian is carrying narcotics in her sports bag, stops her and places her under arrest. The officer seizes the bag and opens it 20 minutes later at the police station.

2. Ned Numbers, an accountant, is suspected of masterminding a major tax fraud scheme. Armed with a warrant for his arrest, Internal Revenue Service (IRS) agents entered his 15-room home in Scarsdale, found Ned sitting at his desk in the study, and placed him under arrest. While one agent removed Ned from the chair, frisked him, and cuffed him, a second opened the drawers of his desk. A list of clients (many of whom were suspected of participation in the fraud scheme) was found in Ned's coat pocket, and an illegally imported pistol was discovered in his desk drawer. Could the agents lawfully seize these items?

3. Speedy was observed driving above the speed limit by Officer Radar and was pulled over. Radar took Speedy's license and registration and went back to her cruiser to run a routine computer check, which revealed that there was an outstanding warrant for Speedy's arrest for burglary. Radar informed Speedy that he was under arrest, handcuffed him, and placed him in the back seat of the cruiser. The officer then returned to Speedy's vehicle and searched the entire passenger compartment. She found burglar's tools in a closed brown paper bag in the back seat, opened the glove compartment and found a pistol, and then searched the trunk and discovered an assault rifle. Which, if any, of these items were lawfully seized? What if the assault rifle had been found in the car's hatchback instead of the trunk?

4. Two police officers arrived at Addison's home with a warrant for his arrest on charges of armed bank robbery. They were informed by the gardener that Addison was inside with two friends. The officers entered the home and encountered Addison as he was on his way upstairs from the basement. He was placed under arrest in the kitchen, and one of the officers went down to the basement, where he observed a pistol on a shelf near the furnace. May this weapon be lawfully seized? What if the gun had been discovered in the closed drawer of a tool cabinet?

EXPLANATIONS

1a. "It is axiomatic that an incident search may not precede an arrest and serve as part of its justification." *Smith v. Ohio*, 494 U.S. 541, 543 (1990) (quoting *Sibron v. New York*, 392 U.S. 40, 63 (1968)). The purpose of the exception is to permit the officer to protect herself and prevent the destruction of evidence while effecting a lawful arrest, *not* to allow searches that then provide the cause to arrest. Keystone's action here violated the Fourth Amendment. See *United States v. Rivera*, 867 F.2d 1261 (10th Cir. 1989) (search invalidated because probable cause to arrest did not exist until it was already underway).

1b. Because the officer had sufficient justification to arrest *prior to* the search of the bag, and thus information obtained through the search is not being used to justify the arrest, the officer's action here would be lawful. See *Rawlings v. Kentucky*, 448 U.S. 98 (1980). With probable cause to arrest already existing, the officer could have chosen to place Patty under formal arrest before he searched the bag, but he was not required to do so. The sequence here does not circumvent the requirement for proper justification prior to the arrest, and *Rawlings* gives the police discretion to delay the formal arrest until the search is conducted.

With regard to opening the sports bag, the officer is permitted to contemporaneously seize and open a container found on the arrestee or within the grabbable space around her. See *United States v. Robinson*, 414 U.S. 218 (1973).

1c. The right to open containers found on or near the person of the arrestee as part of the search incident applies only if done contemporaneously with the arrest. See *United States v. Chadwick*, 433 U.S. 1 (1977). Because the exigency no longer exists at the station house, and there is a reasonable expectation of privacy in containers such as sports bags, a warrant must be obtained in order to open the bag. See, e.g., *United States v. Monclavo-Cruz*, 662 F.2d 1285 (9th Cir. 1981) (warrantless search of arrestee's purse in agent's office one hour after arrest was not permissible).

2. A case-by-case approach to the search incident doctrine would require a determination as to whether in the context of the *particular* arrest, the police had reason to fear the arrestee was armed and dangerous, would reach for a weapon, or would seek to destroy evidence nearby. Such an approach was suggested by Justice

Marshall in dissent in *Robinson*. The Court opted instead for a *categorical* approach, which automatically permits a search (coincident with a lawful arrest) of both the subject and the grabbable space no matter who the subject is or what the underlying offense is. Thus Ned could not successfully argue that the search here was unlawful because the agents had no reasonable basis to fear that he (a mild and meek accountant) was armed or would seek to destroy evidence within his grasp. As long as the arrest warrant was valid, then the entry into his home, the arrest, and the search were all lawful.

With regard to the pistol, if Ned were already cuffed at the time the desk was searched he could argue that the authority to search the space around him had expired because he could no longer reach out. Even if the cuffing had not been accomplished yet, Ned could argue that he was no longer within arm's reach of the desk. The courts have, however, been reluctant to second-guess officers as to the precise timing and contours of a search incident. Illustrative is the observation of the Eighth Circuit Court of Appeals: " A warrantless search incident to an arrest may be valid even though a court, operating with the benefit of hindsight in an environment well removed from the scene of the arrest, doubts that the defendant could have reached the items seized during the search." *United States v. Lucas*, 898 F.2d 606, 609 (8th Cir. 1990). See also *United States v. Abdul-Saboor*, 85 F.3d 664 (D.C. Cir. 1996), in which defendant was taken into custody in the bedroom, then removed from the room and handcuffed in a chair several feet away, at which time the bedroom was searched. Upholding the search, the D.C. Circuit held that a search is conducted incident to an arrest so long as it is an "integral part of a lawful custodial arrest process." Courts should not focus upon whether the suspect could have reached the area, but rather whether the arrest and search are so separated in time or by intervening events that the latter cannot fairly be said to have been incident to the former. See also *In re Sealed Case*, 153 F.3d 759 (D.C. Cir. 1998)

In *United States v. Lucas*, supra, the subject was seated at the kitchen table with two other men as the officers entered to arrest him. He began to rise, and one officer attempted to apprehend him. By the time the officer reached Lucas, the latter's hand was within inches of a cabinet door. A struggle ensued on the floor, and Lucas was finally cuffed and moved into the living room. At the same time, another officer opened the cabinet that Lucas had been attempting to reach and found a pistol inside. Lucas argued that the gun had been unlawfully seized because he had already been handcuffed and removed from the kitchen at the time. Observing that the two other men in the kitchen were being monitored by another officer but had not been cuffed, the court held that the warrantless search was valid.

Other courts have upheld similar searches where the subject had already been handcuffed, even where no confederates were present at the scene. In *United States v. Queen*, 847 F.2d 346, 354 (7th Cir. 1988), the subject was arrested while hiding in a closet, then frisked, handcuffed, and removed from the room. An agent then returned to the closet and seized a loaded revolver. Conceding that the possibility that Queen could have gained access to the weapon at that point was remote at best, the Seventh Circuit nonetheless observed that courts "should not second-guess the agents' on-the-scene determination" and upheld the search as incident to the arrest. See also *United States v. Hudson*, 100 F.3d 1409, 1419 (9th Cir. 1996) (defendant handcuffed and removed from house); *United States v. Mitchell*, 64 F.3d 1105, 1110 (7th Cir. 1995) (defendant handcuffed during search of briefcase); *United States v. Bennett*, 908 F.2d 189 (7th Cir. 1990) (upholding a search of defendants' luggage despite the fact that the subjects were handcuffed and held against the wall of the room); *United States v. Cotton*, 751 F.2d 1146 (10th Cir. 1985) (arrestees were handcuffed and guarded by officers while search was conducted); *United States v. Palumbo*, 735 F.2d 1095 (8th Cir. 1984) (arrestee handcuffed and surrounded by officers while room was searched). But compare *United States v. Lyons*, 706 F.2d 321, 329–330 (D.C. Cir. 1983) (holding that the postarrest search of a coat found in the closet of the suspect's hotel room exceeded constitutional bounds because Lyons was seated handcuffed on a chair at the far end of the wall from the closet, and there were six officers and no confederates in the room).

While Ned's contention that the search of the desk exceeded the proper scope of a search incident may be persuasive given the rationale of *Chimel v. California*, the courts seem quite willing to give the police the benefit of the doubt in such situations.

3. Because the suspect was handcuffed and in a police vehicle, it might appear that the search could not be justified as a search of the immediate vicinity incident to the arrest. In *New York v. Bel-*

ton, 453 U.S. 454 (1981), however, the Court resolved doubts about what constitutes the grabbable space in the context of arrests of automobile occupants by adopting a bright-line rule: The police may search the entire passenger compartment of the vehicle (as well as containers found therein) contemporaneous with a lawful arrest of the occupant. *Belton* would thus seem to authorize the seizure of the burglar tools as well as the pistol, because both were found in containers that were located in the passenger compartment. The trunk, however, is off-limits in a *Belton* search, apparently because it is accessible to occupants only by exiting the vehicle. Thus the rifle was not lawfully seized. If, as the variation suggests, the rifle had been found in the hatchback area, its seizure would probably be deemed lawful. Courts have regarded the hatchback area as an extension of the passenger compartment because occupants can reach it without leaving the car. See, e.g., *United States v. Russell*, 670 F.2d 323 (D.C. Cir. 1982); *Connecticut v. Delossantos*, 211 Conn. 258 (1989).

The twist in our example is that the suspect was not only removed from the vehicle, as in *Belton*, but was handcuffed and secured in the back of the police cruiser. Does the bright-line rule permit a search in such a situation, where the possibility that the arrestee can gain access to the passenger compartment is virtually nonexistent? While the purpose of a standardized approach is to avoid case-by-case adjudication, is Speedy's case simply off the *Belton* scale?

Not surprisingly, the courts are split on this issue. Several decisions uphold searches of the passenger compartment even after the suspect has been cuffed and removed from the immediate vicinity of the vehicle. See *United States v. Karlin*, 852 F.2d 968, 970–972 (7th Cir. 1988) ("Karlin seeks to distinguish *Belton* on the ground that the arrestees in that case appear to have been made less secure than he [Karlin was cuffed and secured in the rear of the police car], and somewhat closer to their car. If those differences in degree are to control, the Court's preference for a straight-forward rule for guidance of police officers and avoidance of hindsight determinations in litigation would be frustrated. . . . We think, under *Belton*, such a search is deemed reasonable, without determining whether the officer had rendered Karlin incapable of reaching into the van."); *United States v. Cotton*, 751 F.2d 1146, 1148–1149 (10th Cir. 1985) ("The Supreme Court expresses quite clearly its goal to formulate a workable rule whereby an officer in the field may be able to evaluate the circumstances surrounding a lawful arrest to determine whether seizure of items in the immediate area of the arrestee is called for. . . . The rule as stated does not require the arresting officer to undergo a detailed analysis at the time of arrest, of whether the arrestee, handcuffed or not, could reach into the car to seize some item within it, either as a weapon or to destroy evidence. . . . In summary, we find that where an officer has made a lawful arrest of a suspect in an automobile, he may seize articles found within the interior of the automobile as part of a search incident to a lawful arrest, *even where the arrestee is outside the vehicle and handcuffed*." (emphasis added)). Contrast *United States v. Lugo*, 978 F.2d 631 (10th Cir. 1992), where defendant was arrested for driving after suspension of license and improper lane usage. He was handcuffed and placed in the back of the patrol car when the search of the truck began. The search produced a gun. An officer later testified that "the gun wasn't an immediate threat to me." The court found the search was not justified as a search of the immediate vicinity incident to arrest. Once Lugo had been taken from the scene, there was obviously no threat that he might reach in his vehicle and grab a weapon or destroy evidence. Thus the rationale for a search incident to arrest had evaporated.

One court has even upheld a warrantless search of a vehicle after the suspect abandoned it, fled on foot, and was apprehended one block from the vehicle. See *United States v. Arango*, 879 F.2d 1501 (7th Cir. 1989). After his arrest, Arango was brought back to the vehicle and it was searched at that point. In ruling that the search was lawful as incident to the arrest, the court noted that there was nothing in the record to indicate that the defendant had been brought back to the car in order to justify searching it; rather the arresting officer returned to the scene to assist an injured comrade. But compare *United States v. Fafowora*, 865 F.2d 360 (D.C. Cir. 1989) (ruling unlawful the search of arrestees' vehicle where they had parked it and were walking away at the time of their arrest, holding that *Belton* does not apply if the arrest occurs away from the immediate area of the vehicle).

Some courts are more willing to take particular circumstances into account. *United States v. Vasey*, 834 F.2d 782, 786–787 (9th Cir. 1987) held unlawful a search of defendant's car 30 minutes after he was arrested, handcuffed, and placed in the police vehicle. The court observed: "The *Belton* Court did not completely abandon Fourth Amendment privacy rights at the expense of establishing a bright line test for law enforcement personnel. . . . The *Belton* holding does have limits and those limits were exceeded here. . . . It was readily apparent to the officers and to this court that Vasey had virtually no opportunity to reach into the vehicle at the time the search occurred.".

If the court in our example were willing to look at the particular context of the search of Speedy's car, it would be hard pressed to conclude realistically that he had access to the passenger compartment at the time of the search. Given the inclination of the courts to take the *Belton* bright-line quite seriously, however, the search would in all likelihood be upheld.

4. *Maryland v. Buie*, 494 U.S. 325 (1990) permits the officers to take two precautionary steps when effecting a home arrest: 1) they may, without any additional justification, look in closets and other spaces immediately adjoining the place of the arrest from which persons might be hiding and might attack them; and 2) beyond that confined area, they may also make a limited protective sweep of other portions of the premises if and only if they have *reasonable suspicion* (that is, articulable facts, which, together with rational inferences from those facts, would warrant a reasonably prudent officer in believing) that persons posing a danger were present there. This sweep is limited in scope to a cursory inspection of those spaces where a person might be found and may last no longer than is necessary to dispel the suspicion.

In our example, the basement area is outside the confined space that the officers may automatically inspect adjacent to the arrest. It would therefore be necessary for them to have specific facts establishing a reasonable suspicion that persons posing a danger were in the basement. The officers knew only that two friends were present with Addison in the home, and that fact would appear inadequate to justify a sweep of the basement. If the officers had information that accomplices from the robbery were present, that would probably suffice.

A determination that the officers did have reasonable suspicion that persons posing a danger were in the basement would justify a cursory sweep of the area for such persons. The weapon in plain view on the shelf would thus be fair game to seize. See §6.8. The officers would not, however, be permitted to open the drawers of a tool chest (where a person obviously could not hide). If the gun had been found there, its seizure would be unlawful.

It should be noted that even if an arrest occurs immediately outside the home, a number of circuits would permit a cursory sweep if the officers have reasonable suspicion that individuals posing a danger to the arrest scene are inside the home. See, e.g., *Sharrar v. Felsing*, 128 F.3d 810, 823–824 (3d Cir. 1997); *United States v. Colbert*, 76 F.3d 773 (6th Cir. 1996).

§6.4 Exceptions that Require Probable Cause: The Automobile Search Exception and the Container Doctrine

Given the central role that the automobile plays in American society as well as its importance in the everyday activities of most citizens, it is not surprising that motor vehicles are a major focus of law enforcement attention. Ever since Prohibition, cars have been closely associated with certain types of criminal activity—from the transportation of bootleg liquor to the importation of illegal aliens. Beginning in the 1920s the courts have increasingly opened the automobile to warrantless search on the basis of several different rationales.

Recognizing the impracticability of obtaining a warrant to search an automobile stopped by police on the open road, the Court in *Carroll v. United States*, 267 U.S. 132 (1925), held that a warrantless search could be conducted if the officers had *probable cause to believe there was contraband or other evidence of criminal activity in the vehicle.* While *Carroll* was premised on the concern that because of their mobility cars were not likely to remain in place while the police obtained a warrant, subsequent decisions have expanded the automobile exception to encompass searches conducted under circumstances where the vehicle has been immobilized and secured. Indeed, by 1999, the Court had explicitly abandoned all reliance on exigency to justify the warrantless automobile search. See *Maryland v. Dyson*, 527 U.S. 465 (1999) (probable cause is only requirement).

In *Chambers v. Maroney*, 399 U.S. 42 (1970), the Court upheld the warrantless search of a car that had been stopped on the road but was searched *subsequently* at the police station, after it had been seized and its occupants arrested and taken into custody. The Court ruled that since the police had probable cause to believe the car contained evidence of a recent robbery, and thus could have lawfully searched it when they stopped it (under *Carroll*), it was constitutionally permissible to conduct the delayed search as well. The Court justified this extension by reference to the nature of the intrusion:

> Arguably, because of the preference for a magistrate's judgment, only the immobilization of the car should be permitted until a search warrant is obtained; arguably, only the "lesser" intrusion is permissible until the magistrate authorizes the "greater." But which is the "greater" and which is the "lesser" intrusion is itself a debatable question and the answer may depend upon a variety of circumstances. For constitutional purposes, we see no difference between on the one hand seizing and holding a car before presenting the probable cause issue to a magistrate and on the other hand carrying out an immediate search without a warrant. Given probable cause to search, either course is reasonable under the Fourth Amendment.

399 U.S. at 51–52.

This dubious equation of the *seizure* of an automobile with the *search* of its contents (which Justice Harlan in dissent characterized as "ignor[ing] the framework of our past decisions circumscribing the scope of permissible search without a warrant" and limiting the scope to the exigency presented, 399 U.S. at 61), pointed the way to the contemporary rationale of the automobile search exception: reduced expectation of privacy.

While *Carroll* and *Chambers* subjected cars to warrantless search (either on the scene or later) when they are stopped on the road and the police have probable cause to believe seizable items are present, *United States v. Ross*, 456 U.S. 798 (1982), and *California v. Acevedo*, 500 U.S. 565 (1991), defined the broad scope of the permissible search. Premised on the assumption that citizens have considerably less privacy expectation in their automobiles than in their homes (because cars travel the open roads and are subject to government license and regulation), these cases permit the warrantless search of the entire automobile as well as containers found within it, limited only by the size and nature of the items for which there is probable cause to search.

In *Ross* the police had probable cause (based on an informant's tip) to believe that narcotics were hidden in Ross's automobile. After stopping the vehicle, they searched it on the scene. In the trunk the police located a paper bag, which they opened to find heroin. They later conducted a second and more thorough search of the car at the station. During this later search they located a leather pouch in the trunk, which they opened to find a considerable amount of cash. The lower court, relying on the *Chadwick*[6] rule that containers are entitled to special protection under the Fourth Amendment because of their owner's heightened expectation of privacy, held that neither the narcotics nor the cash were admissible against Ross. The Supreme Court reversed, holding that if there is probable cause to search a stopped vehicle, that search may extend to *any part of the car* (for example, trunk, glove compartment, interior of upholstered seats) *and any packages, luggage, or other containers* that might contain the object of the search. Probable cause to believe a van is transporting illegal aliens or stolen televisions would not, for example, justify search of the glove compartment or a briefcase found on the front seat. But probable cause to believe the van is carrying narcotics subjects it (and containers in it) to a probing examination.

Acevedo resolved a question left open in *Ross* and held that the police are *not* required to obtain a warrant to open a container found in a car even if their probable cause to search is limited to just that container and not the car itself. Overruling the *Chadwick-Sanders* rule as it applied to automobiles, *Acevedo* represents the triumph of the automobile exception over the more protective container doctrine. With probable cause to believe that a paper bag in Acevedo's car contained narcotics but lacking cause to search the rest of the car, officers stopped the car, seized the bag, and opened it. The lower courts suppressed the narcotics found in the bag, but the Supreme Court reversed. In a reexamination of the law applicable to the search of a closed container found in an automobile, the Court opted for a clear and unequivocal guideline: The police may search an automobile and any containers within it when they have probable cause to believe contraband or evidence of crime is present anywhere inside. The only remaining limit on scope of the permissible search derives from the size and shape of the items sought—the police may search only where such items may be hidden. Moreover, it does not matter that the container in question is known to the officer to be the property of a

---

6. See §6.3. The Court had extended *United States v. Chadwick* in *Arkansas v. Sanders*, 442 U.S. 753 (1979), which held that a warrant was required to search a container found in a motor vehicle if the probable cause to search was directed only at the container and not the car itself. Police had observed Sanders place a suitcase, which they believed contained marijuana, in the trunk of a taxi cab; they followed and stopped the cab, located the suitcase, and opened it. The mere fact that the suitcase was present in an automobile (which they did not have cause to search) did not, the Court held, deprive its owner of the protection of the warrant requirement for the container.

passenger not suspected of criminal activity: Given the reduced expectation of privacy with regard to property transported in cars (as the Court sees it), officers with probable cause to search a car may inspect a passenger's belongings as long as they are capable of concealing the object of the search. *Wyoming v. Houghton*, 526 U.S. 295 (1999).

Two final points regarding the automobile exception should be noted. First, it has been applied to other moving vehicles such as boats and airplanes because of their mobility and the diminished privacy expectation associated with them (as compared to the home). Indeed, a mobile home parked in a parking lot but not fixed to the ground is subject to search under the automobile exception to the warrant requirement. See *California v. Carney*, 471 U.S. 386 (1985). Second, the exception is not the exclusive means of conducting a lawful warrantless search of a vehicle. Other exceptions such as the search incident to an arrest (see §6.3) and the inventory search (see §6.6 and example 4 in §4.5) may also be applicable.

Figure 6–1 summarizes the automobile search exception.

EXAMPLES

In which of the following circumstances has the officer conducted a lawful search under the automobile exception?

a. The police have probable cause to believe Driver had supplied the weapons used by the perpetrators in a bank robbery two weeks before. The officers stop Driver's car, place him under arrest for sale of unlawful weapons, and search the entire vehicle. In the trunk they discover documentary evidence of the weapons deal.

b. Now assume that the police have probable cause to believe that Driver is on his way to a meeting with unknown persons for the purpose of selling illegal weapons to them. They stop his car, place him under arrest, and search the car. In the trunk they find a large green duffel bag, which they open to discover assault rifles.

c. Would it matter in example b if, instead of searching the car at the scene, the officers had it towed to the police garage and searched it there later that day?

d. Would it matter in example b if, instead of probable cause to believe weapons were present *somewhere* in the vehicle, the information known to the police was specifically that the weapons were in the green duffel bag?

e. Would it matter in example b if, instead of probable cause to believe that Driver was on his way to sell rifles, the police had prob-

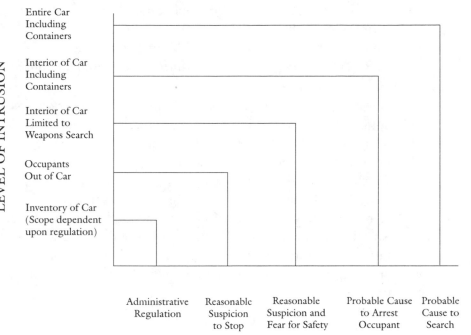

LEVEL OF INTRUSION

Entire Car
Including
Containers

Interior of Car
Including
Containers

Interior of Car
Limited to
Weapons Search

Occupants
Out of Car

Inventory of Car
(Scope dependent
upon regulation)

Administrative
Regulation

Reasonable
Suspicion
to Stop

Reasonable
Suspicion and
Fear for Safety

Probable Cause
to Arrest
Occupant

Probable
Cause to
Search

JUSTIFICATION

Figure 6–1: Automobile Search

able cause to believe he was in possession of a stolen projection television?

EXPLANATIONS

a. The lawful arrest of Driver permits the officers to search the car's passenger compartment, but *not* the trunk, incident to the arrest. See §6.3. To fit within the automobile exception, which would permit search of any part of the car (and any containers) where the items sought might be found, the officers need probable cause to believe contraband or evidence of crime will be found within. In our problem, there is no indication that the police had any cause to believe such items would be found in the vehicle. The alleged crime had occurred two weeks before, and no information ties the car to current criminal activity. In the absence of probable cause to search, the automobile exception does not apply and the search of the trunk would be unlawful.

b. The probable cause to arrest Driver for the impending transaction also provides a basis for concluding that the illegal weapons are present in the vehicle. This probable cause permits a search of the entire vehicle wherever the weapons may be hidden, including the trunk and the duffel bag found within the trunk. See *United States v. Ross*, 456 U.S. 798 (1982); *California v. Acevedo*, 500 U.S. 565 (1991).

c.   While the original rationale for the automobile exception was the impracticality of obtaining a warrant to search a car stopped on the open road and thus capable of being driven off, subsequent decisions discussed above make clear that if there is probable cause to search the car, the police have the option of searching it on the scene *or* impounding it and searching it at a later time. The delayed-search option was made available by the Court even though there is no longer any practical impediment to obtaining a warrant because the present rationale for the automobile exception is rooted in the diminished expectation of privacy inherent in a car compared to a home.

Reference to the original rationale can still occasionally be found in the case law. In *United States v. Williams*, 827 F. Supp. 641 (D. Or. 1993), for example, the engine of the defendant's car had frozen so he had left the vehicle in a repair garage. Because of a previous money dispute with the defendant, the garage owner told police he would not release the car to the defendant. The police also knew the garage was locked and the defendant thus had no access to the car. Could the police conduct a warrantless search of the car if they had probable cause that contraband or other evidence of criminal activity was in the car? The court answered no: "A primary justification for the vehicle exception, the inherent mobility of motor vehicles, is not present here. Without mobility or other exigent circumstances, the government may not invoke the vehicle exception to the warrant requirement." Id. at 645. Contrast *United States v. Hatley*, 999 F.2d 392 (9th Cir. 1993), where although defendant's car was inoperable in his driveway, it appeared to be mobile. If it is reasonable for the officer to believe the car is operable, the court held, the vehicle exception applies.

d.   The distinction between probable cause to search the car and probable cause to search only a container within the car is no longer of significance. Rejecting the distinction that had been drawn in *Chadwick* and *Sanders*, *Acevedo* adopts a uniform rule that permits the search of the entire car, including containers, as long as there is probable cause to believe items related to crime will be found in the place searched.

It should be pointed out that some states interpreting their own constitutions have continued to follow the *Chadwick-Sanders* line of cases. In *State v. Savva*, 616 A.2d 774 (Vt. 1991), for example, the Vermont Supreme Court recognized "a separate and higher expectation of privacy for containers used to transport personal possessions than for objects exposed to plain view within an automobile's interior." The court held that police needed a warrant to search a brown paper bag in the hatchback of a car.

e.   The only remaining limit on the scope of a search conducted pursuant to the automobile exception is defined by the size and nature of the items for which there is probable cause to search. Because a projection television could not be hidden in a duffel bag, opening the bag would not be lawful.

§6.5   Exceptions that Require Reasonable Suspicion: Stop and Frisk and Investigative Detentions

As discussed in Chapter 4, police action such as a stop and frisk that is less intrusive than a full-blown arrest or search may be conducted without a warrant on a showing that the officer had justification amounting to reasonable suspicion. The impracticability of obtaining a warrant in such circumstances is obvious. The permissible scope of the intrusion as well as related issues are discussed in §§4.2–4.4.

§6.6   Exceptions that Require Administrative Justification: Administrative and Inventory Searches

As discussed in Chapter 4, administrative searches are those whose primary purpose is noncriminal, such as safety code inspections. Because this governmental conduct nonetheless intrudes on the citizen's privacy and can uncover evidence that can be used in a criminal trial, the Fourth Amendment is implicated. Having examined the nature of the nonspecific justification required for such searches in Chapter 4, we will now consider the applicability of the warrant requirement.

In its early administrative search cases, the Court indicated a strong preference for warrants. *Camara v. Municipal Court*, 387 U.S. 523 (1967), and *See v. City of Seattle*, 387 U.S. 541 (1967), imposed a requirement for a warrant prior to health and safety inspections of dwellings and commercial premises.[7] The Court observed that requiring a warrant would not frustrate the government purpose because code violations could not be corrected in the time needed to secure a warrant. Subsequent cases have recognized numerous exceptions to the warrant requirement where delay might jeopardize the efficacy of the enforcement scheme. In *United States v. Biswell*, 406 U.S. 311 (1972), for example, the Court authorized warrantless inspections of gun dealers because illegal weapons could be quickly removed.

Similar to the doctrinal evolution we have witnessed in the automobile search exception, the impracticability rationale underlying exceptions to the administrative warrant requirement has given way to a diminished privacy rationale. Pervasively regulated businesses such as gun dealerships are deemed to engender lesser legitimate privacy expectations among their owners, who have implicitly consented to strict governmental scrutiny. "When a dealer chooses to engage in this pervasively regulated business and to accept a federal license, he does so with the knowledge that his business records, firearms, and ammunition will be subject to effective inspection." *Biswell*, 406 U.S. at 316. More recently, the Court explained in dispensing with the requirement for a warrant prior to statutory inspection of automobile junkyards: "Because the owner or operator of commercial premises in a 'closely regulated' industry has a reduced expectation of privacy, the warrant and probable cause requirements, which fulfill the traditional Fourth Amendment standard of reasonableness for a government search, have lessened application in this context." *New York v. Burger*, 482 U.S. 691, 701 (1987).

In determining whether a particular industry is "pervasively regulated" and thus subject to warrantless searches under a statutory administrative scheme, the Court looks to the history of regulation in the industry as well as the hazardous nature of the work. The Court has thus required a warrant prior to Occupational Safety and Health Act (OSHA) inspections because of the absence of a long tradition of close government supervision in that area. See *Marshall v. Barlow's Inc.*, 436 U.S. 307 (1978). The mining industry, which has been sub-

---

7. Administrative warrants issue on the basis of something other than traditional probable cause. See §§4.5 and 5.4.

ject to government regulation and involves hazardous work, could appropriately be subjected to warrantless inspections under a legislative safety program. See *Donovan v. Dewey*, 452 U.S. 594 (1981).

In recent years the Court has been somewhat expansive in classifying businesses as pervasively regulated. The automobile junkyard business has, for example, been placed in this category, prompting the dissenters to protest: "If New York City's administrative scheme renders the vehicle-dismantling business closely regulated, few businesses will escape such a finding. Under these circumstances, the warrant requirement is the exception not the rule." See *New York v. Burger, supra*, 482 U.S. at 721.

Exceptions to the warrant requirement have been carved out in other noncriminal contexts discussed in §4.5. In the "special needs" cases it has been held that there is no requirement for a warrant when a school principal searches a student's purse for drugs,[8] a supervisor searches a government employee's office for evidence of professional misconduct,[9] or a probation officer searches a probationer's home.[10] In holding that no warrant is necessary to conduct drug screening of employees in safety sensitive or narcotic interdiction jobs, the Court observed that a warrant requirement would frustrate the objective of the testing program because evidence of drugs and alcohol in the body dissipates rapidly. *Skinner v. Railway Labor Executives Association, 489 U.S. 602 (1989); National Treasury Employees Union v. Von Raab, 489 U.S. 656 (1989).*

The inventory search exception also permits warrantless examination of impounded automobiles and personal effects. *Colorado v. Bertine*, 479 U.S. 367 (1987); *Illinois v. Lafayette*, 462 U.S. 640 (1983). See §6.4.

§6.7 Warrantless Intrusion Requiring No Justification: The Consent Doctrine

An individual who is protected by a constitutional right may, of course, waive such protection. Just as she may relinquish her Sixth Amendment right to counsel, she may choose not to assert her Fourth Amendment right against unreasonable search and seizure. If there is

---

8. *New Jersey v. TLO*, 469 U.S. 325 (1985).
9. *O'Connor v. Ortega*, 480 U.S. 709 (1987).
10. *Griffin v. Wisconsin*, 483 U.S. 868 (1987).

a valid waiver, the police may proceed uninhibited by *any* of the requirements of that amendment; they may search *without a warrant or justification*, and the *scope* of such search is proscribed only by whatever limits the consenting individual may delineate.

Consent must be *voluntary* to be valid—a coerced waiver at the point of a gun is not an effective abandonment of any constitutional right. Unlike waivers of rights protected by the Fifth and Sixth Amendments, however, a Fourth Amendment waiver need not also be knowing and intelligent. We will see in Chapter 9, for example, that a valid waiver of one's privilege against self-incrimination can occur only after the subject has been specifically informed of the right to remain silent and to counsel, and after she indicates an understanding of those rights.

In contrast, a valid waiver of Fourth Amendment rights is *not* dependent on a showing that the consenter was informed of or understood that she had a right to refuse. In *Schneckloth v. Bustamonte*, 412 U.S. 218 (1973), the occupants of an automobile stopped by police were asked by the officer if he could search the car, one of whom agreed. Rejecting the position that knowledge of the right to refuse is a prerequisite for an effective consent,[11] the Court instead adopted a voluntariness standard evaluated on the basis of the totality of the circumstances (a similar standard applies to confessions, see Chapter 8). Courts are to look to the tactics used by the police to secure consent as well as the particular vulnerabilities of the subject (for example, age, intelligence, level of education, emotional state) to determine whether the consent was coerced or voluntary. Knowledge of the right to "Just Say No" is a factor, but is not by itself determinative in the analysis.

The Court reaffirmed *Schneckloth v. Bustamonte* in another case involving search of an automobile. In *Ohio v. Robinette*, 519 U.S. 33 (1996), a driver was lawfully stopped for speeding and received a verbal warning. After returning the motorist's license, the officer asked for and obtained consent to search the entire car, in the course of which drugs were found. Overturning the Supreme Court of Ohio, which had reversed the defendant's conviction and established a bright-line prerequisite that a citizen must be informed of the right to leave before interrogation may occur or consent be validly obtained, the Court

---

11. In his dissent, Justice Marshall complained that this rejection permitted the police "to capitalize on the ignorance of citizens so as to accomplish by subterfuge what they could not achieve by relying only on the knowing relinquishment of constitutional rights." 412 U.S. at 288.

emphasized again that consent is to be determined from a fact-specific review of the totality of circumstances.

While failure to inform the subject of the right to refuse is not fatal to the validity of her consent, the fact that the police *did* so inform the subject is a strong factor pointing toward the conclusion that the consent was voluntary. In *Florida v. Bostick*, 501 U.S. 429 (1991), the drug sweep case discussed infra, the Court found it "particularly worth noting" that the police specifically advised Bostick that he had the right to refuse consent to search his luggage. See also *United States v. Mendenhall*, 446 U.S. 544 (1980) (in concluding that consent was voluntary the Court considered it "highly relevant" that defendant had been told twice of her right to refuse before she gave her consent to a search). Although the fact that the subject is in custody is relevant in determining voluntariness, custody by itself does not render consent invalid. See *United States v. Watson*, 423 U.S. 411 (1976) (defendant's postarrest consent to search his car was effective).

Because it need not be demonstrated that the waiver was knowing and intelligent as well as voluntary, it is considerably easier for the government to secure a valid waiver of Fourth Amendment rights than is the case with other constitutional protections. The Court has explained this difference in part by emphasizing the practical importance of the consent search to law enforcement work: "In situations where the police have some evidence of illicit activity, but lack probable cause to arrest or search, a search authorized by valid consent may be the only means of obtaining important and reliable evidence." *Schneckloth v. Bustamonte*, supra, 412 U.S. at 227. It would be "thoroughly impractical to impose on the normal consent search the detailed requirements of an effective warning," and "unrealistic to require police officers to always inform detainees that they are free to go before a consent to search may be deemed voluntary." *Ohio v. Robinette*, supra, 519 U.S. at 39.

Moreover, the Court has distinguished the rights protected by the Fourth Amendment from other constitutional rights. The rights to counsel, to a jury trial, and against compulsory self-incrimination, the Court has reasoned, affect the fundamental fairness of the criminal trial, thus making it appropriate to apply a strict standard of waiver to them. The protections against unreasonable search and seizure are "of a wholly different order, and have nothing whatever to do with promoting the fair ascertainment of truth at a criminal trial." *Schneckloth v. Bustamonte*, supra, 412 U.S. at 242. A more lenient standard of waiver is thus deemed appropriate.

To be voluntary, the consent to search must not be the product of official threats, pressure, intimidation, or harassment. Mere submission to authority does not constitute consent. In *Bumper v. North Carolina*, 391 U.S. 543 (1968), for example, the Court held unlawful a search predicated upon the "consent" of a 66-year-old black woman confronted by four white police officers who represented to her (apparently falsely) that they had a warrant to search.

The Court has held that the appropriate inquiry in determining the voluntariness of a consent is whether a reasonable person in the subject's position would have felt free to decline the officers' request. See *Florida v. Bostick*, 501 U.S. 429 (1991). Bostick was a bus passenger confronted by armed officers dressed in green "raid" jackets who were "sweeping" the bus for drugs; when they displayed their badges and asked if they could search his luggage, he agreed. Rejecting the state supreme court's conclusion that such confrontations involve an intimidating show of authority and thus are per se coercive, the Court remanded for application of the reasonable person standard. "The Fourth Amendment," the Court reminded, "proscribes unreasonable searches and seizures; it does not proscribe voluntary cooperation. The cramped confines of a bus are [but] one relevant factor that should be considered in evaluating whether a passenger's consent is voluntary." 501 U.S. at 434. Other factors to be considered on remand militating in favor of a conclusion that Bostick's consent was valid were that he had been advised by the officers that he could refuse their request, and that the officers did not draw their guns or threaten him. See also *United States v. Washington*, 151 F.3d 1354 (11th Cir. 1998) (although there is no per se rule requiring bus passengers to be informed of their constitutional rights before consent to search luggage is requested, the circumstances of the instant search required some indication to passengers that their cooperation was voluntary).

Waiver of Fourth Amendment rights can be made by the person whose property is searched *or* by a third party who shares common authority over and access to the property. One of two cousins who shared use of a duffel bag could, for example, consent to its search and thus waive the rights of the other. See *Frazier v. Cupp*, 394 U.S. 731 (1969). Similarly a girlfriend who shared defendant's bedroom could consent to its search, thereby waiving his rights. See *United States v. Matlock*, 415 U.S. 164 (1974). Indeed, the Court has held that the third party need not have *actual* authority over the area—*apparent authority* will suffice. In *Illinois v. Rodriguez*, 497 U.S. 177 (1990), defendant's former girlfriend, who represented to the police that she shared defendant's apartment, let them in with her key and permitted them to search. In fact, she had moved out one month earlier. Where the facts and surrounding circumstances known to the officer warrant "a man of reasonable caution" to conclude that the consenting party had authority over the premises, consent is valid even if actual authority is absent.

Common authority for purposes of a consent search rests on "mutual use of the property by persons generally having joint access or control for most purposes, so that it is reasonable to recognize that any of the co-inhabitants has the right to permit the inspection in his own right and that the others have assumed the risk that one of their number might permit the common area to be searched." *Matlock*, supra, 415 U.S. at 172. Simply having legal authority to enter the premises is not sufficient. Thus where a hotel clerk permitted the inspection of a guest's room this did not constitute an effective waiver of defendant's Fourth Amendment rights because there was no mutual use of the premises. See *Stoner v. California*, 376 U.S. 483 (1964).

The allowable scope of a consent search is determined by the permission granted. The subject may, for instance, agree to a search of a suitcase but explicitly exclude the opening of a folder found inside. In *Thompson v. Louisiana*, 469 U.S. 17 (1984), the Court held that a daughter's summoning of police to her mother's home to render medical assistance did not constitute an open-ended invitation for detectives to engage in a general exploratory search for evidence of a homicide committed on the scene. As we shall see in §6.8, however, any contraband or evidence observed by police in plain view while they confine themselves to the terms of the consent search may properly be seized.

EXAMPLES

1. Larry Lane, a law student, rents an apartment on the third floor of a three-family private residence. The police suspect Lane of involvement in a criminal enterprise selling stolen copies of the upcoming state bar examination to law school graduates. Unfortunately for the investigators, there is not sufficient probable cause to seek a warrant to search the apartment or arrest Lane. Under which of the following sets of circumstances could a valid consent search be conducted?

   a. Three officers visit Lane and ask his permission to search the apartment. After he becomes exceedingly nervous and indecisive, one of the officers tells him that "it sure won't look good on your law school record if you refuse to let us look around your place." Lane finally agrees to a search, and the officers find and seize copies of the upcoming bar examination in his desk.

b. Three officers visit Lane's apartment in his absence and speak to Kirk, a man Lane has hired to clean for him every other week. The officers explain to Kirk that they would like to look around, and he lets them in. The officers find and seize copies of the upcoming bar examination in Lane's desk.

c. Janis Close, a former (now estranged) live-in girlfriend of Lane's, calls the police and tells them she has proof of his criminal activities. At her suggestion, the officers meet her at Lane's apartment. She opens the door with her key (which she failed to return when she moved out two months prior) and leads the officers into the living room, where they observe several copies of the upcoming bar examination on a coffee table. Close then brings them to the adjoining study and opens the top drawer of Lane's desk, revealing an answer key to the bar examination. The officers seize all the incriminating documents.

d. Officers visit Lane's apartment in his absence and speak to his landlord, who lives on the first floor. The officers ask if they could search Lane's car, which is parked in the driveway. The landlord, who has Lane's permission to enter the car in order to move it if it is blocking other vehicles, agrees and opens the locked doors with a key Lane had provided him. The officers find incriminating evidence under the front seat.

e. Officers visit Lane's apartment, inform him they are investigating unauthorized release of state bar examinations and ask him if they can search his car parked in the driveway. Lane replies: "Sure, go ahead." The officers locate a briefcase in the trunk, which they open to discover copies of the upcoming bar examination. In addition, they came upon a small bottle of pills under the front seat, which they take with them and which, upon further laboratory analysis, turn out to be a controlled substance.

2. Sally White was pulled over on Florida Route 12 when a trooper observed her weaving between the lanes. After White produced her license and registration, the trooper stated: "We've had a lot of trouble with people moving drugs and money along this road. Would you mind if I have a look in your trunk?" White agreed and opened the trunk for the trooper. The officer's attention was

drawn to a spare tire, which appeared unusual—it was the wrong type and size for the vehicle, was extremely heavy when he lifted it, and had white powder residue on its rim. Based on his knowledge that narcotics were often smuggled in such tires, the trooper pulled out his knife and cut open the tire. Inside he found an automatic weapon and several kilograms of cocaine. Was this search lawful?

Would it matter if Sally had been seated in the police cruiser at the officer's request while he ran a routine computer check, and while in the cruiser agreed to the officer's request to search?

3. A Greyhound bus on its way to Miami made a brief stop in Mobile, Alabama. Officer Wallace of that city's drug interdiction unit boarded the bus and announced: "With your cooperation I'd like to check the gear on board for contraband. With your consent, please bring down your luggage from overhead and have it open so I can do a quick on-board inspection." Gus complied, and Wallace discovered cocaine in his carry-on. Arguing that he was never told he could refuse, Gus seeks to suppress. What result?

EXPLANATIONS

1a. A waiver of Fourth Amendment rights need not be knowing and intelligent. Thus, even if Lane had flunked Criminal Procedure and can establish that he in fact did not know he had a right to refuse the officers' request, that in itself will not obviate his consent if it is determined to have been voluntary. *Schneckloth v. Bustamonte*, 412 U.S. 218 (1973). The key issue here is whether Lane's agreement to the search was voluntary or coerced. *United States v. Garcia*, 56 F.3d 418 (2d Cir. 1995) (knowledge of right to refuse consent is not necessary for finding voluntariness).

Voluntariness is determined on the basis of the totality of the circumstances. Given his age and level of education, Lane faces an uphill battle in persuading the court that his consent was compelled. He would point to his nervous state as an indication of his vulnerability, as well as to the officer's statement about ruining his record as a sign that pressure was brought to bear on him. Making a case for coerced waiver usually requires much more, however. See, e.g, *United States v. Talkington*, 843 F.2d 1041 (7th Cir. 1988) (agents burst into defendant's home at night with their guns drawn, confronted him in loud and threatening tones, misrepresented that a search warrant had been applied for and would arrive soon, and threatened to subject his wife to a body cavity search); *United States v. Jones*, 641 F.2d 425 (6th Cir. 1981) (five armed officers kicked and banged on the subject's door and misrepresented to her that they had a search warrant); *United States v. Solomon*, 728 F. Supp. 1544, 1549 (S.D. Fla. 1990) (defendants "were run off the road and their vehicle forcibly stopped. They were yelled at, forced to exit the car, and lie on the ground while facing pointed guns. They were then handcuffed and placed in the back of police vehicles. As a helicopter hovered overhead and the excitement from the stop had not even begun to dissipate, the defendants were then asked to consent to a search of their vehicle. [Defendants were] still handcuffed. In the face of such an overwhelming show of force, any citizen would consent to a search. Further, the police never attempted to advise either defendant that they had the right to refuse consent."). Compare *United States v. Tompkins*, 103 F.3d 117 (5th Cir. 1997) (consent valid even though obtained only after officer told defendant that he would obtain search warrant for premises if defendant refused to permit search).

1b. Assuming that there was no coercion of Kirk, the issue here is whether he is in a position to waive Lane's privacy rights in the apartment. Fourth Amendment rights can be waived by third parties, but only if those persons have (or reasonably appear to have) common authority over and access to the premises. A person on the premises for the purpose of performing a service like cleaning would not have either actual or apparent authority to give effective consent. See *United States v. Chaidez*, 919 F.2d 1193 (7th Cir. 1990) (suggesting in dictum that a person on the premises to do the owner's laundry does not have authority to consent to a search). But compare *United States v. Baswell*, 792 F.2d 755 (8th Cir. 1986) (caretaker of friend's vacation home in which defendant was staying could consent to search of home and opening of defendant's pouch hidden in the attic). Contrast *United States v. Dearing*, 9 F.3d 1428 (9th Cir. 1993), in which the court held that although it was reasonable for the officer to believe a live-in baby-sitter had authority over his own room and the common areas of the house, it was not reasonably apparent that he had authority over the defendant's bedroom. Although the officer knew the sitter had been in the defendant's room on prior occasions, she never inquired into the extent of the sitter's access to the bedroom, or the extent to which the defendant kept his bedroom off-limits. A reasonable officer would have inquired further and it was unreasonable to believe the sitter had authority over the employer's bedroom.

1c. Janis Close's consent to the search could operate to waive Lane's Fourth Amendment rights in either of two situations: 1) she shares *actual* common authority over the apartment with Lane, as in *United States v. Matlock,* 415 U.S. 164 (1974); see, e.g., *United States v. Kim,* 105 F.3d 1579 (9th Cir. 1997) (by instructing his associate to rent storage units in his own name, defendant assumed risk that associate would allow search of units); or 2) she has *apparent* authority to grant permission to search, as in *Illinois v. Rodriguez,* 497 U.S. 177 (1990). Because Close has not lived in the apartment for two months, and thus no longer has joint access or control, she lacks actual authority to consent. Her consent may nonetheless operate effectively against Lane if the facts and surrounding circumstances known to the officers would warrant a reasonable person to conclude that she had authority over the premises. Based on this objective standard for apparent authority, the fact that Close has a key and ready access are important elements in establishing apparent authority, but probably are not sufficient in themselves. It would aid the government's cause if the police had been aware that Close had possessions of her own in the apartment. See *United States v. Trzaska,* 859 F.2d 1118 (2d Cir. 1988) (estranged wife could consent to search of defendant's apartment where she had only recently moved out, still had a key, and removed some of her personal belongings prior to the search).

Assuming Close is held to have had apparent authority over the apartment and, further, that the living room was an area she shared access to and control over, the documents found there in plain view were lawfully seized.

More troublesome is the fact that Close entered the study and opened Lane's desk to police examination. Because that room, and particularly the desk, were most likely the exclusive province of Lane, the search and seizure there would be unlawful. See, e.g., *United States v. Rodriguez,* 888 F.2d 519, 523 (7th Cir. 1989) (wife had no authority, apparent or actual, to consent to a search of closed boxes in an area of the house she did not occupy).

Is it significant that Close acted out of spite against Lane in opening his apartment to a search? Some courts have considered the antagonistic relationship between the third-party consenter and the subject of the search as a factor weighing against waiver, and have held invalid warrantless searches where the cohabitating spouse acted out of anger, spite, and hostility in consenting to the search. See *May v. State*, 780 S.W.2d 866 (Tex. Ct. App. 1989) (and cases cited). But compare *United States v. McAlpine*, 919 F.2d 1461, 1464 n.2 (10th Cir. 1990) (antagonism between the consenter and defendant is not relevant because the *Matlock* test focuses only on the relationship between the consenter and the property searched).

One type of consent case currently attracting publicity is the situation of a child "dropping a dime" on his parents. In *Davis v. State*, 422 S.E.2d 546 (Ga. 1992), the Georgia Supreme Court held that a ten-year-old child did not have sufficient authority to consent to the search of his parents' home. This was the case even though the child had been left alone and had the run of the house. But compare *Rainwater v. State*, 240 Ga. App. 370 (1999) (consent by 15-year-old valid). The Tenth Circuit has held that the minority of the third-party consenter does not per se bar a finding of authority to consent, but is merely a factor to be weighed. See *United States v.Gutierrez-Hermosillo*, 142 F.3d 1225 (10th Cir. 1998) (14-year-old had authority to consent to search of motel room she occupied with father).

The bugging of a hotel room with the consent of defendant's companion was deemed beyond the scope of consent as it was too intrusive and surveillance could occur even without the third party being present. *United States v. Shabazz*, 883 F. Supp. 422 (D. Minn. 1995).

With regard to property specifically owned by a defendant, courts are reluctant to find third-party consent. In *United States v. Welch*, 4 F.3d 761, 764 (9th Cir. 1993), a third party who consented to a search of a car to which he had joint access did not have power to consent to a search of a purse found in the trunk. In *United States v. Chang*, 838 F. Supp. 695 (D.P.R. 1993), a third party's consent to allow agents to search anything in his motel room did not give the agents the authority to search the luggage belonging to his two companions. There must be a clear indication that the property in question belongs to the defendant to constitute valid third-party consent.

A targeted individual's presence at the search would negate a third party's consent, especially where the third party is not present.

[A]n absent third party's consent should not be used to 'waive' another individual's constitutional rights when that individual is present at the search to give or withhold consent in his or her own right. Similarly, the risk that one co-inhabitant might permit the common area of a jointly occupied premises to be searched in the absence of another is qualitatively different from the risk that a warrantless search will be conducted over the objection of a present joint occupant. . . .

In re Welfare of D.A.G., 484 N.W.2d 787 (Minn. 1992). But see *United States v. Rith*, 164 F.3d 1323 (10th Cir. 1999) (consent given by someone with authority cannot be revoked by co-occupant).

1d. Here again the question is whether the landlord's consent operates to waive Lane's rights. Because the landlord's authority to enter Lane's car is limited to moving it around the driveway, and does not constitute mutual use and access, he does not appear to have actual authority to consent to this search. See *United States v. Warner*, 843 F.2d 401 (9th Cir. 1988) (landlord who had permission to enter the property for the limited purpose of making specified repairs and mowing the lawn could not give effective consent to a search of the garage and house). Whether the landlord has apparent authority would depend upon the particular facts and circumstances of his statements to, and actions in front of, the police.

1e. The permissible scope of a consent search is defined by the terms (either explicit or implicit) of the consent. Lane could have agreed to a search either of the passenger compartment only or of the car itself but not the containers within it. Because he did not place any limits on his consent, however, the police are permitted to search anywhere and anything in the vehicle where the items sought (presumably documentary) might be found. That would of course include his briefcase.

The Supreme Court has held that where a motorist is asked by an officer for permission to search his car for narcotics, and the permission is granted, the scope of the search may extend to anywhere in the vehicle where narcotics may be hidden. See *Florida v. Jimeno*, 500 U.S. 248 (1991):

The standard for measuring the scope of a suspect's consent under the Fourth Amendment is that of "objective"

> reasonableness—what would the typical reasonable person have understood by the exchange between the officer and the suspect? The question before us, then, is whether it is reasonable for an officer to consider a suspect's general consent to a search of his car to include consent to examine a paper bag lying on the floor of the car. We think it is.

500 U.S. at 251 (citations omitted). Rejecting Jimeno's argument that the police should be required to seek specific permission for each container they want to examine, the Court held that because a reasonable person may be expected to know that narcotics are generally carried in some kind of container, the driver's consent to search for narcotics implicitly included permission to open the bag. See also *United States v.Coffman*, 148 F.3d 952 (8th Cir. 1998) (in response to officer's question whether there were any weapons on premises, suspect invited officers to look around; consent was broad enough to include search under bed, where weapon was found).

Thus the search of the briefcase and seizure of the bar exams in our example would probably be upheld as a lawful consent search. The seizure and subsequent analysis of the bottle of pills, however, would appear to be beyond the scope of Lane's consent. He had responded positively to a request to search, which was prefaced by reference to the bar exam scheme. His agreement seemed (at least implicitly) limited to a search for evidence of that offense and would not carry over to a laboratory examination of the contents of the bottle.

2. What was the scope of White's consent to search? Arguably, because the officer told White he was looking for narcotics (as opposed to stolen televisions), she could reasonably have expected the search would be thorough. It is questionable, however, whether the consent could be construed as broad enough to cover the slashing of a tire.

Even if the search exceeded the bounds of the consent given, however, there is another basis for upholding its legality. As discussed in §6.3, an automobile stopped on the road (as well as any container found within) is subject to search if the officer has probable cause to believe seizable items are present. While conducting a consent search of the trunk, which properly included an examination of the tire's exterior, the trooper developed probable cause to believe contraband was hidden inside. The automobile exception would thus permit a warrantless search of the tire's interior. See *United States v. Strickland*, 902 F.2d 937 (11th Cir. 1990).

If Sally gave consent to a search while in the confines of the police cruiser, she could of course argue that her will had been overborne. As long as she was not in custody and a reasonable person in her situation would have felt free to leave, her consent is probably still valid. See *United States v. Thompson*, 106 F.3d 794 (7th Cir. 1997); *United States v. Rivera*, 906 F.2d 319 (7th Cir. 1990).

3. The Court in *Florida v. Bostick* refused to require that police inform passengers during a bus stop that they are free to leave and held instead that the appropriate inquiry is whether a reasonable person would believe that consent to search was optional under the circumstances. Factors to weigh are whether the passenger was informed of the right to refuse and whether there was any threat of force. Although Gus was not informed that he could refuse consent, there was no apparent show of force in our problem, probably rendering the search lawful under *Bostick*.

It should be noted, however, that at least one circuit court has concluded that a passenger in this situation would not feel free to disregard the officer's request unless there was some positive indication that the passenger could do so. See *United States v. Guapi*, 144 F.3d 1393 (11th Cir. 1998). The court found it significant that the manner in which the announcement was made by the police appeared designed to convince passengers they had no choice, and that the officer stood at the front of the cramped bus, thus blocking the exit. See also *United States v. Washington*, 151 F.3d 1354 (11th Cir. 1998) (reiterating importance of informing passengers of right to refuse).

§6.8 The Plain View Doctrine

The plain view doctrine permits an officer to make a warrantless seizure of incriminating items that she comes upon while otherwise engaged in a lawful arrest, entry, or search. Unlike the other exceptions to the warrant requirement we have discussed, this doctrine does not permit a *search*, but only a *seizure* of something already discovered. The authorization for the search (as well as its permissible scope) emanates

from the action that the officer is already conducting at the time—
such as a search pursuant to a warrant or a warrantless search incident
to a lawful arrest. The plain view doctrine is premised on the notion
that once the item has been spotted "in plain view" by the officer,
insistence on a warrant authorizing its *seizure* would be a needless
inconvenience that would not significantly serve the privacy interest of
the subject because the item has already been discovered. The Supreme
Court has indicated a willingness to expand the doctrine to senses
other than sight, such as feel and touch. See *Minnesota v. Dickerson*,
508 U.S. 366 (1993).

The three requirements for a lawful plain view seizure are that:

1)   the officer's **original intrusion is lawful**;
2)   the item is **observed while the officer is confining her ac-
     tivities to the permissible scope of that intrusion** (some-
     times referred to as a lawful right of access to the object itself);
     and
3)   it is **immediately apparent that the item is contraband or
     evidence of crime**, without the necessity for any further ex-
     amination or search.

These limitations are designed to ensure that the plain view exception
does not eviscerate the requirements of the Fourth Amendment. Requiring that the original intrusion be lawful ensures that the officer is
in the particular place with proper justification. Requiring that she
confine her action to the parameters of the original intrusion ensures
that the scope is not enlarged. Requiring that it be immediately apparent that the item in question is connected to criminal activity ensures both that the intrusiveness of the search is not increased by a
separate examination of the items found in plain view and that a general
license to seize any of the subject's possessions has not been created.

Suppose, for example, that a warrant is issued authorizing a search
of Peter's home for stolen VCRs of a particular description. The police
enter the home and search those areas in which a VCR might be found.
While doing so, they come upon a large bale of marijuana. A strict
reading of the Fourth Amendment would require that before the officers may seize the contraband, which was not described in the original
warrant, they must seek and obtain another warrant specifying the bale.
The plain view doctrine recognizes that the delay, inconvenience, and
risk that the evidence may be lost by the time the warrant is secured
are generally not justified by the benefit to Peter, given that "the cat

is already out of the bag." We certainly cannot require the police to forget what they saw, and the only issue is whether they may seize it now without a warrant. The plain view doctrine permits such a seizure.

Now suppose instead that police officers are on routine foot patrol when they observe a bale of marijuana through a window in Peter's home. Having seen the contraband in plain view, may they enter the home and seize it? The answer is no. The plain view doctrine requires that *the original intrusion be lawful*—which in the case of entry into a private home means that (absent exigent circumstances) a warrant must be obtained. The observation that the police made through the window must be presented in an affidavit to a magistrate who decides whether probable cause has been made out and, if so, what the scope of the search will be. (Remember that the observation made by the police from the street through the window is not itself a search implicating the Fourth Amendment because Peter can have no reasonable expectation of privacy in this situation. See §3.2.) The plain view doctrine is triggered only *after* the officers have otherwise lawfully entered the premises; it does not provide justification for the entry.

Now suppose that the officers (having observed the marijuana through the window) immediately secure a warrant authorizing entry into Peter's home and seizure of the bale of contraband. They enter and, while one officer locates the bale, the other opens the drawers of Peter's roll-top desk and discovers betting slips, which he immediately recognizes as evidence of unlawful gambling. Since these papers have come into the officer's plain view, may they be seized? The answer is no, because when he opened the desk drawers the officer had expanded the scope of the authorized warrant search for a large bale of marijuana. The bale could not be hidden in a desk drawer (except in the very unlikely event of some very quick repackaging). The plain view doctrine requires that *the discovery occur in the permissible course of the original search and without exceeding its scope*. If the betting slips had been found in open view on top of the bale of marijuana, they could be lawfully seized.

Finally, suppose that the officers, armed with a warrant to search for and seize the marijuana, come across an unmarked vial of white powder in an open area. If they have a hunch that it might be a controlled substance, may they seize it and bring it to the police laboratory for testing? The answer is no. The incriminating nature of the item in question must be *immediately apparent*. That means that the police must, without further inspection or analysis, have probable cause to believe that the thing they have encountered is connected to criminal activity. Lifting stereo components to read the serial numbers on the equipment and matching those numbers (by way of a telephone call) with stolen items was deemed beyond the scope of the plain view doctrine even though the inspection was "cursory." *Arizona v. Hicks*, 480 U.S. 321 (1987). The police did not have probable cause to connect the items to a crime based *solely on what was already exposed to their view* while conducting an otherwise lawful investigation of a shooting.

The plain view doctrine is, in sum, a limited accommodation to the interests of effective law enforcement and not an open license to search and seize *any* items encountered while searching the owner's property.

EXAMPLES

1. Police have a warrant for the arrest of Joseph Barker for the crime of vehicular homicide (a "hit and run"). Armed with reliable information that he was at home, the police entered his two-room apartment and placed him under arrest. While placing Barker in handcuffs, Officer Keen gazed into the open bedroom and observed items (a scale, razor blade, empty plastic bags, and a jar filled with a white powder) that she immediately recognized as paraphernalia used in the preparation and distribution of illegal narcotics. Keen seized the items. They are subsequently offered against Barker at his trial on narcotics offenses. Barker objects, arguing that the seizure of items outside his grabbable space was unlawful and further that the items were not related to the charge of vehicular homicide. Were the items lawfully seized?

2. Assume instead that the officers appeared at Barker's door without a warrant and asked if they could enter to ask him some questions about a traffic accident. He invited them in, and while seated at the kitchen table Officer Keen observed the drug paraphernalia in the open bedroom. She seizes the items. Same result?

3. Assume instead that the officers, armed with a search warrant, entered the private two-car garage where Barker keeps his car. The warrant authorized a search of the vehicle "and the area of the garage immediately surrounding it" for evidence of recent impact with the accident victim. The officers inspected the exterior of the automobile, the floor of the garage, and then turned their attention to a workbench located in a separate alcove at the back of the garage. While examining a shelf above the workbench, the officers discovered a plain white envelope that, when opened, contained

a receipt from an auto body shop indicating that significant repair and painting work was done on the front end of Barker's car the day after the hit and run occurred. Can the officers lawfully seize this receipt?

4. Drug enforcement agents secured a warrant to search Marcus Pepper's residence for narcotics. They also suspected him of trafficking in unlawful assault rifles, which they believed were on the premises, but did not seek authority from the magistrate to search for or seize them. When executing the warrant, the agents (not unexpectedly) came upon the assault rifles, which they removed. Was the seizure proper under the plain view doctrine?

5. Pursuant to a lawful search warrant for stolen wide-screen televisions, officers proceeded to Suspect's home. While in the den conducting the search, the officers smelled what they recognized to be burning marijuana. They then observed a wooden pipe smoldering in the ashtray. May the officers seize the pipe and its contents?

EXPLANATIONS

1. Barker is correct that the search permitted incident to his arrest is limited to the area immediately around him while he is being cuffed and cannot encompass the items in the next room. See §6.3. Given the lawful intrusion into his home (remember that the arrest warrant carries the authority to enter the subject's residence, see §5.5), however, items immediately apparent as contraband that are encountered in plain view while effecting the arrest may be seized. An issue is raised whether the officer, peering in from an adjoining room, had adequate probable cause to believe the items she saw were related to criminal activity. Given their appearance and juxtaposition, as well as the officer's expertise, the "immediately apparent" requirement of the plain view doctrine would appear to be satisfied. See, e.g., *United States v. Peters*, 912 F.2d 208 (8th Cir. 1990).

    The fact that the items seized had no connection to the crime for which Barker was arrested is of no consequence. The plain view doctrine often operates to permit seizure of items unrelated to the reason the officers are on the premises. Nexus to the original investigation is *not* a prerequisite to a plain view seizure.

2. Yes, the seizure would again be permissible under the plain view doctrine. The officers have lawfully entered Barker's apartment by way of his consent (assuming it was voluntary). Once lawfully in-

191

side, the doctrine operates to permit seizure of items observed in plain view that are immediately apparent as contraband. The point of the example is that the initial intrusion, which begins the plain view process, can take any one of the several warrant or warrantless forms we have discussed; it simply must be lawful.

3. There are two problems here. First, the officers may have exceeded their authority under the search warrant at the point at which they discovered the envelope because the workbench was not adjacent to the automobile (the area specified in the warrant). If so, seizure of the envelope would be unlawful because their intrusion into that part of the garage was not authorized. Second, even if the warrant could be read to authorize a search of the workbench and shelves, the officers opened an envelope that was not immediately apparent as evidence or contraband. As in *Arizona v. Hicks*, the police lacked probable cause to connect the envelope to criminal activity based *solely on what was already exposed to their view*. Probable cause to support a plain view seizure has been defined as "more than hunch, guesswork, and cop-on-the-beat intuition, but less than proof beyond a reasonable doubt or a near certainty that the seized item is incriminating. There must be enough facts for a reasonable person to believe that the items in plain view may be contraband or evidence of crime." *United States v. Giannetta*, 909 F.2d 571, 579 (1st Cir. 1990) (citations and internal quotations omitted).

Opening the plain envelope is analogous to lifting Hicks's stereo components to read the serial numbers—both are impermissible searches outside the boundaries of the plain view doctrine.

4. Until recently, inadvertency was a requirement for a lawful plain view seizure. As Justice Stewart explained for the plurality in *Coolidge v. New Hampshire*, 403 U.S. 443 (1971), the rationale of the plain view exception is that the police should not be put to the inconvenience of leaving the place of the original search to procure a warrant to seize contraband or evidence that was inadvertently discovered. "But where the discovery is anticipated, where the police know in advance the location of evidence and intend to seize it, the situation is altogether different. The requirement of a warrant to seize imposes no inconvenience whatever, or at least none which is constitutionally recognizable in a legal system that regards warrantless searches as per se unreasonable in the absence of exigent circumstances." 403 U.S. at 470–471 (citations

and internal quotations omitted). If, in other words, the officers are not surprised by the discovery, but rather anticipated it, they should be bound by the warrant requirement.

In our problem, because the officers had reason to believe they would find the weapons at Pepper's home, the *Coolidge* logic would require them to seek the magistrate's authorization to seize the guns prior to the search. In *Horton v. California*, 496 U.S. 128 (1990), however, the Court dispensed with the requirement that the plain view discovery be inadvertent. In that case, the officers had probable cause to believe stolen jewelry and weapons would be found at the defendant's home, but the search warrant specified only the jewelry. Horton challenged the seizure of the weapons during execution of the warrant on the grounds that, because their discovery was not inadvertent, the plain view doctrine did not apply. Reasoning that the inadvertence requirement added no significant privacy protection beyond the other requirements for a plain view seizure (that is, lawful initial intrusion, limited scope of search, items immediately apparent as incriminating) and further that it required unworkable judicial inquiries into the subjective state of mind of the officers, the Court abandoned it. (It should be noted that some states continue to require inadvertence under their own constitutions. See, e.g., *People v. Manganaro*, 561 N.Y.S.2d 379 (Sup. Ct. 1990)).

After *Horton*, therefore, the fact that the agents in our problem anticipated finding the guns does not preclude their seizure under the plain view doctrine. Officers may seize whatever contraband or evidence of crime they discover in the course of a lawful search provided it is immediately apparent as such and provided the officers have not exceeded the permissible bounds of the original search.

With the abandonment of the inadvertence requirement, the problem of pretext emerges more dramatically. Aware that she may make a warrantless seizure of items immediately apparent as incriminating as long as she has made lawful entry, what is to prevent an officer from gaining such access on a pretext (by, for example, asking Tenant if she could enter the apartment to ask questions relating to a neighbor's complaints about loud noise), but for the real purpose of seeking incriminating items? The problem of pretext is the subject of our next section.

5. The officers are lawfully present on the premises, but are conducting a search for largescreen televisions. The warrant itself

would obviously not authorize a search or seizure of other items. The sight of the wooden pipe does not broaden the range of the search because it is not immediately apparent as an item related to crime. The smell of marijuana, however, should provide the officers with authority to seize the pipe and its contents, as it is now immediately apparent as contraband. In light of the Court's willingness to expand plain view to other senses, see *Minnesota v. Dickerson*, 508 U.S. 366 (1993) (plain touch), plain smell would appear to be justified. It is interesting to note the prediction of the court in *State v. Jones*, 653 A.2d 1040, 1044 (Md. Ct. Spec. App. 1995): "[B]ecause of their common doctrinal base, [the plain view and plain feel doctrines] will in all likelihood come to be seen, probably within a decade, as nothing more than instances or variations of an omnibus Plain Sense Doctrine or Plain Perception Doctrine, which will embrace plain view and plain feel and, by a logically compelling growth process, plain hearing, plain smell, and plain taste."

Keep in mind that smell or hearing can also provide probable cause to search. See, e.g., *United States v. Pierre*, 958 F.2d 1304 (5th Cir. 1992) (smell of burned contraband gave agent probable cause to search vehicle); *United States v. Jackson*, 588 F.2d 1046 (5th Cir. 1979) (conversations overheard from adjoining motel room).

§6.9   The Problem of Pretext

As we have seen, numerous exceptions to the requirement for a search warrant have been carved out in an effort to accommodate the interest of effective and efficient law enforcement. As with any set of rules, the potential for abuse exists. Suppose, for example, that narcotics squad detectives Spanking and Clean have a "cop's hunch" that Dirty Dan is engaged in the distribution of crack cocaine. They would like to search his car but lack sufficient probable cause to do so. The enterprising detectives follow Dan as he drives through the city's streets, and as soon as he commits a traffic infraction (like going 32 m.p.h. in a 30-m.p.h. zone) they pull him over. Because they have authority to arrest for that offense (an authority rarely invoked), Spanking and Clean take Dan into custody. They exercise their prerogative to subject Dan and the interior of his vehicle to a warrantless search incident to the arrest (see §6.3), and they find crack cocaine. Or suppose the detectives follow Dan until he parks his car in a tow-away zone, and as soon as he leaves it, they have it towed back to the station and searched pursuant to the "routine" inventory procedures for impounded automobiles.

Although outwardly the conduct of the detectives in both cases is lawful and "by the book," does the fact that the police actually used the traffic or parking offense as a pretext to search for narcotics invalidate their action? *Whren v. United States*, 517 U.S. 806 (1996), suggests that the answer to that question is no. Defendants conceded that there was probable cause to stop the car for several traffic offenses, but sought to suppress the cocaine found as a result on the ground that the stop was pretextual. Given that the use of automobiles is so heavily and minutely regulated that total compliance with traffic and safety rules is nearly impossible, defendants argued that a police officer will almost always be able to catch a motorist in a technical violation. This, it was asserted, creates the temptation to use traffic stops as a means of investigating other law violations, as to which no probable cause or even articulable suspicion exists. To avoid this danger, defendants argued that the Fourth Amendment test for traffic stops should not be whether probable cause existed to justify the stop, but rather whether a police officer, acting reasonably, would have made the stop for the reason given. A unanimous Supreme Court rejected that proposition and held that ulterior motives do not invalidate police conduct otherwise justified on the basis of probable cause.

Whren did leave open the possibility that in the administrative or inventory search contexts, where probable cause is absent, a pretext inquiry might be appropriate, as had been suggested by previous decisions. *Florida v. Wells*, 495 U.S. 1 (1990), for example, invalidated the opening of a locked suitcase during an inventory search of an automobile because there was no standardized policy regulating the opening of containers; the Court feared that such wide latitude would permit the police to use the inventory as a ruse to search for evidence. Had such a policy been in effect, the Court indicated that the search would have been lawful. In contrast, *Colorodo v. Bertine*, 479 U.S. 367 (1987), upheld a similar search where the police did follow standardized caretaking procedures (although allowing for some discretion regarding the disposition of inventoried vehicles) and there was no evidence that they acted in bad faith for the sole purpose of searching defendant's van for evidence.

In addressing the *Whren* defendants' alternative argument that their car was stopped because they were black,[12] the Court indicated that this issue of selective enforcement would be addressed under the equal protection clause, not the Fourth Amendment. *United States. v. Armstrong,* 517 U.S. 456 (1996), however, would seem to make the establishment of such a claim extremely difficult: in order to prove a selective prosecution defense, the claimant must demonstrate both that the prosecutorial policy had a discriminatory effect—that is, the claimant must show that similarly situated individuals of a different race were not prosecuted, *and* was motivated by a discriminatory purpose.

EXAMPLES

1. The Roane County Sheriff's Department was anxious to stem the transport of drugs into town from the airport. They decided to set up what appeared to be a drunk-driver checkpoint on the exit road from the airport. Jones was stopped at the checkpoint in his rented car, and Lucy, a reliably trained drug-detecting beagle, was brought over to sniff. Lucy's high-pitched bay indicated the presence of narcotics, and a search of the car confirmed her expert opinion. Jones was charged with possession of cocaine, and defendant sought to suppress the evidence before trial. At the hearing, defense counsel established that the checkpoint was staffed by narcotics detectives, not traffic officers, and that there was no breathalyzer at the scene. Moreover, the checkpoint was funded from the department's drug interdiction budget. Conceding that the checkpoint met the outward requirements for a sobriety checkpoint (see 4.5), defense counsel nonetheless argues that the entire operation was pretextual and the fruits of the search should be excluded from evidence. What result?

2. The St. Petersburg police set up a drug interdiction operation in which they would stop cars at a particular location that were in any way in violation of the motor vehicle code (such as an unilluminated license plate). Upon being stopped the motorist would

---

12. Much attention has been given recently to the problem of "race profiling," the targeting of minorities by police. A study of stops along the New Jersey Turnpike indicated that while only 13 percent of the speeders were black, 35–45 percent of those stopped for speeding were black. Similarly, along Interstate 95 in Maryland, blacks represented only 17 percent of the motorists but 73 percent of the persons stopped by police. *USA Today,* June 3, 1999, p. 14a. Several states have enacted laws authorizing the collection of such data. *Nation,* October 11, 1999. 16–1

be approached by narcotics detectives who would identify themselves and request consent to search the vehicle for narcotics. If the motorist refused, the vehicle would be detained while Austin (a reliably trained drug-detecting schnauzer) was summoned to sniff the vehicle. His signal that drugs were present would result in a search of the vehicle by the detectives. Is this operation constitutional?

EXPLANATIONS

1. In *Whren* the Court upheld a pretextual stop, reasoning that since it was based upon probable cause there was some assurance that police discretion was (and in similar cases would be) constrained. Here, however, the stop was justified solely upon an administrative rationale, which turned out to be a ruse. *Whren, Wells,* and *Bertine* suggest that such pretextual administrative searches violate the Fourth Amendment. The Sixth Circuit reached that conclusion in *United States v. Huguenin,* 154 F.3d 547 (6th Cir. 1998). On the topic of drug interdiction programs, see also *Edmond v. Goldsmith,* 183 F.3d 659 (7th Cir. 1999), *cert. granted,* 120 S. Ct. 3519, discussed in §4.5, explanation 2.

2. The fact that the police have probable cause to stop the cars for motor vehicle violations seems to satisfy *Whren,* notwithstanding the real purpose behind the stops. There is no requirement that the police inform drivers that they are free to refuse consent to search (see §6.7), thus rendering the searches of compliant motorists lawful. For those drivers who do refuse consent, the use of Austin to detect drugs would not be considered a "search" because no expectation of privacy would be violated. See *United States v. Place,* 462 U.S. 696 (1983) discussed in §3.2. *Pennsylvania v. Mimms,* 434 U.S. 106 (1977), and *Maryland v. Wilson,* 519 U.S. 408 (1997), discussed in §4.4 permit police to order the driver and passengers out of the vehicle pursuant to a lawful stop. It would appear, therefore, that the only possible constitutional problem with the procedure is if the cars of those drivers who refused consent are detained for an unreasonable period, that is, beyond the time necessary to perform a routine computer check on the vehicle (as discussed in §4.3). See *United States v. Hoffman,* 113 F.3d 192 (11th Cir. 1997).

7

The Exclusionary Rule: Rationale, Operation, and Limitations

The centerpiece of the constitutional criminal procedure framework is the exclusionary rule. Unique to American jurisprudence, the rule requires the suppression of evidence obtained in violation of the defendant's constitutional rights. This remedy has been applied not only to violations of the Fourth Amendment, but to evidence obtained in contravention of the Fifth, Sixth, and Fourteenth Amendments as well. In this chapter we will explore the rationale of the exclusionary rule, its operation (particularly the "fruit-of-the-poisonous-tree" doctrine), and the limitations that have been placed upon it in recent years.

§7.1 The Rationale of the Exclusionary Rule

What purpose is served, one might ask, by keeping from the criminal trial fact finder evidence that is relevant to the question of the defendant's guilt but that was obtained through unlawful means? And are the benefits gained by suppression sufficient to justify the cost, which in some cases is the freeing of a guilty party? These questions have generated a vigorous debate in the years since *Mapp v. Ohio* (see Chapter 1), which applied the exclusionary remedy to the states, and permeate virtually every criminal procedure case decided by the Court from term to term. The following imaginary panel discussion provides a glimpse of the controversy.

Law Professor Moderator *(Well-prepared, erudite, and of course, scrupulously neutral):* We are here today to discuss the relative merits of the exclusionary remedy, which was adopted for federal trials in 1914[1] and was imposed upon the states by *Mapp v. Ohio* in 1961. The *Mapp* Court told us that the exclusionary remedy was constitutionally required to ensure police compliance with the commands of the Fourth Amendment. The theory was that unlawful searches and seizures would be discouraged when the law enforcement community realized they could not use the evidence they obtained when the case went to court. In addition to deterrence, the Court suggested that the "imperative of judicial integrity" also required that the courts not soil their hands with unlawfully seized evidence. Let's start then with the stated purposes for the remedy. Was *Mapp* correct in its assessment that the exclusionary rule would deter police from acting unlawfully?

Police Chief *(Tough, streetwise, and not a big fan of lawyers):* The Supreme Court, with all due respect, was all wet. Let's take a typical case. Two officers on the beat in a large city see a guy they know in their gut is dirty (that is, in possession of drugs). They approach him and shake him down, and sure enough, there's the crack cocaine. Now because there was no probable cause or reasonable suspicion, the search and arrest are technically unlawful, which means that as this guy's case winds slowly through the system, at some point some judge may order the coke excluded and then throw the charges out. Maybe that happens months later at trial, or maybe it happens years later on appeal after trial and conviction, or maybe if the guy pleads or his lawyer misses the issue it never happens. The point is, the cop on the street isn't thinking ahead to possible suppression. He or she just sees somebody who needs to be shaken down and taken off the street.

Prosecutor *(Committed public servant, models herself on Jimmy Stewart in* Mr. Smith Goes to Washington): I'd have to agree with the Chief that the *Mapp* remedy *doesn't* work to deter violations, but I think it *could* work under the right circumstances. The problem is really an institutional one. Let's take the example used by the Chief. Who suffers when the cocaine is excluded from evi-

---

1. *Weeks v. United States*, 232 U.S. 383 (1914).

dence? Obviously, the public, since a bad guy is back on the street. But among the actors in the criminal justice system, it's the prosecutor—not the arresting officer—who is most directly hurt by the suppression. Winning convictions is the coin of the realm for us, and here's a case that's lost before the trial even begins. We might grumble something to the officers about how they screwed up, but we have no real power over them and no way to punish them. Police departments and district attorneys' offices are on the same side of the fight, but they're not the same institution. Unless and until the departments police themselves by disciplining their own officers for violating the rights of citizens, the deterrence function of the exclusionary rule will never be realized because the officer on the street just isn't affected where it hurts—job security and promotion.

That having been said, let me add a couple of my own gripes about *Mapp*. First, there's no language in the Fourth Amendment about excluding evidence. The suppression rule was devised by judges, and if it isn't working, or if the costs of its operation are too high, it can be erased by judges. So even though I personally wouldn't want to prosecute a case with tainted evidence, the drafters of the Bill of Rights provided no constitutional mandate for the rule, and I think the *Mapp* Court overstepped its authority when it suggested otherwise.

Second, there is no proportionality to the *Mapp* sanction. Whether the police commit an egregious violation or a minor indiscretion, whether we're dealing with a terrorist or a shoplifter, the remedy is always the same—the evidence is thrown out. Oh, and by the way, the police can always get around suppression anyway by "testilying"—don't you think they know what they have to say to make the search stick?

Public Defender *(Overworked, underpaid, but wouldn't switch places with anyone):* I couldn't agree more with my worthy opposing counsel about the need for internal enforcement of constitutional standards in our police departments. But just because the *Mapp* rule isn't operating perfectly doesn't mean we should scrap it. The Supreme Court adopted the sanction only after it correctly (and unavoidably) concluded that all other remedies had failed, and after many of the states had developed their own rules of exclusion in frustration at police lawlessness. We all know that both criminal and civil actions against the police for constitutional violations are doomed to failure in front of jurors who are concerned (and rightly so) about crime and violence in our society. The police are *their* protectors, and the jury isn't likely to convict or award damages against the cops for just "doing their job."

So we're really left with the exclusionary remedy as the only real method of discouraging, if not completely deterring, violations of the Constitution. We all can hope that, over time, enforcement of the *Mapp* rule will produce police departments committed to compliance with the Fourth and other amendments, and maybe we can think about abandoning it then. But let's remember that before *Mapp*, little attention was paid to the requirements of the Fourth Amendment. Now all police departments provide their officers with training about probable cause, the permissible bounds of a stop and frisk or a search incident to an arrest, and all the rest. This is no time to retreat to the days before 1961 when freedom from unreasonable search and seizure in this nation was merely an unfulfilled promise.

Average Citizen *(Impatient with lawyer jargon and convinced that violent crime is out of control):* You're never going to convince me that it makes any sense at all to let criminals off just because the police made a mistake. The cops finally get the goods on some dirtbag and the courts throw out the evidence. I'd do some "testilying" myself if I were in their position. No wonder nobody respects the System anymore! Talk about judicial integrity! Letting murderers and rapists off on technicalities is making us the laughing stock of the world. And of course the judges and lawyers go home to the 'burbs at 5 P.M., leaving the rest of us to deal with the low-lifes they set free that day.

Public Defender: I think you're missing the point of the *Mapp* rule. It's not because we want to do the criminals a favor that we "let them off." (And, by the way, it's really only a small percentage of defendants who are actually released as a result of suppression. There's usually other evidence and witnesses available, and so it's mostly just in narcotics possession cases where suppression means dismissal.) The premise is, and I firmly believe it, that the exclusionary rule is protecting *all* of us, innocent as well as guilty. What makes a police officer pause before searching me or you without proper justification, on a lark, or because he doesn't like your face or your attitude? It's the knowledge that if something is found, it can't be used at trial. Now you might say that the innocent don't need protecting because the officer won't find anything anyway. But we all cherish our little bit of privacy in this country. We don't want law enforcement personnel stopping and searching us willy nilly, on the street or in our cars. The only way to prevent that is to take away the goodies when the police *do* find them. Unfortunately that means letting criminals walk sometimes. I should also mention that excluding the evidence is an entirely avoidable result, because if the officers had followed the Fourth Amendment in the first place we wouldn't be talking about the exclusionary rule.

Moderator: I should point out that the *Mapp* rule has been significantly modified since its inception, and those modifications have curtailed its scope. The exclusionary sanction can only be enforced, for example, by someone with "standing" to raise it, which has come to mean that the victim must have had a close connection to the place searched in order to challenge the police action.[2] A "good faith" exception had been carved out by the Court, which removes the exclusionary sanction in situations where the police act in reasonable reliance on a warrant issued by a magistrate, even if it turns out the warrant wasn't valid.[3] And the remedy has been limited to criminal trials and direct appeals; it's not available in habeas reviews, grand jury proceedings, or civil actions.[4] In other words, the Court has not been unmindful of the need to constantly adjust the rule to accommodate the interests of law enforcement and public safety.

Police Chief: Unfortunately Rome is burning while the justices are tinkering, Professor. It's time to get rid of *Mapp*, and I think the Court will do just that. It's just a matter of time.

Moderator: Well, I'll leave prediction to those of you with the tea leaves, but it does seem that the Court is moving in that direction. Anyway, the debate over the suppression sanction won't be resolved here today. The problem is, as always, balancing the public interest in prosecuting crime against the equally important public interest in maintaining a free society, which respects individual rights. We've run out of time, so until next time, I thank you all for your insights.

As we discuss the operation of the exclusionary rule and the limitations that have been placed upon it, do not lose sight of the sharp

---

2. See §7.3.1.
3. See §7.3.3.
4. See §7.3.2.

policy debate that underlies the controversy concerning the rule. Be assured that the Supreme Court never does.

§7.2   The Derivative Evidence ("Fruit-of-the-Poisonous-Tree") Doctrine

The exclusionary remedy applies not only to evidence obtained as a direct result of a constitutional violation, but also to evidence indirectly derived from the violation. In a manner not unlike "but-for" causation analysis in tort law, courts trace the chain of events from the initial violation to its primary and secondary products. For example, if the police conduct an unlawful search of Jones, the ledger book they seize from him indicating his involvement in narcotics transactions is rendered inadmissible against Jones at trial. In addition, evidence that is derived from the book is deemed tainted by the initial constitutional violation and, as the "fruit of the poisonous tree," is also subject to suppression. If, therefore, the police use the information in the ledger book to obtain warrants to search the homes of the buyers listed, evidence obtained from those searches is not admissible against Jones because its discovery derived from the book illegally seized from him. (A discussion of the critical issue of who has standing to raise the illegality follows in §7.3.)

As in the tort doctrine of proximate cause, there are limits on how far courts will trace the taint of a Fourth Amendment illegality. As we shall see, if the taint becomes too attenuated, or there is an independent source for the evidence, or the evidence would have been inevitably discovered anyway, exclusion is deemed inappropriate.

In *Wong Sun v. United States*, 371 U.S. 471 (1963), James Toy was arrested on suspicion of narcotics trafficking. At the time of his arrest, Toy made a statement to the police implicating Johnny Yee. The police then proceeded to arrest and search Yee. After they discovered narcotics in his bedroom, Yee made a statement implicating Wong Sun. Wong Sun was then arrested, released on his own recognizance, and several days later he made a statement concerning the narcotics transactions. The arrest of Toy was subsequently held to be unlawful because it was not based on probable cause. The question before the Court was how far the taint of that illegality should travel down the road of subsequent events. Were the statements and evidence obtained from Yee and Wong Sun rendered inadmissible against Toy because they could all be traced back to his unlawful arrest?

To make this determination, the Court adopted the following test: whether the secondary evidence was discovered by *exploitation* of the initial illegality (in which case it must be suppressed), or instead by means sufficiently *attenuated* to be purged of the original taint. The Court held that the statement made by Toy must be excluded from evidence because it was the direct product of his unlawful arrest, having occurred immediately thereafter. The statement of Yee as well as the narcotics found in his home were suppressed because the federal agents got to them solely and directly by using the information illegally obtained from Toy. Wong Sun's statement, however, was held admissible in evidence against Toy because, although it was the fruit of the poisonous tree, its connection to the initial illegality was attenuated: Wong Sun had been released on his own recognizance and had voluntarily returned days later to make the statement. The taint of Toy's unlawful arrest had dissipated, the Court concluded, with the passage of time and the intervention of Wong Sun's own free will.

The Court elaborated on the concept of attenuation in *United States v. Ceccolini*, 435 U.S. 268 (1978). An unlawful search in a flower shop led months later to the discovery of a prosecution witness. The issue before the Court was whether that testimony should be suppressed as the fruit of the poisonous tree. The Court held that a live witness willing to testify requires "a closer, more direct link between the illegality and that kind of testimony" in order to justify suppression than is required for physical evidence. The rationale for the distinction is that the witness's free will in deciding to testify is a significant intervening act thus breaking the chain of causation from the initial illegality. The Court also expressed its concern about any application of the derivative evidence doctrine that would "permanently disable" a cooperative witness from testifying. "Witnesses are not like guns or documents which remain hidden from view until one turns over a sofa or opens a filing cabinet. Witnesses can, and often do, come forward and offer evidence entirely of their own volition. And, evaluated properly, the degree of free will necessary to dissipate the taint will very likely be found more often in the case of live-witness testimony than other kinds of evidence." 435 U.S. at 276–277.

Mindful of the deterrence rationale behind the exclusionary rule as well as the societal costs of excluding relevant evidence from the trial, courts weigh a number of factors in assessing whether the poison of a constitutional violation has been purged:

1) *The time period between the illegality and the acquisition of the secondary evidence*—The longer the period, the more likely

attenuation will be found. In *Ceccolini*, for example, where four months elapsed between the initial illegality and the interview of the live witness, the Court concluded that the taint had dissipated.

2) *The occurrence of intervening events*—The more links (or should we say kinks) in the chain between the illegality and the secondary evidence, the more attenuated the connection. Events representing an individual's free choice, such as Wong Sun's decision to make a statement or a suspect's consent to a search, are likely to be viewed as breaking the connection. Similarly, the giving of *Miranda* warnings is viewed as an intervening event to be considered in the attenuation analysis.

3) *The flagrancy of the initial illegality*—The more deliberate and flagrant the constitutional violation, the more reason there is to suppress *all* evidence that can be traced back to the illegality. Conversely, where the violation is unintentional and minor, the necessity for deterrence of future misconduct is less compelling. In *Ceccolini*, for example, where the offending officer inadvertently discovered evidence of gambling while conversing with a friend in the flower shop, the Court observed: "[There is] not the slightest evidence to suggest that Biro entered the shop or picked up the envelope with the intent of finding tangible evidence bearing on an illicit gambling operation. . . . Application of the exclusionary rule in this situation could not have the slightest deterrent effect on the behavior of an officer such as Biro." 435 U.S. at 279–280.

In addition to the concept of *attenuation*, there are two other important limitations on the operation of the derivative evidence doctrine. If the prosecution can establish that the secondary evidence was obtained from an *independent source*, and not solely by exploiting the original illegality, then the evidence will not be suppressed. In this case, it can be said that the fruit does not derive from the poisonous tree. If, for example, the police learn of the whereabouts of narcotics from the ledger book unlawfully seized from Jones, but they can demonstrate that they also had independent knowledge of these locations from an informant, suppression of the narcotics would not be required.

In *Murray v. United States*, 487 U.S. 533 (1988), the police illegally entered a warehouse without a warrant and observed bales, which they believed to be marijuana. Without disturbing the bales, the police left and sought a warrant to search. In their affidavit in support of the warrant, the police relied solely on information they would later contend they had *prior to* the illegal entry (and, indeed, the officers neglected to mention the previous entry in their affidavit). The warrant was issued and executed, and the bales were "rediscovered." On review, the Court ruled that the bales would be admissible at trial if the warrant affidavit was in fact based on sources independent of the illegal entry (to be determined on remand). The Court set aside the concerns expressed by Justice Marshall in his dissent that *Murray* would encourage police to circumvent the warrant process and, further, that the independent source exception is too vulnerable to manipulation by the police because they alone know what information was secured independently and what was discovered through the illegality.

Another limitation on the reach of the derivative evidence doctrine is the *inevitable discovery* exception. Even if the evidence in question is found to have been the fruit of the poisonous tree—evidence that can be traced directly back to the initial illegality and for which there is no independent source—suppression can nonetheless be avoided if the prosecution can establish that the evidence would have ultimately been discovered anyway by lawful means. In *Nix v. Williams*, 467 U.S. 431 (1984), the initial illegality was the violation of the suspect's Sixth Amendment rights[5]—the officers deliberately elicited an incriminating statement from him in the absence of his counsel. See discussion of *Brewer v. Williams*, in §10.1. Specifically, the detective's "Christian burial speech" prompted Williams to provide information that led the police to the homicide victim's body. Evidence concerning the body was later introduced at trial and Williams was convicted. Despite the straight line of causation from constitutional violation to secondary evidence, the Court held the evidence was properly admissible because the body would have been discovered anyway within a short period of time by a search party of volunteers that was operating in the area. Casting aside suggestions that inevitable discovery will generally be a matter of speculation, the Court indicated that there must be a basis in fact, readily verifiable, for the conclusion that discovery would have occurred. The search party provided that basis in *Nix*. The lower courts concluded that, had the search not been

---

5. As noted previously, the Court has applied the same exclusionary rule doctrines to violations of the Sixth Amendment as it has to those of the Fourth.

suspended when the body was found, it would have been discovered "within a short period of time" in the same condition as it was actually found (because of the freezing temperature, tissue deterioration would not have occurred).

The limitations that have been placed on the derivative evidence doctrine reflect the Court's continuing concern about the costs of the exclusionary rule. The deterrence rationale does not, it is argued, require suppression of evidence that the police obtained, or would have obtained, even if the unconstitutional action had not occurred. Such "overkill" would unfairly deprive the prosecution of relevant evidence without achieving the corresponding benefit of educating the police. Offending law enforcement officers must not be placed in a *better* position as a result of an illegality (and must therefore be deprived of the fruits of their violation); but they should also not be placed in a *worse* situation because of the error. They should not, in other words, be deprived of evidence that they actually secured through an independent source, or would have inevitably secured, notwithstanding the illegality. See *Nix v. Williams*, supra.

The suppression remedy is triggered, therefore, only where: 1) the connection between the secondary evidence and the original violation is close and unattentuated; and 2) there is no independent lawful means that led, or would have led, the police to the evidence.

Figure 7–1 illustrates the operation of the derivative evidence doctrine.

EXAMPLES

1. Which of the following situations raise potential application of the derivative evidence doctrine? How should each be analyzed?

   a. The police make a warrantless entry into *A*'s apartment and place her under arrest. Days after being taken into custody (and after receiving *Miranda* warnings), *A* volunteers an incriminating statement, which the prosecution proposes to use at trial.

   b. The police make a warrantless entry into *B*'s apartment and seize a diamond tiara, which they suspect has been stolen. They take the tiara to a jewelry store that had previously reported a theft, and the proprietor recognizes it as the one taken from his establishment. The proprietor also selects *B*'s photograph from an array the police show him and is prepared to identify *B* in court as the person he had observed suspiciously "casing" the store the day before the burglary.

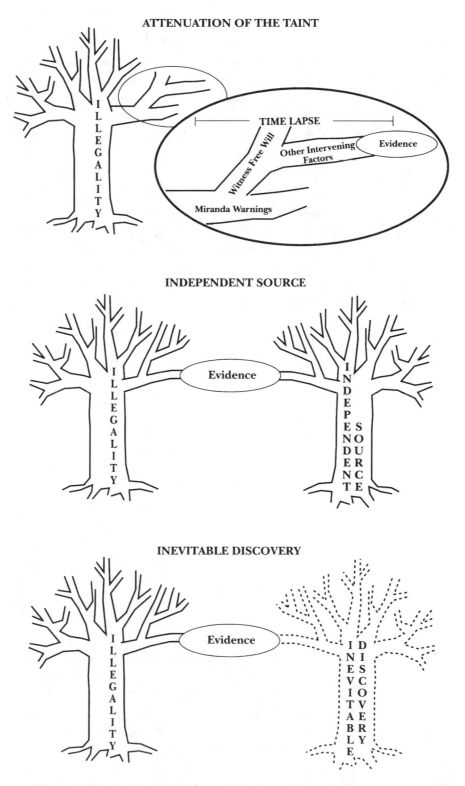

Figure 7–1: Derivative Evidence Doctrine—Exceptions

      c. The police lawfully arrest *C* but then coerce a confession from her that she has been operating an illegal gambling business from her pharmacy. The officers report her confession in their affidavit in support of an application for a warrant to search *C*'s store. The warrant is issued, the search conducted, and evidence of gambling operations is seized.

      d. The police forcibly (and without a warrant or probable cause) enter *D*'s RV trailer, which is parked unoccupied in her driveway. They conduct an intensive search and, in a hidden compartment behind a cabinet, they locate dozens of bottles containing heroin. Days later the police apprehend *D* and, when confronted with the bottles by her interrogators, *D* confesses to possession and sale of the unlawful drug.

2. Based on a tip from a neighborhood resident, Los Angeles Police Officer Rodriguez suspected that a blue van parked at the same downtown location each evening after midnight was involved in the smuggling of illegal aliens. Rodriguez and his partner approached the van and ordered the occupants out. He then looked inside and observed several sheets of paper hanging from the sun visor. Reaching in, the officer removed the papers and noted that they contained a long list of names and numbers. Rodriguez asked the van's occupants what the numbers next to the names meant, and one of the men (later identified as Juan Colon) responded that he had just been transported into the United States from Mexico and the number next to his name represented the amount of money he had paid the driver. The officers then placed the driver, Hector Ortiz, under arrest for illegal transportation of aliens. The prosecution proposes to use Colon's statement made at the scene of the arrest as well as his live testimony in court against defendant Ortiz at trial. Will this evidence be admissible?

3. Working under cover, narcotics squad detective Roland Rambo purchased a large quantity of crack cocaine from Lance Spear at his home on Elm Street. The detective reported this information to his supervisor, Sergeant Brady, who immediately proceeded to the courthouse to seek warrants to arrest Spear and to search his home. In the meantime, Rambo and several of his colleagues returned to Spear's home where they were to wait for Brady and the warrants. When the sergeant failed to appear after one hour, the officers decided to act on their own. With their guns drawn, they knocked on Spear's door and told him he had no choice but to

let them in. Spear relented, and the officers entered. They discovered a large cache of cocaine and weapons in plain view in the hallway.

At that point Sergeant Brady finally appeared with the arrest and search warrants. She arrested Spear, searched the home, and "rediscovered" the items previously found by Rambo. Spear has moved to suppress the evidence on the grounds that it was the fruit of a coerced consent and illegal entry. What result?

4. State police officers, armed with a valid warrant to arrest Peter Swope for the crime of defrauding the state welfare agency of $10,000, stopped Swope in his car on the Thruway. He was taken into custody, and his automobile was locked and left on the shoulder of the road. Later that day the state troopers returned and searched Swope's car. They located a plastic trash bag on the passenger seat, which they brought back to the station and opened to find a large quantity of marijuana. Although the welfare fraud charges have been dropped, the prosecution intends to use the marijuana against Swope at his upcoming trial for possession with intent to distribute an unlawful substance. Swope's counsel has filed a motion to suppress and has persuaded the court that because there was no probable cause to believe seizable items were present in the car, the search was unlawful. Is there any way the prosecution can nonetheless avoid suppression of the marijuana? What if state police regulations require that vehicles of persons taken into custody on the open road be impounded and subjected to a prescribed inventory inspection?

5. Wilma is driving a rental car accompanied by her husband Fred. The car is lawfully stopped for speeding. On request the officer is shown the rental agreement, which is in Wilma's name, as well as her license. The officer issues Wilma a warning, but when she appears unusually nervous, he asks if she has any narcotics in the car. She says no, but upon the officer's request she gives him the keys for the trunk, which he opens to find a garment bag that has a tag labelled "Fred" on it. The officer feels the bag, removes a large manilla envelope, and asks Fred if he can open it. Although Fred hesitates, the officer threatens to get a drug-sniffing dog, and Fred finally relents (muttering he doesn't really have a choice) to the opening of the envelope, which contains cocaine. What are the chances of suppression at trial?

EXPLANATIONS

1. The point here is that the derivative evidence doctrine is poten-
    tially applicable in *any* situation where there has been an initial
    illegality followed by a chain of events leading to incriminating
    evidence. The illegality can take the form of a violation of any of
    the constitutional commands we have discussed throughout this
    book—Fourth, Fifth, or Sixth Amendment.[6] It may be an unlawful
    search or arrest, a coerced confession, or the deliberate elicitation
    of incriminating statements in the absence of counsel. The sec-
    ondary evidence can take the form of physical evidence, a confes-
    sion, testimony of a live witness, or an eyewitness identification.

    For any illegality identified in a given fact situation, the ana-
    lytical task is to trace and identify its ripple effects. With regard to
    each item of evidence that is causally connected to the illegality, it
    must be determined 1) whether the chain has become too long or
    otherwise attentuated so it can be said that the taint has dissipated;
    2) whether the police secured the evidence through an independent
    source; and 3) whether the police would have inevitably secured
    the evidence through another means. If the answer to each of these
    questions is no, then the derivative evidence doctrine applies and
    the evidence will be suppressed as the fruit of the poisonous tree.
    (An additional inquiry must often be made into the question of
    who has standing to raise the issue of illegality. See §7.3.1.)

    In each of the fact situations presented in example 1, there
    are indirect products that flow from the unlawful police action. In
    example 1a, the suspect's confession can be traced back to the
    unlawful entry and arrest. Thus even if the confession was vol-
    untary and not subject to challenge on due process grounds (see
    Chapter 8), it appears to be the fruit of a Fourth Amendment
    violation. Certain factors, however, point toward a conclusion that
    the connection is too attenuated to support application of the
    exclusionary rule. First, several days passed between the arrest and
    the confession. It could therefore be said that the original taint
    has dissipated. What this means in reference to the deterrence goal
    of the exclusionary rule is that the offending officers are less likely

---

6. Violations of the *Miranda* requirements are treated somewhat differently
and the fruits of such violations are not subject to suppression under the same
standards as fruits of an illegal search or coerced confession. See §9.3.3.

to be educated by the suppression of a confession remote in time from the unlawful arrest than they would be if the confession had followed immediately. Compare *Brown v. Illinois*, 422 U.S. 590 (1975) (suppressing a confession that occurred within two hours of defendant's unlawful arrest). Second, *A* volunteered the confession, and this (apparently) free choice on her part can be viewed as a break in the chain of causation. See *Wong Sun*, supra. A third factor to be weighed would be the flagrancy of the initial violation: Did the police, for example, merely misjudge a situation they reasonably believed was an emergency that justified immediate entry into *A*'s apartment, or did they deliberately disregard the commands of the Fourth Amendment?

A fourth factor to be considered in cases such as the one set out in example 1a, where the secondary evidence is a confession, is whether the suspect received proper *Miranda* warnings prior to the statement. *Brown v. Illinois*, supra, rejected the conclusion that such warnings are sufficient to purge the taint of a prior illegal arrest. The Court explained:

> If *Miranda* warnings, by themselves, were held to attenuate the taint of an unconstitutional arrest, regardless of how wanton and purposeful the Fourth Amendment violation, the effect of the exclusionary rule would be substantially diluted. [Illegal arrests] would be encouraged by the knowledge that evidence derived therefrom could well be made admissible at trial by the simple expedient of giving *Miranda* warnings. Any incentive to avoid Fourth Amendment violations would be eviscerated by making the warnings, in effect, a "cure-all."

422 U.S. at 602. The provision of *Miranda* warnings to *A* is nonetheless a factor weighing against application of the derivative evidence doctrine.

In a decision dealing with a confession as the fruit of an unlawful arrest, the Court emphasized the need to weigh the costs of exclusion against the deterrent purpose served. See *New York v. Harris*, 495 U.S. 14 (1990). Police, armed with probable cause but without an arrest warrant (as required by *Payton v. New York*, see §5.6), arrested the suspect in his home. Harris then made incriminating statements both at home and later at the station house. The Court refused to apply the poisonous tree doctrine to the station house statement, reasoning that the purpose of the *Payton* warrant requirement, that is, protection of the privacy of the home, was fully accomplished by suppressing the statement made in the home. "Because the officers had probable cause to arrest Harris for a crime, Harris was not unlawfully in custody when he was removed to the stationhouse, given *Miranda* warnings and allowed to talk." 495 U.S. at 18. The Court distinguished *Brown v. Illinois*, where the police lacked probable cause to arrest and thus suppression of all subsequent confessions was deemed justified.

Turning to example 1b, the unlawful search yielded the tiara, which would be excluded as the direct product of the illegality. The officers further exploited that illegality to obtain an identification of *B* from the proprietor. Thus even if the identification process was not unnecessarily suggestive and violative of the suspect's rights (see §11.1), it could be challenged as evidence derived from the initial unlawful search. Because the selection of *B*'s photograph followed closely in time from the unlawful seizure of the tiara, which indeed was used by the police to obtain the identification from the proprietor, that identification may very well be suppressed as fruit of the poisonous tree. The proposed in-court identification, however, may be held admissible because it is much further removed in time from the initial illegality and may have been based on an independent source, that is, the proprietor's observation of the person casing the store prior to the burglary. See *United States v. Crews*, 445 U.S. 463 (1980) (holding admissible an in-court identification despite the fact that both a photographic and a lineup identification were suppressed because of their closer proximity to defendant's unlawful arrest), discussed in §11.1.

It should be remembered that whenever the derivative evidence in question is the testimony of a live witness, as in example 1b, suppression requires a closer link to the initial illegality than is the case with physical evidence. *United States v. Ceccolini*, 435 U.S. 268 (1978).

In example 1c, the initial illegality is the coercion of the confession, which must be excluded from evidence. See Chapter 8. Because information from that tainted confession was used to secure the search warrant, the items seized during the search are subject to suppression under the derivative evidence doctrine. Even if the search and seizure met constitutional standards, they may be poisoned because of their genesis in the violation of the suspect's right against compelled self-incrimination. The deterrence rationale supports exclusion here—that is, unless the police are deprived of *all* the fruits of a coercive interrogation, they will not be sufficiently discouraged from conducting another one in the future. The items seized in *C*'s store should therefore be excluded from evidence. See, e.g., *Commonwealth v. White*, 374 Mass. 132, 371 N.E.2d 777 (1977), *aff'd by an equally divided court*, 439 U.S. 280 (1978) (the Massachusetts Supreme Judicial Court suppressed evidence seized pursuant to a search warrant because the affidavit in support of the warrant had been based on information obtained during an unlawful interrogation of defendant).

In example 1d, the police clearly exploited the illegal search by confronting D with the evidence seized, and thereby obtained her confession. Thus, even though the confession may have been secured without coercion, it nonetheless is subject to suppression under the derivative evidence doctrine. This connection between the illegality and the confession argues in favor of suppression: In order to deter future unlawful searches, the police must be deprived of *all* the evidence they gained from it, directly and indirectly. Arguing against suppression is that several days separate the search from the confession, and that *D*'s confession may be an intervening act of free will. The provision of *Miranda* warnings (if they had been given) would also weigh against exclusion of the confession.

2. While the officers might have had reasonable suspicion to stop and briefly detain the occupants of the vehicle (see §4.4), their intrusion into the vehicle required either 1) reasonable fear for their safety (see §4.4); or 2) probable cause either to arrest and conduct a search incident to that arrest (see §6.3) or to search the vehicle (see §6.4). All such justification would seem to be lacking here. The intrusion into the van and removal of the papers thus becomes the initial illegality, the ripples of which can clearly be traced to the statement made by Colon implicating the defendant. Given the short time frame between the search and the on-the-scene statement, as well as the actual use of the unlawfully seized list to obtain the statement, it is unlikely a court would find that the taint had become attenuated. The statement would be inadmissible.

    On the separate question of the admissibility of subsequent in-court testimony from Colon, there is obviously a looser temporal connection. Moreover, as *Ceccolini* teaches, live testimony is less likely than physical evidence to be suppressed as the fruit of the poisonous tree. In our example, however, the witness was questioned immediately following the illegal search, the officer's question was prompted by the very fruits of the search, and the witness himself was discovered only as a result of the search. This contrasts sharply with the situation in *Ceccolini* where the officer's unlawful discovery of the betting slips was far removed from the questioning of the witness months later, the slips were not used during the questioning, and the witness was known to the investigators before the illegal search occurred. Further, unlike *Ceccolini*, it is unlikely that Colon would have come forward as a witness on his own initiative to inform the police of his illegal alien status; he spoke in the pressure of the moment as the officer read the papers removed from the van. Compare *Satchell v. Cardwell*, 653 F.2d 408, 409 n.7 (9th Cir. 1981) (the court concluded that a brutally beaten rape victim would probably have come forward to testify even if she had not been discovered as a result of an unlawful entry, and thus her testimony was admissible). There was no likelihood here, in short, that the witness would have been inevitably discovered without the occurrence of the unlawful search. It is likely that the in-court testimony would therefore be suppressed under the derivative evidence doctrine. See *United States v. Ramirez-Sandoval*, 872 F.2d 1392 (9th Cir. 1989) (suppressing both the on-the-scene statement and live testimony under similar circumstances).

3. Rambo and his colleagues discovered the contraband as a direct result of their forced unlawful entry into Spear's residence, thus rendering the evidence presumptively inadmissible. The prosecution might avoid suppression, however, through the independent source exception. Sergeant Brady, without knowledge of Rambo's actions, secured the warrants with information separate from and untainted by Rambo's entry, and she seized the evidence pursuant to those valid warrants. As *Murray v. United States*, 487 U.S. 533 (1988), teaches, evidence that is initially discovered through unlawful means but is later acquired through genuinely independent and lawful means may be admissible in evidence. In *United States v. Curtis*, 931 F.2d 1011 (4th Cir. 1991), on facts similar to our example, the court concluded:

> [T]he warrant authorizing a search of Curtis' residence was issued solely upon information known to the officers before the [illegal] entry. . . . [And] the record clearly demonstrates that a search warrant would have been sought regardless of the entry because detective McCracken had already departed to obtain a warrant prior to the entry and had no knowledge of the actions of the other officers.

Thus, the search pursuant to the warrant was independent of the entry, and the district court did not err in refusing to suppress the evidence seized pursuant to it.

931 F.2d at 1014.

United States v. Markling, 7 F.3d 1309 (7th Cir. 1993), involved a variation of this situation. Information found as a result of an unlawful search of defendant's briefcase was included in an affidavit to obtain a warrant to search defendant's hotel room. Unlike *Murray,* the warrant application in *Markling* was partially based on what was seen during the illegal search. The Seventh Circuit, however, found that the independent source doctrine still applied and the warrant was valid. The test the court used involved two questions: 1) Did the illegally obtained evidence affect the magistrate's decision? 2) Was the officer's decision to seek a warrant prompted by the illegal search? With regard to the first question, the court found that the application, minus the illegally obtained evidence, still showed sufficient probable cause of illegal activity. With regard to the second question, the court remanded to determine whether the officer would have sought a warrant even if he had not conducted the illegal search.

4. Even if the search of Swope's car was unlawful because a) it was not contemporaneous with the arrest and b) there was no probable cause to search, and the fruits of the illegality were therefore presumptively inadmissible, the prosecution may nonetheless use the evidence if it can demonstrate that the police would have inevitably discovered it anyway in the normal course of their work. See *Nix v. Williams,* 467 U.S. 431 (1984). Because Swope was arrested, his automobile was subject to impoundment and inventory under police regulations. As long as such procedures are not a pretext for a search for evidence of crime (see §§4.5 and 6.9), the inventory would be lawful. The marijuana would thus have been discovered by routine (lawful) procedures even if the police had not conducted their unlawful search on the highway. In similar situations where an illegality resulted in the discovery of evidence that would have been found in any event pursuant to a lawful inventory, courts have applied the inevitable discovery exception and admitted the evidence. See, e.g., *United States v. Kirk,* 111 F.3d 390 (5th Cir. 1997); *United States v. Mancera-Londono,* 912 F.2d 373 (9th Cir. 1990) (and cases cited).

Although the Court warned in *Nix v. Williams* that inevitable discovery cannot rest on mere speculation as to what might have been, some courts seem to be doing just that. See, e.g., *United*

217

States v. Lamas, 930 F.2d 1099 (5th Cir. 1991) (holding that the agents would have inevitably discovered the contraband, even if they had not done so by way of defendant's involuntary consent, because they had probable cause to search and one of the officers testified that he was about to seek a warrant when defendant made that unnecessary by agreeing to the search); *United States v. Ivey*, 915 F.2d 380 (8th Cir. 1990) (holding that records were properly admitted into evidence, despite the fact that they were seized during an unlawful search of the defendant's purse, because the government had "an alternative line of investigation," that is, the police had suspicions and leads that would inevitably have led them to the lawful discovery of the evidence).

Sometimes, on the other hand, the inevitability is hard to dispute. In *United States v. Oakley*, 731 F. Supp. 1363 (D. Ind. 1990), the court held that even if the digital rectal cavity probe of the prisoner was unlawful, the balloons containing narcotics that were found were nonetheless admissible because they would have been inevitably discovered as a result of the isolated prisoner's normal excretory process. "Although physically and mentally capable humans learn at an early age to postpone the call of nature at most times, this control mechanism merely delays the inevitable release of our body's metabolic by-products. If Oakley was to survive, it was inevitable that he pass the balloons through his system. Once eliminated from Oakley's system, the balloons were destined for discovery by prison authorities." 731 F. Supp. at 1372–1373.

The inevitable discovery exception significantly curtails, and has the potential to emasculate, the operation of the exclusionary rule and its derivative evidence component. Mindful of this, one circuit has required, as part of the analysis, consideration of the following question: "Does the application of the inevitable discovery exception [in this case] either provide an incentive for police misconduct or significantly weaken fourth amendment protection?" *United States v. Silvestri*, 787 F.2d 736, 744 (1st Cir. 1986). Following this mandate the district court refused to apply the inevitable discovery exception where the defendant's gun had been found as a direct result of his coerced admissions but would have been discovered anyway when the police searched the area of the arrest: "Application of the inevitable discovery doctrine here would encourage law enforcement officers to believe they can avoid the burden of a prolonged area search by physically abusing a suspect, without significant risk of forfeiting the admissibility of any physical evidence. . . . Thus, this is the type of case in which the exclusionary rule has a substantial potential deterrent effect which would be significantly weakened if the inevitable discovery doctrine were applied." *United States v. Rullo*, 748 F. Supp. 36, 44 (D. Mass. 1990).

It should be noted that the inevitable discovery exception is now cropping up in cases such as *Oakley*, supra, where the issue is the admissibility of a *direct* fruit of an illegal search, as opposed to the indirect derivative result (the balloons were obtained as the direct result of the rectal search). Extending the inevitable discovery exception beyond the derivative evidence context to cases involving direct fruits of the illegality raises a serious question about the continued viability of the exclusionary rule.

5. Since Wilma is driving and the car is rented in her name, she clearly has authority to consent to the search of the trunk. This permission extends to any closed containers in the car. See *Florida v. Jimeno*, 500 U.S. 248 (1991), discussed in §6.7. The complication arises here because the garment bag is labelled with Fred's name. Does Wilma have apparent authority to consent to the opening of Fred's bag? A reasonable officer under the *Illinois v. Rodriguez* standard (see §6.7) would probably not conclude that she does. Fred's consent under threat of the dreaded sniffer-dog may very well be deemed coerced under the totality of the circumstances analysis.

Assuming that the consents are invalid, what about the possibility of applying the inevitable discovery doctrine to justify admission of the cocaine? Would the evidence have ultimately been discovered by lawfuls means? The Eighth Circuit answered yes in the similar case of *United States v. Hammons*, 152 F.3d 1025 (8th Cir. 1998), concluding that the officer would have called upon a drug-detection dog, which would have sniffed out the contents of the envelope. Application of the inevitable discovery exception required, in the Eighth Circuit's view, not only a showing that there was a reasonable probability that the evidence would have been discovered by lawful means but also that the government was pursuing a substantial, alternative line of investigation at the time of the police misconduct. (*Hammons* notes that the circuits are split on this issue, some requiring only the first prong.) The officer's assertion that he would call a drug-sniffing dog was deemed sufficient showing that he had initiated an alternative plan.

§7.3   Limitations on the Exclusionary Rule

The tension between the goal of effective law enforcement (that is, apprehending and convicting the bad guys) and the protection of individual rights and privacy has played itself out over past decades in judicial expansion or contraction of the exclusionary rule. The suppression remedy reached its high-water mark in the Warren Court era, and the years since have witnessed a slow but steady recession. Thus although the Supreme Court has chosen to maintain the rule excluding unlawfully obtained evidence at trial, it has chipped away at it by imposing a number of substantial limitations on its scope, coverage, and operation.

§7.3.1   Standing

One major restriction on the operation of the exclusionary rule is the doctrine of standing. Only those who are actual victims of the alleged violation have standing to challenge it. In its most basic form, the doctrine prevents *A* from complaining about an infringement of *B*'s rights. If, for example, *B*'s home is subjected to an unlawful search and items are seized that implicate *A* in criminal activity, *A* is not permitted to seek exclusion of that evidence at his trial based on the Fourth Amendment violation. Although the search certainly has consequences for *A*, because his rights were not directly violated when the police entered *B*'s home he lacks standing to seek suppression. Only if the evidence were offered against *B* would the exclusionary remedy be available, and then only to *B*.[7] As the Court has put it, "a person who is aggrieved by an illegal search and seizure only through the introduction of damaging evidence secured by a search of a third person's premises or property has not had any of his Fourth Amendment rights infringed." *Rakas v. Illinois*, 439 U.S. 128, 134 (1978).

The definition of a victim who has standing to challenge a violation has been expanded and then narrowed over the past three decades. While initially tied to property law concepts, the decision in *Jones v. United States*, 362 U.S. 257 (1960), rejected that analysis and broadened the definition by conferring standing on anyone "legitimately on the premises" where the search occurs, even if they are not owners or

---

7. The concept is also reflected in the requirement of Fed. R. Crim. P. 41(e) that a party moving to suppress evidence must be a "person aggrieved."

lessees of the property. Thus the fact that Jones was merely staying at his friend's apartment at the time of the search did not mean that he lacked standing to challenge the admission into evidence against him of narcotics seized there.

Together with expanding the general category of victims to include those without enforceable property interests in the premises searched, *Jones* also established a rule providing automatic standing to any defendant charged with a possessory offense. Recognizing the dilemma faced by such defendants—that in order to establish standing to challenge the search, the accused oftentimes had to admit the contraband was his and thus incriminate himself—the Court conferred standing categorically and without regard to the particular circumstances of each case.

Neither prong of the *Jones* analysis survives today. The automatic standing doctrine was overturned in *United States v. Salvucci*, 448 U.S. 83 (1980).[8] And the "legitimately on the premises" standard has been replaced by a new standard based on the expectation of privacy analysis adopted in *Katz v. United States*, 389 U.S. 347 (1967) (see §3.2).

In *Rakas v. Illinois*, 439 U.S. 128 (1978), passengers in a car stopped by the police sought to suppress a rifle and shells found in the glove compartment and under the front seat. They based their standing to challenge the search of the car (which they did not own) and the seizure of the incriminating items (which they did not claim were theirs) on the theory that they were legitimately on the premises. Concluding that the *Jones* standard was "too broad a gauge for measurement of Fourth Amendment rights," the Court abandoned it and held instead that the standing requirement "is more properly subsumed under substantive Fourth Amendment doctrine." 439 U.S. at 139, 142. The question of standing thus becomes merged into the question of whether the challenged action infringed an interest protected by the amendment, which in turn becomes the question of whether *this particular defendant's* reasonable expectation of privacy was intruded upon.

Applying this analysis, the Court concluded that the search of the car did not violate the rights of the *Rakas* passengers. The passengers asserted neither a property interest in the place searched (the car) nor

---

8. The Court had previously held in *Simmons v. United States*, 390 U.S. 377 (1968), that an admission by an accused during the suppression hearings that the contraband was his could no longer be used against him at trial. Some states have retained their own automatic standing rules under the state constitution. See, e.g., *Commonwealth v. Amendola*, 406 Mass. 592 (Sup. Jud. Ct. 1990).

in the items seized, and thus were held to have had no expectation of privacy in either. The Court emphasized that the places searched—the glove compartment and under the seat—were areas in which mere passengers (in contrast with the car's owner) would not normally have a legitimate expectation of privacy.[9]

While the *Rakas* Court purported to agree with *Jones* that property interests should not control standing analysis, property concepts focusing on the defendant's relationship to the place searched do indeed appear to dominate contemporary standing analysis. In *Rawlings v. Kentucky*, 448 U.S. 98 (1980), for example, defendant challenged a search of his female companion's purse in which drugs that he had hidden inside were found. Despite the fact that Rawlings admitted ownership of the drugs on the scene and during the suppression proceedings, the Court ruled that he did not have standing to challenge the search. While observing that Rawlings's claim of ownership of the items seized was a factor to be considered in the standing analysis, the Court held that he had no reasonable expectation of privacy in the place searched (the purse), and thus his rights were not implicated. In reaching this conclusion, the Court emphasized the following facts relating to defendant's interest in the purse: 1) Rawlings had known his companion for only a few days at the time of the "sudden bailment"; 2) he had never sought nor received access to the purse before; 3) he had no right to exclude others from access to the purse, and indeed on the very morning of the search, another friend of Cox's had rummaged through the purse for a hairbrush; 4) the "precipitous nature of [Rawlings's placing of the drugs in the purse] hardly supports a reasonable inference that [he] took normal precautions to maintain his privacy"; and 5) Rawlings admitted in testimony that he had no subjective expectation that Cox's purse would be free from governmental intrusion. 448 U.S. at 105.

Those with standing to enforce Fourth Amendment protections appear, on the whole, to be limited to the group of victims who either own or have some other close connection to the place searched. The latter group has included the defendant in *Jones*[10] who, although he did not own the apartment searched, was nonetheless alone there with

---

9. Distinguishing searches of homes and automobiles, the Court pointed out that "cars are not to be treated identically with houses or apartments for Fourth Amendment [expectation of privacy] purposes." See §3.2.

10. The *Rakas* Court indicated that the *Jones* case would come out the same way—that is, with Jones having standing—under the new expectation of privacy analysis.

his friend's permission at the time of the search, had a key, and kept some of his possessions there. An overnight guest who did not have a key and was never alone in the home was similarly held to have standing to challenge his warrantless arrest in *Minnesota v. Olson*, 495 U.S. 91 (1990), where the Court reasoned that society recognized a guest's legitimate expectation of privacy in the host's home in such a situation. Where, however, individuals went to an apartment for the sole purpose of packaging cocaine in exchange for some of the product, spent only two hours there, and had never been to the apartment before, the Court refused to confer standing to challenge a search. See *Minnesota v. Carter*, 525 U.S. 83 (1998). In sum, lacking a possessory interest in or a close connection to the place searched, defendants will not be permitted to pursue their claims of unconstitutional search and seizure.

On a final note, it should be added that while *Rakas* purported to merge the standing question with substantive Fourth Amendment analysis, it still makes sense conceptually to keep them separate. As Justice Blackmun has observed, it is possible for a defendant to demonstrate standing to challenge a search and yet fail to prove that the search was unlawful, and conversely for a defendant to show that an illegality occurred but fail to establish that he has standing to challenge it. See *Rawlings v. Kentucky*, 448 U.S. at 112 (Blackmun, J., concurring). Analytically, therefore, the standing issue should be resolved first and separate from the substantive issue of the illegality.

EXAMPLES

1. In which of the following situations does the defendant have standing to challenge the police action?

    a. Acting on an unsupported hunch that he was involved in gambling activities, officers arrested Clyde as he left his downtown office. A search of his briefcase turned up documents linking his friend, Bonnie, to a major bookmaking ring, and the prosecution now proposes to use the evidence against Bonnie at trial.

    b. Harry Homicidal hid a hatchet (which he had used on his latest victim) in a garage owned and used by his landlord. Police investigating the murder conducted a warrantless search of the garage and found the weapon. May Harry challenge the search if the hatchet is offered into evidence at his murder trial?

    c. Narcotics detectives had Dealer under surveillance as she rented a room at the Fleabag Hotel and entered it with a key. One hour later they observed Buyer knock and enter. The detectives waited five minutes and then stormed the hotel room, interrupting a narcotics transaction. Does either Dealer or Buyer have standing to challenge the seizure of narcotics and cash during this search when offered in evidence against them at trial? Would it help either's argument if she admitted that the items seized belonged to her?

d. Bill was a passenger in the rear of a sedan owned by Ted (who was seated in the front) and driven by Cynthia. Believing there was "something suspicious" about the car, state police officers stopped it, ordered the occupants out, and subjected the car to an intensive search. They discovered several opaque plastic bags containing marijuana on the rear seat, Cynthia's purse containing drug paraphernalia in the locked glove compartment, and a large quantity of hashish in the trunk. Bill, Ted, and Cynthia are charged with drug offenses and the prosecution proposes to use the items seized against each of them. Which of them, if any, have standing to object on Fourth Amendment grounds?

e. Bill rented a Honda from Ace Car Rental, which under the contract was to be returned by January 20. On January 24, now in unlawful possession of the Honda, Bill was stopped for speeding. Officer Jones asked for and was given the rental agreement, from which he learned that the car was overdue. Jones impounded the Honda, and pursuant to policy conducted a full inventory search, uncovering a gun in the glove compartment and narcotics in the trunk. Does Bill have standing to challenge the search?

Derivative Evidence Meets the Standing Doctrine

2. Having heard rumors to the effect that John was involved in the unlawful distribution of "underground" record albums, police officers made a warrantless entry into his apartment and found him in the kitchen. When the officers threatened to arrest him, John stated that he had nothing to do with such activities but that his friend, Paul, was involved. Because this information confirmed other reliable sources and thus established probable cause, a warrant was issued to search Paul's apartment. Inside the police discovered bootleg record albums and documents connecting John to the illegal scheme.

a. The evidence seized is offered against Paul at trial. Does he have standing under the Fourth Amendment to object?

b. The evidence seized is offered against John at trial. Does he have standing under the Fourth Amendment to object?

Standing in the Electronic Age

3. Jackie Accountant worked for All-American Defense Products, overseeing the preparation of sealed bids for contracts with Uncle Sam. Unbeknownst to her employer, Jackie was disclosing (by way of a computer link) pricing information to a competitor, Military Hardware, Inc. The disclosed information helped Military Hardware underbid All-American. Jackie charged a tidy fee for this service. The FBI got wind of this illegal scheme and, without bothering to seek a warrant, entered and searched the offices of Military Hardware. The agents seized several computer disks, which contained files evidencing Jackie's communications. May Jackie challenge the admission of these files into evidence against her?

EXPLANATIONS

1a. It is axiomatic that the Fourth Amendment confers personal rights that may not be vicariously asserted. While Clyde may challenge his unlawful arrest and search, Bonnie has no standing to do so. No matter how egregious the violation, the exclusionary sanction is unavailable to Bonnie in these circumstances. Although she is a victim of the police action in the sense that the fruits of the arrest are being used against her, *her* right to be free of unreasonable search or seizure has not been invaded by a search of another's briefcase. See *Rawlings v. Kentucky*, 448 U.S. 98 (1980).

1b. In order to determine whether Harry's *own* rights have been violated, *Rakas v. Illinois*, 439 U.S. 128 (1978), requires us to determine whether his expectation of privacy was infringed upon when the officers entered and searched the garage. This in turn requires us to explore whether (by way of his lease or otherwise) Harry had a possessory interest in, use of, or control over the garage. If not, he will likely be deemed to have no reasonable expectation of privacy in the place searched and thus lack standing to raise objections under the Fourth Amendment. The standing doctrine prevents Harry from complaining about a search of someone else's garage, even when the fruits of that search are used against Harry and not the garage owner.

Note that the Landlord, who obviously does have standing to challenge the search, has no way to do so through the suppression remedy because the hatchet is not being used against him. (Landlord may of course be able to pursue a civil action for the violation.)

1c. Unlike the first two problems, the individuals here were actually on the premises (and legitimately so) at the time of the search. While that would meet the *Jones* test for standing, it is no longer sufficient. Rather, to invoke the exclusionary remedy each party must demonstrate that *his* reasonable expectation of privacy was violated by the police action. See *Rakas v. Illinois*, supra.

Dealer, who rented and had a key to the room, and spent an hour in it, was in possession and control and thus had a reasonable expectation of privacy there. That would establish her standing to challenge the search. Buyer, on the other hand, had a more tenuous connection to the place searched. She neither had a possessory interest in it nor had she spent more than a few minutes there. Although Buyer may seek to analogize her situation to the invited guests in *Jones v. United States*, 362 U.S. 257 (1960), and *Minnesota v. Olson*, 495 U.S. 91 (1990), both of whom were held to have standing to challenge searches of their hosts' dwellings, her attachment to the hotel room appears far more remote and short-term, and thus more analogous to the passengers in *Rakas*, who were held to lack standing. Compare *Rose v. United States*, 629 A.2d 526 (D.C. 1993), where defendant was arrested without a warrant while within the home of his aunt and uncle. The arresting officer was aware that the defendant had a key to the apartment but was not an overnight guest. The court focused on three factors in determining whether the defendant had standing to challenge the warrantless arrest: the defendant's close kinship with the owners of the apartment, his regular visits (several times a week), and his possession of a key. These factors added up to essentially the same expectations of privacy that an overnight guest might have.

Another problem for Buyer is the purpose of her presence at the Fleabag. *Minnesota v. Carter*, 525 U.S. 83 (1998), ruled that a person in a normally protected area such as a home may nonetheless not have a reasonable expectation of privacy if there for purely commercial purposes, for example, the purchase of narcotics. See also *United States v. Macias-Treviso*, 42 F. Supp. 2d 1206,

1212 (D.N.M. 1999), where defendant had his brother's permission to use the garage located near his brother's unoccupied home still under construction, had worked on cars and stored his tools there for almost a year, and was the only one using a key to the garage. Because of the commercial nature of his activities in the garage and the lack of any residential connection there, defendant had no standing to challenge the search.

Although property used for commercial purposes is treated differently for Fourth Amendment purposes than residential property, *Minnesota v. Carter* notes that there are some circumstances in which a worker can claim protection over his own workplace, citing *O'Connor v. Ortega*, 480 U.S. 709 (1987), discussed in §§3.2 and 4.5. See, e.g., *United States v. Evaschuck*, 65 F. Supp. 2d 1360 (M.D. Fla. 1999), where defendant was found to have standing to challenge a search of offices his company rented because he was the owner and operator of the company, the only person who used those offices, and the only person who had the keys.

What if a visitor to the searched premises has a *dual* purpose, both social and commercial, for his presence? Since Justice Kennedy's decisive fifth vote in *Minnesota v. Carter* was expressly based on its reasoning which was "consistent with [his] view that almost all social guests have a legitimate expectation of privacy, and hence protection against unreasonable searches, in their host's home," it may be argued that the dual-purpose visitor has standing to challenge a search.

The automatic standing rule of *Jones*, which would have conferred standing to raise a Fourth Amendment challenge for any possessory offense Buyer is charged with, has been abandoned. See *United States v. Salvucci*, 448 U.S. 83 (1980). Moreover, *Rawlings v. Kentucky*, supra, raises substantial doubt as to whether an admission by Buyer that the narcotics and cash were hers would establish standing for her—such admission did not accomplish that result for Rawlings because of his lack of possessory interest in the place searched, his companion's purse.

1d. Ted, as the owner of the vehicle (who was also present during the search), would clearly have standing to challenge the search because his possessory interest creates a reasonable expectation of privacy on his part in all areas of the car. See *Rakas v. Illinois*, supra. He could thus object to the entry into the car and the subsequent seizure of the plastic bags, the purse, and the hashish in the trunk. (Some courts would hold that he lacked standing to challenge the *opening* of the purse or the plastic bags, which belonged to the other occupants and in which he had no reasonable expectation of privacy. See, e.g., *United States v. Maling*, 746 F. Supp. 223 (D. Ma. 1990).)

As a mere passenger, Bill will not be able to establish a privacy interest in the trunk of the vehicle or the glove compartment, and thus will not be able to challenge the use of the items seized there against him at trial. Bill probably will be able to demonstrate a legitimate privacy expectation in the rear seat area, where he had been seated, and thus could challenge the seizure and opening of the trash bags. See *United States v. Salazar*, 805 F.2d 1394 (9th Cir. 1986) (defendant, although a mere passenger in a car, had standing to challenge the search of a closed container placed out of sight on the floor near where he had been seated). Compare *United States v. Paulino*, 850 F.2d 93 (2d Cir. 1988) (holding that a passenger in the back seat, who had been seen by an officer placing something on the floor, did not have standing to challenge the search and seizure of the counterfeit money he had hidden underneath the floor mat). The *Paulino* court reasoned that, while defendant had clearly evidenced his desire to keep the item private and, further, admitted ownership of the money, other *Rawlings* factors militated against conferring standing on him: 1) he had only known the owner-driver for a week; 2) as a passenger he had no right to exclude others from the vehicle; and 3) he had quickly secreted the money only moments before the police discovered it. The court was thus "unprepared to hold that Paulino's expectation of privacy is one that society willingly accepts as reasonable." 850 F.2d at 97.

Cynthia, as the car's driver, falls somewhere in between Ted and Bill. While lacking the ownership interest that Ted had, she did have control over the vehicle as well as possession of the ignition key, which probably gave her access to both the glove compartment and the trunk. She can probably challenge the seizure of items in those areas as well as the rear seat. See *Maling*, supra. Compare *United States v. Kopp*, 45 F.3d 1450 (10th Cir. 1995) (holding that driver of a pickup truck did not have standing to contest a search of an attached trailer rented by the passenger who kept sole possession of the only key). She may lack standing to challenge the opening of the plastic bags located next to Bill in the rear, an area in which she might be deemed to lack a legitimate privacy interest.

If Cynthia has no key or other access to the glove compartment, then *Rawlings* suggests that because she has no control over the place searched, she lacks standing to challenge the search.

What if the opaque bags were in Bill's dufflebag? Would the owner and driver of the car have an expectation of privacy in a dufflebag owned and held by a passenger sitting in the back seat? *Rakas* suggests that the answer is no: If a passenger lacks a privacy expectation in the glove compartment, the driver probably lacks such expectation in a passenger's bag.

The Supreme Court has recently held that a police officer with probable cause to search a vehicle may also search the belongings of any passenger. *Wyoming v. Houghton*, 526 U.S. 295 (1999). Writing for the Court, Justice Scalia extended prior precedent, which authorized the search of any containers in the car that might contain the object of the search (see §6.4, infra), to include containers (in *Houghton* a purse) owned by passengers as well. One might argue from *Houghton* that if probable cause opens all containers to search, whether owned or controlled by the driver or not, then the driver should have standing to contest search of any container.

On an alternative theory of standing for the occupants of a vehicle, Justice Powell suggested in his concurring opinion in *Rakas* that the passengers there might have had standing had they challenged *the stop* of the car and the order to get out, as opposed to the search and seizure that followed. The fruits of the stop could then be challenged under the derivative evidence doctrine. The occupants in our example (and most particularly Bill, who stands lowest on the standing hierarchy) could thus argue that they had a reasonable expectation of freedom from an arbitrary stop without justification and therefore standing to challenge the officer's initial action. See, e.g., *United States v. Erwin*, 875 F.2d 268 (10th Cir. 1989) (holding that defendant had standing to challenge the stop of an automobile in which he was merely a passenger even though he lacked standing to object to a search of the tailgate area: "Drivers and passengers have similar interests in seeing that their persons remain free from unreasonable seizure.").

As examples 1a through 1d illustrate, the standing doctrine operates to separate the victims of a search into those privileged to challenge it, by virtue of their connection to the place searched, and those not so privileged. It has been suggested that this division encourages the police to engage in unlawful activity with the knowledge that the evidence seized, while inadmissible as to some, may nonetheless be used against others. See *Rakas v. Illinois*, 439 U.S. at 168–169 (White, Brennan, Marshall, and Stevens, JJ., dissenting). This is precisely what occurred in *United States v. Payner*, 447 U.S. 727 (1980). In order to obtain confidential information on bank customers, Internal Revenue Service (IRS) agents entered the hotel room of a visiting bank official, removed his briefcase, and photocopied documents inside. Based on evidence so obtained, Payner was charged with income tax violations. Despite the district court's finding that Payner was a victim of a deliberate IRS policy exploiting the Fourth Amendment standing limitation—agents were counseled that they could violate the constitutional rights of one individual in order to secure admissible evidence against *another*—the Supreme Court held that he lacked standing to challenge the search of the bank official's briefcase.

1e. The Eleventh Circuit held in *United States v. Cooper*, 133 F.3d 1394 (1998), that a driver of an overdue rental vehicle does have a legitimate expectation of privacy (and thus standing) in the car where he could have renewed the agreement by simply telephoning the rental company and where the company had not taken any affirmative steps to repossess the car. The situation is distinguishable from that in which the driver is not listed on the rental agreement. See *United States v. Wellons*, 32 F.3d 117 (4th Cir. 1994) (as unauthorized driver, defendant lacked standing to challenge search).

Derivative Evidence Meets the Standing Doctrine

2a. Paul clearly has standing to complain about the search of his apartment. If, however, the warrant was (as it appears to have been) lawful, Paul lacks a substantive claim of illegality. Moreover, Paul does not have standing to raise any illegality experienced earlier by John.

2b. It may appear at first glance that John lacks standing because he is objecting to evidence obtained in a search of Paul's apartment. The information that led the police to Paul, however, was derived from the initial unlawful entry into John's own apartment. Since the evidence offered against John is the fruit of an illegality that was directed *at him* and his apartment, he does have standing to pursue a Fourth Amendment challenge. The situation is similar to that of defendant Toy who successfully challenged the use of heroin seized from defendant Yee in *Wong Sun v. United States,* 371 U.S. 471 (1963). The police were led to Yee only through declarations made by Toy in the face of his unlawful arrest, and thus the evidence could not be used against Toy.

The derivative evidence doctrine thus expands the realm of standing for defendants who can trace actions directed against *others* to initial illegalities directed against *themselves.* A defendant who has standing to challenge the initial illegality also has standing to challenge the use of evidence derived from that illegality.

The prosecution might argue in response in our example that the other reliable sources concerning Paul's activities established (or would eventually have established) sufficient probable cause for the search of Paul's apartment, and thus the independent source or inevitable discovery exceptions to the derivative evidence doctrine should apply. These issues would have to be resolved based on the particular factual circumstances.

Standing in the Electronic Age

3. Jackie can contest this search and seizure only if it infringed on *her own* personal Fourth Amendment rights—that is, only if *her* privacy interest was violated. Because the search occurred in a location in which she had no possessory interest and over which she had no control, it would appear that Jackie is in the same situation as Bonnie in example 1a, that is, attempting to rely vicariously on the violation of someone else's Fourth Amendment rights. Even if Jackie can establish a property interest in the information on the computer tape, such interest in the item seized does not make out standing in the absence of a close connection to the place searched. See *Rawlings v. Kentucky,* supra (although Rawlings admitted ownership of the drugs seized, his lack of possessory interest in the purse from which they were taken defeated his claim of standing to object).

In the case upon which this example is based, *United States v. Horowitz,* 806 F.2d 1222 (4th Cir. 1986), defense counsel argued creatively that the search challenged was not really that of Military Hardware's office but rather of "the intangible space where images and sounds are recorded in a computer memory disc," and that the computer images seized constituted defendant's "electronic file cabinet." 806 F.2d at 1224–1225. Applying the traditional analysis, however, the court ruled that Horowitz lacked standing because the search occurred in the offices of a third party, the tapes seized were taken from that third party's files, and whatever interest Horowitz had in the information contained on the disks was lost when he sold it to a third party. Moreover, Horowitz failed to establish that he had any control over the computer tapes:

> The defendant lacked any ability to exclude others from the tapes; on the contrary, his own access was controlled by EMI. The defendant had no keys to either EMI's building or EMI's computer room. His only access to the RER file was by an electronic hookup through the use of a password. But employees of EMI could bar his access simply by removing the tapes from the computer or by changing the password. The defendant could not effectively exclude anyone from access to the tapes since any of several EMI employees knowing the password could give it to others and any employee with a key to the computer room could remove the tapes.

Id. at 1226. Because the defendant lacked standing to challenge the search and seizure, the court did not reach the question of its conformity with Fourth Amendment requirements. For more on computer searches, see Chapter 12.

§7.3.2   *Limitation to Criminal Trial versus Other Proceedings*

A criminal trial is only one of several types of judicial proceedings in which evidence obtained during a search might be offered against a party. Does the exclusionary remedy apply in other criminal contexts, such as grand jury or habeas corpus proceedings? Does it apply in proceedings of a civil nature, such as deportation or tax penalty cases? A series of Supreme Court cases have consistently answered no to these questions and limited the rule to the criminal trial context.

In *United States v. Calandra*, 414 U.S. 338 (1974), a witness called before a grand jury refused to answer questions based on evidence that had been obtained from him during an unlawful search. Expressing concern that utilization of the exclusionary remedy would seriously impede the operation of the grand jury in its investigative function, the Court held that the rule could not be applied in those proceedings. Premised on the notion that the exclusionary rule is a judicially created remedy rather than a constitutional right, the Court utilized a cost-benefit analysis now typical in cases curtailing operation of the rule. It weighed what it viewed as the minimal deterrent effect of suppression in grand jury proceedings against the cost of keeping relevant information from the grand jury. As long as law enforcement officials know that illegally obtained evidence cannot be used at the ultimate trial, the Court reasoned, there is little incentive to violate constitutional requirements merely for the purpose of securing evidence for the grand jury: "A prosecutor would be unlikely to request an indictment where a conviction could not be obtained." 414 U.S. at 351.

The exclusionary remedy has also been held inapplicable in habeas corpus proceedings. The habeas corpus device permits a state prisoner to challenge his conviction in federal court on the grounds that his constitutional rights were violated during the state trial. In *Stone v. Powell*, 428 U.S. 465 (1976), the Court removed Fourth Amendment violations from those that can be raised as long as the petitioner had a "full and fair" opportunity to assert the violation during the state proceedings. The deterrent effect of the rule will be achieved (if at all), the Court reasoned, by having the suppression remedy available at trial and on direct appellate review; the incremental deterrence that might result from the availability of the remedy during habeas proceedings is remote and speculative. "The view that the deterrence of Fourth Amendment violations would be furthered rests on the dubious assumption that law enforcement authorities would fear that federal habeas review might reveal flaws in a search or seizure that went undetected at trial and on appeal." 428 U.S. at 493. Police officers do not, the Court suggested, think this far in advance in the conduct of their daily affairs. The costs of applying the rule, on the other hand, are the deflection of the truth-finding process, diversion from the central question of guilt or innocence, and the exclusion of relevant evidence. It is interesting to note that one of the factors that the Court relied on in allowing the exclusionary remedy in habeas corpus proceedings for a *Miranda* violation was the potential for such a violation to distort the truth-finding process. See *Withrow v. Williams*, 507 U.S. 680 (1993). See §9.3.

The same balancing analysis has led the Court to hold the exclusionary rule unavailable in civil actions brought by the IRS to collect taxes, *United States v. Janis*, 428 U.S. 433 (1976), in deportation administrative hearings, *INS v. Lopez-Mendoza*, 468 U.S. 1032

(1984); and most recently in parole revocation hearings. *Pennsylvania Board of Probation and Parole v. Scott*, 524 U.S. 357 (1998). As is typical in this line of cases, the majority and dissent in *Scott* disagree on the costs and benefits of applying the exclusionary rule, particularly around the question of deterrence. In his decision for the Court, Justice Thomas concludes that the social costs of allowing convicted criminals who violate their parole to remain at large outweigh whatever marginal deterrence the rule may create for the officer on the street (beyond enforcement of the exclusionary rule in the criminal trial). The dissenters (in an opinion by Justice Souter) see a significant potential for deterrence if the rule is applied at the revocation hearing, because police are often aware of the parole status of the subject of their search and thus quite concerned with the admissibility of evidence in those proceedings, which may very well end up being the only action taken against the subject.

In refusing to apply the exclusionary rule in these situations the Court has cast aside the argument that, even in the absence of demonstrable evidence of deterrence, the suppression remedy nonetheless serves the noble purpose of preserving judicial integrity and preventing the courts from acting as partners with law enforcement officials in the violation of constitutional rights.

EXAMPLES

1. Detectives investigating a gambling ring had long heard rumors that insurance executive Maxwell Coffee was the main brain at the center of the operation. Lacking sufficient cause to obtain a warrant, but impatient to crack the ring, the detectives broke into Coffee's insurance agency at night and thoroughly searched his office. They discovered records of extensive illegal gambling activities as well as $120,000 in cash.

    Because they were seized during an illegal search, the district attorney who subsequently prosecuted Coffee agreed not to offer the documents or cash into evidence at his trial. Coffee was, however, convicted on the basis of other evidence and testimony from former colleagues in crime. A sentencing hearing has been scheduled. The district attorney, desiring to bring before the judge all information relating to Coffee's deep involvement in the gambling ring, would like to offer into evidence the illegally obtained items. Will they be admissible during the sentencing proceedings?

2. Proceeding under a statute that permits prosecutors to seek forfeiture of property used in the perpetration of criminal activities,

the district attorney has moved in a civil action to seize Coffee's office condominium on the grounds that it was actually the front for his gambling ring. Will the documents and cash illegally seized be admissible during forfeiture proceedings?

EXPLANATIONS

1. The courts are split on the question of the exclusionary rule's applicability during sentencing proceedings. Concluding that the "desirability of reaching an appropriate decision in sentencing outweighs what little deterrent effect may be present," the Third Circuit Court of Appeals held the exclusionary remedy inapplicable at a postconviction sentencing hearing. See *United States v. Torres*, 926 F.2d 321 (3d Cir. 1991) (holding that in determining the amount of cocaine involved in defendant's offense for purposes of setting the appropriate sentence under the Sentencing Guidelines, the court could consider cocaine that had been suppressed at trial because of its unlawful seizure). See also *United States v. McCrory*, 930 F.2d 63 (D.C. Cir. 1991) ("Where there is no showing of a violation of the Fourth Amendment purposefully designed to obtain evidence to increase a defendant's base offense level at sentencing, this police misconduct is not sufficient to justify interfering with individualized sentencing. . . . The exclusion of that evidence from the trial sufficed in this case to vindicate the purpose of the rule." 930 F.2d at 69).

   Concerned that admission of illegally obtained evidence on the question of sentencing would encourage police officers to violate defendants' rights, U.S. District Judge Martin reached the opposite conclusion in *United States v. Cabrera*, 756 F. Supp. 134 (S.D.N.Y. 1991). Rejecting precedent established prior to the adoption of the Sentencing Guidelines holding that illegally seized evidence could be considered in imposing sentence, see *United States v. Schipani*, 435 F.2d 26 (2d Cir. 1970), Judge Martin held that the exclusionary rule would be applied. Alluding to the judicial integrity theme sounded in *Mapp v. Ohio*, Judge Martin wrote:

   > Winston Cabrera has been convicted of a serious crime and he will receive a substantial sentence. If we are to ask him to accept that sentence and, in the future, conform his conduct to the requirements of the law, he is entitled to know that the courts also require law enforcement officials to

> conform their conduct to the law's requirements and will
> not sanction the illegal search and seizure that took place
> here by using the evidence seized to increase his sentence
> by over 2⅓ years.

756 F. Supp. at 136. See also *Vedugo v. United States*, 402 F.2d
599 (9th Cir. 1968) (evidence was excluded from sentencing consideration where the warrantless search was "blatantly illegal").

In light of *Pennsylvania Board of Probabtion and Parole v.
Scott*, supra, refusing to apply the exclusionary rule to parole revocation hearings, and decisions like *United States v. Armstrong*,
187 F.3d 392 (4th Cir. 1999), extending *Scott* to federal supervised release revocation proceedings, it is unlikely that the sanction
will be applied during sentencing hearings.

2. When the Court took this issue up some years ago it concluded
that the evidence could not be used. *One 1958 Plymouth Sedan v.
Pennsylvania*, 380 U.S. 693 (1965), held that evidence obtained
in violation of the Fourth Amendment may not be relied upon to
sustain a forfeiture. In that case, forfeiture of an automobile used
in the transport of illegal liquor was reversed because the evidence
upon which it was based—the liquor—had been seized during a
search conducted without a warrant or probable cause. The Court
reasoned that it "would be anomalous indeed . . . to hold that in
the criminal proceeding the illegally seized evidence is excludable,
while in the forfeiture proceeding, requiring the determination
that the criminal law had been violated, the same evidence would
be admissible. [F]orfeiture is clearly a penalty for the criminal offense and can result in even greater punishment than the criminal
prosecution. . . ." 380 U.S. at 701. The government may, however, proceed against the property with independent evidence not
tainted by the illegality. See *United States v. $37,780 in U.S. Currency*, 920 F.2d 159 (2d Cir. 1990).

Given the trend of cases over recent years, it is unclear
whether the Court would follow *One 1958 Plymouth Sedan* if the
issue came before it today.

§7.3.3   The "Good Faith" Exception

As we have seen, the primary justification for the exclusionary rule is
the goal of deterring violations of constitutional rights. This purpose

is best achieved when the violation is knowing and deliberate because in that situation the offending officer could have conformed his conduct to legal mandates and will, presumably, do so in the future, rather than again face loss of relevant evidence. Where, however, the officer has made an "honest mistake" and was not even aware that he was violating the Fourth Amendment, the deterrent effect of suppressing the evidence is much harder to identify. Should the rule apply in such situations?

In *United States v. Leon*, 468 U.S. 897 (1984), a decision representing a major constraint on the scope of the exclusionary remedy, the Court held (at least in cases involving search warrants) that the exclusionary rule should not apply when the officers acted in "good faith." Expressing the majority's frustration with the rule (which it characterized as a judicially created remedy and not a constitutional mandate),[11] Justice White wrote:

> We have frequently questioned whether the exclusionary rule can have any deterrent effect when the offending officers acted in the objectively reasonable belief that their conduct did not violate the Fourth Amendment. No empirical researcher, proponent or opponent of the rule, has yet been able to establish with any assurance whether the rule has a deterrent effect. But even assuming that the rule effectively deters some police misconduct and provides incentives for the law enforcement profession as a whole to conduct itself in accord with the Fourth Amendment, it cannot be expected, and should not be applied, to deter objectively reasonable law enforcement activity.

468 U.S. at 918–919 (internal quotation and citations omitted). Recognizing that police officers are not lawyers and must often make quick judgments under considerable pressure, the Court held that probative evidence should not be excluded when the officers make reasonable mistakes regarding the legality of warrants.

Leon involved a search conducted pursuant to a warrant issued by a magistrate. The warrant was subsequently found to have been issued

---

11. In their dissent Justices Brennan and Marshall sharply disagreed: "Because seizures are executed principally to secure evidence, and because such evidence generally has utility in our legal system only in the context of a trial supervised by a judge, it is apparent that the admission of illegally obtained evidence implicates the same constitutional concerns as the initial seizure of that evidence. Indeed, by admitting unlawfully seized evidence, the judiciary becomes a part of what is in fact a single governmental action prohibited by the terms of the amendment." 468 U.S. at 933.

without an adequate showing of probable cause (the affidavit in support was based primarily on the word of a confidential informant of unproven reliability),[12] and defendants sought suppression of the evidence seized. Finding that the warrant appeared to be valid on its face, the police officers were deemed to have reasonably relied upon it in their execution of the search. In such a situation, the Court concluded, the minimal possibility of deterrence of such violations in the future is outweighed by the substantial costs of suppressing the evidence, namely, interference with the truth-finding function of the trial and the freeing of guilty parties.

Even if a reviewing court disagrees with the issuing magistrate's conclusion that probable cause existed, it may no longer exclude the evidence seized if the police officer's reliance on the warrant was reasonable. The exclusionary remedy, the Court reminded, is directed against police officers, *not* judges and magistrates who are "neutral judicial officers" with "no stake in the outcome of particular criminal prosecutions." Because the "threat of exclusion thus cannot be expected significantly to deter" judges and magistrates, it makes no sense to exclude evidence because of their mistakes. Suppression remains appropriate, of course, where the police officer's reliance upon the warrant was unreasonable (as explained below).

This good faith exception adopted in *Leon* was extended to cover the case of a warrant that erroneously described the items to be seized where the officer conducting the search reasonably relied upon on the assurance of the issuing judge that the warrant was proper. See *Massachusetts v. Sheppard*, 468 U.S. 981 (1984). Officers conducting a homicide investigation applied for a warrant to search Sheppard's residence for evidence connecting him to the murder of his girlfriend. Because it was a Sunday, the only standard application form the officers could locate was for a narcotics search. In their affidavit they described the items sought as the murder weapon and rope used to bind the victim. The judge promised to modify the narcotics search form so as to properly authorize the seizure of these items, but he failed to do so and the warrant thus listed narcotics as the target of the search.

The warrant was executed and evidence of the homicide was discovered, but the state courts suppressed the evidence because the warrant failed to correctly describe the items sought and seized. Concluding, however, that the officers had acted in reasonable reliance

---

12. It should be pointed out that this decision on probable cause was rendered before *Illinois v. Gates*, 462 U.S. 213 (1983). See §4.1.

upon the judge's assurance, the Supreme Court reversed: "We refuse to rule that an officer is required to disbelieve a judge who has just advised him, by word and by action, that the warrant he possesses authorizes him to conduct the search he has requested." 468 U.S. at 989-990. (Other decisions involving the interaction of the particularity requirement and the good faith exception are discussed in §5.2.3.)

The good faith exception does not apply (and thus the exclusionary remedy remains available) in the following cases:

1) where the police misled (either deliberately or in reckless disregard of the truth) the magistrate in their application for the warrant (see §5.2.2);

2) where the warrant was so obviously invalid (either because probable cause is lacking or because it fails to particularize the place to be searched or the things to be seized) that no officer could reasonably rely on it; and

3) where the magistrate abandoned his neutral and detached posture.

As a consequence of *Leon* and *Sheppard*, an additional level has been added to Fourth Amendment analysis in cases involving search warrants. In those cases where it is determined that the warrant was defective because probable cause was lacking (see §4.1) or the particularity requirement was not complied with (see §5.2.3), it is now necessary to add the good faith dimension: Despite the defect(s), were the searching officers reasonable in relying upon the warrant? Was their mistake, in other words, a reasonable one (measured against the benchmark of what *Leon* refers to as the "reasonably well-trained officer")? If the answer is yes, then the exclusionary remedy may not be invoked.

Although *Leon* created a good faith exception only in the context of searches conducted *pursuant to a warrant*,[13] the rationale of the

---

13. In his separate dissent, Justice Stevens found it particularly ironic that the exception was carved out for warrant searches: "The notion that a police officer's reliance on a magistrate's warrant is automatically appropriate is one the Framers of the Fourth Amendment would have vehemently rejected. The precise problem that the Amendment was intended to address was *the unreasonable issuance of warrants*. . . . The fact that colonial officers had magisterial authorization for their conduct when they engaged in general searches surely did not make their conduct 'reasonable.' The Court's view that it is consistent with our Constitution to adopt a rule that it is presumptively reasonable to rely on a defective warrant is the product of constitutional amnesia." 468 U.S. at 970-971.

decision could arguably support a more general exception to the exclusionary rule that applies to warrantless searches as well. Indeed, Justice Brennan described the decision in global terms as "the Court's victory over the Fourth Amendment," the culmination of a "gradual but determined strangulation of the [exclusionary] rule." 468 U.S. at 929 (Brennan and Marshall, JJ., dissenting).

The Court has in fact subsequently applied the good faith exception in a warrantless search context. In *Illinois v. Krull*, 480 U.S. 340 (1987), the officer performed a warrantless search pursuant to a statute that was later declared unconstitutional. The Court explained:

> The approach used in *Leon* is equally applicable in the present case. The application of the exclusionary rule to suppress evidence obtained by an officer acting in objectively reasonable reliance on a statute would have as little deterrent effect on the officer's actions as would the exclusion of evidence when an officer acts in objectively reasonable reliance on a warrant. Unless a statute is declared unconstitutional, an officer cannot be expected to question the judgment of the legislature that passed the law.

480 U.S. at 349–350.

A further expansion of the good faith exception can be found in *Arizona v. Evans*, 514 U.S. 1 (1995). During a routine traffic stop the patrol car's computer erroneously indicated that there was an outstanding arrest warrant for the driver. The driver was placed under arrest and pursuant to a search incident thereto marijuana was found. See §6.3. The defendant moved to suppress the marijuana on the grounds that the arrest warrant was invalid. Erroneous information resulting from a court employee's clerical error had been conveyed to the patrol car's computer. The Court focused on the narrow purpose of the exclusionary rule—deterrence of law enforcement personnel—and held the rule did not apply to mistakes by court employees. The Court indicated that there was no basis to believe that the application of the exclusionary rule would have a significant effect on court employees who were not engaged in law enforcement.

In a decision based on a similar rationale, the Court in *Illinois v. Rodriguez*, 497 U.S. 177 (1990), held that the proper test for determining the validity of a warrantless search justified by third-party consent is not simply whether that party had *actual* authority over the premises, but rather whether there was *apparent* authority—that is, whether the facts known to the officer would justify "a man of reasonable caution in the belief that the consenting party had authority over the premises." (This case is discussed in §6.7.) If the mistake by the police officer was reasonable, the exclusionary remedy will not apply.

These cases have moved beyond the narrow holding of *Leon*. No longer are search warrants needed to trigger the good faith exception. By focusing exclusively on the goal of deterring individual police officers, as opposed to others also involved in the criminal justice system, the Court has opened the door to further limitations on the use of the exclusionary rule and thus has insulated these violations from judicial review.

Some states have refused to read a good faith exception into their own constitutions. See, e.g., *Commonwealth v. Upton*, 394 Mass. 363, 476 N.E.2d 548 (1985); *State v. Novembrino*, 105 N.J. 95 (1987); *Commonwealth v. Edmunds*, 526 Pa. 374, 586 A.2d 889 (1991); *New Hampshire v. Canelo*, 653 A.2d 1097 (N.H. 1995).

EXAMPLES

1. Officer Jumpthegun has been investigating a string of credit card burglaries. While at a local supermarket she overhears another shopper say to his companion that "my neighbor Ralph Rabbit has been spending money like it's going out of style." Jumpthegun concludes that Rabbit must be the burglar she is seeking and she applies for a warrant to search Rabbit's home, setting forth the conversation she heard in the supermarket as her probable cause showing. Magistrate Rubberstamp quickly reviews the application and issues the warrant, which, when executed by Jumpthegun, turns up evidence connecting Rabbit to the burglaries. On the defendant's motion to suppress on the grounds that the warrant was defective, the prosecution concedes (as it must) that probable cause to search was lacking but contends nonetheless that Jumpthegun acted in good faith and thus the *Leon* exception should apply. What result?

2. Officer Nixon was summoned to the home of Chamber Whittaker who had received three anonymous typewritten letters setting out threats to bomb his house and car. Whittaker informed the officer that the letters appeared to have been written on the old Underwood typewriter that he had given his former wife, Janet, before they split up one month before. Nixon's investigation developed probable cause to believe that Janet Whittaker had in fact sent the letters. He also learned that Janet had no permanent residence but

had been staying for short periods of time with various relatives and friends. Having a hunch that she might be at the home of her father, Fred Findley, Nixon set out the information known to him, as well as his hunch, in an application for a warrant to search Findley's residence for the Underwood typewriter.

The warrant was issued, and Nixon conducted the search. The officer's hunch bore fruit—Janet was living at her father's home, and the typewriter was found and seized. An expert is prepared to testify at trial that the letters sent to Chamber were typed on the Underwood. Janet's attorney has moved to suppress the typewriter, but the prosecution is relying on the good faith exception. What result?

3. Based on an adequate showing of probable cause to believe that large amounts of cocaine would be found at the home of Dennis Demon, 100 Main Street, Magistrate Careless issued a search warrant. Although Demon's address was set out in the police officer's affidavit requesting the warrant, the magistrate neglected to fill in the address to be searched in the space provided on the form warrant she issued. The police officers conducted the search and seized 600 grams of cocaine. Defendant Demon challenges the use of the evidence at trial on the grounds that the warrant was facially defective in that it did not indicate the place to be searched. What result?

    Would it make a difference if the officers executing the warrant were not the same officers who had conducted the investigation and filed the application?

4. While on routine cruiser patrol Trooper Thomas's attention was drawn to a late-model luxury sedan being driven by a very young driver. His suspicions aroused, Thomas radioed in the license plate of the vehicle. When he did so, however, he transposed two digits of the plate number and reported it incorrectly as RT-234 (the actual number was RT-324). The dispatcher ran a check on RT-234 and reported back to Thomas that the plate had been issued to a 1995 Chevy Impala. Erroneously concluding that the vehicle he had under observation had been stolen, the trooper pulled it over. When he approached the driver, Thomas observed drug paraphernalia and a large quantity of marijuana on the seat next to the driver. The trooper placed the driver under arrest and seized the contraband. Conceding that there were no proper grounds to stop the vehicle, the prosecution nonetheless argues the good faith exception to avoid suppression. What result?

EXPLANATIONS

1. Despite the name it has been given, the good faith exception applies only where the police officer's reliance on the warrant was *objectively* reasonable. The subjective good intentions of the officer are not relevant to the inquiry. Because no reasonably well-trained police officer could rely on the warrant issued by Magistrate Rubberstamp (given the clear absence of adequate probable cause), the *Leon* exception would not apply here.

   Needless to say, most cases will fall in a more gray area than example 1. Although Justice White asserted in *Leon* that the good faith exception "should not be difficult to apply in practice" because it turns on "objective reasonableness," lawyers and law students are all too aware of the wide room for disagreement that such a concept imparts.

   Given the flexible probable cause standard established by *Illinois v. Gates* (discussed in §4.1), together with the elastic good faith exception to the operation of the exclusionary sanction, the issue that must be resolved in such cases is: Should a reasonably well-trained police officer have recognized that there was *not* a fair probability that contraband or other evidence of a crime would be found at the place to be searched? Put another way, evidence seized pursuant to a warrant will be suppressed if 1) probable cause was lacking under the totality of the circumstances–fair probability standard of *Gates*; and 2) a reasonably well-trained officer would have recognized this deficiency.

   Another issue could arguably be raised if Magistrate Rubberstamp (as his name would indicate) did not bother to read the affidavit before issuing the warrant. This factor would bring into question whether Rubberstamp was the "neutral and detached" magistrate required by the Fourth Amendment. See §5.2.1. The *Leon* Court indicated that the good faith exception does not apply if the magistrate has abdicated his role as a neutral and detached evaluator. Although the example used in *Leon* for a lack of neutrality cited *Lo-Ji Sales* (see §5.2.1), in which the magistrate actually participated in the execution of the warrant, is distinguishable from Magistrate Ruberstamp's actions, at least a credible argument could be made as to the neutrality of the magistrate. However, the Court's emphasis in *Arizona v. Evans*, 514 U.S. 1 (1995), on the deterrence of individual police officers as opposed to other officials such as magistrates might signal a willingness by the Court to reconsider this limitation on the good faith exception.

243

2. Probable cause to search Findley's home (that is, facts and circumstances that would lead a reasonable person to conclude that items related to the bomb threats would be found there) was clearly lacking because Nixon disclosed to the magistrate no solid information to connect Janet or the typewriter to that location. The only question to be resolved, therefore, is whether Officer Nixon reasonably relied upon the warrant when he conducted the search. *Leon* made clear that an officer cannot manifest objective good faith if the warrant he is relying upon was "so lacking in indicia of probable cause as to render official belief in its existence entirely unreasonable." 468 U.S. at 923 (citation omitted). A reasonably well-trained officer would have recognized that this affidavit, which failed to concretely link the place to be searched with the items sought, was in that category and that consequently the warrant was not properly issued. The good faith exception should thus not apply here.

As the Ninth Circuit Court of Appeals explained in a case involving similar facts (where the affidavit "offer[ed] no hint as to why the police wanted to search *this* residence") and holding the good faith exception inapplicable: "*Leon* creates an exception to the exclusionary rule when officers have acted in reasonable reliance on the ruling of a judge or magistrate. The point is that officers who present a colorable showing of probable cause to a judicial officer ought to be able to rely on that officer's ruling in executing the warrant. When the officers have not presented a colorable showing, and the warrant and affidavit on their face preclude reasonable reliance, the reasoning of *Leon* does not apply." *United States v. Hove*, 848 F.2d 137, 140 (9th Cir. 1988). Compare *United States v. Ramos*, 923 F.2d 1346 (9th Cir. 1991) (although probable cause to search the particular apartment was lacking, the officers reasonably relied on the warrant because the affidavit in support had set forth *some* facts connecting the apartment to the criminal enterprise).

The complexity of the issue as well as the wide room for disagreement concerning what a "reasonably well-trained" police officer should know about probable cause to search is illustrated by *United States v. Savoca*, 761 F.2d 292 (6th Cir. 1985). The affidavit in support of the warrant merely recited that two persons who had just been arrested for a bank robbery, which occurred 2,000 miles away, had been seen recently in the motel room to be searched. Conceding that probable cause to search *that particular location* was lacking, a majority of the court of appeals nonetheless concluded that a reasonably well-trained officer could have properly relied on the warrant:

> [T]he defect in the affidavit was that it only tenuously connected the place to be searched with two persons for whom arrest warrants were outstanding. It failed to describe the relationship of the persons to the premises and it did not state how recently the bank robberies had occurred. On these facts, our *Hatcher* decision [emphasizing the "well-established" legal principle that probable cause to arrest will not necessarily establish probable cause to search] is controlling on the question of probable cause. Whether a reasonably well-trained officer could believe that this affidavit stated probable cause for the search thus depends in part on whether such an officer would be aware of *Hatcher* and related decisions and the principle for which those cases stand. *We conclude that a reasonably well-trained officer would be aware of the principle which* Hatcher *amplifies [sic]; we also conclude, however, that such an officer could conclude that* Hatcher *and related decisions are distinguishable and that the warrant was not, therefore, invalid.*

761 F.2d at 297 (emphasis added). Dissenting Circuit Judge Jones, on the other hand, viewed the affidavit as so lacking in indicia of probable cause as to render official belief in its existence entirely unreasonable: "[T]he general principle requiring a nexus between the evidence sought and the place to be searched, in addition to the mere presence of a suspect, is sufficiently clear that *a reasonably well-trained police officer should have known that the mere presence of Savoca at the hotel room could not constitute probable cause for a search warrant of the hotel room.*" 761 F.2d at 302 (emphasis added).

A factor weighed by the courts in determining the reasonableness of an officer's conduct is the time pressure under which he operated. In *Ramos*, supra, for example, the court observed that the officers who had obtained the warrant had generated a nine-page affidavit in a matter of hours after the arrest of several perpetrators: "Under the circumstances it is not entirely inscrutable that the affidavit failed to include some information which officers observed and which may have bolstered a finding of probable cause." 923 F.2d at 1355 n.18. In *United States v. Weber*, 923 F.2d 1338, 1346 (9th Cir. 1991), in contrast, "since the government planned the undercover delivery of the items that provided the occasion for the search, the government had complete control over the timing of the search. Under these circumstances, there was no need for the hurried judgment upon which law enforcement decisions must often be based. Although we do not question the subjective good faith of the government, it acted unreasonably in preparing the affidavit it presented." (Citation and internal quotes omitted.)

3. The warrant, which fails to indicate the address to be searched, unquestionably violates the Fourth Amendment mandate that the place to be searched be particularly described. The prosecution can avoid suppression, however, if it can establish that the officers acted in objectively reasonable reliance on the invalid warrant. Suppression is required, on the other hand, if the warrant was so facially deficient—in failing to particularize the target premises—that the executing officers could not reasonably presume it to be valid.

    The courts have tended to view errors such as the one here as more clerical than substantive, and in the absence of evidence that the police officers acted in bad faith (by, for example, deceiving the magistrate, or with knowledge that the warrant was defective, or in reckless disregard for the requirements of the Fourth Amendment), the *Leon* exception has been applied. See *United States v. Kelly*, 140 F.3d 596 (5th Cir. 1998) (an unsigned and undated warrant due to magistrate's error); *United States v. Curry*, 911 F.2d 72 (8th Cir. 1990) (failure of the magistrate to indicate the address to be searched in the warrant); *United States v. Gordon*, 901 F.2d 48 (5th Cir. 1990) (warrant listed incorrect street name for home to be searched); *Maryland v. Garrison*, 480 U.S. 79 (1987) (discussed in §5.2.3; warrant incorrectly authorized search of entire floor where probable cause existed for only one of the two separate apartments); *Massachusetts v. Sheppard*, 468 U.S. 981 (1984) (discussed supra; failure of the warrant to correctly describe the items sought because of magistrate's clerical error). The decision in each of these cases reasoned that exclusion of the evidence would not significantly deter future violations because the officers had reasonably relied on facially sufficient warrants issued by magistrates. While deliberate police dishonesty or gross negligence can (and of course should) be discouraged, the theory goes, objective reasonable reliance cannot (and should not) be deterred. As for errors made by a magistrate, the suppression remedy is not (as *Leon* emphasized) directed at those players in the criminal justice process.

Would it make a difference if the officers executing the warrant in example 3 were not the same officers who had conducted the investigation and filed the application? In assessing whether reliance on a search warrant was objectively reasonable under the circumstances, the courts take into account the knowledge that the searching officer possessed at the time. In *Sheppard* the Court emphasized that Detective O'Malley, the officer who conducted the search, was also the officer who had filed the affidavit requesting the warrant and therefore "knew what items were listed in the affidavit presented to the judge, and he had good reason to believe that the warrant authorized the seizure of those items." 468 U.S. at 989 n.6. "Whether an officer who is less familiar with the warrant application or who has unalleviated concerns about the proper scope of the search would be justified in failing to notice a defect like the one in the warrant in this case is an issue we need not decide. We hold only that it was not unreasonable for the police in this case to rely on the judge's assurances that the warrant authorized the search they had requested." Id. Similarly in *Curry*, supra, the court found it significant that the search was conducted by the same officer who had prepared the application for the warrant. 911 F.2d at 78. Although the warrant itself omitted the address, the officer was aware that Curry's correct address was stated in the affidavit, and his reliance upon the warrant was deemed reasonable despite its facial deficiency. See also *Gordon*, supra, in which the court emphasized that the officer who conducted the search was the one who had initially provided the information for the supporting affidavit, and he thus knew the correct location of defendant's residence. 901 F.2d at 50.

Consequently, the good faith exception might *not* apply in example 3 if the officer conducting the search had not been the same officer who had filed the earlier application for the warrant. The searching officer would then have been faced with a warrant that did not specify any address, and he would not have known that the address had been provided to the magistrate in the supporting affidavit. An officer under those circumstances would *not* be acting in reasonable reliance upon the facially defective warrant.

4. As a threshold matter it must be determined whether the good faith exception applies at all in the context of *warrantless* police conduct. A good part of the rationale expressed in *Leon* and *Sheppard* is limited to situations involving warrants—the major premise being that police officers, as nonlawyers, should be able to rely on the judgment of trained magistrates as to the proper circumstances for a search and should not be penalized for the errors of the magistrate. Moreover, an officer's objective reasonableness is easier to measure against the benchmark of a warrant and supporting documentation than it is where the officer simply acts on his own. For these reasons, several circuit courts had refused to extend the good faith exception to warrantless searches. See, e.g., *United States v. Scales*, 903 F.2d 765 (10th Cir. 1990); *United States v. Curzi*, 867 F.2d 36 (1st Cir. 1989); *United States v. Winsor*, 846 F.2d 1569 (9th Cir. 1988). The Supreme Court, however, has extended the good faith exception to warrantless police conduct. See *Illinois v. Krull*, 480 U.S. 340 (1987), and *Arizona v. Evans*, 514 U.S. 1 (1995).

In the case upon which example 4 is loosely based, *United States v. De Leon-Reyna*, 930 F.2d 396 (5th Cir. 1991), the court sitting en banc held the exception applicable to a stop made in good faith reliance on information that was inaccurate because of an error by the police officer in reporting the subject's license number. Despite the negligence, the officer was deemed to have acted reasonably when he stopped the vehicle he believed to have been stolen. Under this view, the suppression remedy is unavailable for *any* police error, whether in reliance on a warrant or otherwise, where the officer "maintains a good faith and objectively reasonable belief that he has an adequate foundation [to act]."

The same result would follow if the mistake in our example had originated with a clerk, and not the police officer. *Arizona v. Evans*, supra, teaches that because the deterrence behind the exclusionary rule is directed *only* at law enforcement personnel, there would be no basis for suppression as long as the officer reasonably relied upon the clerk's erroneous report. See also *United States v. Santa*, 180 F.3d 20 (2d Cir. 1999) (arresting officers' reliance on statewide computer database record erroneously showing existence of outstanding arrest warrant for defendant was objectively reasonable). At least one circuit court has extended the good faith exception to a reasonable mistake attributed to a police dispatcher. See *United States v. Shareef*, 100 F.3d 1491 (10th Cir. 1996).

§7.3.4   *The Impeachment Exception*

We have seen (in §7.3.2) that the Court has limited the exclusionary sanction to the context of criminal proceedings. Within that context, the Court has imposed a further structural limitation: Evidence unlawfully obtained is admissible when it is used solely to impeach the defendant's testimony at trial. As with its counterpart in the *Miranda* doctrine (see §9.3.2), the impeachment exception is premised on a cost-benefit analysis: Whatever marginal deterrence is achieved by excluding the evidence for impeachment (as well as substantive) purposes is outweighed by the cost of permitting a defendant to perjure himself without effective challenge from the prosecution.

United States v. Havens, 446 U.S. 620 (1980), illustrates the operation and rationale of the exception. Havens was subjected to a search, and a T-shirt was seized that linked him to cocaine carried by his traveling companion. Prior to trial, the court held the search unlawful and ruled that the T-shirt could not be used in evidence. After the government presented its case, however, Havens took the stand in his own defense and during cross-examination denied having any connection to the incriminating T-shirt. At that point, the prosecution was permitted to introduce the shirt for the limited purpose of challenging Havens's credibility. "It is essential . . . to the proper functioning of the adversary system," the Court held, "that when a defendant takes the stand, the government be permitted proper and effective cross-examination in an attempt to elicit the truth." 446 U.S. at 626–627.

Thus, while the prosecution cannot use illegally obtained evidence during its case-in-chief, once the defendant chooses to testify and (either on direct or cross) raises an issue regarding the evidence, it may then be admitted for impeachment. Concerned that extension of this opening would too significantly undercut the deterrent function of the exclusionary rule, the Court has limited the impeachment exception to testimony by the defendant—it does *not* apply to the use of unlawfully obtained items to impeach *other* defense witnesses. See *James v. Illinois*, 493 U.S. 307 (1990). In a rare instance in which the cost-benefit balancing approach resulted in a decision in favor of the exclusion of relevant evidence, Justice Brennan reasoned for a closely divided Court (5-to-4) that the costs of extending the impeachment exception to defense witnesses would be greater than those involved in impeachment of the defendant himself, and the benefits would be less. Among the costs are the risk of discouraging defendants from calling defense witnesses, knowing that this might bring in otherwise inadmissible evidence, and the risk of encouraging police misconduct by making unlawfully seized evidence more valuable to the prosecution. The main benefit achieved—the enhancement of the truth-seeking function of the trial—is less compelling in the case of the defense witness than that of the defendant himself, because the former is far more likely to be deterred from perjury by the mere threat of a perjury prosecution.

Illustrating the elasticity of the cost-benefit analysis, four dissenters reached the opposite conclusion in *James*. Justice Kennedy reasoned that the cost to the truth-seeking function of excluding relevant impeaching evidence is greater in the case of the defense witness than that of the defendant, whom the jurors are less likely in any event to credit as an impartial witness. Moreover, he asserted it was unrealistic to believe that police officers would be encouraged to violate a defendant's constitutional rights by the knowledge that evidence obtained (although otherwise inadmissible) could be used to impeach a defense witness—the officer's decision to conduct an illegal search does not turn on such "a precise calculation of the possibilities of rebuttal at some future trial." 493 U.S. at 318.

§7.3.5   *Harmless Error*

It is well established that not *all* errors committed during trial proceedings, even if of constitutional dimension, automatically require a reversal of the conviction. Rather, if it appears that a conviction would have resulted *in any event* because of the overwhelming weight of the prosecution's case, the verdict will not be overturned. See *Chapman v. California*, 386 U.S. 18 (1967). The burden is on the prosecution to establish beyond a reasonable doubt "that the error complained of did not contribute to the verdict obtained,"—that the error was "harmless."

Exhibiting its continuing concern with the costs of the exclusionary rule (particularly the freeing of apparently guilty defendants), the Court in *Arizona v. Fulminante*, 499 U.S. 279 (1991), broke with precedent and extended the harmless error doctrine for the first time to the admission at trial of a coerced confession. If the reviewing court determines that the jury would have convicted the defendant even in the absence of the coerced statement, then the conviction will be affirmed. In making this determination, courts are directed to consider the following factors: whether the conviction depended on the jurors believing the confession; whether the jury's evaluation of an additional uncoerced confession relied on its relation to the coerced confession; and whether the admission of the coerced confession led to the admission of other evidence.

The *Fulminante* dissenters would have "adher[ed] to the consistent line of authority that has recognized as a basic tenet of our criminal justice system . . . the prohibition against using a defendant's coerced confession against him at his criminal trial." 499 U.S. at 295. In addition to the risk that coerced confessions may be untrustworthy, they argued: "More importantly, however, the use of coerced confessions, whether true or false, is forbidden because the methods used to extract them offend an underlying principle in the enforcement of our criminal law: that ours is an accusatorial and not an inquisitorial system—a system in which the State must establish guilt by evidence independently and freely secured and may not by coercion prove its charge against an accused out of his own mouth." 499 U.S. at 293 (internal quotations and citations omitted; White, Marshall, Blackmun, and Stevens, JJ., dissenting).

PART TWO

Interrogation and Confessions

8

The Voluntariness Standard

What are the rights of an individual who is being questioned by the police about suspected criminal activity? This problem, like that of search and seizure, requires the delicate balancing of conflicting goals. On the one hand, is the legitimate interest of the police in obtaining information about crime, information that may be available only from the suspect? On the other hand, is the concern in a democratic society for protecting the individual from governmental coercion and over-reaching? Unlike the inquisitorial criminal justice systems of Continental Europe, which place primary reliance on statements elicited from the suspect herself, the American accusatorial process reflects a long-standing aversion to convictions obtained solely through the accused's own mouth and a preference for "evidence independently secured through skillful investigation." *Watts v. Indiana*, 338 U.S. 49, 54 (1949) (Frankfurter, J.).

The Supreme Court has over time approached the interrogation dilemma from a variety of constitutional perspectives. The Fifth and Sixth Amendment approaches will be discussed in the chapters that follow. Our focus here is on the earliest approach of the Court, which focused on the voluntariness of the statement obtained from the suspect. Invoking the fundamental fairness concept of the Fourteenth Amendment due process clause, the Court ruled in 1936 that a statement obtained by police that was not the product of voluntary choice by the suspect would be inadmissible at trial. See *Brown v. Mississippi*, 297 U.S. 278 (1936).[1]

---

1. The suspects in *Brown* were physically beaten until they confessed.

While initially the rationale for exclusion seemed to be the unreliability of an involuntary confession, it shifted over time to a focus on the unfairness of the police tactics. Justice Frankfurter explained that involuntary statements were suppressed "not so much because such confessions are unlikely to be true but because the methods used to extract them offend an underlying principle in the enforcement of our criminal law: that ours is an accusatorial and not an inquisitorial system." *Rogers v. Richmond*, 365 U.S. 534, 540 (1961).[2] Thus the critical issue became "whether the [police behavior] was such as to overbear petitioner's will to resist and bring about confessions not freely self determined—a question to be answered with complete disregard of whether or not petitioner in fact spoke the truth." 365 U.S. at 543.

How is it to be determined whether the accused's will was overborne at the time he confessed? The Court has adopted a totality-of-the-circumstances analysis that weighs numerous considerations. One set of factors concerns the suspect's peculiar characteristics and vulnerabilities such as her age, level of education, mental stability, state of sobriety, and familiarity with the criminal justice process. The other factors concern the manner in which the police conducted the interrogation such as the length of the suspect's detention, the duration and intensity of the questioning, the use of trickery, deception, threats, or promises of leniency, the deprivation of access to family, friends, or nourishment, whether the police advised the suspect of her rights (see Chapter 9), and whether she was subjected to any physical or psychological mistreatment. While the use of physical force to extract a confession would clearly violate the voluntariness requirement, most cases fall in the gray area requiring close attention to the particular characteristics of the accused and the details of the interrogation. Thus, for example, a seriously wounded suspect who was questioned in the hospital intensive care unit while in considerable pain and barely conscious was held to have made an involuntary (and thus inadmissible) confession, even though the police did not engage in any "gross abuses" during the interrogation. See *Mincey v. Arizona*, 437 U.S. 385 (1978).

A significant elaboration (if not modification) of the voluntariness standard occurred with the case of *Colorado v. Connelly*, 479 U.S. 157 (1987). Connelly had initiated contact with the police when he told an officer on the street that he had killed someone and wanted to talk

---

2. Rogers confessed to murder after his interrogator went through the pretense of summoning Rogers's ill wife to the police station for questioning.

about it; he later confessed to an unsolved murder that had been committed months earlier. Prior to trial, Connelly moved to suppress the confession on the grounds that it was involuntary. A psychiatrist testified that Connelly suffered from command auditory hallucinations, a mental disorder that rendered him unable to resist the instructions he "hears" in his head, and that Connelly had been commanded by the "voice of God" to confess to the murder. Deeming this confession "involuntary," and not the product of free choice, the state courts ruled it inadmissible. The U.S. Supreme Court reversed. The Court (per Chief Justice Rehnquist) ruled that admission of the confession did not violate due process because it was not the product of overreaching by the police. "Coercive police activity," the Court held, is a "necessary predicate to a finding that a confession is not 'voluntary' within the meaning of the Due Process Clause of the Fourteenth Amendment." 479 U.S. at 166. While the susceptible mental condition of the subject is a factor to be weighed in the balance, suppression is appropriate only where it can be demonstrated that the police exploited that condition by means of coercion and that the confession resulted from that exploitation.[3] Challenging a confession under the contemporary voluntariness standard therefore requires a showing that

1) the police subjected the suspect to coercive conduct; and
2) the conduct was sufficient to overcome the will of the accused, given her particular vulnerabilities and the conditions of the interrogation, and resulted in an involuntary statement.

The second requirement incorporates the totality-of-the-circumstances analysis discussed above.[4]

As the examples will illustrate, the totality-of-the-circumstances standard is by its very nature subjective, imprecise, and ad hoc, thus providing the police (and the lower courts) with little guidance as to what conduct is constitutionally acceptable during interrogation. Indeed the "voluntariness rubric has been variously condemned as 'use-

---

3. Emphasizing the absence of volition on Connelly's part, Justice Brennan in his dissent characterized the decision as "inconsistent with the Court's historical insistence that only confessions reflecting an exercise of free will be admitted into evidence." 479 U.S. at 180.

4. For cases applying this analysis, see *McCall v. Dutton*, 863 F.2d 454, 459 (6th Cir. 1988); *Green v. Scully*, 850 F.2d 894, 903–904 (2d Cir. 1988); *United States v. Rohrbach*, 813 F.2d 142, 144 (8th Cir. 1987).

less,' 'perplexing,' and 'legal double-talk.' " *Miller v. Fenton*, 474 U.S. 104 (1985) (O'Connor, J.). Because it is so fact-specific, moreover, application of the standard to questioning invariably conducted incommunicado frequently leaves courts with credibility contests between the suspect's and the interrogator's versions of the events leading up to the challenged confession. "Such disputes," Justice Black observed, "are an inescapable consequence of secret inquisitorial practices." *Ashcraft v. Tennessee*, 322 U.S. 143, 152 (1944). *Connelly* brings into the picture an additional level of uncertainty explored in the examples that follow: what constitutes coercive activity for purposes of the due process standard?

Despite these shortcomings, and its partial eclipse by the *Miranda* and *Massiah* doctrines (discussed in Chapters 9 and 10), the voluntariness standard remains an important aspect of constitutional analysis of interrogation and confessions. It currently provides an alternative method of challenging confessions where *Miranda* is not applicable (because, for example, the suspect is not in custody or subjected to interrogation). In *Arizona v. Fulminante*, 499 U.S. 279 (1991), the defendant challenged a confession he made to a fellow inmate who, unbeknownst to him, was cooperating with the government to obtain evidence against Fulminante. The confession was obtained by playing on the suspect's fears of other inmates and then promising him protection from them. Because there was no interrogation, *Miranda* was not an available avenue of challenge. Fulminante was nonetheless able to attack the confession as involuntary.[5] Even where *Miranda* applies and has been complied with, a statement shown to have been involuntary must be suppressed under the due process clause.

The Supreme Court has recently held that the voluntariness test does not replace the *Miranda* framework, as Congress had sought to do in 1968 with §3501 of the Crime Control Act. The Court ruled that Congress has no power to supersede *Miranda* legislatively.

EXAMPLES

1. The police arrested Carey Corn on suspicion of homicide and transported him to the police station. He is 30 years old, dropped out of school in the ninth grade, and has an extensive criminal record. Corn suffers from diabetes, requiring him to take medi-

---

5. The Supreme Court used that case to apply the harmless error doctrine to coerced confessions. See §7.3.4.

cation twice daily and to eat at regular intervals. He arrived at the police station at 9 P.M. and was interrogated in a small room for four hours by Officer Maple, during which time Corn refused to respond to questions. He was taken to a cell in which a plank fastened to the wall served as a bed. Corn was not able to sleep. At 7 A.M. he was taken again to the interrogation room where he waited alone for two hours before Officer Maple appeared and resumed questioning. At 11:30 A.M. he confessed orally to involvement in the homicide. During the entire time at the police station, Corn received coffee and water but neither requested nor was offered food or medication. Could Corn prevent this statement from being admitted as evidence at trial under the due process voluntariness standard?

Promises, Promises

2. Assume the same facts as example 1. In addition, while conducting the interrogation, the officer tells Carey: "Look, I'm your only friend now. I can make the difference between you doing hard time and getting off easy. But I need your cooperation if you want me to make the right things happen for you. You've got to admit what you did, then I'll help you." Carey makes an incriminating statement. What effect if any should the officer's comments have on the voluntariness analysis?

Threats

3. Assume the same facts as example 1. In addition, while conducting the interrogation the officer tells Carey: "This looks like first degree murder from where I sit. You're looking at the gas chamber here, Carey. You can admit you did the crime and avoid the gas with second degree murder, or go the silence route and take your chances." Corn makes an incriminating statement. What effect if any should the officer's comments have on the voluntariness analysis?

Deception and Trickery

4. Assume the same facts as example 1 except that during the interrogation the officer falsely tells Corn that his close friend, McCoy, has implicated him in the crime. Corn then makes an incriminating statement. What effect if any should the officer's comments have on the voluntariness analysis?

Drug-Induced Confession

5. A homicide suspect in custody attempted to hang herself while in her cell. She was rescued and taken to a hospital where she was injected with a powerful tranquilizer. Officers later appeared in the suspect's hospital room and questioned her concerning the crime. Unbeknownst to the officers, the tranquilizer in the suspect's system had the properties of a truth serum, and she soon confessed. In support of her motion to suppress the statement as violative of her rights under the due process clause, the suspect-now-defendant has presented medical testimony indicating that an individual under the influence of that drug would not be capable of withholding information or resisting questioning. Should her motion be allowed?

EXPLANATIONS

1. This example (as well as example 5) illustrates the substantial change that *Colorado v. Connelly* has wrought. Prior to *Connelly*, suppression required a showing that under the totality-of-the-circumstances analysis, Corn did not speak of his own free will. Corn would point to his limited education and medical condition, together with the deprivation of sleep, food, and medication during interrogation, as evidence that he was vulnerable and his will had been overborne. The prosecution would respond by noting that he is a mature adult who had had considerable experience dealing with the police and was thus not likely intimidated by them. The court would make a finding as to whether Corn's free will had been overcome in these particular circumstances.

    After *Connelly*, however, that traditional analysis is not even reached unless Corn can demonstrate that the police resorted to coercive action. As one court put it: "*Connelly* makes it clear that such personal characteristics of the defendant are constitutionally irrelevant absent proof of coercion brought to bear on the defendant by the State." *United States v. Rohrbach*, 813 F.2d 142, 144 (8th Cir. 1987). Thus several courts have refused to consider the mental disorders of the suspect, even where they rendered him highly vulnerable to suggestion, in the absence of evidence of physical or psychological coercion. See *Bell v. Lynaugh*, 828 F.2d 1085 (5th Cir. 1987); *United States v. Gordon*, 638 F. Supp. 1120 (W.D. La. 1986), *aff'd*, 812 F.2d 965 (5th Cir. 1987). Compare *Jackson v. United States*, 404 A.2d 911 (D.C. App. 1979) (a pre-

Connelly case in which compelling evidence of the defendant's mental illness, together with the long duration of the interrogation, its late hour, and the fact that defendant was isolated from family, friends, and counsel, combined to require a finding that the statements were involuntary and inadmissible). One court has weighed the suspect's mental instability in determining whether the police interrogation amounted to coercion, holding that the police action must be evaluated in light of the defendant's condition where the police are aware of that condition. Thus a tactic deemed noncoercive when used against a suspect of normal intelligence may amount to coercive action when the suspect has mental shortcomings. See *State v. Carrillo*, 750 P.2d 883 (Ariz. 1988).

To suppress his statement, therefore, Corn must establish that it was extracted from him by means of coercion and was thus not the product of voluntary choice. Specifically, he must 1) make a showing that the police subjected him to coercive conduct; and 2) demonstrate that the conduct operated on him (given his particular characteristics and the conditions of the interrogation) to produce the involuntary statement.

What conduct is deemed coercive? Some courts have taken a rather narrow view as to what constitutes coercion. In *McCall v. Dutton*, 863 F.2d 454 (6th Cir. 1988), for example, the court concluded that there was no showing of coercive activity despite the fact that the interrogation was conducted by five officers who surrounded McCall with their guns drawn while he lay handcuffed on the ground and was semiconscious as a result of gunshot wounds he had received earlier. There was "no evidence that the officers used these weapons in any way to force a confession out of the petitioner." 863 F.2d at 458. Although this reading of *Connelly* seems to set an unduly high threshold for the type of police conduct that amounts to coercion, the Court provided little guidance on this point. Because the facts of *Connelly* involved only passive police action (listening to defendant's self-initiated confession), there appears to be considerable room for disagreement as to what police conduct is coercive.

Corn would argue that the deprivation of food, sleep, and medication, coupled with the duration of the separate interrogations, constituted coercive activity. It is highly unlikely that these circumstances (short of an equally unlikely admission by the police that there was a deliberate scheme to extract a confession) would satisfy the *Connelly* threshold. See *People v. House*, 141 Ill. 2d 323

(1990) (refusing to suppress a confession obtained after defendant had been held and repeatedly questioned in a starkly furnished interview room for 37 hours).

If the court were to find the police conduct here coercive, we would then turn to the question of whether the action played upon Corn's particular characteristics to result in a statement that was not the product of his free choice. Under *Connelly*, such causal nexus is a prerequisite to a finding of involuntariness. In *Hawkins v. Lynaugh*, 844 F.2d 1132 (5th Cir. 1988), for example, the court found the possibility of coercion because of the duration of the interrogation and the fact that the police were seeking psychological advantage by sending a black officer to interview the black suspect and express sympathy for his plight. Although such tactics "undoubtedly contributed to Hawkins' urge to confess," the court nonetheless ruled that "the sum of the events are not such that those statements would have produced psychological pressure strong enough to overbear the will of a mature, experienced man." 844 F.2d at 1140–1141 (citation omitted). The confession was held to be voluntary.

In sum, Corn would have considerable difficulty challenging the statement here under the contemporary voluntariness standard.

Promises, Promises

2. The Supreme Court in *Bram v. United States*, 168 U.S. 532, 542–543 (1897), held that a confession may not be "extracted by any sort of threats or violence, *nor obtained by any direct or implied promises, however slight*." (Emphasis added.) Modern decisions, however, have not been that inflexible in evaluating the importance of promises in the voluntariness calculus, and there is no longer a per se proscription against promises made during interrogation. As one court put it: "Under the totality of the circumstances test, the existence of a promise made to the defendant is not dispositive. . . . [R]ather, all the facts must be examined and their nuances assessed to determine whether, in making the promise the police exerted such an influence on the defendant that his will was overborne." *State v. Reynolds*, 471 A.2d 1172, 1175 (N.H. 1984). *Colorado v. Connelly* adds the threshold question as to whether the promises of leniency amounted to coercive activity, now a prerequisite to suppression under the due process clause.

Thus while courts have sometimes found that an officer's exploitation of a defendant's ignorance through promises of leniency rendered a statement involuntary, see *United States v. Pinto*, 671 F. Supp. 41 (D. Me. 1987), confessions have frequently been admitted despite the fact that they were made after such promises. See, e.g., *United States v. Jorgensen*, 871 F.2d 725 (8th Cir. 1989) (although the police made promises of leniency to the suspect, the court reasoned that the atmosphere of the interrogation—in an FBI office building rather than a police station—coupled with defendant's previous criminal experience, the fact that he chose the time and place of the interrogation, and that he had appeared there voluntarily, precluded a finding that defendant's will was overborne).

Mere representations to the suspect that cooperation is the best course of action have not been held improper. See *United States v. Shears*, 762 F.2d 397 (4th Cir. 1985); *United States v. Pomares*, 499 F.2d 1220 (2d Cir. 1973). Where the suspect speaks in the hope of leniency, and not in response to a promise of it, the statement will be held voluntary. See *Rachlin v. United States*, 723 F.2d 1373 (8th Cir. 1983). Where, however, the confession occurs in response to a direct promise of leniency, a close review of the record is required to determine whether it was involuntary. See *State v. Strain*, 779 P.2d 221 (Utah 1989) (the detective's "guarantee" of a lesser charge and threat of a first-degree murder indictment were held improper and the case remanded to the trial court to determine whether the confession was involuntary; the court noted that while the threats and promises were coercive, the suspect was a mature adult in his 40s, was familiar with the criminal justice system, and gave indications that the officers' conduct did not induce his confession).

Treating the officer's statement in example 2 as a promise of leniency, the court would have to engage in a fact-specific inquiry as to whether, in view of all the circumstances (including the suspect's particular vulnerabilities), the promise constituted coercion, which induced him to make an involuntary confession.

Threats

3. Threats to pursue a more serious criminal charge can certainly constitute coercion in the context of an interrogation. Like promises, however, they do not automatically render the statement

involuntary. As one court put it: "No single criterion controls whether an accused's confession is voluntary: whether a confession was obtained by coercion is determined only after careful evaluation of the totality of the surrounding circumstances." *Green v. Scully*, 850 F.2d 894, 901 (2d Cir. 1988).

If it is determined that the threats constituted coercive conduct within the meaning of *Connelly*, the court must proceed with a totality-of-the-circumstances analysis to determine whether Corn's confession was in fact induced by the threats. See, e.g., *State v. Garner*, 294 N.W.2d 725 (Minn. 1980) (where the police told the suspect that unless he gave them a truthful statement he would be charged with additional crimes, this was an important factor in the court's determination that the statement was involuntary).

Deception and Trickery

4. Again, the fact that the police engaged in deception during the interrogation does not automatically invalidate the confession on grounds of involuntariness. In *Frazier v. Cupp*, 394 U.S. 731 (1969), for example, although it was determined that the police had falsely told the suspect that his accomplice had already confessed, that action was held to be an insufficient reason to suppress the confession as involuntary given the totality of the circumstances, including the short duration of the questioning and the fact that Frazier was a mature adult of normal intelligence. Similarly, where the interrogating officer leaned toward the suspect (who had just denied knowing that a package delivered to her house contained narcotics), hit his fist on the table and accused her of lying, and then falsely told her that her accomplice had already implicated her (when in fact the accomplice had not even been questioned), the court concluded nonetheless that the statement she made was voluntary given the totality of the circumstances. See *United States v. Lux*, 905 F.2d 1379 (10th Cir. 1990).

Miller v. Fenton, 796 F.2d 598 (3rd Cir. 1986), *rev'd on other grounds*, 474 U.S. 104 (1985), involved an interrogation in which the detective falsely told the murder suspect that the victim was still alive and could identify her attacker and that blood stains had been found at the suspect's home. Throughout the interrogation the officer portrayed himself as sympathetic to Miller's plight and told the suspect that he did not consider him a criminal deserving of punishment but rather a sick person in need of medical help.

Eventually Miller confessed. Despite the deception and the obvious psychological ploys, the Third Circuit Court of Appeals (on a writ of habeas corpus) concluded that the confession was voluntary: "[I]n our view, [the manipulative tactics used here] did not produce psychological pressure strong enough to overbear the will of a mature, experienced man, who was suffering from no mental or physical illness and was interrogated for less than an hour at a police station close to his home." 796 F.2d at 613. The complexity and fact-specific nature of the totality-of-the-circumstances calculus is reflected in the court's elaboration:

> Detective Boyce's method of interrogation might have overborne the will of another detainee, for example, a young, inexperienced person of lower intelligence than Miller, or a person suffering from a painful physical ailment. It might have overcome the will of Miller himself if the interrogation has been longer or if Miller had been refused food, sleep, or contact with a person he wished to see. Moreover, if Miller had made remarks that indicated that he truly believed that the state would treat him leniently because he was "not responsible" for what he had done or that he believed that he would receive psychiatric help rather than punishment, we might not find the confession voluntary. We hold simply that, under the totality of the circumstances of this case, the confession was voluntarily given.

796 F.2d at 613.

Thus in example 4, the court would consider the deception along with Corn's personal characteristics and the atmosphere of the interrogation in assessing whether his statement was voluntary. The open-ended nature of the totality-of-the-circumstances standard permits courts considerable leeway in assessing the importance of deception. Moreover, whether deception will be treated as coercion for purposes of the critical *Connelly* threshold showing remains to be seen.

Drug-Induced Confession

5. In *Townsend v. Sain*, 372 U.S. 293 (1963), the Supreme Court held that a confession induced by a "truth serum" drug is by definition involuntary and therefore inadmissible. This was the case even though it did not appear from the record that the police knew the suspect was under the influence of such a drug when they questioned him.

After *Colorado v. Connelly*, however, it would appear necessary in order to suppress the confession to establish that the police knew of and exploited the suspect's helpless condition. Indeed, Chief Justice Rehnquist in the *Connelly* opinion portrayed *Townsend* as a case of "police wrongdoing" in which the officers *did* know about the drug and its effects. While the dissenters disagreed with this revisionist reading of *Townsend*, the important point for us is that a majority of the Court is clearly of the view that the actual involuntariness of a statement in circumstances such as these is not sufficient to require suppression. Rather, there must be police misconduct, at least in the form of knowledge that the suspect cannot resist answering. Evidence that the police directed the use of the drug for the purpose of inducing a statement would clearly constitute coercion.

9

The Miranda *Approach*

§9.1   The *Miranda* Decision

Given the amorphous and ad hoc nature of the voluntariness standard, it is not surprising that several members of the Court sought a more precise and efficient method of treating the problems arising out of police interrogation. Using its supervisory powers over the federal courts, the Supreme Court in 1957 adopted an automatic rule of exclusion for statements extracted from a federal defendant if he had not been brought before a judicial officer "without unnecessary delay" after arrest.[1] This approach was premised on the view that lengthy incommunicado interrogation creates an atmosphere ripe for coercion of the suspect.

In devising an alternative to the voluntariness doctrine that would apply to state prosecutions as well as federal, the Supreme Court turned to the Sixth Amendment right to counsel provision.[2] The opportunity arose in the case of Danny Escobedo, a suspect in a murder investigation who was interrogated at the police station despite repeated requests to consult with his attorney, who was present at the station and

---

1. This approach was known as the "*McNabb-Mallory*" rule after the two cases that created it. See *McNabb v. United States*, 318 U.S. 332 (1943); *Mallory v. United States*, 354 U.S. 449 (1957).
2. The Sixth Amendment had already been incorporated against the states in *Gideon v. Wainwright*, 372 U.S. 335 (1963).

attempting to see his client. Escobedo made inculpatory statements,[3] which were later admitted at trial, and he was convicted. On review the Court reversed, holding that the statement had been obtained in violation of Escobedo's Sixth Amendment right to counsel. *Escobedo v. Illinois*, 378 U.S. 478 (1964). A suspect who has become the focus of an accusatory interrogation is entitled, the Court held, to the "guiding hand of counsel" during that process. "[N]o system of criminal justice can, or should, survive if it comes to depend for its continued effectiveness on the citizens' abdication through unawareness of their constitutional rights." 378 U.S. at 490. The applicability of the decision was, however, explicitly limited to situations where an investigation had already focused on a suspect and where the suspect requests counsel prior to interrogation. Clearly *Escobedo* would not serve as the elusive all-purpose alternative to the voluntariness analysis.[4]

Miranda v. Arizona, 384 U.S. 436 (1966), decided two years later, represented the adoption of a comprehensive scheme designed to limit the abuses of incommunicado interrogation. In this watershed decision, the Court concluded (in an opinion by Chief Justice Earl Warren) that "the very fact of custodial interrogation exacts a heavy toll on individual liberty and trades on the weaknesses of individuals." Id. at 455.[5] Thus protective measures were necessary to dispel the coercion inherent in such questioning. Relying on the Fifth Amendment privilege against compelled self-incrimination,[6] the Court mandated that the four now-familiar warnings be given prior to any police interrogation of a suspect held in custody. Two of the warnings advise the suspect of his right to remain silent and of the implications of not doing so—that anything he says can be used against him in court. The other two warnings advise the suspect of the right to have an attorney

---

3. The statements were made by Escobedo after the police had arranged a confrontation between him and his accomplice, whom the police told Escobedo had already implicated him.

4. The Sixth Amendment approach is still applicable to interrogation occurring after a "critical stage" of the criminal justice process has been reached. See Chapter 10.

5. The Court reached this conclusion after examining various police interrogation manuals, which had been submitted together with the briefs and which the Court described as a "valuable source of information about present police practices." 384 U.S. at 448. The manuals described numerous tactics designed to obtain confessions from unwilling suspects, including deception, trickery, promises, and threats.

6. The Fifth Amendment had already been applied to the States in *Malloy v. Hogan*, 378 U.S. 1 (1964).

present during questioning and to have one appointed at state expense if he cannot afford to retain an attorney. If the individual decides to exercise his right to silence, *Miranda* dictates that the interrogation must cease; if he requests an attorney, the interrogation must cease until an attorney is present. The suspect, in short, has the right to cut off questioning. If the police do obtain a statement from the interrogation, *Miranda* requires the prosecutor (as a condition of its admissibility at trial) to meet a "heavy burden" to "demonstrate that the defendant knowingly and intelligently waived his privilege against self-incrimination and his right to retained or appointed counsel." Id. at 475. A statement obtained in violation of these requirements may not be admitted into evidence.

The conclusion that a suspect has "not merely a right to consult with counsel prior to questioning but also to have counsel present during any questioning" represented the Court's resolution of what Justice Jackson had previously described as "a real dilemma in a free society," namely, that to "subject one without counsel to questioning which may and is intended to convict him, is a real peril to individual freedom," but to "bring in a lawyer means a real peril to the solution of crime." *Watts v. Indiana*, 338 U.S. 49, 58 (1949).[7] The *Miranda* dissenters (Justices Clark, Harlan, Stewart, and White) suggested that the presence of counsel would indeed prevent the police from gaining useful information from an accused. They strongly disagreed with the majority's categorical approach, which they characterized as a "constitutional straitjacket" motivated by "a deep seated distrust of all confessions." The dissenters asserted that the extent to which abuses were occurring in the interrogation process had been vastly exaggerated, and they argued that continued resort to the voluntariness standard could remedy proven instances of coercion. For these members of the court, the cost of excluding reliable and uncoerced statements was simply too great a price for society to bear. The majority answered that the limits being placed on the interrogation process "should not constitute an undue interference with a proper system of law enforcement," particularly because they viewed as an overstatement the need for confessions in the prosecution of most crimes. 384 U.S. at 481.

One court would later describe the innovation of the 1966 decision as follows:

---

7. "If the ultimate quest in a criminal trial is the truth and if the circumstances indicate no violence or threats of it, should society be deprived of the suspect's help in solving a crime merely because he was confined and questioned when uncounseled?" 338 U.S. at 58.

Prior to *Miranda*, the Supreme Court attempted to protect an accused from improper police questioning by holding inadmissible statements that appeared to have been involuntary in light of the totality of their surrounding circumstances, including the characteristics of the accused and the details of the interrogation. . . .

But in *Miranda*, the Court found the totality of the circumstances approach inadequate. Recognizing that in-custody questioning has inherently coercive tendencies, the Court adopted in its place a set of rigid procedural rules. It held that until these rules have been followed, and an accused has been adequately informed of and waived his rights, he may not be questioned. If he is questioned, any statements he makes in response cannot be presented by the prosecution as part of its proof at trial.

The rigidity of the *Miranda* rules and the way in which they are to be applied was conceived of and continues to be recognized as the decision's greatest strength. The decision's rigidity has afforded police clear guidance on the acceptable manner of questioning an accused. It has allowed courts to avoid the intractable factual determinations that the former totality of the circumstances approach often entailed. When a law enforcement officer asks a question of an accused and the accused, without the benefit of *Miranda*'s safeguards, answers, the totality of the circumstances is irrelevant. The accused's answer is simply inadmissible as part of the prosecution's case in chief.

Mayfield v. State, 293 Ark. 216, 736 S.W.2d 12, 13–14 (1987) (citations omitted).

Perhaps the most accurate prediction made by the dissenting Justices in *Miranda* was that the new construct would not provide the bright-line approach sought by the Court. Rather than saving judicial time and effort as compared with the due process analysis, the dissenters asserted the *Miranda* approach would actually generate more litigation over issues of whether the suspect was "in custody," whether he had been "interrogated," and whether he had "effectively waived" his rights. As we will see, each of these components has indeed occupied the significant attention of the courts. And, ironically, the recent approach interpreting *Miranda* is very reminiscent of the totality-of-the-circumstances approach rejected in 1966.

Only two years after *Miranda*, Congress purported to "overrule" it by enacting the Crime Control Act of 1968, 18 U.S.C. §3501, which imposes the voluntariness standard as the exclusive method of weighing the admissibility of confessions in federal prosecutions. The administration of the *Miranda* warnings are relegated to just one of several factors to be considered under §3501. Although the statute was for the most part ignored for decades and not relied upon by federal prosecutors in pressing for the admission of confessions, the Fourth Circuit Court of Appeals "rediscovered" §3501 in *United States v. Dickerson*, 166 F.3d 667 (4th Cir. 1999). Drawing upon Supreme Court decisions characterizing the *Miranda* construct as merely prophylactic and remedial, but not constitutionally mandated (see, e.g., *Oregon v. Elstad*, discussed in §9.3.3), the Fourth Circuit upheld the validity of §3501. It should be noted that *Miranda* itself encouraged the development of alternative remedies: "Our decision in no way creates a constitutional straitjacket which will handicap sound efforts at reform, nor is it intended to have this effect. We encourage Congress and States to continue their laudable search for increasingly effective ways of protecting the rights of the individual while promoting efficient enforcement of our criminal laws." 384 U.S. at 467.

United States v. Dickerson, ___ S. Ct. ___ (2000), however, decisively affirmed the constitutional basis of *Miranda*. Writing for the 7 to 2 majority, Chief Justice Rehnquist both rejected the Fourth Circuit's reading of *Miranda* as merely remedial, and declined the invitation to overrule the controversial decision. The Court recognized that *Miranda* provides "concrete constitutional guidelines for law enforcement and the courts to follow," and has indeed "become embedded in routine police practice to the point where the warnings have become part of the national culture." As a rule of constitutional dimension, Congress had no power to overrule it.

§9.2 The Components of *Miranda*

Miranda held that the warnings and other protective measures would be required whenever there was "questioning initiated by law enforcement officers after a person has been taken into custody or otherwise deprived of his freedom of action in any significant way." 384 U.S. at 443. Any statement obtained during such questioning would be admissible at trial only after a demonstration that the warnings were given and that the suspect subsequently waived his rights. It was left for later decisions to define the concepts of custody " and "questioning," as well as to spell out the elements of a valid waiver.

§9.2.1 *Custody*

Miranda sought through the prescribed warnings to neutralize an atmosphere viewed by the Court as inherently hostile and intimidating. While in custody, the Court observed, the suspect is "cut off from the outside world" and in an environment that is "police dominated." "An individual swept from familiar surroundings into police custody, surrounded by antagonistic forces and subjected to the techniques of persuasion described above, cannot be otherwise than under compulsion to speak." 384 U.S. at 460.

It is only in the context of "*custodial* interrogation" that the *Miranda* protections are triggered. How do we define "custody"? Is a person stopped by officers in an airport terminal in custody when they ask him to identify himself and answer a few questions? Is a person questioned by agents in his own living room in custody and thus entitled to the warnings?

The ultimate inquiry is whether there is either a formal arrest or "restraint on freedom of movement of the degree associated with a formal arrest." *New York v. Quarles*, 467 U.S. 649, 655 (1984). The actual place in which the interrogation occurs is not determinative. One need not be in a police station to be deemed in custody. In *Orozco v. Texas*, 394 U.S. 324 (1969), it was held that the suspect had been in custody when interrogated (concerning a gun used in a recent murder) by four officers in his bedroom at 4 A.M. The Court, emphasizing the officers' testimony at pretrial proceedings that Orzoco would not have been free to leave had he made the attempt, determined that there was a "potentiality for compulsion" equivalent to a station house interrogation.[8]

Conversely, the fact that the questioning occurs in a police station does not automatically lead to the conclusion that it is custodial. In *Oregon v. Mathiason*, 429 U.S. 492 (1977), the defendant, then a parollee, reported to the police station at the telephone request of an officer. He was told upon his arrival that he was not under arrest, but he was asked questions concerning a burglary. Mathiason confessed to the crime and was then released pending review of his case. On review of his conviction the Court held that *Miranda* warnings were not re-

---

8. Compare *Beckwith v. United States*, 425 U.S. 341 (1976), involving interrogation in the suspect's occasional residence. The Court reached the opposite result on the custody issue, concluding that the pressures associated with a police-dominated station house interrogation were absent.

quired because the suspect had come to the station voluntarily, was informed that he was not under arrest, and had not been restricted in his freedom to depart.

Even where the police accompany the suspect to the station, questioning there may be deemed noncustodial (and thus no warnings necessary) if the suspect goes along voluntarily and is informed that he is not under arrest. In *California v. Beheler*, 463 U.S. 1121 (1983), the suspect, having made an incriminating statement to the police regarding a robbery-murder, agreed to accompany them to the police station for further questioning. He was informed that he was not under arrest. After brief questioning at the station, during which he made additional incriminating statements, Beheler was allowed to leave. The Court concluded that there had not been custodial interrogation because there was neither a formal arrest nor restraint on the suspect's freedom of movement "of the degree associated with formal arrest," and thus the absence of *Miranda* warnings did not preclude the admissibility of the statements at trial.

In the absence of a formal arrest, how then do we determine whether there has been a restraint on the subject's freedom of movement which is the equivalent of an arrest? The answer turns on whether a reasonable person in the suspect's position would have believed himself in custody or deprived of his freedom in a significant way. Only if the answer is yes will it be deemed necessary to neutralize the pressures of the interrogation by way of the *Miranda* warnings. The Supreme Court reiterated the objective test in *Stansbury v. California*, 511 U.S. 318 (1994) (per curiam), indicating that the subjective view harbored by the police officer or the suspect has no place in the analysis of custody.

Based on this objective test it has been held that the warnings are not generally required in routine encounters between motorists and police. *Berkemer v. McCarthy*, 468 U.S. 420 (1984), dealt with roadside questioning of a driver stopped on the highway because he had been observed weaving in and out of the lane. The officer failed to provide the warnings, but the Court nevertheless held that the incriminating statements obtained were properly admitted at trial of the drunk driving charge because the interrogation was not custodial. Routine traffic stops, which are ordinarily brief and occur in the public view, do not create the police-dominated, coercive environment critical to the triggering of the *Miranda* protections. Similarly, *Pennsylvania v. Bruder*, 488 U.S. 9 (1988), held that roadside sobriety tests are not custodial in nature. In both cases the Court emphasized that the actual intention of the police officer to detain the particular suspect and take him into custody is irrelevant to the custody issue unless the intention is communicated to the suspect. The standard to be applied is an objective one based on the suspect's perceptions, and the determinative question is "how a reasonable man in the suspect's position would have understood his situation?"

Among the factors the courts have looked to in applying the reasonable person test to a particular interrogation are the location (that is, is it familiar or unfamiliar to the suspect?), the duration, and the persons present (that is, was it just law enforcement personnel?). Despite the effort in *Miranda* to devise a categorical approach, the determination of custody remains a fact-specific and ad hoc inquiry, as illustrated by the following examples.

EXAMPLES
The Basics

1. As you will recall from the scenario set out in Chapter 1, the police arrested Michael Chestnut, transported him to the police station, and interrogated him there concerning his involvement in narcotics trafficking. Would such an interrogation require *Miranda* warnings?

2. Assume instead that the police chased Chestnut and, immediately upon overtaking him, asked what he was doing. He responded: "I ain't taking this drug rap myself. I'm just the little guy." Could this statement be introduced against Chestnut at trial in light of the absence of *Miranda* warnings? Does it matter whether the officers intended to hold Chestnut indefinitely at the time they asked the question?

3. Assume instead that the police were unable to catch Chestnut. Later that day, however, he decided to find out why the police were after him and went to the police station. After introducing himself and explaining the reason for his appearance, he was taken to an interrogation room and questioned by two detectives. Chestnut ultimately made an incriminating statement and was then placed under arrest. Could this statement be introduced against Chestnut at trial in light of the absence of *Miranda* warnings?

4. Assume instead that the police appeared at Chestnut's apartment and requested entry. He allowed them in, and they questioned

him regarding his involvement in narcotics dealing. Could any statement thus obtained be introduced against Chestnut at trial in light of the absence of *Miranda* warnings? What factors would the court look to?

5. The police were called by paramedics to the scene of an apparent shooting. Upon arrival they found the victim in the bedroom and a 16-year-old boy standing outside the room. In response to the officers' question as to what happened, the youth stated that the victim had fallen and hit his head. After one of the officers discovered a spent bullet next to the victim, the boy and his mother were taken to the patrol car and seated inside. The boy was confronted with the bullet and asked again what had happened. He changed his story and stated that he had accidentally shot the victim. When the youth was charged with homicide, he sought to suppress both statements on the grounds that they were obtained without the *Miranda* warnings. What result?

A Couple of Curveballs

6. Assume that our old friend Chestnut was being held in jail while awaiting trial. The police, who had thus far been unable to get him to make an incriminating statement, decided to place an undercover agent in his cell. The two men engaged in conversation and the agent asked his cellmate: "So, what do you do for spending money?" Chestnut responded by bragging about his role as a kingpin in a narcotics ring. Could this statement be used against Chestnut at trial in light of the absence of the *Miranda* warnings?

7. Assume the same facts as in example 2 except that upon overtaking Chestnut, the police read him the *Miranda* warnings and then asked what he is doing. He responded: "I ain't taking this drug rap myself. I'm just the little guy." Does the reading of the warnings convert a noncustodial situation (our conclusion in example 2) into a custodial one, thus triggering the other protection of the *Miranda* scheme requiring demonstration of a knowing, intelligent, and voluntary waiver?

EXPLANATIONS
The Basics

1. This is clearly the type of situation envisioned by *Miranda*: the suspect is deprived of his freedom and finds himself in a police-dominated environment. The suspect is clearly in custody. The

Miranda warnings are required here, and a statement obtained by the police without the warnings would be excluded at trial.

2. Unlike example 1 the suspect here is neither under formal arrest nor being held in the police station, the threatening environments that the *Miranda* Court concluded were inherently coercive. "General on-the-scene questioning as to the facts surrounding a crime" is not regarded as custodial in nature. 384 U.S. at 477. Custody attaches only where the subject reasonably believes that his freedom to depart has been curtailed by the police.

Chestnut would argue that when he was chased and stopped by the police, the degree of constraint on his liberty was more than that associated with general on-the-scene questioning and that he reasonably believed himself in custody, thus entitling him to warnings prior to any questioning. It is unlikely, however, that a court would treat Chestnut as having been in custody. Routine roadside stops of motorists (see *Berkemer v. McCarthy*, supra, and *Pennsylvania v. Bruder*, supra) and *Terry* stops and frisks (see *United States v. Galberth*, 846 F.2d 983, 994 (5th Cir. 1988)) have generally been treated as noncustodial for purposes of *Miranda*.[9]

If the brief public stop grows into something of longer duration or the police escalate the restraint on Chestnut (such as drawing their guns or placing him in a cruiser), he will likely be considered in custody and therefore entitled to the *Miranda* protections. In *United States v. Jones*, 846 F.2d 358, 361 (6th Cir. 1988), for example, the court concluded that the suspect was in custody for *Miranda* purposes "when three police officers in three separate cars, lights flashing, surrounded Jones' car, blocking him from leaving the scene." In applying the objective reasonable person standard, the unstated intention of the officers to detain Chestnut (assuming that they subsequently admitted to it) is irrelevant to the custody question. The determinative issue is whether a reasonable person in Chestnut's position, knowing what he knew then, would have believed himself in custody.

---

9. A subject being chased by police is not considered seized for purposes of the Fourth Amendment unless and until there is an actual application of force upon him or he submits to police authority. See *Michigan v. Chesternut*, 486 U.S. 567 (1988), and *California v. Hodari D.*, 499 U.S. 621 (1991), discussed in §4.3. The Court applies a similar reasonable person standard to determine both the seizure question within the Fourth Amendment context and the custody question within the *Miranda* doctrine.

3. If the interrogation here is deemed custodial, the absence of *Miranda* warnings would preclude use of the statement at trial. The fact that the questioning occurs in a police station is not itself sufficient to establish custody. Rather, the determinative inquiry remains whether a reasonable person in the suspect's position would have believed himself in custody or deprived of his freedom in a significant way. Because Chestnut had come voluntarily to the station and was not told he was under arrest, the court would most likely conclude that Chestnut could not reasonably have believed himself to be in custody. Although Chestnut (unlike the suspects in *Mathiason* and *Beheler*) was placed under arrest immediately upon making the incriminating statement, that fact would seem to make no material difference in the result, since the only relevant inquiry is the suspect's objective state of mind at the time of the questioning.

4. Questioning in one's own home can constitute custodial interrogation when there is the "potentiality for compulsion" equivalent to a station house interrogation. Where, for example, an interrogation was conducted in the suspect's bedroom by four officers at 4 A.M., the Court concluded that it was custodial. See *Orozco v. Texas*, 394 U.S. 324 (1969). Compare *Beckwith v. United States*, 425 U.S. 341 (1976), where questioning in a home that was the occasional residence of the suspect was deemed noncustodial. The determinative question is whether a reasonable person in the suspect's position would have felt his freedom significantly constrained by the police action.

5. The initial inquiry as to what happened constituted general on-the-scene questioning. The officers had just arrived and were not certain at that point whether a crime had been committed. Their inquiry did not focus on the boy as a suspect and there was no custodial atmosphere surrounding the conversation.

    The questioning in the patrol car was an entirely different situation. By then the police had reason to believe that a crime had been committed and, further, that the boy had lied in his initial response to them. Moreover, the questioning occurred inside a police vehicle. The defendant would thus argue that a reasonable person in these circumstances would believe his freedom constrained in a significant way. While this position seems compelling, the court that decided the case upon which this problem is based concluded that neither instance of questioning was custodial in nature and that the warnings were thus not required in either instance. See *In re Shannon*, 483 A.2d 363 (Md. Ct. Spec. App. 1984). The factors found determinative were 1) that the interrogation in the police car was brief and conducted while still in front of the youth's house in the presence of his mother; 2) that no weapons, handcuffs, or other physical constraints were used; and 3) that in his subsequent testimony the defendant did not indicate that he had believed his freedom constrained at the time of the questioning.

A Couple of Curveballs

6. Even though it is clear that Chestnut was in a custodial environment at the time he responded to the question, the Supreme Court concluded in a similar situation that the *Miranda* protections did not apply. In *Illinois v. Perkins*, 496 U.S. 292 (1990), the Court turned to the original rationale for these protections — namely, the need to neutralize the coercive aspects of interrogation in a police-dominated environment. When an incarcerated inmate speaks freely to a fellow inmate, *Perkins* concludes, this unique environment does not exist. "*Miranda* was not meant to protect suspects from boasting about their criminal activities in front of persons whom they believe to be their cellmates. . . . Respondent viewed the cellmate-agent as an equal and showed no hint of being intimidated by the atmosphere of the jail." 496 U.S. at 298. The Court distinguished *Mathis v. United* States, 391 U.S. 1 (1968), holding inadmissible statements obtained from a prison inmate questioned by Internal Revenue Service agents in the absence of the warnings, on the grounds that Mathis was acutely aware he was speaking to a government agent and thus likely felt the coercive pressure inherent in that situation.

7. If the police provide *Miranda* warnings when they do not have to (because the setting is not custodial), do they then have to abide by the other mandates of that decision (including the requirement for a valid waiver)? Do the warnings themselves create a custodial environment? At least one court has held that the warnings themselves do not create custodial intimidation. See *United States v. Gordon*, 638 F. Supp. 1120 (W.D. La. 1986), *aff'd*, 812 F.2d 965 (5th Cir. 1987). "To suggest that the mere administration of the *Miranda* warnings converts a legally non-custodial situation into custody is to completely strip from *Miranda* its original intention which was to protect a citizen from the coercive effects of police custody." 638 F. Supp. at 1133.

§9.2.2 *Interrogation*

The *Miranda* protections are triggered by "interrogation" of a suspect (who, as we have already seen, must be in custody). This component was defined by the Court as "questioning initiated by law enforcement officers." Statements volunteered with no such questioning are not covered by the doctrine. The police are not, for instance, required to interrupt a person who is about to blurt out a confession and inform him of his right to silence and an attorney. Moreover, *Miranda* has been read to permit the police to conduct limited follow-up questioning to clarify a volunteered statement. The question "Who did you kill?" would probably be permitted in response to the volunteered statement "I killed him."

Rhode Island v. Innis, 446 U.S. 291 (1980), expanded the concept of interrogation to include police conduct which, while not formal questioning, amounts to its functional equivalent. The broader definition includes "any words or actions on the part of the police (other than those normally attendant to arrest and custody) that the police should know are reasonably likely to elicit an incriminating response from the suspect." 446 U.S. at 301. Despite the breadth of this definition, the Court has been narrow in its application. In *Innis*, no interrogation was found where two officers, while transporting the accused to the police station in a cruiser, engaged in a conversation in which they discussed the compelling need to locate a shotgun believed to have been the weapon used by Innis in a recent robbery-murder. Referring to a nearby school for handicapped children, one officer expressed his concern that "God forbid one of them might find a weapon with shells and they might hurt themselves." Innis interrupted the officers and stated that he would show them where the gun was located, which he proceeded to do. Concluding that the police had engaged in a subtle yet effective form of interrogation, the Rhode Island Supreme Court held that his statement should not have been admitted at trial and reversed Innis's conviction. *State v. Innis*, 120 R.I. 641 (1978).

The U.S. Supreme Court disagreed and held that the statement was outside the scope of *Miranda* because the officers could not reasonably have expected their conversation to elicit an incriminating statement. The Court found "nothing in the record to suggest that the officers were aware that was peculiarly susceptible to an appeal to his conscience concerning the safety of handicapped children" or that the officers' remarks were designed to elicit a response. 446 U.S. at 302.[10]

In defining interrogation to include conduct that the officers should reasonably have foreseen would elicit such a response, the Court observed that where the police practice is *deliberately designed* to evoke a confession, such foreseeability is highly likely. 446 U.S. at 310. In assessing foreseeability, courts are directed to focus on both the particular susceptibilities of the suspect and the knowledge the officers had of these at the time of their action. The police, the Court added, cannot be held accountable when their conduct *unforeseeably* results in a confession.

Arizona v. Mauro, 481 U.S. 520 (1987), brought to prominence in the definition of interrogation a factor alluded to in *Innis*—that is, the perception of the suspect that he is being subjected to psychological pressures. The police permitted Mauro and his wife (at her request) to talk together in the police station where he was being held. Both were suspects in the murder of their child. The conversation occurred in the presence of a police officer and a tape recorder. Seeking a reversal of his conviction, which was based in part on incriminating statements made during the conversation, Mauro argued that he had been subjected to the functional equivalent of interrogation and thus was entitled to the *Miranda* protections. In rejecting this contention, the Court focused both on the perception of the suspect and on the conduct of the police. With regard to the suspect's perception, the Court concluded: "We doubt that a suspect, told by officers that his wife will be allowed to speak with him, would feel he was being coerced to incriminate himself in any way." 481 U.S. at 528. With regard to the police conduct, Mauro had not been subjected to compelling influences or psychological ploys, and the Court found the police action in permitting the conversation with his spouse reasonable under the circumstances.[11]

Where an undercover agent posing as a fellow prisoner was placed in the suspect's cell in order to elicit an incriminating statement and the ploy worked, the Court nonetheless held that *Miranda* protections

---

10. Dissenting Justices Marshall, Brennan, and Stevens concluded that the officers' conduct was such that they should reasonably have expected an incriminating response to result.

11. The dissenters in *Mauro*, convinced that the police had set up a confrontation designed to take advantage of the dynamics between the defendant and his wife and to thus elicit an incriminating statement, concluded that the *Miranda* protections should apply.

did not apply because the suspect did not perceive himself as being questioned and thus did not feel the coercive pressures that trigger the protections. See *Illinois v. Perkins*, 496 U.S. 292 (1990). Writing for the Court, Justice Kennedy explained:

> The essential ingredients of a "police dominated atmosphere" and compulsion are not present when an incarcerated person speaks freely to someone that he believes to be a fellow inmate. Coercion is determined from the perspective of the suspect. [When] a suspect considers himself in the company of cellmates and not officers, the coercive atmosphere is lacking. . . .
>
> It is the premise of *Miranda* that the danger of coercion results from the intersection of custody and interrogation. We reject the argument that *Miranda* warnings are required whenever a suspect is in custody in a technical sense and converses with someone who happens to be a government agent. [When] the suspect has no reason to think that the listeners have official power over him, it should not be assumed that his words are motivated by the reaction he expects from listeners.

496 U.S. at 296.

Thus while *Miranda* originally sought to standardize the constitutional approach to police questioning by resort to a uniform set of prophylactic measures, recent decisions defining "interrogation" represent a move back toward the fact-specific focus on compulsion and police conduct that characterized the voluntariness standard.

One additional point should be made regarding the interrogation component of *Miranda*. It had long been held that routine background questions regarding the suspect's name, address, and related matters were not within the *Miranda* doctrine because they were generally not investigatory, did not involve psychological intimidation, and were not likely to elicit an incriminating response. See, e.g., *United States v. Doe*, 878 F.2d 1546 (1st Cir. 1989). The existence of such an exception was confirmed in *Pennsylvania v. Muniz*, 496 U.S. 582 (1990), in which a majority of the Court (albeit for different reasons)[12]

---

12. The Court was evenly divided between those who regarded the process as interrogation but created an exception for it, and those who treated the responses to such questions as nontestimonial, and therefore not within the constitutional privilege against compelled self-incrimination. This latter group concluded that the incriminating slurred speech of the suspect in response to the sobriety test questions was analogous to the disclosure of the physical characteristics of voice or handwriting, which had been held not protected by the Fifth Amendment because it constituted "real or physical" evidence, and not content-based testimony.

held that warnings were not required prior to "routine booking questions," which are asked for administrative reasons as part of the arrest process. Similarly, incriminating responses made to the "carefully scripted instructions" that typically accompany field sobriety tests were held to be outside *Miranda*'s coverage.

EXAMPLES

1. Assume that Chestnut was arrested and transported to the station house. Without being administered any warnings, he blurted out: "I ain't taking this rap myself. I'm just the little guy in the operation." Could this statement be introduced against Chestnut at trial? What if the arresting officer responded: "What operation are you talking about?" and Chestnut then spilled all the beans. Could that statement be used?

2. Assume that Chestnut was arrested and transported to the station house. The police sat him in a room and showed him a videotape of one Jane Oak implicating Chestnut in a major narcotics ring. Detective Elm stated to Chestnut at the end of the viewing: "It sure looks like you're being played for a patsy to take the whole rap for the gang." Chestnut then stated: "I ain't taking this rap myself. I'm just the little guy in the operation." Could this statement be introduced against Chestnut at trial in light of the absence of *Miranda* warnings?

3. Police see Chestnut fleeing the scene of a crime he has reportedly committed. An officer chases Chestnut and observes him bend down along a wooden door that opens into the street. Chestnut approaches the officer and is arrested and the officer then looks behind the door and finds a gun. Chestnut asks what is happening; the officer tells him that he is to be charged and that he saw Chestnut bend over by the door. Chestnut then makes a statement that no one had seen him throw away the gun. Chestnut has not been read his *Miranda* rights. Is the officer's statement about seeing Chestnut bend over the equivalent of interrogation, making Chestnut's response inadmissible?

4. Assume that Chestnut was arrested at his girlfriend's apartment. Before being removed he insisted that his girlfriend was not involved in any of his activities and pleaded with the police to leave her alone. As he was being transported to the police station in a cruiser, the two officers accompanying him engaged in conversa-

tion in which they expressed concern that Chestnut's girlfriend would have to be brought in for questioning and perhaps kept in custody. At this point Chestnut interrupted and made incriminating statements absolving his girlfriend of any wrongdoing. Are these statements admissible in evidence against him, in light of the absence of *Miranda* warnings?

5. Assume that the police entered Chestnut's empty apartment with a lawful search warrant and found cocaine. He subsequently returned home and was immediately placed under arrest. He was then seated at the kitchen table and several officers brought in the cocaine and placed it on the table in front of him. Upon seeing this, Chestnut stated "O.K., the stuff is mine." Was the use of the cocaine in this situation the functional equivalent of interrogation?

6. Hemlock was involved in a fight with Maple in which Maple was stabbed and later died. Hemlock was arrested but not advised of his rights under *Miranda*. The police transported him to the hospital for treatment of injuries he received in the fight. While being treated by Nurse in the emergency ward in the presence of the arresting officers, Hemlock was asked several questions by Nurse. She first asked how he had been injured, and he responded that Maple had hit him. She then asked if he had stabbed Maple, and he replied that he had. She inquired as to what type of knife he used, and he described it. The police officer then asked Hemlock if he knew the location of the knife, and he said he did not. Was Hemlock subjected to interrogation?

7. Following a car chase, police apprehended Drake, who was suspected of having just robbed the Northern Bank & Trust Company of $10,000. The police asked him to identify himself, and he answered falsely that his name was Smathers. Later on at the police station Drake gave the officers his real name. The prosecution seeks to use the fact that Drake initially provided a false name as evidence against him at trial. Defendant argues that because he had not been advised of his *Miranda* rights before being asked to identify himself, his response must be suppressed. How should the court rule?

8. Responding to a radio call, police officers arrived on the scene of a domestic dispute and found Husband on the sidewalk yelling up to Wife, who was at the window of a third-floor apartment. One officer asked Husband: "What's going on here? You're making a lot of noise." Husband replied: "She's my wife and I can do any-

thing I want to her." Wife then came down to the street. Looking like she had been beaten, she accused Husband of assaulting her and the police arrested him. Wife was transported to the police station in another cruiser. At the station (and before *Miranda* warnings were read) as he was being led from the front desk toward a back room, Husband passed Wife, who was seated at a bench. Upon passing Wife, Husband stated: "They can't do anything to me because I'm your legal husband. When I get out tomorrow, I'll finish what I started, and you'll get one right between the eyes."

Can either statement made by Husband be introduced against him at trial in light of the absence of *Miranda* warnings?

EXPLANATIONS

1. Chestnut's first statement would be admissible against him. Although he was clearly in custody, there was no questioning initiated by the police and thus *Miranda* is inapplicable. The admissibility of the subsequent confession in response to the officer's question is a closer issue. Because the suspect himself initiated the conversation, some clarification or follow-up is permitted and the officer's question may fall within this permissible area. If, however, the officer had probed further or initiated questioning in new areas, warnings would be required.

2. Even though there has been no direct questioning by the police, their conduct here might be deemed "the functional equivalent of interrogation," thus triggering the *Miranda* protections. Chestnut would have to establish that the showing of the videotape and the subsequent comment by the officer was either deliberately designed to elicit an incriminating statement or that such statement was the reasonably foreseeable result. See *Rhode Island v. Innis*, 446 U.S. 291 (1980). In addition, *Arizona v. Mauro*, 481 U.S. 520 (1987), would seem to require demonstration that he had been subjected to psychological pressures or felt coerced into talking.

In the absence of an (unlikely) admission from the police that they had engaged in a deliberate ploy to compel a confession, Chestnut would ask the court to infer such intent or, in the alternative, to conclude that officers in those circumstances should reasonably have foreseen the result. It would be helpful to his argument if he could demonstrate that the police were aware of his peculiar susceptibility to the showing of the tape because of his relationship to Oak. If, for example, they knew of bad blood between Chestnut and Oak or of another relationship between the two, which would cause Chestnut to feel betrayed and vulnerable upon viewing the taped accusation, that would be an important factor in determining whether the officers should have foreseen that their actions would elicit an incriminating response. This type of knowledge, found missing in *Innis*, may well result in a conclusion that the suspect had been subjected to the functional equivalent of interrogation.

The showing of the tape and the subsequent statement directed at Chestnut seems more clearly within the concept of the functional equivalent of questioning than either the conversation and "few off-hand remarks" between the officers in *Innis* or the facilitation of a meeting between spouses in *Mauro*. Justice Stevens, dissenting in *Mauro*, stated that "it is undisputed that a police decision to place two suspects in the same room and then listen to or record their conversation may constitute a form of interrogation even if no questions are asked by any police officers." 481 U.S. at 535.

Where the police have set up a confrontation between the suspect and an alleged accomplice and either inform the suspect that the accomplice has already implicated him or instruct the accomplice to do so, that action has been regarded as interrogation under the *Innis-Mauro* standard. See *Nelson v. Fulcomer*, 911 F.2d 928 (3d Cir. 1990). Where, however, the encounter between the suspects does not appear to have been deliberate and the officers did not inform each of the other's accusations or prime one to do so himself, no interrogation was held to have occurred. See *United States v. Vazquez*, 857 F.2d 857, 862 (1st Cir. 1988) ("simply placing two individuals in the same area does not focus the police attention on a suspect in such a way that the suspect necessarily would feel added pressure—pressure above and beyond that inherent in custody itself—to say something"). Something more than merely bringing the persons in proximity is required for the action to be regarded as the functional equivalent of interrogation.

The something more in example 2 is the detective's statement directed at Chestnut immediately after the showing of the video. The police conduct here would likely be deemed the functional equivalent of interrogation, thus triggering the *Miranda* protections.

3. There was no direct question asked by the officer in this case. The Third Circuit, in the case on which these facts are based, looked at the totality of the circumstances to determine if the officer's conduct constituted interrogation and concluded that it did not. Although it was not necessary for the officer to mention that he had seen Chestnut bend over when Chestnut asked what was going on, there was no evidence that the officer intentionally created circumstances likely to elicit a response. The Court reasoned that the officer's remark gave Chestnut no incentive to say that no one had seen him throw away the gun. In fact, Chestnut's remark was described as "unforeseeable" and "gratuitous" and therefore admissible as evidence. *United States v. Benton*, 996 F.2d 642 (3d Cir. 1993).

4. Does the fact that the police were aware of Chestnut's particular concern regarding his girlfriend compel the conclusion that they subjected him to interrogation by conversing as they did? At least one court has indicated that the desire to keep family and friends out of a criminal investigation is so common that it does not by itself create the "peculiar susceptibility" envisioned in *Innis*. See *United States v. Thierman*, 678 F.2d 1331 (9th Cir. 1982). The officers did not ask Thierman any questions but they discussed in his presence their intention to contact his family and get them involved in the investigation, a prospect that Thierman had previously sought to avoid. At that point the suspect interrupted and said he would like to make a statement, which he later did. Rejecting the argument that the police had interrogated him by playing upon this concern, the court ruled that the peculiar susceptibility required by *Innis* must be something more than commonly held concerns to protect family and friends. It must be shown, for example, that the police knew the suspect was easily susceptible to psychological pressures or that he was unusually upset or disoriented at the time.

   The fact-specific focus of the interrogation issue in such cases is reminiscent of the voluntariness standard. In *United States v. Calisto*, 838 F.2d 711, 717–718 (3d Cir. 1988), the officer, having just discovered cocaine in the daughter's bedroom, stated in front of her father that "we'll have to get an arrest warrant for the daughter." This caused the father to respond: "Don't lock my daughter up. She has nothing to do with that stuff. That's mine. I'm the one you want." The court subsequently held that officer's statement did not constitute interrogation: "[the officer's] remark was not directed to Calisto, was the kind of remark that an officer would normally make in carrying out his duties under the circumstances that confronted him, and was not made in a provocative manner. Moreover, it was a single isolated remark made in the presence of a suspect who showed no signs of being emotionally upset or overwrought. Finally, even if it could be said that reasonable officers might have expected a protest of some kind from Calisto upon hearing of his daughter's possible arrest, we do not think it was reasonable to expect an inculpatory response from Calisto."

Dissenting in the *Thierman* case, supra, Judge Wallace concluded that the police, capitalizing on their knowledge of the suspect's concern, deliberately elicited the incriminating statement. Quoting from *Innis*, he emphasized that "where a police practice is designed to elicit an incriminating response from the accused, it is unlikely that the practice will not also be one which the police should have known was reasonably likely to have that effect." 678 F.2d at 1339. The contrast between the dissent's focus on the intent of the police and the majority's focus on the vulnerability of the suspect reflects a basic (and yet unresolved) ambiguity in the *Innis* analysis.

5. Did the police action here amount to asking Chestnut: "Is this cocaine yours?" Translated into *Innis* terms, did the police deliberately display the cocaine as a ploy to prompt a confession or, if not, should they have reasonably foreseen that result? Clearly in custody and surrounded by the officers, it is certainly conceivable that Chestnut would feel himself subjected to pressure to make a statement. It is equally conceivable that the police recognized this and took advantage of it. On similar facts a Massachusetts court ruled that the display of incriminating evidence constituted interrogation. See *Commonwealth v. Rubio*, 540 N.E.2d 189 (Mass. App. Ct. 1989). Similarly, where the police showed a suspect photographs of two suspected accomplices and told him "these two guys were arrested and you are going to be charged with the robbery," his statement was deemed to be a foreseeable result and thus the action constituted interrogation. See *State v. Ward*, 573 A.2d 505 (N.J. Super. Ct. App. Div. 1990).

The fact-contextual nature of the inquiry is illustrated by the opposite conclusion in *People v. Rowen*, 314 N.W.2d 526 (Mich.

Ct. App. 1981). The police officer's action in showing the suspected car thief a dent puller (a device frequently used to steal cars), which had been found in his car, was held not to be interrogation because it was not viewed as reasonably likely to elicit an incriminating response under the circumstances.

6. In *Arizona v. Mauro* the police officer's presence during the suspect's conversation with his wife was not held to be interrogation because there was no evidence that the police instigated it or used the wife for the purpose of eliciting incriminating statements. Nor did the officer participate in that discussion. In example 6, the officers sat back and listened to the questioning by the nurse without advising the suspect of his right to remain silent. They awaited the outcome of the questioning and then asked their own question. On these facts the New Mexico Supreme Court found that the conduct constituted interrogation. See *State v. Ybarra*, 111 N.M. 234, 804 P.2d 1053 (1990). The court concluded that the atmosphere in the emergency room, given the police presence, was more coercive than that inherent in custody itself, and that the police had taken advantage of that compulsion to obtain incriminating statements. A dissenting judge, observing that the officers brought the suspect to the hospital for treatment and not to elicit statements, disagreed that interrogation had taken place.

Involvement of third parties in the interrogation process has raised difficult questions for the courts. In *Endress v. Dugger*, 880 F.2d 1244 (11th Cir. 1989), defendant was visited in his jail cell by a detective who was a friend. The detective initiated the visit on his own to inquire about Endress's well-being and not at the direction of officers connected with the homicide investigation. Although the detective asked no questions regarding the crime, Endress made incriminating statements about it. The detective advised him to say nothing more, but reported the statements to his supervisor. Endress sought to suppress the statements as the product of unlawful interrogation. Since the meeting was not initiated by the investigating officer and the only purpose of the meeting was personal, the court concluded that the investigating officers (who were apparently aware of the detective's upcoming visit) should not have known that the visit was reasonably likely to elicit an incriminating response.

7. Drake's response will be suppressed only if it was the result of custodial interrogation. As he was clearly in custody, the pivotal

issue turns on whether he was interrogated. Unlike the previous examples, the police clearly directed a question at the suspect. *Innis* instructs, however, that words and actions "normally attendant to arrest and custody" fall outside the definition of interrogation. 446 U.S. at 301. Taking basic personal information from the suspect—such as name, age, and date of birth—does not constitute interrogation but is merely incident to the arrest and booking process. See *Pennsylvania v. Muniz*, 496 U.S. 582 (1990).

The twist in example 7 is that while such routine questions generally do not result in incriminating statements, the suspect's response here (by giving a false name) *did* provide evidence that could be used to assess his guilt. *Innis* teaches, nonetheless, that the police "cannot be held accountable for the unforeseeable results of their words or actions." 446 U.S. at 301. Because the question concerning identity was routine and not investigatory, the absence of warnings should not prevent the admissibility of Drake's response. See *United States v. Taylor*, 799 F.2d 126 (4th Cir. 1986). See also *United States v. Adegbite*, 846 F.2d 834 (2d Cir. 1988) (suspect's acknowledgment of a nickname in response to officer's question was not interrogation).

Where it appears that the law enforcement officer was using the routine background questions to elicit incriminating evidence, courts have held the *Miranda* protections applicable. Thus where a Coast Guard officer asked several persons taken off a foreign ship suspected of carrying narcotics for their identity and citizenship, the court concluded that warnings should have been provided:

> [Q]uestions about citizenship, asked on the high seas, of a person present on a foreign vessel with drugs aboard would (in our view) seem "reasonably likely to elicit an incriminating response." When, or whether, the United States can prosecute a person found on such a ship is not immediately obvious; and the possibility that prosecution will turn upon citizenship is great enough (and should be well enough known to those in the drug enforcement world) that Coast Guard officers ought to know that answers to such questions may incriminate. In this particular case, the likelihood of an incriminating response was rather evident.

United States v. Doe, 878 F.2d 1546, 1551–1552 (1st Cir. 1989). See also *United States v. Gonzalez-Sandoval*, 894 F.2d 1043 (9th Cir. 1990) (when border patrol agents questioned person suspected of being an illegal alien about his place of birth and immigration status, it constituted interrogation because it was likely to lead to incriminating information).

Statements taken from John Hinckley shortly after his arrest for the attempted assassination of President Reagan were suppressed because, although taken during a "background" interview, they were found to be the result of questions that had a clear investigatory purpose and were asked without regard to the *Miranda* safeguards. See *United States v. Hinckley*, 672 F.2d 115, 123 (D.C. Cir. 1982). The interview, which took 25 minutes and covered a wide range of biographical data (including his psychiatric treatment) as well as recent activities, "bore none of the indicia of a clerical operation." Moreover, the officers, knowing that Hinckley would likely raise an insanity defense, were aware of his peculiar susceptibilities and thus should have known that their interview was likely to result in incriminating evidence.

Skeptics have suggested that the distinction between questions that are clerical and those that are investigative is illusive and unworkable. Justice Marshall predicted that the distinction "would necessitate difficult, time-consuming litigation over whether particular questions asked during booking are 'routine,' whether they are necessary to secure biographical information, whether that information is itself necessary for record-keeping purposes, and whether the questions are—despite their routine nature—designed to elicit testimony." *Pennsylvania v. Muniz*, supra, 496 U.S. at 610 (Marshall, J., concurring in part and dissenting in part). Chief Judge Winter also expressed "serious doubts about defining interrogation according to the tenuous distinction between administrative and investigatory questioning." *United States v. Taylor*, supra, 799 F.2d at 130 n.1 (Winter, C.J., dissenting). "Because," he observed, "such 'routine' information may provide the critical link between the suspect and the crime, it is a substantial dilution of the principles established in *Miranda*." Id. Moreover, Judge Winters detected investigatory purpose in the "routine" questions directed at Taylor because they were asked at the scene of the arrest, not the station house, and because the officers already had information from an accomplice that made the suspect's nickname, "Snake," more than a mere administrative matter, but rather a direct connection to the crime being investigated.

In any event, it is interesting to note that the administrative/investigatory distinction that plays so critical a role in Fourth

Amendment jurisprudence (see §4.5) has now been incorporated into *Miranda* analysis as well.

8. Was either statement the product of custodial interrogation? The first statement in response to the officer's on-the-scene question was clearly not. Husband was not in custody at that time and could not have reasonably believed that his freedom was being restrained. The police, as far as we know, did not draw their guns or overwhelm him with their presence. *Miranda* permits such general nonaccusatorial questioning of citizens as part of the fact-finding process.

     The more difficult issue relates to the second statement made by Husband in the police station. Husband will contend that the police deliberately provoked the statement by confronting him with the alleged victim of his assault, conduct that they should reasonably have foreseen would accomplish that result. If Husband can establish that the encounter was arranged by the police, he may succeed in this contention. If, however, it appears that the encounter was not planned and that the action in leading Husband past the bench where Wife was seated was a routine part of the processing of arrestees and thus normally attendant to arrest and custody, then there was no functional equivalent of interrogation. See *People v. Reyes*, 506 N.Y.S.2d 541 (Sup. Ct. 1986).

     Whether the encounter between victim and offender was an intentionally coercive tactic or not was deemed the determinative issue in *Spann v. United States*, 551 A.2d 1347 (D.C. 1988). Spann was apprehended at the scene of a purse snatching and was being held by an officer within a few feet of the victim, who was asked by another officer whether the suspect was the man who had taken her purse. She responded, "That's the one." Upon hearing the woman's statement, Spann admitted that he took her purse because she owed him money. The court rejected Spann's effort to suppress his admission of guilt on the theory that the questioning of the victim within his earshot was the functional equivalent of interrogation. Rather, the court concluded that "the challenged question and answer were merely part of a dialogue between the officer and the victim to which appellant's response was neither invited nor expected," not a deliberate ploy to encourage a statement. 551 A.2d at 1349. The police were reacting to a confused arrest scene, and it was the victim herself who had moved within earshot of the suspect. Moreover, the court found that Spann had no obvious peculiar susceptibilities to pressure (such as alcohol or drug intoxication or mental disability) that were known to the officers. Thus from both perspectives of the *Innis* analysis—the officers' intent and the suspect's perceptions—there had been no interrogation.

§9.2.3   *The Substance and Adequacy of the Warnings*

Miranda mandates that specific warnings be given prior to any police interrogation of a person held in custody. Two warnings advise the suspect of his right to remain silent and of the implications of not doing so: that anything he says can and will be used against him in court. Two other warnings advise of the right to have an attorney present during questioning and to have one appointed at government expense if the suspect cannot afford to retain his own. The four warnings were deemed essential to counteract the compelling pressures inherent in the process of in-custody interrogation and thus to meaningfully protect the privilege against self-incrimination and the right to counsel.

Many police departments provide their officers with "*Miranda* cards" from which they can read the warnings now so familiar to viewers of television crime shows. In the heat of the moment during an arrest, however, the police may deviate from the routine language. Or the officers may respond to questions from the suspect in which they elaborate on and explain the warnings. How strictly must the police adhere to the exact language of the warnings as they are set out in *Miranda*?

The *Miranda* Court in 1966 provided some general flexibility to the entire prophylactic approach when it indicated that it was not establishing a "constitutional straitjacket" and suggested that there might be "potential alternatives" or "fully effective equivalents" to its chosen measures. There were also specific indications that the warnings did not have to be intoned in precisely the manner set out. Thus the warning concerning the appointment of counsel at state expense could be dispensed with, the Court suggested, if the suspect was known to have an attorney or sufficient funds to hire an attorney. Nevertheless the Court observed that the "expedient of giving a warning is too simple and the rights involved too important to engage in ex post facto inquiries into financial ability," and thus urged that the warning be given in all cases. 384 U.S. at 468.

More generally the Court admonished that "no amount of circumstantial evidence that the person may have been aware of [his rights to remain silent and to have the assistance of counsel during interrogation] will stand in [the] stead [of the warnings] ." Id. at 472. "We will not pause to inquire in individual cases whether the defendant was aware of his rights without a warning being given. Assessments of the knowledge the defendant possessed, based on information as to his age, education, intelligence, or prior contact with authorities, can never be more than speculation; a warning is a clearcut fact." Id. at 468.

Years later the Court addressed the issue of deviation from the original warnings. In *California v. Prysock*, 453 U.S. 355 (1981), the state appellate court had reversed the defendant's murder conviction because the police officer, while providing warnings to the juvenile suspect, did not explicitly advise him that he was entitled to the services of a free lawyer *prior to* questioning and made some additional comments, which arguably could have been interpreted as meaning that such a lawyer would not be available until the defendant appeared in court. The Supreme Court reinstated the conviction, emphasizing that "no talismanic incantation" of precise language is necessary to satisfy *Miranda*. Rather, what is required is that the police reasonably convey to the suspect his rights to remain silent and to counsel, which the Court found was done in *Prysock*:

> It is clear that the police in this case fully conveyed to respondent his rights as required by *Miranda*. He was told of his right to have a lawyer present prior to and during questioning, and his right to have a lawyer appointed at no cost if he could not afford one. These warnings conveyed to respondent his right to have a lawyer appointed if he could not afford one prior to and during the interrogation.

453 U.S. at 361.

If, however, the reference to the right to counsel is linked to some future point in time *after* the interrogation, the Court indicated that the *Miranda* dictates would not be satisfied. This latter situation came before the Court in *Duckworth v. Eagan*, 492 U.S. 195 (1989). Faced with the pragmatic reality that they were not able to immediately provide a lawyer to advise suspects taken into custody at all times of the day and night, the local police modified the warnings in a form that stated:

> Before we ask you any questions, you must understand your rights. You have the right to remain silent. Anything you say can be used against you in court. You have the right to talk to a law-

yer for advice before we ask you any questions, and to have him with you during questioning. You have this right to the advice and presence of a lawyer even if you cannot afford to hire one. *We have no way of giving you a lawyer, but one will be appointed for you, if you wish, if and when you go to court.* If you wish to answer questions now without a lawyer present, you have the right to stop answering at any time. You also have the right to stop answering at any time until you've talked to a lawyer.

492 U.S. at 198 (emphasis added).

Eagan, a murder suspect, was read this form and later argued (in an attempt to suppress his statement) that the warnings were inadequate because the "if and when you go to court" language violated the proscription in *Prysock* against linking the appointment of counsel to a future point in time after interrogation. The Court (in a 5-to-4 decision) disagreed, concluding that the warnings did in fact convey the substance of the rights required by *Miranda*. The suspect was informed of his right to talk to a lawyer for advice *before* any questioning and of his right to stop the questioning at any time *until* he talked to a lawyer. *Miranda* does not mandate that each police station have a "station house lawyer" present at all times to advise suspects; it requires simply that the suspect be advised of his right to counsel and provides that he cannot be questioned unless and until he validly waives that right.

In sum, considerable flexibility is permitted in the administration of the warnings as long as the fundamental points of the protections are conveyed.

EXAMPLES

1. A suspect in custody at the police station was given a written form to read that advised her of her right to remain silent and further stated: "You have the right to talk privately to a lawyer before, during, and after questioning and to have a lawyer present with you during questioning. However, you must make your own arrangements to obtain a lawyer and this will be at no expense to the Government. If you cannot afford to pay for a lawyer, one *may* be appointed to represent you." (Emphasis added.) Suspect, having made an incriminating statement during interrogation, now seeks to suppress it on the grounds that she was not adequately informed of her absolute right to appointed counsel. Should her confession be admitted?

2. A suspect in custody at the police station was given a written form to read that advised him of his right to remain silent and further stated: "You have the right to talk with an attorney, either retained by you or appointed by the court, before giving a statement, and to have your attorney present when answering any questions." Suspect, having made an incriminating statement during interrogation, now seeks to suppress it on the grounds that he was not explicitly informed of his right to appointed counsel at state expense if he were indigent. Should his confession be admitted?

3. A suspect in custody at the police station was given complete and adequate *Miranda* warnings. She then stated that she could not afford an attorney and asked the officer how and when one could be appointed for her. The officer replied that she could get a lawyer appointed when she went to court. Suspect, having made an incriminating statement during interrogation, now seeks to suppress it on the grounds that she was not adequately informed of her right to counsel. Should her confession be admitted?

4. Defendant contends that the warnings he was given at the police station prior to questioning were inadequate because he was advised that "anything you say *can* be used against you in court" instead of "anything you say *can and will* be used against you in court." He argues, therefore, that he did not understand the consequences of making a statement. Should his statement obtained during questioning be admitted?

EXPLANATIONS

1. While "talismanic incantation" of the precise language of the original *Miranda* warnings is not required, the suspect must be informed of the basic rights in a manner meaningful to the unlearned lay person. *Miranda* dictated that the suspect be warned prior to any questioning "that he has *the right* to the presence of an attorney, and that if he cannot afford an attorney one will be appointed for him prior to any questioning if he so desires." 384 U.S. at 479 (emphasis added). The use of the word *may* in this example was equivocal and open to misinterpretation, and could have conveyed the impression that the appointment of counsel at state expense was *discretionary*. This is particularly the case here because of the previous statement that "you must make your own arrangements to obtain a lawyer and this will be at no expense to the government." The suspect's statement should not be admitted because

of the inadequacy of the warnings. See *United States v. Connell*, 869 F.2d 1349 (9th Cir. 1989).

2. *Miranda* requires that the suspect be warned "that he has the right to the presence of an attorney, *and that if he cannot afford an attorney one will be appointed for him* prior to any questioning if he so desires." 384 U.S. at 479 (emphasis added). Although the suspect was informed of his right to a court-appointed attorney, he was not told that this lawyer would be free of charge if he was unable to afford private counsel. This omission goes to the core of the protection of right to counsel for all suspects, including indigents. To be adequate, a warning must convey to the accused that if he is indigent, he has the same right to counsel as a person who can afford to retain a lawyer. The suspect's statement should not be admitted because of the inadequacy of the warnings. See *Mayfield v. State*, 293 Ark. 216, 736 S.W.2d 12, 15 (1987).

   Some courts have held, however, that the omission of the specific language regarding indigency does not require suppression of the statement where the suspect was not in fact indigent and could afford his own attorney anyway. See *Chambers v. Lockhart*, 872 F.2d 274 (8th Cir. 1989). The Eighth Circuit Court of Appeals, however, in urging that the full warnings be given to all future suspects, cautioned the police (as did the *Miranda* Court) not to rely on their estimate of a suspect's financial resources in deciding which warnings to provide.

3. The defendant here would appear to have a more compelling argument than either Prysock or Eagan that her right to appointed counsel had been conditioned on the future event of appearing in court. She specifically told the officer that she needed appointed counsel free of charge, and was told in response to her request that this could not be arranged until she went to court. Thus while the Court has ruled favorably on the "if and when you go to court" language in *Duckworth*, the context of that advice here was much more likely to leave the impression with the suspect that she was not entitled to a free lawyer prior to and during questioning. As one state court ruled in a similar case, "rights of which the suspect was informed were, in the next breath, denied him when he was told he would only have a lawyer 'if he went to court.' " *State of Alabama v. O'Guinn*, 462 So. 2d 1052 (Ala. Ct. App. 1985).

   In *State v. Strain*, 779 P.2d 221 (Utah 1989), the suspect was warned that "if you cannot afford an attorney, you have the right to have an attorney appointed for you by the court *at a later date*" (emphasis added). The court rejected the contention that this was constitutionally inadequate, observing that he was also advised of his right to remain silent and that he had the right to the presence of counsel prior to and during questioning: "[The] immediate right to counsel which defendant envisions is not within the scope of the *Miranda* decision. Once the accused requests court-appointed counsel, it is treated as a wish to remain silent, and the police cannot proceed to interrogate him until such counsel has been obtained or until defendant initiates the interview." 779 P.2d at 224.

It should be pointed out that the suspect's inquiry about an attorney might be regarded as an exercise of his right to counsel. If this were the case, interrogation would have to cease. See §9.2.5.

4. *Miranda* emphasized that "the warning of the right to remain silent must be accompanied by the explanation that anything said can and will be used against the individual in court" because this is necessary to "make him aware not only of the privilege, but also of the consequences of foregoing it." 384 U.S. at 469. Further, the Court noted that this warning may make the suspect "more acutely aware that he is faced with a phase of the adversary system—that he is not in the presence of persons acting solely in his interest." Id.

The language used in example 4 probably sufficed to reasonably convey the substance of the right to remain silent and the implications of not doing so. Indeed, when the *Miranda* Court summarized its holding it used the very language challenged here. See id. at 444 ("the person must be warned that he has a right to remain silent [and] that any statement he does make *may be* used against him"). The statement should thus be admissible at trial. See *Ex parte Siebert*, 555 So. 2d 780 (Ala. 1989).

§9.2.4   *Waiver of* Miranda *Rights*

As discussed above, *Miranda* sought to eliminate the case-by-case, open-ended approach of the due process voluntariness analysis. Despite the Court's clear intention to provide bright-line standards for the interrogation process, that goal has not been achieved. One reason is that the doctrine of waiver of *Miranda* rights has evolved into its own totality-of-the-circumstances approach. A second reason is that the due process challenge to an involuntary confession survives *Miranda* as an independent avenue of attack. See Chapter 8. As one court put it: "The question of the voluntariness of a waiver of *Miranda* rights is separate and differs from the determination of the voluntariness of a confession. Once it is clear that a defendant has made a knowing and voluntary waiver of his or her *Miranda* rights, the issue then becomes whether the confession itself was voluntary." *Smith v. Duckworth*, 856 F.2d 909, 911 (7th Cir. 1988) (citations omitted). A confession may, for example, be suppressed because, although the suspect freely signed a *Miranda* waiver form permitting questioning, he was subsequently coerced into confessing.

Turning to the waiver question, *Miranda* held that if a statement is obtained from a suspect during custodial interrogation following provision of the warnings, the statement may be admitted as evidence at trial only if the prosecution demonstrates that the suspect "knowingly, intelligently and voluntarily" waived his privilege against self-incrimination and right to counsel.[13] There is strong indication in *Miranda* that the Court, seeking to avoid the ambiguities of the past, envisioned that such waivers would be explicit. Thus it observed that "an express statement that the individual is willing to make a statement and does not want an attorney followed closely by a statement could constitute a waiver," but that "a valid waiver will not be presumed simply from the silence of the accused after warnings are given or simply from the fact that a confession was in fact eventually obtained." 384 U.S. at 475.

Subsequent decisions have nonetheless opened the courthouse doors to implied waivers. *North Carolina v. Butler*, 441 U.S. 369 (1979), held that a waiver may be found even in the absence of an express statement to that effect if the suspect's words and actions *implicitly* constitute a decision to forgo his rights. While mere silence in the face of the warnings is not sufficient, "the defendant's silence, coupled with an understanding of his rights and a course of conduct

---

13. The *Miranda* decision characterizes this as a "heavy burden" for the prosecution to meet. The Court has since defined it as proof by a preponderance of the evidence. See *Colorado v. Connelly*, 479 U.S. 157 (1987). Some states in interpreting their own laws have established a heavier burden. New Jersey, for example, interprets the state constitution to require that waiver be proven "beyond a reasonable doubt." *State v. Bey*, 112 N.J. 123 (1988). See also *Commonwealth v. Day*, 387 Mass. 915 (1983).

indicating waiver" may suffice. 441 U.S. at 373.[14] Butler was administered the warnings and responded that he understood his rights. He refused to sign the written waiver form, but nevertheless agreed to talk about the robbery being investigated and proceeded to admit participation in it. When his statement was offered against him at trial, Butler claimed that in the absence of an explicit waiver the statement could not be used; the North Carolina Supreme Court agreed. The U.S. Supreme Court reversed and remanded, rejecting a per se requirement that a waiver be explicit and instead holding that a valid waiver could be inferred from appropriate conduct of the suspect. In determining whether a suspect has implicitly waived his *Miranda* rights, the Court (in a manner reminiscent of the due process voluntariness standard) directed trial judges to look at "the particular facts and circumstances surrounding [the] case, including the background, experience, and conduct of the accused." 441 U.S. at 374.[15]

Whether express or implied, a waiver must be shown to have been 1) knowing, 2) intelligent, and 3) voluntary in order to be valid. The first two components are treated together by the courts and focus on whether the waiver was made with an awareness of the rights being abandoned and the consequences of doing so. The third component requires a determination of whether the waiver "was the product of a free and deliberate choice rather than intimidation, coercion or deception." *Moran v. Burbine*, 475 U.S. 412, 421 (1986).

With regard to the requirement that the waiver be knowing and intelligent, it must be shown that: 1) the suspect understood that he had the right not to talk to the police or to talk only with counsel present; and 2) that he appreciated the consequences of foregoing these rights and speaking to the police. The Court has held that the prosecution may not rely on any presumption that the warnings were understood by the suspect, but rather must affirmatively demonstrate such understanding by showing, for example, that he answered affirmatively when asked by the officer whether he understood the rights just read to him. *Tague v. Louisiana*, 444 U.S. 469 (1980).

---

14. A number of states have departed from this standard and require explicit waivers under their own laws. See, e.g., *Commonwealth v. Bussey*, 486 Pa. 221, 404 A.2d 1309 (1979) ("by explicit waiver, we mean an outward manifestation of a waiver such as an oral, written or physical manifestation").

15. The dissenters in *Butler* would have imposed a "simple prophylactic rule requiring the police to obtain an express waiver," and they criticized the doctrine of implying waivers from conduct that is often of "uncertain meaning." 441 U.S. at 379.

The Court has taken a narrow view in recent years of the information that must be disclosed to the suspect prior to a knowing and intelligent waiver. In *Moran v. Burbine*, 475 U.S. 412 (1986), the fact that the police failed to inform the suspect that an attorney retained by a relative to represent him was trying to see him at the police station was held not to undercut the validity of his written waiver. The police had assured the attorney that the suspect would not be questioned until the next day, but then proceeded to interrogate him. While the First Circuit Court of Appeals had reversed Burbine's conviction, reasoning that he had been deprived of information necessary for a knowing and intelligent waiver, the Supreme Court disagreed: "Events occurring outside of the presence of the suspect and entirely unknown to him surely can have no bearing on the capacity to comprehend and knowingly relinquish a constitutional right." 475 U.S. at 421. The Court added:

> No doubt the additional information [that an attorney was seeking to meet with him] would have been useful to respondent; perhaps even it might have affected his decision to confess. But we have never read the Constitution to require that the police supply a suspect with a flow of information to help him calibrate his self interest in deciding whether to speak or stand by his rights. *Once it is determined that a suspect's decision not to rely on his rights was uncoerced, that he at all times knew he could stand mute and request a lawyer, and that he was aware of the state's intention to use his statements to secure a conviction, the analysis is complete and the waiver is valid as a matter of law.*

Id. (emphasis added).[16] *Moran* did leave open the possibility that "on facts more egregious than those presented here police deception might rise to the level of a due process violation." Id. at 432.

Other decisions similarly indicate that the suspect need only have a minimal understanding of his *Miranda* rights and the consequences of relinquishing them. Like Butler in the case discussed above, the suspect in *Connecticut v. Barrett*, 479 U.S. 523 (1987), indicated after receiving the warnings that he would not make a written statement but would talk about the sexual assault being investigated. He later

---

16. Justice Stevens, writing for the dissenters, criticized the Court's "what the suspect doesn't know can't hurt him" approach, 475 U.S. at 453 n.38, and concluded that "the failure to inform Burbine of the call from his attorney makes the subsequent waiver of his constitutional rights invalid." Id. at 450.

confessed orally. Barrett challenged the admission of his statement into evidence on the grounds that his inconsistent conduct demonstrated that he did not understand the implications of speaking to the police, and thus his waiver was not knowing and intelligent. The Supreme Court held otherwise, ruling that the police could properly take the opportunity opened by his ambiguous actions to obtain an oral confession: "[The] fact that some might find Barrett's decision illogical is irrelevant, for we have never embraced the theory that a defendant's ignorance of the full consequences of his decisions vitiates their voluntariness." 479 U.S. at 530.

The Court held in *Colorado v. Spring*, 479 U.S. 564 (1987), that a suspect need not be aware in advance of all the possible subjects of the interrogation in order to make a valid waiver of his *Miranda* rights. Spring, arrested by federal agents in Missouri on a firearms charge, signed a written waiver form after being advised of his rights. The focus of the interrogation ultimately changed, however, from the firearms transactions to an unsolved homicide in Colorado, to which Spring then confessed. Rejecting his assertion that he could not have knowingly waived his right to remain silent when he was unaware that he would be questioned about the unrelated crime, the Court reaffirmed its position that a valid waiver does not require that an individual be informed of all information that would be useful in making his decision or that might affect his decision to confess. The information withheld by the police, the Court observed, might go to the "wisdom" of the waiver but not to "its essentially voluntary and knowing nature." 479 U.S. at 577.

Turning to the separate requirement that the waiver be voluntary, *Colorado v. Connelly*, 479 U.S. 157 (1987) equated this with the due process standard discussed in Chapter 8. "The sole concern of the Fifth Amendment, on which *Miranda* was based, is governmental coercion. Indeed, the Fifth Amendment privilege is not concerned with moral and psychological pressures to confess emanating from sources other than official coercion. The voluntariness of a waiver of this privilege has always depended on the absence of police overreaching, not on 'free choice' in any broader sense of the word." 479 U.S. at 170 (citations and internal quotations omitted). Thus to invalidate a waiver as involuntary it is not enough to show a lack of free choice on the suspect's part; it must be demonstrated that the waiver resulted from police coercion that overcame the suspect's will. If the accused was subjected to compulsion such as intimidation or threats, then the impact of those tactics will be examined in light of the totality of the circumstances surrounding the interrogation (including the suspect's age, mental state, experience, and intelligence) to determine the voluntariness of the waiver. See *Fare v. Michael C.*, 442 U.S. 707 (1979). Absent evidence of objectionable police methods, however, *Connelly* signals that the waiver will be found voluntary regardless of the defendant's peculiar vulnerabilities or internal compulsions to confess.

The *Miranda* Court stated that "any evidence that the accused was threatened, tricked, or cajoled into a waiver will of course show that the defendant did not voluntarily waive his privilege." 384 U.S. at 476. In recent years, however, such deceptive activity by the police has been treated by the courts as only one factor among the totality of circumstances in the decision as to the validity of the waiver and does not result in an automatic finding of involuntariness. This development parallels the treatment of deception for purposes of the due process voluntariness standard. See Chapter 8.

EXAMPLES

1. Suzanne Suspect was arrested near the scene of a robbery and was transported to the police station. She was advised of her *Miranda* rights and signed a "Waiver Form" indicating that she understood her rights to remain silent and to counsel but chose to waive those rights and submit to interrogation. After two hours of questioning, Suspect admitted participation in the robbery. What legal issues are involved, and what standards apply to those legal issues, when the prosecution offers that statement into evidence at trial?

2. Assume instead that Suspect was advised of her rights, stated that she understood them, but refused to sign the waiver form. The detective on the case then said to Suspect: "You don't have to sign the form, but we would like you to answer some questions for us." The detective proceeded to interrogate Suspect about the robbery, and she made several incriminating responses. How does the analysis of the admissibility of these statements differ from the confession in example 1?

3. Assume instead that after Suspect was advised of her *Miranda* rights, she stated that she would answer questions about the crime but would not give or sign a written statement because "that could be used against me." She then proceeded to make several incriminating statements during questioning. How does the analysis of the admissibility of these statements differ from the confession in example 2?

4. Now assume that when Suspect arrived at the police station, she appeared to be very disoriented, fatigued, and obviously under the influence of narcotics. She was advised of her rights and nodded affirmatively when the detective asked whether she understood them. The detective then said to Suspect: "The sooner you come clean with us, the quicker we can get you help." The detective proceeded to question Suspect about the robbery, reminding her several times in a forceful manner that it would be easier on her if she confessed. Suspect finally agreed to answer questions and eventually admitted committing the crime. How does the analysis of the admissibility of this statement differ from the confession in example 3?

5. Daniel Bernard, a 22-year-old with a fourth-grade education and no prior experience with the police, confessed to a robbery-murder during questioning at the station house. He had been advised of his rights after being arrested, and signed a *Miranda* waiver form prior to interrogation. His attorney, who has filed a motion to suppress the confession, has learned that Bernard is of subnormal intelligence and (according to expert witnesses) could not have understood the terminology of the warnings. The police, however, did not engage in any coercive conduct either before or during the interrogation. Is the confession admissible at trial?

6. Suppose instead that Bernard is a 15-year-old of normal intelligence. Assuming again that there is no police coercion, would his waiver be valid?

7. Ned Nave was arrested for embezzlement, taken to the police station, and advised of his *Miranda* rights. He responded that he wished his attorney, Walter Willow, was available to advise him but was out of town for the week. Nave said that in light of Willow's unavailability he "might as well talk," and during the subsequent questioning he made several incriminating statements. Unbeknownst to Nave, Attorney Willow had in fact already arrived back in town, heard about Nave's arrest, and tried unsuccessfully to meet with him prior to his questioning. The police had steadfastly refused to let Willow see his client and had failed to advise Nave of his lawyer's presence. Are his statements admissible at trial?

8. Rodney Ring was arrested for aggravated rape, taken to the police station, and advised of his *Miranda* rights. Before waiting for a response from Ring, the detective told him that he had already

been positively identified by the victim from a photograph. Ring replied: "I guess there's no sense keeping quiet then," and signed a waiver form. After ten minutes of questioning, Ring confessed. It turns out that the detective lied about the victim having identified Ring. Is his statement admissible in court?

EXPLANATIONS

1. There are two basic issues that must be resolved concerning the admissibility of the confession 1) Did Suspect make a legally effective waiver of her *Miranda* rights? 2) Was Suspect's confession voluntary or the result of police coercion? The second issue is controlled by the due process standard discussed in Chapter 8 and is distinct from the *Miranda* waiver issue. A suspect may, for example, make a valid waiver ("knowing, intelligent, and voluntary") of his *Miranda* rights and submit to questioning, but then be intimidated by the police into making a confession. That statement could be challenged under the due process standard even though the waiver was lawfully obtained.

   Regarding the first issue, *Miranda* held that "an express statement that the individual is willing to make a statement and does not want an attorney followed closely by a statement could constitute a waiver." 384 U.S. at 474. The validity of Suspect's written waiver depends upon whether it was knowing, intelligent, and voluntary. The prosecution bears the burden of establishing this by a preponderance of the evidence. The waiver will be considered knowing and intelligent as long as it appears that Suspect generally understood the warnings and the rights described (which she acknowledged at the time she did) and that she appreciated the consequences of undergoing interrogation—that is, that the prosecution would use her statements against her in court. The waiver will be considered voluntary as long as it was not the product of police coercion or pressure.

2. Unlike example 1, Suspect did not make an explicit waiver (either written or oral) here. The statement may nonetheless be admitted if the prosecution can establish 1) that Suspect's conduct constitutes an *implied* waiver; and 2) that the waiver was knowing, intelligent, and voluntary.

   Although *Miranda* held "that a valid waiver will not be presumed simply from the silence of the accused after warnings are given or simply from the fact that a confession was in fact eventually obtained," 384 U.S. at 474, silence together with conduct by the accused indicating that he understands his rights and wishes to relinquish them may constitute a valid implied waiver. *North Carolina v. Butler*, 441 U.S. 369 (1979). Courts must look at the particular facts and circumstances surrounding the questioning—including the suspect's age, education, background, and prior experience with the police—to determine if he intended to forgo his rights.

Like Butler (in *North Carolina v. Butler*) and Barrett (in *Connecticut v. Barrett*), Suspect's conduct in refusing to sign a waiver but then responding to questions appears inconsistent and ambiguous (it would no doubt be described by the dissenters in *Butler* as of "uncertain meaning"). The Court held in both cases, however, that a waiver may be inferred from the facts that the accused was advised of his rights, indicated he understood them, and then proceeded to answer the detective's questions. This is particularly so where the accused is a mature adult of reasonable intelligence and has had prior experience with the criminal justice system.

Although Suspect's conduct seems hardly the product of rational deliberation and indeed may reflect a lack of understanding that her responses could be used against her by the prosecution, under the prevailing narrow definition of "knowing and intelligent" it probably makes the grade. She stated that she understood her rights and submitted to questioning. Moreover, the detective's prompting here falls far short of coercion undercutting the voluntary nature of the waiver. See *Colorado v. Connelly*, 479 U.S. 157 (1987). As the Court held in *Moran v. Burbine*: "Once it is determined that a suspect's decision not to rely on his rights was uncoerced, that he at all times knew he could stand mute and request a lawyer, and that he was aware of the state's intention to use his statements to secure a conviction, the analysis is complete and the waiver is valid as a matter of law." 475 U.S. at 422–423.

3. There is a much clearer indication here than in the previous example that the accused misunderstood the warnings and the consequences of submitting to interrogation. Unlike example 2 or *Connecticut v. Barrett*, Suspect explicitly expressed her misunderstanding (that only written statements could be used against her and not oral responses) to the police and they failed to correct it. She thus has a more persuasive argument that her waiver was not knowing and intelligent.

4. Suspect, in agreeing to answer questions, has made an explicit oral waiver. The validity of that waiver must be analyzed, however, in light of the pressures placed on Suspect by the detective's remarks, as well as Suspect's apparent vulnerability. In other words, it must be determined whether the waiver was voluntary under a totality-of-the-circumstances analysis: Did the police conduct themselves in such a manner as to overcome the will of the accused, given her personal characteristics? See *Fare v. Michael C.*, supra. For a waiver to be voluntary it must be "the product of a free and deliberate choice rather than intimidation, coercion or deception." *Moran v. Burbine*, 475 U.S. at 421. The detective's encouragements may very well have worn down Suspect's resistance to being questioned, particularly given her apparently impaired state of mind. *Colorado v. Connelly* teaches, however, that a waiver may be deemed involuntary only if the police used *coercive tactics* to overcome the accused's will. The detective's conduct here probably does not rise to the level required by *Connelly*. See Chapter 8.

    It is possible, nonetheless, that a court would conclude that Suspect's waiver was not knowing and intelligent because her impaired mental state (exhaustion and the effect of narcotics) precluded her from understanding the warnings and the consequences of answering questions. Unlike the voluntariness requirement, coercive tactics are *not* a prerequisite to such a finding under the separate knowing and intelligent standard. See example 5.

5. Because the waiver was not the product of police coercion it cannot be considered involuntary. The requirement that a waiver be knowing and intelligent is, however, a distinct prerequisite to validity and has *not* been held dependent upon a finding that the police engaged in coercive conduct. See *Illinois v. Bernasco*, 138 Ill. 2d 349, 562 N.E.2d 958 (1990). Even under the minimal standard set by the Supreme Court—that the suspect be mentally aware that he may remain silent and request a lawyer and, further, that the prosecution will use his statements against him in court—Bernard could probably not make a knowing and intelligent waiver on his own (assuming, of course, that the court accepts the conclusion of the expert witnesses).

    The extent to which mental defect may foreclose a knowing and intelligent waiver depends upon the nature of the defect and the other factors peculiar to the situation. In *United States v. Gaddy*, 894 F.2d 1307 (11th Cir. 1990), where there was no contention that the *Miranda* waiver was involuntary, there was serious question as to whether it was knowing and intelligent. Factors weighing against the validity of the waiver in this regard were the suspect's addiction to drugs and his mental illness. Weighing in favor of the waiver were his above-average intelligence, his previous experience with the law (he was "no novice to law enforcement procedures"), and the fact that he did not exhibit scattered thinking or panicky behavior. The court concluded that the waiver was knowing and intelligent.

A moderately retarded and functionally illiterate individual was similarly held to have made a voluntary, knowing, and intelligent waiver of his *Miranda* rights in *Dunkins v. Thigpen*, 854 F.2d 394 (11th Cir. 1988). Under the *Connelly* standard, mental retardation by itself does not render a waiver involuntary without the element of police coercion. And mental retardation is just one of the factors to consider in the determination of whether the waiver was knowing and intelligent. The court concluded that a person functioning as Dunkins in the high mild range of retardation could understand his rights and intelligently waive them.

In *Smith v. Zant*, 887 F.2d 1407 (11th Cir. 1989), the court came to the opposite conclusion when it held that a mentally retarded suspect had not knowingly and intelligently waived his *Miranda* rights. The court-appointed psychiatrist who examined Smith testified that a person functioning at his level of intelligence would have difficulty understanding his rights and the consequences of relinquishing them unless those rights were slowly and carefully explained to him, which they were not. See also *State v. Flower*, 539 A.2d 1284, 1288 (N.J. Super. 1987) (holding that a mentally retarded 26-year-old, with the intelligence of a child of six, could not "knowingly and intelligently waive a right that he cannot understand or appreciate.")

6. If Bernard were a 15-year-old of normal intelligence, the concern would be whether he had the maturity to appreciate the nature of his rights and the implications of waiving them. Courts weigh the presence of a parent or other helpful adult as an important factor when determining the validity of a waiver by a juvenile. See, e.g., *State v. Jimenez*, 799 P.2d 785 (Ariz. 1990). Some states, in their desire to establish at least some bright lines, have adopted per se rules requiring that the consequences of the waiver be explained to the juvenile by a parent or other interested adult in order for

the waiver to be valid. See *State v. Stone*, 570 So. 2d 78, 80 (La. 1990). See also *Commonwealth v. Juvenile*, 389 Mass. 128, 134 (1983) (a determination that a juvenile has made a valid waiver requires a showing either that he consulted with an adult or that he possesses a high degree of intelligence, experience, knowledge, or sophistication).

7. *Moran v. Burbine*, 475 U.S. 412 (1986), held that neither the refusal of the police to allow an attorney to see her new client nor the failure to inform the suspect of the lawyer's request invalidated a subsequent waiver because "events occurring outside of the presence of the suspect and entirely unknown to him surely can have no bearing on the capacity to comprehend and knowingly relinquish a constitutional right." 475 U.S. at 421. Our example, however, is distinguishable in several material respects. The suspect explicitly stated to the police his desire to have the assistance of counsel before deciding on a waiver, and the police (at least passively) misled him by failing to disclose that his attorney was available and indeed present. This may therefore be considered the case left open in *Moran* where "on facts more egregious than those presented here police deception might rise to the level of a due process violation." Id. at 432. It is difficult to categorize Nave's waiver as knowing and intelligent when he made explicit his desire to confer with counsel. Moreover, as we will see in the next section, a suspect's equivocal request for counsel should cut off further questioning beyond clarification of that request. Under *Davis v. United States*, 512 U.S. 452 (1994), the police are not obligated to clear up the ambiguity.

It should be pointed out that some state courts have held that withholding information on the presence or availability of a lawyer retained on behalf of a suspect will render invalid the suspect's waiver of the privilege of self-incrimination. See, e.g., *State v. Reed*, 627 A.2d 630 (N.J. 1993), in which the court held that this knowledge is essential to making a knowing waiver and withholding such information violates the defendant's state constitutional rights; *People v. McCauley*, 645 N.E.2d 923 (Ill. 1994).

8. This case raises the issue of the effect of police deception on the validity of a *Miranda* waiver. As is the case with the due process voluntariness standard (see Chapter 8), trickery weighs in as one factor (but not an automatically determinative one) in the totality-of-the-circumstances analysis. Where the issue in the confession

context is whether the trickery produced an involuntary confession, the issue in the *Miranda* context is whether it produced an invalid waiver.

The court in *United States v. Velasquez*, 885 F.2d 1076, 1086 (3d Cir. 1989), observing that "the analytical framework applied in the confession context—the totality of the circumstances—is also the proper approach to the waiver issue," concluded that the suspect had validly waived her rights even though the officer seeking her waiver had lied when he told her a companion was being released because he had given a statement implicating Velasquez and planned to testify against her. While this misinformation greatly inflated the state's evidence against Velasquez and was probably a partial cause of her waiver, the court did not find that "her will was overcome or her capacity for self-control vitiated." 885 F.2d at 1089. In support of this conclusion the court emphasized that the suspect, who had worked as a journalist, was a mature adult with a college degree and thus possessed a full awareness both of the nature of her rights and the consequences of abandoning them. Moreover, she had asked to speak with the police officer prior to her waiver, "thus indicating that it was likely that she wanted to discuss the investigation and less likely that the statement was a spontaneous reaction to [the officer's] falsehood." Id. at 1089. Finally, she was in custody for only two hours and was not subjected to any threats, promises, or ill-treatment.

A similar conclusion was reached in *Shedelbower v. Estelle*, 885 F.2d 570 (9th Cir. 1989), where despite the fact that the police falsely told the accused that he had been identified by the rape victim, his waiver was held to have been knowing, intelligent, and voluntary. Shedelbower had already made incriminating statements before the deception and had said that he was anxious to speak to someone about his involvement in the events to get it off his chest. Therefore "the false statement by the police was clearly an unimportant element in the mind of Shedelbower when he said that he had to tell someone what had happened. . . . [I]t is indeed doubtful that the officer's statement to Shedelbower that he had been identified, played any role in motivating him to want to talk to them then or later to confess." 885 F.2d at 574. See also *Foster v. Commonwealth*, 380 S.E.2d 12 (Va. 1989) (suspect who was falsely told that his fingerprints were found on the weapon had already indicated his intention to talk and thus validly waived his rights).

In our problem, however, the waiver seems quite clearly the product of the police deception. The officer's false indication of the strength of the case against Ring gave him a feeling of hopelessness, which he expressed immediately before signing the waiver. Unlike *Velasquez* and *Shedelbower*, Ring gave no indication prior to the deception that he wanted to speak about the crime, nor had he already made any incriminating statements. His waiver should therefore be held invalid.

§9.2.5   *Waiver After Invocation of the Right to Silence or to Counsel*

The flip side of waiver is invocation—the individual *exercises* rather than *relinquishes* his rights. *Miranda* mandated that "if the individual indicates in any manner, at any time prior to or during questioning, that he wishes to remain silent, the interrogation must cease." 384 U.S. at 473–474. The Court envisioned that no questioning could properly be conducted after that point because any statement obtained would likely be "the product of compulsion, subtle or otherwise." Id. at 474. Invocation of the right to silence would, therefore, prevent any further interrogation of that suspect.

Subsequent decisions have, however, read this right to terminate questioning more narrowly. *Michigan v. Mosley*, 423 U.S. 96 (1975), rejected the concept of a permanent termination and held instead that interrogation could resume as long as the right to cut off questioning was "scrupulously honored." Mosley, under arrest for robbery, was Mirandized and declined to be questioned. Two hours later another officer gave him a fresh set of warnings and Mosely agreed to talk about an unrelated murder. Rejecting Mosely's challenge to the admission of the incriminating statement he made during this interrogation, the Court held that his right to cut off questioning had been scrupulously honored because the police had immediately ceased questioning when he exercised his right to remain silent and had resumed questioning about a different crime only after the passage of significant time and with the provision of fresh warnings.

Thus if the prosecution seeks to introduce a statement from a suspect who had initially invoked his right to remain silent, it must be demonstrated: 1) that his right not to speak, once invoked, had been scrupulously honored; and 2) that a knowing, intelligent, and voluntary waiver subsequently occurred (see §9.2.4). Where it is shown that the police failed to cease interrogation immediately, or engaged in repeated efforts to get the suspect to change his mind, his right to cut off questioning will be considered not to have been honored and his resulting statement will be deemed inadmissible.

Somewhat different consequences flow from invocation of the right to counsel. *Miranda* held that if (upon being administered the warnings) the suspect states that he wants the assistance of counsel, then interrogation must cease *until an attorney is present*. This prohibition against the resumption of questioning until counsel arrives is premised on the view that invocation of the right to counsel indicates that the suspect is unwilling to decide on his own whether to submit to interrogation. Subsequent decisions have, again, modified this firm rule.

Edwards v. Arizona, 451 U.S. 477 (1981), permits the police to resume interrogation even in the absence of counsel if the suspect himself initiates further communication with the police. The questioning of Edwards (who had initially waived his rights) was terminated when he asserted his right to counsel. He was taken to a jail cell where, the following morning, two other detectives sought to talk to him, but he refused. A guard then told Edwards that he "had to" talk with the detectives and took him to meet them. The detectives informed Edwards of his rights and then played a taped statement of an alleged accomplice who implicated him in the crime. He then indicated a willingness to talk and later made an incriminating statement. Concluding that the playing of the tape constituted the functional equivalent of questioning under *Innis*, the Court ruled that his statement was inadmissible. When a suspect invokes his right to counsel, a valid waiver of that right cannot be established merely by showing that he received additional warnings and then responded to further police-initiated custodial interrogation. Rather, the Court held, additional safeguards are necessary to protect the right to counsel. Specifically, the suspect may not be questioned further until counsel has been made available to him "unless the accused himself initiates further communication, exchanges, or conversations with the police." 451 U.S. at 484. Because Edwards's second meeting with the police had occurred at *their* insistence, his statement made without having had access to counsel did not amount to a valid waiver. Id. at 487.

Thus if the prosecution seeks to introduce a statement from a suspect who had initially invoked his right to counsel, it must be demonstrated: 1) that counsel was made available to him; or 2) the suspect himself initiated the further communication; and 3) that a knowing, intelligent, and voluntary waiver subsequently occurred.

What constitutes "invocation" of the right to counsel? "I'd like to speak to a lawyer before answering questions" would clearly suffice. A request by a juvenile to see his probation officer was held, however, not to be the equivalent: "It is [the] pivotal role of legal counsel [in the administration of justice] that justifies the per se rule established in *Miranda* and that distinguishes the request for counsel from the request for a probation officer, a clergyman, or a close friend." *Fare v. Michael C.*, 442 U.S. 707, 722 (1979).

In *Smith v. Illinois*, 469 U.S. 91 (1984), the Court liberally construed an ambiguous statement to find an invocation of counsel. See explanation 5, below. In the more recent case of *Davis v. United States*, 512 U.S. 452 (1994), however, the Court held that the police were under no obligation to clarify an ambiguous request for counsel. Defendant's statement, "Maybe I should talk to a lawyer," was deemed not a request for counsel. Even though the five-Justice majority ruled that police were not obligated to clarify an ambiguity, they nonetheless went on to praise the police for obtaining clarification. However, Justice Souter, concurring in the judgment, argued that all questioning should stop until the police determine whether a suspect's ambiguous statement was meant as a request for counsel.

In *McNeil v. Wisconsin*, 501 U.S. 171 (1991) (discussed in §10.3), the Court held that a defendant's invocation of his Sixth Amendment right to counsel during a court appearance did not constitute an invocation for purposes of *Miranda* when he was subsequently questioned about a different crime. The Court reasoned that the exercise of the right to representation under the Sixth Amendment is offense-specific and distinct from the prophylactic right provided under *Miranda* to have counsel present during custodial interrogation. Moreover, in order to effectively invoke one's rights, the invocation must occur either during interrogation or immediately preceding it: *Miranda* rights cannot be invoked in an anticipatory manner, as at a preliminary hearing. Id. at 182 n. 3; see also *United States v. Grimes*, 142 F.3d 1342 (11th Cir. 1998) (claim of rights form signed by defendant when he was arrested on worthless check charges could not anticipatorily invoke defendant's Fifth Amendment right to remain silent).

What constitutes "initiation" of further communications by the suspect? "I changed my mind and want to talk about the crime now without a lawyer" would clearly suffice. But statements by persons in police custody are often more ambiguous. In *Oregon v. Bradshaw*, 462 U.S. 1039 (1983), for example, the defendant asserted his right to counsel, but shortly afterwards, while being transferred to jail, he inquired of an officer: "Well, what is going to happen to me now?" The officer responded: "You do not have to talk to me. You have requested an attorney and I don't want you talking to me unless you so desire because anything you say—because—since you have requested an attorney, you know, it has to be your free will." 462 U.S. at 1042. Bradshaw replied that he understood. The two then conversed about where Bradshaw would be taken and what he would be charged with, and the officer then suggested that he take a lie detector test, which he agreed to. The next day, following new warnings, Bradshaw took the test and subsequently made incriminating statements.

Reversing the state appellate court, which had suppressed the statements, the Supreme Court concluded that the *Miranda* doctrine as elaborated by *Edwards* had not been violated. A four-Justice plurality, noting that questions "relating to routine incidents of the custodial relationship" (such as request for water or access to a telephone) would generally not constitute initiation, nevertheless found that Bradshaw's question to the jailer "evinced a willingness and desire for generalized discussion about the investigation," thus permitting interrogation to resume. Id. at 1045. The plurality then addressed the separate waiver issue and found it to be knowing, intelligent, and voluntary. The four dissenting Justices were "baffled [at] the plurality's application of [the initiation] standard to the facts of this case" and concluded that Bradshaw's inquiry was plainly designed simply "to find out where the police were going to take him," and did not "demonstrate [the requisite] desire to discuss the subject matter of the criminal investigation." Id. at 1055.

The constraint upon further interrogation once a suspect has invoked his right to counsel applies even if the second interrogation would concern an offense *unrelated* to the subject of the initial arrest and questioning. In *Arizona v. Roberson*, 486 U.S. 675 (1988), the defendant was arrested for burglary and exercised his right to counsel after receiving the warnings, thus foreclosing interrogation. Three days later, while the defendant was still in custody, he was again Mirandized and questioned by a different officer about a different burglary. This officer was not aware that defendant had previously invoked his right to counsel. An incriminating statement was obtained. The state argued that the *Edwards* rule should not apply when the police-initiated interrogation following the suspect's request for counsel regards a *different* crime. The Supreme Court, emphasizing the importance of maintaining clear and unequivocal guidelines to law enforcement officers, rejected this approach. "[W]hether a contemplated reinterrogation concerns the same or a different offense, or whether the same or different law enforcement authorities are involved in the second investigation, the same need to determine whether the suspect has requested counsel exists. The police department's failure to honor that request cannot be justified by the lack of diligence of a particular officer." 486 U.S. at 687.

What does the *Edwards* rule mean when it mandates that a suspect who has invoked his right to counsel may not be interrogated until counsel has been "made available" to him? The Court has held that merely providing the opportunity to consult with counsel outside the interrogation room is not sufficient. Rather, the accused is entitled to have his attorney present with him during the questioning. See *Minnick v. Mississippi*, 498 U.S. 146 (1990). Minnick, in custody on suspicion of murder, terminated interrogation by requesting a lawyer. He later consulted with an appointed attorney two or three times. The police subsequently told Minnick that he would "have to talk" to them, and they reinitiated interrogation. Refusing to suppress the resulting confession, the Mississippi Supreme Court read *Edwards* as being satisfied by permitting consultation with an attorney. In reversing, the U.S. Supreme Court observed that the purpose of the "clear and unequivocal guidelines" of *Edwards* was to protect the suspect's right to have counsel present at the interrogation; a consultation with counsel is not enough to remove the pressures inherent in custody. "[T]he need for counsel to protect the Fifth Amendment privilege comprehends not merely a right to consult with counsel prior to questioning, but also to have counsel present during any questioning if the defendant so desires." 498 U.S. at 154 (citation omitted). Police-initiated reinterrogation cannot take place until counsel is "present" in that sense.

EXAMPLES

1. Sylvia Suspect was arrested, taken to the police station, and booked for selling narcotics. She was advised of her *Miranda* rights by Detective Oak and responded: "I don't have anything to say." No questioning was attempted, and she was placed in a holding cell. One hour later Oak approached her, read her her rights again, and stated: "Have you had enough time in there yet?" Suspect replied that she was "tired of rotting in this cell alone" and would talk.

During questioning she admitted her participation in the narcotics ring. Is her statement admissible in court?

2. Assume instead that after Sylvia Suspect was advised of her *Miranda* rights by Detective Oak, she responded: "I won't say anything until I talk to my lawyer." No questioning was attempted, and she was placed in a holding cell. One hour later Oak approached her, read her her rights again, and asked: "Are you ready to talk now?" Suspect submitted to interrogation and made an incriminating statement. Is her statement admissible in court? Would it make any difference in your answer if Suspect had sent word through her guard that she wanted to see Detective Oak?

3. Assume instead that after Sylvia Suspect was advised of her *Miranda* rights by Detective Oak, she orally agreed to waive those rights. After several minutes of interrogation, Suspect interrupted and said: "When will you let me go home? I really need to talk to someone about this before I answer your questions." The detective responded: "Why don't we get this over with, it'll be easier on you if you just tell me what happened out there?" The detective continued questioning and elicited an incriminating statement from Suspect a short time later. Is Suspect's statement admissible in court?

4. Lyle Loser was taken into custody on suspicion of rape and read his *Miranda* rights. At first he agreed to answer questions, but after ten minutes stated: "You know, I'd better talk to my lawyer before I say anything more." As the two interrogators were gathering up their papers to leave, Officer Mutt said to Officer Jeff: "Let's go see the victim. I heard she picked Loser's photo out of the array." Upon hearing this, Loser stated: "I've changed my mind, guys. I don't need to talk to anyone. Let me tell you what happened and let's work something out." Loser proceeded to respond to questions and confessed. Is his statement admissible at trial?

5. Steven Smith was arrested and taken to the interrogation room of the police station by two detectives. The following conversation occurred:

   Q. Steve, I want to talk with you in reference to the armed robbery that took place at McDonald's restaurant on the morning of the 19th. Are you familiar with this?
   A. Yeah. My cousin Greg was.

Q. Okay. But before I do that I must advise you of your rights. Okay? You have a right to remain silent. You do not have to talk to me unless you want to do so. Do you understand that?

A. Uh. I was told to get my lawyer. I was told you guys would railroad me.

Q. Do you understand that as I gave it to you, Steve?

A. Yeah.

Q. If you want to talk to me I must advise you that whatever you say can and will be used against you in court. Do you understand that?

A. Yeah.

Q. You have a right to consult with a lawyer and to have a lawyer present with you when you're being questioned. Do you understand that?

A. Uh, yeah. I'd like to do that.

Q. Okay. If you want a lawyer and you're unable to pay for one a lawyer will be appointed to represent you free of cost, do you understand that?

A. Okay.

Q. Do you wish to talk to me at this time without a lawyer being present?

A. Yeah, and no, uh, I don't know what's what, really.

Q. Well. You either have to talk to me this time without a lawyer being present and if you do agree to talk with me without a lawyer being present you can stop at any time you want to.

A. All right. I'll talk to you then.

In subsequent questioning Smith admitted participation in the robbery. Can his admission be offered into evidence against him at trial?

6. Barry Bash was arrested at a train station on probable cause to believe he was a narcotics dealer and was taken to an Amtrak police interrogation room at the station. He was advised of his *Miranda* rights and agreed to submit to questioning. After a specific question about the identity of his supplier, however, Barry responded that he was pleading "the Fifth." At this point questioning stopped, and he was transported by the arresting officer to the police station. En route in the cruiser, Barry inquired as to where he was being taken. The officer responded and described the procedure that would take place when they arrived at the police station. The officer then asked Barry what he did for a living, and he

said he was studying electronics. The officer observed that "it's a shame you got mixed up in this, because you're young and have a trade and you're going to screw up your whole life." Barry responded that "I am just doing it to see how much money I can make." The officer then asked: "Where does a kid like you get the drugs to sell?" Barry responded: "Somewhere uptown." Can these incriminating answers be used against Barry at trial?

EXPLANATIONS

1. If a subject in custody indicates in any manner at any time prior to or during questioning that he wishes to remain silent, the interrogation must cease.[17] Sylvia Suspect's statement, "I don't have anything to say," appears to be an exercise of this right to remain silent, and the police properly complied. Her right to terminate questioning is, however, neither permanent nor irrevocable. Rather, *Michigan v. Mosley*, 423 U.S. 96 (1975), teaches that interrogation may resume as long as the right to cut off questioning is scrupulously honored.

   The prosecution would argue that that was the case here because no questioning occurred when Suspect invoked her right to silence and questioning began only after a fresh set of warnings some time later. However, Suspect would argue that, unlike *Mosley*, the resumption of questioning here was for the same crime, by the same officer, and with the passage of less time. Moreover, she would seek to portray the police conduct and statement to her as an effort to wear down her resistance to further questioning.

   The analysis to determine if the right to cut off interrogation was scrupulously honored is fact-specific. The courts consider a variety of factors including 1) the amount of time elapsed between interrogations; 2) the provision of a fresh set of warnings; 3) the subject matter and scope of the second interrogation; and 4) the officer's zealousness in attempting to pursue questioning after the suspect has invoked his rights. Generally, no one factor is determinative, but the provision of fresh warnings is considered the

---

17. Some courts have permitted routine personal information questions even after the suspect has exercised the right to terminate interrogation. See, e.g., *United States v. Thompson*, 866 F.2d 268 (8th Cir. 1989) (officer's question "Where are you from?" did not violate the suspect's already invoked right to silence).

most important and critical. New Jersey has even adopted a per se rule that the failure to administer new warnings will result in a finding that the right to cut off questioning was not scrupulously honored. See *New Jersey v. Hartley*, 511 A.2d 80 (1986).

It is useful to look at examples of the *Mosley* analysis in action. In *United States v. Hsu*, 852 F.2d 407 (9th Cir. 1988), the suspect invoked his right to remain silent while being questioned by federal drug agents at the scene of an arrest. Thirty minutes later he was questioned again by different agents at a different location after another set of warnings. The court ruled that Hsu's right to cut off questioning was scrupulously honored because fresh warnings had been given, the agents had conducted themselves in a deferential manner and did not harass or pressure him to change his mind, and the location and atmosphere of the second interrogation was different than the first. The court observed that "the change in scenery served as an intervening event to help alleviate any pressure that Hsu may have felt to waive his rights at the [first location]. The fresh warnings, of course, furthered this same end in a powerful way, as did the agents' restraint after Hsu asserted his *Miranda* rights." 852 F.2d at 412. Thus "[a]lthough the passage of time in this case [only 30 minutes] might ordinarily incline us toward a conclusion that right to cut off questioning was not respected, the clear evidence of scrupulous conduct by the DEA agents and free informed choice by Hsu militates against such a judgment." Id.

In contrast, the court in *Charles v. Smith*, 894 F.2d 718 (5th Cir. 1990), found that the police had not scrupulously honored the suspect's refusal to speak when the same police officer asked two questions just a few minutes after invocation of the right to silence. The questions concerned the same crime that the suspect had just refused to discuss, and the officer admitted that he had used "psychology" on the suspect to obtain an admission. The court in *Nelson v. Fulcomer*, 911 F.2d 928 (3rd Cir. 1990), reached a similar conclusion that the police had failed to respect the suspect's right to remain silent:

> While the Commonwealth argues that it fulfilled its duty to scrupulously honor Nelson's right to cut off questioning, its confrontation ploy [in which the suspect was confronted with an accomplice who had just confessed, and which was deemed the functional equivalent of interrogation,] bears none of the indicia of respect identified in *Mosley*. The

Commonwealth failed to contend, let alone to demonstrate, that it waited a significant amount of time after Nelson cut off questioning, that it gave Nelson a fresh set of *Miranda* warnings, that Nelson had invoked his right in connection with an offense other than the rape and murder, or that the officers who engineered the confrontation were different from those to whom Nelson initially refused to talk.

911 F.2d at 939–940.

Getting back to example 1, despite the provision of fresh warnings, it is likely the court would conclude that Suspect's right to silence was not properly respected when the same officer resumed questioning only one hour later, concerning the same crime, and after needling Suspect about her time in the cell. We would therefore not have to reach the issue of whether Suspect's subsequent waiver was valid (that is, knowing, intelligent, and voluntary), which, it must be remembered, is a separate determination from the question of whether the right to silence was properly respected.

2. Like the right to remain silent, invocation of the right to counsel is not irrevocable. The police may resume interrogation in the absence of counsel *if the accused himself initiates* further communication, exchanges, or conversations with the police. *Edwards v. Arizona*, 451 U.S. 477 (1981). Further *police-initiated* custodial interrogation is forbidden, even if the accused is again advised of his rights and makes a valid waiver. In example 2, therefore, it is of determinative significance whether the subsequent interrogation was instigated by the police or Suspect. When the detective, without any prompting from Suspect, asked whether she was ready to talk, the right to counsel was clearly violated and the confession would not be admissible.

    In the variation posed where Suspect summoned Detective Oak, it must be determined whether that constituted initiation. We would have to uncover more details regarding Suspect's request and the subsequent conversation. Merely requesting to see the detective, without indicating a willingness to discuss the crime, would not constitute a sufficient green light under *Edwards v. Arizona* to resume interrogation. Suspect may simply have had a question relating to the routine incidents of the custodial relationship ("Where can I get a drink of water?"). It is significant, however, that Suspect asked to see the officer investigating the case, as opposed to another officer or guard, because that makes it more likely she desired to discuss the investigation. See *United States v. Velasquez*, 885 F.2d 1076 (3d Cir. 1989).

Given *Oregon v. Bradshaw*'s broad interpretation of what constitutes a willingness to discuss the crime ("Well, what is going to happen to me now?"), any communication from Suspect that arguably reflects a desire to talk about the investigation could be deemed initiation. If that were the case here, the separate issue of waiver would have to be addressed—that is, having initiated further discussions and thus revoked her exercise of the right to counsel, did Suspect then knowingly, intelligently, and voluntarily waive her right to remain silent and submit to questioning? Again, more details of the interrogation would have to be learned.

3. A suspect undergoing interrogation after waiver of his rights may cut off that interrogation by invoking *in any manner* and *at any time* his right to silence or to counsel. An accused need not rely on talismanic phrases or magic words to invoke those rights. The issue in example 3 is whether Suspect's ambiguous statement constituted invocation of either of those rights.

Suspect's inquiry, "When will you let me go home," will probably be considered an understandable expression of concern, and *not* an invocation of the right to remain silent. See *United States v. Lux*, 905 F.2d 1379 (10th Cir. 1990) (suspect's question during interrogation as to how long it would take if she wanted a lawyer and whether she would have to remain in jail while she waited for one was held not to be an invocation of the right to counsel); *Moore v. Dugger*, 856 F.2d 129, 134 (11th Cir. 1988) ("We are not persuaded that this statement evidences a refusal to talk further."); compare *Commonwealth of Pennsylvania v. Zook*, 553 A.2d 920, 922 (1989) (when the suspect asked to use the phone to call his mother "to see if she could get him an attorney," this was a clear invocation of the right to counsel and should have terminated the interrogation). Suspect's indication of a desire to talk to "someone" may have been an attempt to exercise the right to remain silent or to counsel. Although a request to see a probation officer was not deemed to be an exercise of the right to counsel in *Fare v. Michael* C., 442 U.S. 707 (1979), Suspect's statement here may very well have been referring to an attorney.

Given the importance of the rights involved, the courts have permitted (and indeed encouraged) the police to seek clarification of such equivocal statements to determine whether they do in fact constitute an exercise of *Miranda* rights. There is, however, no obligation to do so. See *Davis v. United States*, 512 U.S. 452 (1994). "Are you saying you want to consult with an attorney?" would be an appropriate response from the officer. Such questioning is, however, strictly limited to clarifying the ambiguous request and must not coerce or intimidate the suspect into waiving his rights. See *Campaneria v. Reid*, 891 F.2d 1014 (2d Cir. 1989); *Nash v. Estelle*, 597 F.2d 513 (5th Cir. 1979) (en banc). Interrogation concerning the crime must of course cease until the accused makes clear that he is *not* invoking his rights.

A suspect's claim that the police violated his *Miranda* rights by failing to immediately terminate interrogation is not negated by the fact that he answered additional questions. See *Christopher v. State*, 824 F.2d 836 (11th Cir. 1987); *Smith v. Illinois*, 469 U.S. 91, 100 (1984) ("[A]n accused's *post-request* responses to further interrogation may not be used to cast retrospective doubt on the clarity of the initial request itself."). Compare *Bradley v. Meachum*, 918 F.2d 338 (2d Cir. 1990) (when the suspect initially stated that he did not wish to discuss his involvement in the crime but then denied any connection to it and explained his whereabouts at the time of the crime, this conduct did *not* constitute an invocation of the right to silence, but rather evidenced a willingness to discuss his involvement). Any doubts concerning a suspect's desires must be resolved in favor of protecting *Miranda* rights. Cf. *Michigan v. Jackson*, 475 U.S. 625 (1986). But see *Davis v. United States*, 512 U.S. 452 (1994). Defendant initially waived his right to remain silent and to counsel when he was interrogated. He later said, "Maybe I should talk to a lawyer." Agents asked if he was requesting a lawyer and he replied he was not. He was reminded of his rights and the interview continued. The Court held that when "a suspect makes a reference to an attorney that is ambiguous or equivocal in that a reasonable officer in light of the circumstances would have understood only that the suspect *might* be invoking the right to counsel, our precedents do not require the cessation of questioning." Id. at 464. A suspect must unambiguously request counsel for the interrogator to be required to stop. The Court stated that although it is good police practice for officers to clarify whether the suspect wants an attorney, it is not required.

In our example, Detective Oak ignored Suspect's statement that, while equivocal, at least arguably *in some manner* invoked her right to cut off questioning. Rather than seek clarification, Oak tried to persuade Suspect to talk and continued questioning her concerning the crime. Arguably Suspect's rights to remain silent and to counsel were not scrupulously respected, and her subsequent confession should be inadmissible. See *United States v. Pena*, 897 F.2d 1075, 1078 (11th Cir. 1990) (the Court found that the police had not scrupulously honored the defendant's right to cut off questioning when they continued to question him rather than clarify his ambiguous statement that "I want to [cooperate]. I really want to but, I can't. They will kill my parents."). Whether *Davis v. United States*, supra, changes this result remains to be seen.

4. Because Loser made a clear invocation of his right to counsel, all interrogation must cease. The issue raised here is whether the police complied. While formal questioning terminated, the statement by one officer to the other regarding the identification of Loser arguably constitutes the functional equivalent of interrogation, which is equally violative of the *Edwards* rule. If the statement was one the police should know was reasonably likely to elicit an incriminating response from Loser, then interrogation continued improperly and the confession is inadmissible.

    If, however, the statement does not fall within the *Innis* standard, then the police (having discontinued interrogation) were permitted to resume interrogation upon initiation from Loser of further communications. Loser's statement to the officers that he wished to talk about the case would certainly constitute such initiation (that is, it clearly evinced a willingness to discuss the investigation). Assuming, therefore, that Loser is found to have made a knowing, intelligent, and voluntary waiver, his confession would be admissible.

    Based on similar facts, the court in *Shedelbower v. Estelle*, 885 F.2d 570 (9th Cir. 1989), concluded that the officer's statement did *not* constitute the functional equivalent of questioning, and thus interrogation ceased and was properly resumed after the suspect initiated the further communication. The court also concluded that the waiver was valid despite the fact that the officer's statement indicating the witness had identified the accused was actually false: "[T]he totality of the circumstances compels the conclusion that Shedelbower's taped confession was not the product of that falsehood, and that he was fully aware of the nature and consequences of his actions." 885 F.2d at 574. The court reached a similar conclusion in *Plazinich v. Lynaugh*, 843 F.2d

836 (5th Cir. 1988), where the suspect exercised his right not to submit to questioning, but while being transported to a cell was told by the officer that his alleged accomplice had just attempted suicide. The suspect then asked to speak to an assistant district attorney and confessed shortly thereafter. Rejecting Plazinich's argument that he had been improperly subjected to the functional equivalent of interrogation after exercising his right to silence, the court held that the officer's statement was merely informational ("food for thought") and not reasonably likely to elicit an incriminating response.

5. The threshold issue here is whether Smith effectively invoked his right to counsel, in which case questioning would have to cease and not begin again until either counsel were present or Smith initiated further communication. Upon being advised that he had a right to counsel, Smith said, "Uh, yeah. I'd like to do that." This appears to be a clear and unequivocal assertion of his right, and thus all interrogation should have stopped.

The Illinois Supreme Court in the case upon which this problem is based ruled, however, that Smith's subsequent hedging— "Yeah, and no, uh, I don't really know what's what, really"— undercut and nullified his initial request, and thus held that the police could properly continue their interrogation. The U.S. Supreme Court reversed:

> No authority, and no logic, permits the interrogator to proceed . . . on his own terms and as if the defendant had requested nothing, in the hope that the defendant might be induced to say something casting retrospective doubt on his initial statement that he wished to speak through an attorney or not at all. . . . [A]n accused's post-request responses to further interrogation may not be used to cast doubt on the clarity of the initial request itself. Such subsequent statements are relevant only to the distinct question of waiver.

Smith v. Illinois, 469 U.S. 91, 98–99 (1984). Because the suspect had invoked his right to counsel and did not himself initiate the further communication, the confession was not admissible.

In *Davis v. United States*, 512 U.S. 452 (1994), the Court was more inflexible about interpreting an ambiguous communication as a request for counsel. Although the facts are distinguishable from *Smith*, in which there was a direct invocation of counsel and a later equivocation, Davis's statement, "Maybe I should talk to a lawyer," was at least arguably an invocation. *Davis* thus seems to be a shift from the more flexible approach of resolving ambiguity in favor of right to counsel.

6. The pivotal issue here is whether by pleading "the Fifth" Barry effectively exercised his right to remain silent. If so, questioning should have ceased and the suspect's right not to speak should have been scrupulously honored.

It could be argued that Barry intended only to plead the Fifth in response to the specific question directed at him, and not to cut off all interrogation. Because his equivocal statement at least arguably constituted exercise of his *Miranda* right, however, further police inquiry should have been limited to clarification of his wishes.

Assuming Barry did invoke his right to silence, the police could resume questioning if, having scrupulously honored the right by terminating interrogation, the suspect subsequently waived his right in a knowing, intelligent, and voluntary manner. Under the *Michigan v. Mosley* analysis, it would be very difficult for the police to demonstrate such a waiver. Only a short period of time elapsed between the invocation of the right to silence and the resumed questioning, which involved the same crime. And, most importantly, the suspect was not afforded a fresh set of warnings, which would have served to alleviate the continued pressures of custody.

The prosecution would argue that the officer in the cruiser was merely engaging in idle chatter (not interrogation) with the accused, who spontaneously incriminated himself. In this scenario, the right to cut off questioning was thus scrupulously honored. Alternatively, it could be argued that Barry himself initiated the conversation with the question as to where he was being taken. While the definition of initiation is quite broad in *Oregon v. Bradshaw*, 462 U.S. 1039 (1983), and the statement there ("Well, what is going to happen to me now?") is similar to Barry's, the latter would seem more clearly related to the routine incidents of the custodial relationship and not an indication of a desire to discuss the crime. Moreover, it was the officer who turned the conversation to the subject of the crime by making a statement reasonably likely to elicit an incriminating response ("it's a shame you got mixed up in this . . ."), and then asked the specific question concerning the source.

It is likely, therefore, that Barry's statements would not be admissible in evidence. See *United States v. Carey*, 952 F.2d 393 (2d Cir. 1991).

§9.3 Limitations on the Scope of the *Miranda* Exclusionary Rule

From its inception, the *Miranda* doctrine (like the Fourth Amendment exclusionary rule) has acted as a lightning rod for criticism of the criminal justice system.[18] The requirement of the warnings has been attacked as an undue interference in the investigative work of law enforcement officers, and the suppression of noncomplying statements as inconsistent with the search for the truth at trial. In the face of persistent challenge it is not surprising that the original *Miranda* scheme has been significantly modified and limited by an increasingly conservative Supreme Court in recent years.

Like the debate over the Fourth Amendment exclusionary rule, the doctrinal controversy over *Miranda* has centered on the question whether the rules adopted in 1966 are themselves *constitutionally required* or merely constitute particular *remedies* chosen at that time to enforce the right against compelled self-incrimination. If the *Miranda* scheme represents remedy and not a right, modification of the rules by the Court or through legislation[19] is obviously more easily accomplished.

The *Miranda* Court appeared to suggest that the protective devices adopted were more remedy than constitutional imperative:

> It is impossible to foresee the potential alternatives for protecting the privilege which might be devised by Congress or the States in the exercise of their creative rule-making capacities.

---

18. The Reagan Justice Department under Attorney General Meese adopted the following policy position: "We accordingly regard a challenge to *Miranda* as essential, not only in overcoming the detrimental impact caused directly by this decision, but also as a critical step in moving to repudiate a discredited criminal jurisprudence. Overturning *Miranda* would, accordingly, be among the most important achievements of this administration—indeed of any administration—in restoring the power of self-government to the people of the United States in the suppression of crime." Office of Legal Policy, U.S. Dept. of Justice, Report to The Attorney General on the Law of Pre-Trial Interrogation (February 12, 1986).

> Therefore we cannot say that the Constitution necessarily requires adherence to any particular solution for the inherent compulsions of the interrogation process as it is presently conducted. Our decision in no way creates a constitutional straitjacket which will handicap sound efforts at reform, nor is it intended to have this effect.

384 U.S. at 467.

In the years since *Miranda*, the Court has increasingly emphasized the *right vs. remedy* distinction as justification for cutting back on the protective scheme mandated in 1966. Characterizing the warnings and associated rules as "not themselves rights protected by the Constitution" but merely "procedural safeguards" designed to reinforce the right against compelled self-incrimination, see *Michigan v. Tucker*, 417 U.S. 433, 443–444 (1974), the Court has limited the scope of *Miranda* in the manner outlined below.

United States v. Dickerson, ___ S. Ct. ___ (2000) has now resolved the debate resoundingly in favor of *Miranda* as a constitutional mandate, and not merely as a remedy subject to Congressional tinkering (as in 18 U.S.C. §3501). *Dickerson* does, however, put the Court's stamp of approval of the limitations imposed on the *Miranda* scheme, which are discussed below.

It should be noted, however, that the Court has refused to limit *Miranda* violation reviews in habeas corpus proceedings in a manner similar to that used for Fourth Amendment violations (see §7.3.2). In *Withrow v. Williams*, 507 U.S. 680 (1993), the Court distinguished *Miranda* violations from those involving search and seizure by pointing out that the former do affect the ascertainment of truth.

§9.3.1 *Public Safety Exception*

In a significant limitation on the original scope of *Miranda*, the Supreme Court has created an exception for questioning conducted in "public safety" situations. The incriminating statement at issue in *New York v. Quarles*, 467 U.S. 649 (1984), resulted when the police pursued a rape suspect believed to be armed with a gun into a supermarket and captured him. Upon frisking Quarles and finding an empty shoul-

---

19. See, e.g., Title II of the Crime Control Act of 1968, 18 U.S.C. §3501, which purports to repeal *Miranda* and impose in its place a return to a voluntariness standard.

der holster, the officer questioned him about the location of the missing gun. No warnings were given. Quarles responded: "The gun is over there." The officer, following the suspect's direction, then retrieved the loaded pistol. On the defendant's motion the statement and the gun were both excluded at his state court trial on the grounds that they were obtained in violation of *Miranda*.

The U.S. Supreme Court reversed, holding that the state court had erred in excluding the evidence because "under the circumstances involved in this case, overriding considerations of public safety justify the officer's failure to provide *Miranda* warnings before he asked questions devoted to locating the abandoned weapon." 467 U.S. at 651. Reflecting the cost/benefit analysis typical of the Court's cutback on Warren-era decisions, the right of the suspect to be free from compelled self-incrimination was measured against the risk to the public if the dangerous weapon were not retrieved: "[T]he need for answers to questions in a situation posing a threat to public safety outweighs the need for the prophylactic rule protecting the Fifth Amendment's privilege against self-incrimination." Id. at 657. The Court was careful to emphasize that the public safety exception (like the impeachment exception, see §9.3.2) does *not* apply to an involuntary or coerced statement.

Where the officer's questions are *reasonably prompted by a concern for safety*, therefore, he may engage in noncoercive questioning without complying with *Miranda*'s dictates. Applicability of the exception does not, the *Quarles* Court indicated, depend upon the actual motivation of the officers, but rather on the objective facts of the case. Despite the potential uncertainty with this standard, the Court asserted that it would be easy to apply as "officers can and will distinguish almost instinctively between questions to secure their own safety or the safety of the public and questions designed solely to elicit testimonial evidence from a suspect." Id. at 658.

In a separate opinion, Justice O'Connor disagreed with the adoption of a public safety exception, suggesting that it "unnecessarily blurs the edges of the clear line heretofore established and makes *Miranda*'s requirements more difficult to understand." Id. at 663. She predicted:

> In some cases, police will benefit because a reviewing court will find that an exigency excused their failure to administer the required warnings. But in other cases, police will suffer because, though they thought an exigency excused their noncompliance, a reviewing court will view the "objective" circumstances differ-

ently and require exclusion of admissions obtained. The end result will be a finespun new doctrine on public safety exigencies
incident to custodial interrogation, complete with the hair-
splitting distinctions that currently plague our Fourth Amendment jurisprudence.

Id. Indeed, the New York Court of Appeals had concluded in its
Quarles decision that the missing gun did *not* pose an imminent threat
to public safety because the suspect had been overpowered by police,
no accomplices were thought to be nearby, and the supermarket was
empty at 12:30 A.M. when Quarles was apprehended.

Justice O'Connor also observed that *Miranda* never prohibited
the police from asking questions to protect the public or themselves.
It simply required that in the absence of warnings, the answers to those
questions could not be used as evidence at trial. Id. at 664.

EXAMPLES

1. Drug enforcement agents had developed probable cause to believe
    that Dudley Dealer was selling narcotics in his neighborhood in
    lower Manhattan. Based on reliable information that he was pres-
    ently plying his trade at the corner of 5th Street and Broadway,
    and, further, that the heroin he was selling from a large brown
    suitcase was (unbeknownst to him) laced with a deadly chemical,
    the agents immediately proceeded to the scene. They found Dud-
    ley there, but he was empty-handed. After placing him under arrest
    (and without *Miranda* warnings) the agents asked Dudley where
    the brown suitcase "with the stuff in it" was. He told them he had
    hidden it in a nearby alleyway, and they recovered the suitcase in
    the location he indicated. The suitcase was filled with plastic bags
    containing heroin. Could Dudley's statement be admitted against
    him at trial?

2. Newark police responded to reports of a man beating a woman.
    An investigation on the scene revealed that the man had forced
    the woman into a black Thunderbird and driven off. The police
    located the car parked down the block and approached it. As the
    woman jumped out and ran, the officers asked the man to step
    out and they frisked him, finding nothing. By that time a crowd
    of people had gathered around the car, and the officers became
    anxious about a potential confrontation. Holding their pistols
    pointed at the suspect, the officers asked if he had any weapons in

the car, and he responded that he had a revolver under the seat. The police reached in and seized the unregistered weapon. Given the absence of *Miranda* warnings, may the suspect's statement be used against him at trial?

3. Stevens summoned the police to her home, advising them that a shooting had occurred. Upon arrival the police found two wounded persons lying in the living room. The officers asked where the shooter was, but Stevens was evasive. After explaining that the ambulance crew would not treat the victims until the scene was safe, Stevens admitted that she had shot the persons, believing them to be burglars. In response to a later question, Stevens told the officers she had left the gun in the bedroom, where they retrieved it. May these responses be used against Stevens at trial?

EXPLANATIONS

1. Although the product of custodial interrogation and thus obtained in apparent violation of *Miranda*, Dudley's statement may nevertheless be admissible under the public safety exception created by *New York v. Quarles*. Given the deadly nature of the narcotics here, the prosecution would likely contend that the officers' questioning was reasonably prompted by a concern for public safety—that is, to retrieve the lethal substance before it got into other hands (or veins).

   This example illustrates some of the uncertainties Justice O'Connor warned of in *Quarles*. Does the public safety exception embrace deadly chemicals as well as weapons? If so, would questioning be permissible regarding *any* narcotic (even if not laced with a deadly chemical), given the inherently dangerous nature of such substances? How important is the setting of the interrogation when applying *Quarles* (contrast the same confrontation in a sparsely populated rural area as opposed to a crowded urban street corner where the risk of someone discovering the missing item is greater)? Will the officers questioning Dudley (and the courts reviewing their action) realistically be able to distinguish between questions necessary to protect the public safety and those designed to elicit evidence to be used to prove the suspect's guilt?

   While the contours of the public safety exception are yet to be definitively drawn, some courts have already extended it beyond the "missing weapon" scenario. See *State v. Vickers*, 159 Ariz. 532, 768 P.2d 1177 (1989). Vickers, a prisoner on death row, became angry with another inmate and set him on fire. Responding to the ensuing alarm, a guard pulled Vickers out of the burning cell and asked what had happened. He responded: "I burned Buster [the other inmate]." Asked whether Buster was dead, the defendant responded: "He should be, he's on fire." The guard proceeded to rescue the other trapped inmates. Both statements were held admissible despite the lack of warnings because the court concluded that the guard's questions were motivated by a desire to devise a rescue plan, and not to develop evidence of guilt.

Like the administrative search doctrine in Fourth Amendment jurisprudence, the *Quarles* exception is based on the often illusive distinction between action taken to obtain evidence of crime and action taken for noninvestigative public-protection reasons. In *United States v. Carrillo*, 16 F.3d 1046 (9th Cir. 1994), the court held that a police officer's inquiry before a search incident to an arrest as to whether the arrestee had any drugs or needles fell within the public safety doctrine and did not require *Miranda* warnings. The danger of transmission of disease or contact with a dangerous substance was a real and serious risk and therefore there was an objectively reasonable need to protect the public and police from immediate danger. In finding the public safety exception applicable, the court relied on the noninvestigatory nature of the officer's question.

2. Because it appears that the suspect was in custody at the time the question was asked, the response must be suppressed unless it falls within the public safety exception. Unlike *Quarles* (where the police had captured a suspect believed to be armed and had found an empty holster), the police in this example had no reason to believe that the suspect had disposed of a weapon in a place where it posed an immediate threat to the public. In a case involving similar facts, the Ninth Circuit Court of Appeals nonetheless held that the public safety exception applied. See *United States v. Brady*, 819 F.2d 884 (9th Cir. 1987). Focusing on the potential danger of the crowd gathering around the police in a "rough" neighborhood, as well as the possibility that a passerby could seize a weapon in the car, the court concluded that the officers reasonably believed that prompt action was necessary and that the purpose of their

question was not to elicit testimonial evidence but to secure their own safety and that of the public. Ignoring other available alternatives (such as securing the car until it could be impounded and removed), the court refused to suppress the suspect's response.

Brady illustrates the real potential for expansion of *Quarles*. See also *People v. Gilliard*, 234 Cal. Rptr. 401, 189 Cal. App. 3d 285 (1987) (a man under arrest for public drunkenness was brought to the nearby scene of a shooting and was asked by the officer where the gun was; his incriminating response was held admissible under the public safety exception even though there was no hot pursuit of the suspect, nor imminent danger to the officers, nor even any basis for believing the suspect had disposed of a weapon in a place accessible to the public). Like the emergency exception to the warrant requirement in the Fourth Amendment context (see §6.2), the public safety exception to *Miranda* could quite easily swallow the rule.

Not all courts have taken an expansive view. In *People v. Roundtree*, 482 N.E.2d 693 (Ill. App. Ct. 1985), a white Cadillac slammed into the rear of a police cruiser parked on the highway. When the officers approached the car, they heard a gunshot and observed two men in the front seat fighting over a gun. The officers disarmed and arrested the men. When a search of the car turned up an aluminum suitcase in the back seat, the officers asked whose suitcase it was. Roundtree admitted it was his; when it was opened it was found to contain narcotics. At trial, Roundtree moved to suppress his response because the question had been asked of him while in custody, but no *Miranda* warnings had been given. The court excluded the statement, rejecting the state's argument that the public safety exception applied:

> The State, relying on *Quarles*, argues that the question asked by Trooper Martinez was only meant to secure control of the scene and was not designed to elicit testimonial evidence from defendant. However, the record establishes that all the suspects in the present case were handcuffed and positioned away from the car and its contents when Trooper Martinez asked the question. It is evident that Trooper Martinez had secured control of the scene before he asked the question. Furthermore, the record does not support the inference that either the suitcase or its contents posed a threat to the public safety or that Trooper Martinez perceived such a threat. Thus, the limited *Quarles* exception to *Miranda* is inapplicable under the facts of this

case, and defendant's response to Trooper Martinez's question should have been excluded from evidence.

482 N.E.2d at 697-698.

Similarly, a New York state court refused to apply the exception to the questioning of a juvenile in an apartment that was the scene of a shooting. After finding the victim on the bedroom floor, the officer asked the juvenile if he had shot the victim, and he said yes. The officer then escorted him to the living room and questioned him as to the location of the gun; after approximately one hour he told the officers he had given it to a friend who lived across the street. Emphasizing that *Quarles* is a "narrow" exception and that "[i]f inquiry as to the location of weapons were permitted in every case without the police being required to first give *Miranda* warnings, the exception would overcome the rule," the Appellate Division reversed the trial court's ruling that it applied to the questioning here. See *In the Matter of John C.,* 130 A.D.2d 246, 252, 519 N.Y.S.2d 223, 227 (App. Div. 1987). Noting that the questioning about the gun occurred after the suspect had been removed from the immediacy of the crime scene and the apartment had been secured by 14 police officers, the court concluded that there did not exist "the type of volatile situation calling for immediate action upon which the Supreme Court predicated the narrow public safety exception to the *Miranda* rule." 519 N.Y.S.2d at 228. Further, the court concluded that the officer's motivation in asking the questions was based on the need to solve the crime, and not upon any objective need to protect the public.

Thus the *immediacy of the threat to public safety* and the *motivation of the officers* (viewed from an objective perspective) are the important factors weighed by the courts in determining the applicability of *Quarles*.

It must be emphasized that *Quarles* represents an exception only to the *Miranda* requirements, and *not* to the basic due process clause requirement that confessions be voluntary in order to be admitted into evidence. See Chapter 8. Thus, in our example, if it is determined that the questioning of the suspect at gunpoint was coercive, his response would be inadmissible regardless of the applicability of the public safety exception.

3. Unlike *Quarles*, the incident in this example occurred in a *private* residence, not a public place. The state court that decided a case on similar facts concluded that the distinction was determinative

and refused to apply the *Quarles* exception: "In *Quarles*, the accused entered a *public* place carrying a gun. . . . Here, we have a man's private residence which is not open to the public at large. Furthermore, there were no other persons around who could have gained access to the gun and the trial court found there was an opportunity to get a search warrant. Therefore the 'public safety' exception to *Miranda* is inapplicable here." *State v. Stevenson*, 784 S.W.2d 143, 145 (Tex. Ct. App. 1990).

This distinction is not universally recognized. In *State v. Jackson*, 756 S.W.2d 620 (Mo. Ct. App. 1988), also involving a shooting at a private residence, the court suggested that the *Quarles* decision was not limited to those incidents taking place in a public setting, but applied in any situation where there was a threat to police or public safety.

§9.3.2 Use of the Statement for Impeachment

The *Miranda* decision indicated that statements obtained in violation of the protections set out could not be used at trial *for any purpose*. In its first modification of the *Miranda* scheme, however, the Burger Court held in *Harris v. New York*, 401 U.S. 222 (1971), that statements obtained in violation of *Miranda* (but otherwise voluntary and uncoerced) could be used to impeach the defendant's testimony at trial. Harris made incriminating statements at the time of his arrest for the sale of heroin but had not received complete warnings. While Harris could thus prevent the statements from coming into evidence during the prosecution's case-in-chief, the Court held that he could not prevent the prosecutor from confronting him with these admissions on cross-examination when he chose to testify. "[The] shield provided by *Miranda* cannot be perverted into a license to use perjury by way of a defense, free from the risk of confrontation with prior inconsistent utterances." 401 U.S. at 226.[20] In such a situation the judge will instruct the jury (for whatever it is worth!) that they are to consider the prior statement only in weighing the credibility of the defendant's trial testimony, and not for the truth of the matters asserted.

Four years later in *Oregon v. Hass*, 420 U.S. 714 (1975), the Court extended the impeachment exception to a situation where the

---

20. The Court has ruled that statements obtained in violation of the Sixth Amendment right to counsel may similarly be introduced for impeachment purposes. See *Michigan v. Harvey*, 494 U.S. 344 (1990), discussed in §10.4.

suspect, after receiving the warnings, invoked his right to counsel, which the police ignored as they persisted in questioning him. Despite the deliberate nature of the *Miranda* violation, the Court held that the statements obtained (which were found to have been voluntary) could be used to challenge the defendant's testimony on the stand.

The Court has refused to extend *Harris* to situations where the prosecution seeks to use defendant's postwarning *silence* for purposes of impeachment. In *Doyle v. Ohio*, 426 U.S. 610 (1976), the arrestee remained silent after receiving *Miranda* warnings. When Doyle later testified at his trial on narcotic offenses that he had been framed by a police informant, the prosecution elicited (over objection) on cross-examination that he had not protested his innocence at the time of arrest. Reversing the conviction, the court held that it would be "fundamentally unfair and a deprivation of due process to allow the arrested person's silence to be used to impeach an explanation subsequently offered at trial." Because the mandated warnings advise the suspect that he has the right to remain silent and that anything he says may be used against him, the Court recognized that his silence may simply represent an exercise of those rights and should thus carry no penalty.

As with all other limitations, the impeachment exception does *not* apply if the statement obtained was not only in violation of *Miranda*'s dictates, but was also coerced and involuntary. Statements procured in that unconstitutional manner are inadmissible for *all* purposes.

EXAMPLES

Talia Teller was arrested on suspicion of embezzlement from the bank she worked for. She was questioned for five hours at the police station without being advised of her *Miranda* rights, and she finally confessed. As defense counsel in her upcoming trial, what would you advise her with regard to whether she should testify or not? What further information would you seek?

EXPLANATIONS

Talia's confession was clearly obtained in violation of the *Miranda* dictates and thus is inadmissible in the prosecution's case-in-chief. Under *Harris v. New York*, 401 U.S. 222 (1971), however, the statement may be used for purposes of impeachment during cross-examination if Talia chooses to testify. She would have to be advised, therefore, that if she elects to testify and denies the charges, that would permit the prosecutor to bring to the jury's attention the otherwise inadmissible confession as a prior inconsistent statement.

The impeachment exception does not apply to *Miranda*-violation statements that are also found to have been involuntary under the due process totality of the circumstances standard. It would thus be necessary to further explore the circumstances of the five-hour interrogation and the manner in which Talia was treated to determine whether her testimony would trigger the impeachment exception or not.

§9.3.3 *Suppression of the Fruits of a Statement Obtained in Violation of* Miranda

As discussed in §7.2, constitutional doctrine mandates that the indirect as well as the direct products of unlawful police activity (the "fruit of the poisonous tree") are subject to the exclusionary rule. Thus if the police conduct an unlawful search of Sam's home and find a map that describes the location of buried loot from a burglary, both the map and the evidence the police derive from the map (the loot) must be suppressed under the Fourth Amendment. Similarly, if the police unlawfully coerce a statement from Sam describing where the loot may be found, both the statement and the loot found as a result of it must be suppressed under the Fifth Amendment. The rationale for the exclusion of derivative evidence is deterrence—in order to ensure compliance with constitutional mandates, the prosecution must be deprived of the use at trial of *all* the goodies gained from a violation, both immediate and more remote.

Consistent with the Supreme Court's pre-*Dickerson* theme that *Miranda* violations are not *constitutional* in nature, the Court pruned back the application of the poisonous fruit doctrine in this area. *Oregon v. Elstad*, 470 U.S. 298 (1985), held that while the failure to comply with *Miranda* requires suppression of the unlawfully obtained statement, evidence derived from the statement is not rendered inadmissible. Police obtained an oral admission from Elstad, an 18-year-old burglary suspect, while he was in custody at his home and without advising him of his rights. One hour later at the station house the suspect received *Miranda* warnings, indicated that he understood them, and made a detailed statement (which was reduced to writing and signed by him) describing his involvement in the crime. Elstad argued that the second statement, although obtained in compliance with *Miranda*, was the tainted fruit of the first statement, which was not in compliance, and thus should be suppressed. The Oregon Court of Appeals agreed, holding that after Elstad's first admission the "cat was sufficiently out of the bag to exert a coercive impact on later admissions." 61 Or. App. 673, 678.

The U.S. Supreme Court reversed. Reasoning that the *Miranda* remedy sweeps more broadly than the Fifth Amendment protection against compelled self-incrimination, and that *Miranda* thus represents a "prophylactic rule" and not a constitutional right (a view ultimately abandoned in *Dickerson*), the Court confined suppression to the immediate product of the *Miranda* violation and not its indirect fruits. Thus while Elstad's unwarned first statement must be excluded from evidence, the Court held that his second statement (even if derived from the first) was admissible.

The *Elstad* Court emphasized that the consequences are different if the statement is not only obtained in violation of *Miranda* but also through coercion. Where the police elicit an *involuntary* statement in violation of the *constitutional right* against compelled self-incrimination (see Chapter 8), then all fruits, both indirect as well as direct, must be suppressed. Because the context of Elstad's first statement had "none of the earmarks of coercion," the Court held that no unconstitutional taint carried to the second statement; because the second statement was itself in compliance with *Miranda* as well as voluntary, it was admissible against defendant at trial. 470 U.S. at 316.

In sum, while a statement obtained in violation of *Miranda*'s dictates is not itself admissible in the prosecution's case, evidence (both testimonial as well as tangible)[21] derived from it *is* admissible provided that the statement is found to have been voluntary and uncoerced.

EXAMPLES

After extensive investigation into the theft of a priceless Impressionist painting from the City Museum, police concluded that it was an "inside job" and that Sticky Finger, a security guard at the museum, was

---

21. The *Elstad* Court appeared to reject any distinction between the forms of evidence for purposes of the *Miranda* derivative-evidence doctrine. 470 U.S. at 308. A distinction between tangible items and live witnesses is made under the Fourth Amendment fruits analysis. See *United States v. Ceccolini*, 435 U.S. 268 (1978), discussed in §7.2. The dissenters in *Elstad* would have made a similar distinction for *Miranda* violations. 470 U.S. 298, 347 n.29 (Brennan, J., dissenting) ("[T]oday's opinion surely ought not be read as also foreclosing application of the traditional derivative-evidence presumption to physical evidence obtained as a proximate result of a *Miranda* violation.").

involved. Finger was taken into custody and questioned without being advised of his *Miranda* rights. After some time he admitted that he had unlocked the museum to let his accomplice in to steal the painting, and he finally told the police where they had hidden it in the museum gift shop stock room. Detectives immediately went to the location and discovered the painting wrapped in old newspaper. Would the painting be admissible against Finger at trial?

EXPLANATIONS

Because Finger was subjected to custodial interrogation without the benefit of the warnings, the statement obtained from him must be suppressed. Under the rationale of *Elstad*, exclusion of the painting would not be required even though it was discovered as a result of the *Miranda* violation. The painting would be tainted fruit only if, in addition to that violation, Finger's statement had also been unconstitutionally *coerced*. We would need more information as to how the interrogation was conducted to determine whether under the due process voluntariness standard that was the case. See Chapter 8.

In *United States v. Cherry*, 794 F.2d 201 (5th Cir. 1986), a statement was obtained from the suspect in violation of *Miranda*, and the statement led the police to the murder weapon. While the statement itself could not be used at trial, the court held that the gun would be admissible because the statement (while not in compliance with the *Miranda* rules) passed muster under the due process voluntariness test.

Cherry represents the rejection of the distinction between testimonial and physical evidence, which Justice Brennan sought to draw in *Elstad*. See n.21, supra. This distinction would parallel the one drawn for purposes of the Fourth Amendment derivative evidence doctrine. See §7.2. In Finger's case it would permit the argument that the physical evidence obtained from his statement (that is, the painting) should be suppressed even though testimonial evidence derived from it would not be subject to exclusion. The Court has yet to definitively resolve this issue.

§9.4 Summary—What's Left of *Miranda*?

A statement obtained in violation of the *Miranda* rules (warnings, waiver, etc.) may not be admitted against the suspect *except* in the following situations: The statement was voluntary and either 1) the interrogation falls within the *Quarles public safety exception*; or 2) the response is used solely to *impeach defendant's testimony* at trial, and not as substantive evidence of the defendant's guilt during the prosecution's case-in-chief.

Where a *Miranda*-violation statement does not fall within either of the above, it cannot itself be used at trial. Evidence derived from the statement (either physical or testimonial) will be admissible as long as the statement was not coerced and involuntary.

10

The Sixth Amendment "Right to Counsel" Approach

§10.1   The *Massiah* Doctrine

The Sixth Amendment, which guarantees an accused the "assistance of counsel for his defense," provides another approach to the problem of interrogation and confessions that supplements (and at times overlaps) the two approaches previously discussed—due process voluntariness and *Miranda*.

The role of the Sixth Amendment in this area can be traced to *Massiah v. United States*, 377 U.S. 201 (1964). The prosecution admitted into evidence at trial incriminating statements that Massiah (charged with narcotics offenses) had made to his codefendant, Colson. Unbeknownst to Massiah, Colson was cooperating with the government and had initiated the conversation at the request of federal agents, who recorded it. The conversation occurred after both men had been indicted, retained counsel, pled not guilty, and were released on bail. Massiah challenged his conviction on the ground that the damaging admissions should have been suppressed. The Supreme Court agreed, holding that once adversary judicial proceedings have commenced against an individual, government efforts to "deliberately elicit" statements from him in the absence of his attorney (whether done openly or surreptitiously) violate the Sixth Amendment. The Court reasoned that the right to the assistance of counsel at trial would be rendered meaningless if the prosecution could obtain incriminating statements from an uncounseled defendant prior to trial.

Although the *Massiah* doctrine appeared to have been displaced by *Miranda* (decided two years later), it reemerged in 1977 with the decision in *Brewer v. Williams*, 430 U.S. 387 (1977). Williams, a suspect in a child murder in Des Moines, Iowa, surrendered to police in Davenport, following the issuance of a warrant for his arrest. He spoke by telephone to an attorney in Des Moines and was advised not to make any statements to the police until he could consult in person with the attorney upon his return to that city. After being booked, arraigned, and advised of his *Miranda* rights, Williams was transported the 160 miles to Des Moines by police officers who had expressly agreed with Williams's lawyer that he would not be questioned en route. During the trip a detective (who knew that Williams was a former mental patient and that he was deeply religious) suggested that since Williams was the only person who knew where the missing girl's body was, he was obliged to take the police to her so that she could get a decent burial (the "Christian burial speech"). Williams subsequently led the police to the victim and made incriminating statements.

Despite the admission of the detective that he had acted with the design to obtain incriminating evidence from the suspect, the evidence related to the discovery of the body and the accompanying inculpatory statements were admitted at trial. On review of Williams's conviction, the Supreme Court reversed. Concluding that there was no need to consider Williams's claims that his rights under *Miranda* had been violated or that his statements were involuntary, the Court instead relied on *Massiah*: Williams had been denied his Sixth Amendment right to assistance of counsel when, after the initiation of judicial proceedings (his arraignment), the police deliberately elicited information from him without affording him the opportunity to consult with his attorney. His incriminating statements were therefore not admissible in evidence.

Unlike the due process standard, the Sixth Amendment approach does not require a finding of coercion (which was not present in either *Massiah* or *Williams*). Unlike *Miranda*, neither custody nor interrogation are prerequisites to applicability. (Neither Massiah nor Williams were subjected to interrogation in any traditional sense, and Massiah was not even in custody at the time he incriminated himself.) What is required for invocation of the *Massiah* doctrine is: 1) that the government *deliberately elicited* incriminating statements from the accused in the absence of counsel (or a waiver of counsel); and 2) that this occurred *after the initiation of judicial proceedings* (which is the point at which the right to counsel is triggered).

§10.2 The "Deliberately Elicit" Standard

The constitutional wrong committed by the police in both *Massiah* and *Williams* was the intentional pursuit of incriminating information from the suspect *after* his right to counsel had attached. The fact that no actual questioning occurred in either case was not considered significant; it was sufficient that the officers had "deliberately elicited" the inculpatory statements.

Although "deliberate elicitation" seems to bear a resemblance to the "functional equivalent of interrogation" concept under *Miranda* (see §9.2.2), the Court has observed that the two concepts "are not necessarily interchangeable." *Rhode Island v. Innis,* 446 U.S. 291, 300 n.4 (1980). The emphasis in the Sixth Amendment context is on the *deliberate or intentional* nature of the officer's effort to gain incriminating evidence, while the test for interrogation in the *Miranda* context is broader: whether the police engaged in conduct that they could reasonably have foreseen would elicit an incriminating response from the suspect (even if it was not designed to achieve that result).

A second (and more subtle) difference between the two concepts is that the functional equivalent of interrogation focuses more on the susceptibilities and perceptions of the suspect, while the *Massiah* doctrine looks more to the state of mind of the officer (that is, did she intend to elicit the confession?). Both *Rhode Island v. Innis* and *Arizona v. Mauro* (discussed in §9.2.2) refused to find that the police conduct constituted the functional equivalent of interrogation—in *Innis* because the suspect had not been shown to be particularly vulnerable to the expressed concern for the handicapped children; in *Mauro* because the suspect could not reasonably have felt coerced by the confrontation with his wife. In contrast, the determinative factor in both *Massiah* and *Williams* appeared to be the deliberate nature of the police effort to secure a confession. In any event, the distinction between interrogation under *Miranda* and deliberate elicitation under *Massiah* has yet to be clearly drawn by the Court.

The *Massiah* doctrine has been applied to the deliberate elicitation of evidence from a suspect by means of an informant placed in his prison cell. In *United States v. Henry*, 447 U.S. 264 (1980), the FBI arranged to have Nichols, a paid informant, placed as Henry's cellmate. Although the agents instructed Nichols not to question Henry about the crime, he was told to report incriminating statements to them (for payment), which he did. The Court suppressed the statements, concluding that the government had intentionally set up a situation likely to induce Henry to make incriminating statements and thus violated his Sixth Amendment right to counsel. Nichols was not, the Court determined, "a passive listener" but rather had "stimulated" conversations with the defendant, which were designed to (and did) obtain incriminating admissions. 447 U.S. at 271.

Where the informant is merely a passive listener, the Sixth Amendment is not violated. In *Kuhlman v. Wilson*, 477 U.S. 436 (1986), the informant did nothing to stimulate the conversation in which the suspect made incriminating statements, and thus there was no deliberate elicitation. A defendant does not make out a Sixth Amendment violation "simply by showing that an informant, either through prior arrangement or voluntarily, reported his incriminating statements to the police." 477 U.S. at 459. Rather, it must be shown that the police and their informant took some deliberate action (beyond merely establishing a "listening post") that was designed to elicit incriminating remarks. The "primary concern of the *Massiah* line of decisions is secret interrogation by investigatory techniques that are equivalent to direct police interrogation." Id.

§10.3   At What Point Does the *Massiah* Doctrine Apply?—The Initiation of Judicial Proceedings

The triggering event for the application of the *Massiah* doctrine is the initiation of "adversary judicial criminal proceedings"—meaning either indictment, information, arraignment, or preliminary hearing. Only at that point is the suspect an accused in a criminal prosecution and thus entitled to the assistance of counsel under the Sixth Amendment. See *Kirby v. Illinois*, 406 U.S. 682 (1972).

The government may, therefore, deliberately elicit admissions from a suspect *prior to* the initiation of formal proceedings against him without running afoul of *Massiah*. In *Moulton v. Maine*, 474 U.S. 159 (1985), for example, the prosecution obtained incriminating statements from the defendant by recording a meeting between him and a codefendant who was cooperating with the government.[1] The statements related to the charges that were already pending against Moulton (he had been indicted for receiving stolen property), to other similar crimes, and to a plan to kill state witnesses expected to testify in the upcoming trial. Concluding that the government had deliberately elicited these statements from Moulton, the Court ordered that the admissions concerning *the pending charges* must be suppressed. "[T]he Sixth Amendment is violated when the State obtains incriminating statements by knowingly circumventing the accused's right to have counsel present in a confrontation between the accused and a state agent." 474 U.S. at 176. Those incriminating remarks about crimes not yet charged at the time of the elicitation, but that were *subsequently* brought, were not subject to exclusion. No judicial proceedings had been initiated and thus no right of counsel had yet attached. These statements, the Court held, could thus be used against Moulton at trial of those other charges.

The "offense-specific" nature of Sixth Amendment protection was underscored in *McNeil v. Wisconsin*, 501 U.S. 171 (1991). McNeil was represented by a public defender at a bail hearing on charges of armed robbery. While in jail on that charge, he was questioned by police about an unrelated murder in another town. McNeil executed a written *Miranda* waiver and made statements implicating himself in the murder. When he was subsequently charged with the murder, McNeil moved to suppress these admissions, arguing that his invocation of the right to counsel at the bail hearing prevented the police from any subsequent questioning of him in the absence of counsel. The Court disagreed: "The Sixth Amendment right, however, is offense-specific. It cannot be invoked once for all future prosecutions, *for it does not attach until a prosecution is commenced, that is, at or after the initiation of adversary judicial proceedings—whether by way of formal charge, preliminary hearing, indictment, information, or arraignment.*" 501 U.S. at 175 (emphasis added, internal quotations omitted). Because the murder charges had not yet been brought against McNeil, questioning in the absence of counsel did not violate the *Massiah* doctrine.

There are suggestions in the case law that once the right to counsel attaches, it lasts. See *People v. West*, 615 N.E.2d 968 (N.Y. 1993) (where right to counsel attaches on original charge, defendant arrested

---

1. Because there was no custodial interrogation, *Miranda* was not applicable.

three years later on unrelated charge still has right to counsel on original charge).

§10.4   Waiver Under the *Massiah* Doctrine

As with any constitutional right, the Sixth Amendment right to counsel may be waived. Even if the *Massiah* doctrine is applicable, therefore, a statement deliberately elicited by the police in the absence of counsel may nonetheless be admissible if the prosecution can demonstrate a voluntary relinquishment of the right to counsel. The Court has equated the standard for waiver under the Sixth Amendment with the knowing, intelligent, and voluntary standard of the *Miranda* waiver (discussed in §9.2.4). See *Patterson v. Illinois*, 487 U.S. 285 (1988). A showing that defendant had been advised of, understood, and voluntarily waived his *Miranda* rights (which includes, of course, the right to an attorney) also suffices to establish a waiver of his rights under the Sixth Amendment (at least where he has not yet, as in *Patterson*, retained counsel).

Where the suspect has requested counsel, however, the *Edwards* rule (see §9.2.5) applies. The police, in other words, may not conduct further interrogation until counsel has been made available or *the accused herself initiates further communication* with the police. In *Michigan v. Jackson*, 475 U.S. 625 (1986), the Court held that confessions had been improperly obtained when police questioned the suspects three days after they were arraigned and requested the appointment of counsel. The Court rejected the notion that a valid waiver could be made out in such circumstances by providing a fresh set of Miranda warnings and obtaining a written waiver: "Just as written waivers are insufficient to justify police-initiated interrogations after the request for counsel in a Fifth Amendment analysis, so too are they insufficient to justify police-initiated interrogations after the request for counsel in a Sixth Amendment analysis." 475 U.S. at 634.

In another analogy to the *Miranda* doctrine (see §9.3.2), the Court has held that a statement obtained in violation of the *Michigan v. Jackson* rule (forbidding police-initiated interrogation once the suspect requests counsel) may be used by the prosecution to impeach the defendant's testimony at trial, even though the statement is inadmissible in the prosecution's case-in-chief. See *Michigan v. Harvey*, 494 U.S. 344 (1990). The rationale for permitting limited use of the statement to contradict the defendant on the witness stand, as in the *Mi-*

randa context, is that the *Jackson* rule is merely prophylactic and not constitutional in nature. Thus suppression of the statement for *all* purposes is not required, and weighing the costs of exclusion against benefits, the Court concluded that use of the statement for impeachment was appropriate.

It is interesting to note that the Court has refused to adopt a Sixth Amendment counterpart to the *Quarles* public safety exception (see §9.3.1). The Court rejected the government's argument in *Moulton v. Maine* (discussed in §10.3) that the violation of the Sixth Amendment should be excused because the police had a compelling reason to listen in on the defendant's conversation independent of the gathering of evidence—that is, to investigate Moulton's plan to kill state witnesses and thereby protect the safety of the informant. In an unusual expression of cynicism regarding law enforcement officials, the Court explained: "To allow the admission of evidence obtained from the accused in violation of his Sixth Amendment rights whenever the police assert an alternative, legitimate reason for their surveillance invites abuse by law enforcement personnel in the form of fabricated investigations and risks the evisceration of the Sixth Amendment right recognized in *Massiah*." 474 U.S. at 180.

EXAMPLES

1. Arrest warrants were issued for Tommy Tucker and Max Malone on a charge of armed robbery of a gas station. Police, who had been unable to locate either suspect, received a call from Malone in which he offered to turn himself in if "he could get a good deal." Detective Simpson told Malone that they would consider "giving him a break" if he could "get the goods on Tucker." Malone agreed to wear a wire and engage Tucker in a conversation concerning the gas station robbery. Simpson also directed Malone to "get Tucker talking about that First National bank heist last month, because I think he's our man on that job, too."

   Malone met Tucker the next day, wearing a recorder the police fitted him with, and turned the conversation to reminiscing about the gas station robbery. Tucker made several incriminating statements. Malone also got Tucker talking about other crimes he had been involved in, and Tucker boasted about his participation in the First National robbery.

   May the prosecution use these statements against Tucker at trial on the gas station robbery? Or the bank robbery? Would it make a difference if Tucker had already been indicted for the gas station robbery at the time the conversation with Malone occurred?

2. Chatty Charlie, who has been an informant on a number of occasions for the Drug Enforcement Administration (DEA), was sharing a cell at City Jail with Loose Lips, who was under indictment for first degree murder. Lips and Charlie had a conversation in which Lips shared the details of his involvement in the murder. Charlie, seeking to benefit from this information, informed his DEA contact of the conversation and enthusiastically offered to testify about it in court. Would this evidence be admissible against Lips?

EXPLANATIONS

1. Because Tucker was not subjected to custodial interrogation or coerced against his will into speaking, he is not protected by either *Miranda* or the due process voluntariness requirement. The only challenge he could mount to the admission of this evidence would be based on the Sixth Amendment *Massiah* doctrine, which prohibits the police from deliberately eliciting incriminating statements from an accused in the absence of counsel after the right to counsel has attached.

   There is little question here that the deliberate elicitation requirement has been met. The police used Malone as their agent to gather evidence from Tucker's mouth, as Colson was used against Massiah. It is not so clear, however, whether the right to counsel had attached at the time of the conversation. The issuance of an arrest warrant, which is an early step in the criminal justice process and does not commit the government to go forward with a prosecution, has been generally held not to constitute the commencement of federal adversary criminal proceedings for purposes of the *Massiah* doctrine. See, e.g., *United States v. Langley*, 848 F.2d 152 (11th Cir. 1988); *United States v. Pace*, 833 F.2d 1307 (9th Cir. 1987); *United States v. Muzychka*, 725 F.2d 1061 (3d Cir. 1984) (and cases cited). Some federal courts reviewing state prosecutions in habeas cases have, however, looked to state law and concluded that the issuance of an arrest warrant under that law constitutes initiation. See, e.g., *Meadows v. Kuhlman*, 812 F.2d 72 (2d Cir. 1987).

The requirement for initiation in the federal criminal justice process generally is either 1) a formal charge (an indictment or information); or 2) the defendant's appearance at an arraignment or preliminary hearing. Because such proceedings had not yet begun in example 1, the government was free to gather evidence from Malone in the manner they did, and his incriminating statements could be used against him at both the gas station robbery and bank robbery trials.

The situation would of course be different if Malone had already been indicted for the gas station robbery. That event would have triggered his right to the assistance of counsel on that charge, and the deliberate effort to obtain evidence from him in the absence of counsel would violate the proscriptions of the *Massiah* doctrine. Even in that situation, however, the statements implicating him in the bank robbery would be admissible at trial because no judicial proceedings had been commenced for that crime, and thus no right to counsel had yet attached. See *Moulton v. Maine*, 474 U.S. 159 (1985).

2. The *Massiah* doctrine applies only where *the government* deliberately elicits incriminating statements from the accused; it does not prevent the government from accepting information offered by a private individual who obtained it on his own initiative and not as agent for the government. (See discussion of the analogous private search doctrine in the Fourth Amendment context, §3.1.) Unless there is evidence that the DEA encouraged Charlie to elicit these statements, the Sixth Amendment is not implicated. The fact that Charlie has worked as an informant on other occasions is not determinative. If the evidence is acquired "by luck or happenstance" and not by design, there is no constitutional violation. See *Moulton v. Maine*, supra. See also *United States v. Watson*, 894 F.2d 1345 (D.C. Cir. 1990); *Brooks v. Kincheloe*, 848 F.2d 940 (9th Cir. 1988).

    In *State v. Bey*, 610 A.2d 403 (N.J. Super. Ct. App. Div. 1992), defendant, a death row inmate, made incriminating statements in response to questions asked by a state prison guard. The court held that in order to establish a violation of right to counsel, a defendant must show that there was deliberate elicitation by a law enforcement agent. Unlike another prisoner, the guard in this case is considered a law enforcement agent. The next question is whether the guard deliberately elicited the defendant's statements.

The court, in holding that the guard did not deliberately elicit the incriminating statements, found that the guard was never instructed to obtain information, nor did he make a report to the prosecuting authorities (only a later investigation turned up this evidence). It was also relevant that the conversation was casual. The court concluded that the state did not "knowingly exploit the custodial situation or intentionally create the opportunity to intrude into the unavailability of counsel on the cellblock." Id. at 415. Quoting from *United States v. Henry*, 447 U.S. 264, 276 (1980): "Thus, the Sixth Amendment is not violated whenever—by luck or happenstance—the State obtains incriminating statements from the accused after the right to counsel has attached." Discovering defendant's admission to the guard was described as luck and not a product of deliberate elicitation by a government agent. If the guard had been under direction by the state to question the defendant, the decision would have been different.

§10.5   Overview of Interrogation and Confessions

In analyzing any interrogation or confession problem, one must keep in mind the three approaches discussed in Chapters 8, 9, and 10. As Figure 10–1 indicates, the due process voluntariness standard applies to *all* interrogation and confession contexts, overlapping in coverage with both the *Miranda* and *Massiah* approaches, as well as filling in the gaps where, for whatever reason, the other doctrines do not apply. Put another way, neither the Fifth Amendment nor the Sixth Amend-

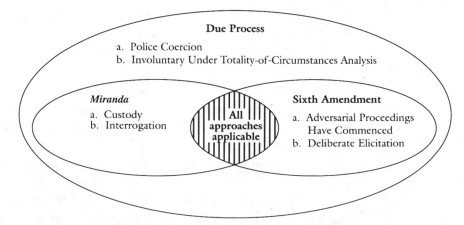

Figure 10–1: Approaches to Interrogation and Confession

ment doctrine relating to self-incrimination supplants the due process requirement that the statement be shown to have been voluntary and uncoerced as a condition of its admission into evidence. Rather, those doctrines supplement the voluntariness standard.

Thus if *Miranda* is not applicable because the statement did not result from custodial interrogation (or because the public safety or impeachment exceptions applies), and the Sixth Amendment is not applicable because there was no deliberate elicitation after initiation of adversary proceedings, admission of the statement into evidence may nonetheless be challenged on the grounds that it was the product of police coercion (either physical or mental).

PART THREE

Other Investigative Procedures

11

Other Investigative Procedures—Eyewitness Identification, Bodily Intrusions, Examination of Physical Attributes, and Entrapment

We have discussed in previous chapters two general methods by which law enforcement officers seek evidence for use in criminal prosecutions—search and seizure, and interrogation of suspects. In this chapter we turn to two other categories of investigative procedures—eyewitness identification and the examination of physical attributes of the suspect (including bodily intrusions). As we will see, various constitutional constraints have been applied to such police work. We also take up the problem of entrapment.

§11.1   Eyewitness Identification

Suppose the police would like to present Suspect to Victim to deter-mine whether the latter recognizes the former as the perpetrator. May the police require Suspect to participate in a lineup?

While arguably the lineup implicates his Fourth Amendment pri-vacy concerns as well as his Fifth Amendment right not to be com-pelled to incriminate himself, it has long been established that neither protection applies to eyewitness identification procedures. The Fourth Amendment is inapplicable because the attributes in question—namely, the suspect's physical appearance—are constantly on public display and thus carry no reasonable expectation of privacy. See §3.2.[1] The Fifth Amendment is not triggered because it only protects an accused from being compelled to *testify* against himself, or otherwise provide the government with evidence of a *testimonial or communi-cative* nature. "[C]ompelling the accused merely to exhibit his person for observation by a prosecution witness prior to trial involves no com-pulsion of the accused to give evidence having testimonial signifi-cance." *United States v. Wade*, 388 U.S. 218 (1967). For the same reasons, neither the Fourth nor Fifth Amendments is implicated when the suspect is required to speak certain words uttered by the perpetra-tor (*Wade*, supra) or to provide voice exemplars (*United States v. Dio-nisio*, 410 U.S. 1 (1973)) or handwriting exemplars (*United States v. Mara*, 410 U.S. 19 (1973)) for purposes of identification.

Concerned about the risk of mistaken identification because of unreliable or unfairly suggestive procedures,[2] the Court has invoked two other constitutional sources to protect the suspect in the identi-fication process. In a preventive approach, the right to have counsel present at lineups conducted after the initiation of formal criminal pro-ceedings has been derived from the Sixth Amendment. More generally, all eyewitness identification procedures are subject to review to ensure

---

1. Unless the suspect consents, it is necessary to have justification in the form of probable cause to hold him in custody at the station house while engaging in the identification procedures. See *Davis v. Mississippi*, 394 U.S. 721 (1969) (fingerprinting). But see *Hayes v. Florida*, 470 U.S. 811 (1985) (suggesting that a brief detention in the field for the purpose of fingerprinting may be permissible where there is only "reasonable suspicion" not amounting to probable cause.)

2. "Usually the witness must testify about an encounter with a total stranger under circumstances of emergency or emotional stress. The witness' recol-lection of the stranger can be distorted easily by the circumstances or by later actions of the police." *Manson v. Brathwaite*, 432 U.S. 98, 111 (1977).

that they were not so unnecessarily suggestive and conducive to mistaken identification so as to deny the defendant the due process of law guaranteed by the Fifth and Fourteenth Amendments.

The Court has recognized that the pretrial lineup is a critically important stage in the prosecution of a case, but that it is also susceptible to both intentional abuse by the police and the limitations and dangers inherent in eyewitness identification. Effective assistance of counsel is thus required by the Sixth Amendment at the lineup. See *Wade*, supra. The attorney's presence serves two basic purposes: 1) avoiding intentional as well as inadvertent prejudice to the suspect at the time of the lineup (as, for example, placing a short, black, bearded suspect in a line of tall, white, clean-shaven men), and 2) ensuring that counsel will be sufficiently familiar (from firsthand observation) with what actually occurred to mount a meaningful confrontation of the witnesses at trial. Unless the suspect is afforded the opportunity to have counsel present (or waives that right), therefore, evidence of an identification at the lineup is not admissible at trial.

The *Wade* requirement for counsel has been extended beyond lineups to other live presentations (dubbed "trial-like confrontations") of the suspect to witnesses, such as one-on-one "show-ups." See *Moore v. Illinois*, 434 U.S. 220 (1977). The right to counsel does not, however, apply to photographic arrays shown to witnesses because the defendant is not present. See *United States v. Ash*, 413 U.S. 300 (1973).

As we have previously seen with regard to the *Massiah* doctrine (see Chapter 10), the Sixth Amendment right to counsel does not attach until the commencement of adversary judicial proceedings.[3] Consequently the requirements of *Wade* are inapplicable to lineups held prior to indictment or other formal charges against the suspect. See *Kirby v. Illinois*, 406 U.S. 682 (1972). Because many lineups take place earlier in the criminal justice sequence, the right to counsel protection is of limited practical application.

Of wider application is the requirement that any identification procedure (whether conducted before or after the initiation of formal charges) conform to due process standards of fundamental fairness. Utilizing a totality-of-the-circumstances approach, the court must determine whether the procedure was: 1) unnecessarily suggestive; and 2) likely to lead to a mistaken identification. See *Stovall v. Denno*, 388

---

3. Some states have applied the right to counsel at lineup to all suspects in custody even if formal proceedings have not been commenced. See, e.g, *Blue v. State of Alaska*, 558 P.2d 636 (Alaska 1977).

U.S. 293 (1967). If so, evidence of the identification is inadmissible at trial.

The first element involves an analysis of both the prejudicial nature of the procedure and the circumstances that necessitated resort to it. In *Stovall*, for example, the handcuffed suspect (a black man) was brought into the stabbing victim's hospital room by several white police officers and asked if he was "the man." While conceding that this one-on-one confrontation procedure was indeed "suggestive," the Court nevertheless concluded that it was not "unnecessarily" so —that is, the police were faced with a situation where they were not sure that the victim would survive and thus had to act quickly to obtain the identification from her hospital bed.

The second element has come into increasing prominence in recent years as the Court has described *reliability* as "the linchpin in determining the admissibility of identification testimony." *Manson v. Brathwaite*, 432 U.S. 98 (1977). Identification evidence, even if the result of unnecessarily suggestive procedures, is nonetheless admissible if it possesses certain indicia of reliability that reduce the possibility of mistaken identification. The factors to be considered by the courts in assessing reliability include: 1) the opportunity of the witness to view the perpetrator at the time of the crime; 2) the witness's degree of attention; 3) the accuracy of his prior description of the perpetrator (if any); 4) the level of certainty demonstrated at the confrontation; and 5) the elapsed time between the crime and the confrontation. These factors are to be weighed against "the corrupting effect of the suggestive identification itself." *Manson*, supra.

Because an identification procedure must be shown defective on *all* three grounds [(that is, 1) suggestive; 2) unnecessarily so; and 3) unreliable)], the Court has rarely found a violation of the due process standard. Even in cases of highly suggestive one-on-one show-ups, such as *Stovall*, the totality-of-the-circumstances approach usually results in a decision in favor of the prosecution.

If a pretrial identification is suppressed because of either a Sixth Amendment or due process violation, the question arises as to whether the witness may nonetheless identify the defendant from the witness stand at trial. Because of the probability that the in-court identification would be greatly influenced by the prior tainted procedure, it too is inadmissible unless the prosecution can establish that the courtroom identification was independently based upon another source, such as observations made at the time of the crime. (The premise is similar to the independent source exception to the fruit-of-the-poisonous-tree doctrine, discussed in §7.2.) The analysis to determine whether the courtroom testimony is tainted uses the same reliability factors discussed above—a witness who had a good opportunity to view the perpetrator when the crime occurred and who accurately described the defendant prior to the tainted lineup would, for example, likely be permitted to identify him at trial.

EXAMPLES

1. Victoria was robbed of her wallet at gunpoint while waiting for a bus at 1 P.M. The robber, the only other person at the bus stop, had previously engaged Victoria in conversation lasting about ten minutes. Immediately following the incident Victoria reported it to the police and described the robber as a slim black man, approximately six feet tall, wearing a long tweed coat and a woolen hat, and approximately 20 years old. A man of that description was observed in the vicinity shortly after the robbery and was taken into custody by the police. A search of the suspect turned up a wallet with Victoria's identification inside.

    Victoria was bought to the police station at 3 P.M. and shown her wallet. She was told that it was found on the suspect, and the police asked her to observe the man in his cell. Victoria did so and immediately identified him as the robber. The suspect was the only person in the cell and the only individual the police asked Victoria to observe.

    a. Is Victoria's station house identification admissible in evidence?
    b. Assume instead that the suspect had been indicted and arrested pursuant to a warrant prior to Victoria's station house identification of him. How would this change your analysis?
2. Johnson is arrested pursuant to an indictment for armed robbery of Cozy's Convenience Store. The police also suspect him of an unsolved robbery of a nearby gas station.

    a. If the police wish to display an array of photographs including Johnson's to customers who were at the convenience store at the time of the crime, must counsel be present?
    b. If the police wish to display Johnson in a lineup to the witnesses of the gas station robbery, must counsel be present?

EXPLANATIONS

1a. Does this identification pass muster under the due process standard or was it conducted in so unnecessarily suggestive a manner

357

that there was a substantial likelihood of mistaken identification? *Stovall v. Denno*, 388 U.S. 293 (1967). There is no question that the procedure here was highly suggestive. The victim was shown only one individual—the suspect—and the show-up occurred while the suspect was in a jail cell and after the police had informed the victim that her wallet had been found on the suspect. The message from the police was, in effect, "He's the man, isn't he?" Moreover, unlike *Stovall* (where the elderly stabbing victim appeared to be dying in her hospital bed), in our problem there is no compelling justification for shortcutting the identification process. Although it could be argued that the police were faced with a serious crime and had to quickly determine if the felon was still at large, there appears no necessity for resorting to the jail cell show-up as opposed to a fairer method, such as a lineup.

As *Manson v. Brathwaite* teaches, however, even though the procedures were *unnecessarily suggestive*, they may still satisfy the due process standard if the identification is shown to have been *reliable*. Victoria's identification may be admissible, in other words, if it can be demonstrated that it was based on her adequate observation of the accused at the time of the crime and was not influenced by the promptings and suggestions of the police at the tainted confrontation. The analysis of the reliability question is informed by the following factors: 1) Victoria's opportunity to view the robber at the time of the crime; 2) her degree of attention at that time; 3) the accuracy of her description of the robber prior to the identification; 4) the level of certainty demonstrated at the time of the identification; and 5) the time lapse between the crime and the confrontation.

These factors point to a conclusion that Victoria's identification of the suspect was reliable. Victoria had a clear view of the perpetrator while standing next to him and conversing in broad daylight for ten minutes. This was an adequate opportunity to form an accurate mental impression of the robber's appearance. Victoria's degree of attention was high and focused on the person she was speaking to, the only other individual in the immediate area. Victoria was thus able to give a detailed description of the robber to the police.

The accuracy of the description given prior to the identification helps the court determine if the witness had a fixed picture of the perpetrator in mind before the suggestive identification procedure. Here we would have to know what the suspect actually looked like and compare that to Victoria's detailed description before the jail cell confrontation. Assuming a close fit between the description and the defendant's actual appearance (the courts usually discount minor discrepancies), the accuracy of the description bolsters the reliability of the subsequent identification.

While it is recognized that the witness's level of certainty in making a positive identification may reflect the corrupting effect of the suggestive procedures, courts nonetheless weigh a high level of certainty in favor of the reliability of an identification. A prompt, spontaneous "He's definitely the guy!" counts considerably toward a conclusion that the identification was trustworthy. Victoria's immediate identification in our example would thus support a conclusion of reliability.

Finally, the greater the time lapse between the event and the identification, the less reliable the identification is thought to be. In our example Victoria identified the defendant only two hours after the robbery, and this would provide further support for a finding of reliability.

The *Manson* analysis requires the court to weigh the indicia of reliability against the corrupting effects of the suggestive procedures to determine whether there was a substantial likelihood of misidentification. This would likely result in a conclusion that Victoria's station house identification would be admissible. See *Walton v. Lane*, 852 F.2d 268 (7th Cir. 1988).

As with any fact-specific analysis, a change in the circumstances regarding Victoria's encounter might well change the result. If, for example, the crime had occurred in dark of night and Victoria had only a few fleeting seconds to view the robber, or if Victoria's description did not fit the suspect ultimately identified, the reliability factors might well be outweighed by the suggestive nature of the identification. See, e.g., *Dispensa v. Lynaugh*, 847 F.2d 211 (5th Cir. 1988) (suppressing as unreliable an identification where the witnesses' prior description failed to include several striking features of the defendant's appearance).

1b. The initiation of formal proceedings by way of an indictment triggers the *Wade* rule, which entitles the suspect to the presence of an attorney at a lineup or other physical exhibition. Because the station house confrontation proceeded without the presence of counsel or the suspect's waiver of that right, that out-of-court identification would not be admissible at trial.

There is a separate question as to whether Victoria would nonetheless be permitted to identify the defendant from the witness stand at trial. Admissibility of an in-court identification would depend on an "independent source" analysis: If we remove the influence of the tainted station house confrontation, is there a sufficiently reliable independent basis for the identification testimony? This analysis is based on the same *Manson v. Brathwaite* reliability factors discussed above. Because Victoria got a good look at the perpetrator and accurately described the suspect before the station house identification, there is a substantial likelihood that an in-court identification would be allowed.

2a. No, Johnson would not be entitled to the presence of counsel. The right to counsel applies at any postindictment identification procedure where the suspect is displayed live. A photo array has not, however, been included in the *Wade* rule. See *United States v. Ash*, 413 U.S. 300 (1973). Some states have interpreted their own constitutions to require the presence of counsel at a photo array. See, e.g., *Commonwealth v. Ferguson*, 475 A.2d 810 (Pa. Super. Ct. 1984).

2b. No, Johnson would not be entitled to the presence of counsel. The Sixth Amendment right to counsel is offense-specific, as we have seen with regard to the *Massiah* doctrine. (See §10.3.) Because no formal proceedings have been initiated against Johnson for the gas station robbery, the *Wade* rule would not apply to this lineup.

§11.2   Excessive Police Actions, Bodily Intrusions, and Examination of Physical Attributes

Certain investigative procedures involve examination of, and sometimes intrusion into, the suspect's body and its functions. We have already discussed, for example, drug screening that uses urine and blood tests. See §4.5. Other procedures involve the extraction of blood or analysis of breath for purposes of testing alcohol content. What constitutional protections are implicated with regard to such investigative techniques?

The Sixth Admendment right to counsel is not implicated, the Court has held, because, unlike lineups (see §11.1), "knowledge of the techniques of science and technology is sufficiently available and the variables in techniques few enough that the accused has the opportunity for a meaningful confrontation" even though counsel is not present at the procedure. *United States v. Wade*, 388 U.S. at 227.

If the police conduct is "shocking to the conscience," the due process clause comes into play. In *Rochin v. California*, 342 U.S. 165 (1952), the police sought to forcibly remove from the suspect's mouth capsules that he had just swallowed, which they believed contained narcotics. Unable to retrieve them, the officers forcibly took Rochin to a hospital and had doctors pump his stomach with a chemical that brought the capsules up. The Supreme Court reversed his conviction for possession of the unlawful substance, concluding that Rochin's right to due process of law had been violated by the outrageous actions of the police, and thus the capsules should not have been used in evidence. Because of the egregious nature of the police conduct, however, *Rochin* has proven to have limited applicability.

It has long been established that intrusions into the body constitute searches and seizures, implicating the Fourth Amendment. See *Schmerber v. California*, 384 U.S. 757 (1966) (involuntary extraction of a sample of the motorist's blood to establish whether he was intoxicated was a search and seizure requiring justification). Thus the procedure in question must be conducted pursuant to a warrant or fit within a recognized exception to the warrant requirement. *Schmerber* held that the warrantless extraction of blood in that case was not "unreasonable" because 1) the police had probable cause to believe the driver (who had just been involved in an accident) was intoxicated; and 2) the delay necessary to secure a warrant would *risk the destruction of the evidence* of blood-alcohol content. Given the existence of these two elements of the emergency exception (see §6.2), together with the fact that the procedure was routine, harmless, and had been performed by medical personnel, the Fourth Amendment was not violated. Since *Schmerber*, minor intrusions into the body have been measured against these Fourth Amendment standards. See, e.g., *Cupp v. Murphy*, 412 U.S. 291 (1973) (warrantless extraction of scrapings underneath the suspect's fingernails was held lawful because the police had probable cause to believe he had just strangled his wife and the spots of blood were easily removeable by him, making resort to the warrant process impracticable).

The Court has emphasized, however, that major bodily intrusions are subject to special scrutiny. "Notwithstanding the existence of probable cause, a search for evidence of a crime may be unjustifiable if it endangers the life or health of the suspect." *Winston v. Lee*, 470 U.S. 753, 761 (1985). In *Lee* the government sought an order (in effect a search warrant) requiring the suspect to undergo surgery to remove a bullet lodged in his chest muscle. There was probable cause to believe the bullet would connect him to a robbery. Emphasizing that surgical search procedures are not per se unreasonable, the Court stated that a case-by-case approach was necessary to determine the reasonableness of intrusions beneath the skin. The Court weighed the intrusiveness and risks of the surgery (and anesthesia) against the government's need for the bullet (the prosecution had other evidence including an eyewitness identification by the victim) and concluded that the proposed procedure would be unreasonable under the Fourth Amendment.

While applying the Fourth Amendment to searches of the body, *Schmerber* held that such procedures do not implicate the Fifth Amendment's protections. This conclusion derives from the testimonial vs. physical evidence dichotomy discussed above (see §11.1): The privilege against self-incrimination applies only to compelled communications that relate factual assertions or disclose information. The Fifth Amendment does not apply where the suspect is merely the source of physical evidence, as in the case of a blood test or breathalyzer.[4] Nor (as we have seen in §11.1) is the privilege implicated where the physical characteristics of the suspect's communications are used to identify him (such as requiring him to speak certain words in a lineup or to provide a handwriting or voice exemplar).

Some investigative procedures do not fall neatly on one or the other side of the "testimonial/physical" evidence line. *Pennsylvania v. Muniz*, 496 U.S. 582 (1990) (discussed in §9.2.2), involved field sobriety tests commonly used by police to determine whether a driver is intoxicated. Muniz sought to suppress evidence that his speech was slurred while he performed these tests and later in response to routine booking questions. The Court had little difficulty concluding that because this evidence was not "testimonial" in nature, but rather was used to reveal the suspect's lack of physical and muscular coordination, the Fifth Amendment was not implicated. More troublesome, however, was Muniz's answer to the "sixth birthday" question: "Do you know what the date was of your sixth birthday?" The defendant argued that his "I don't know" response to this question should have been suppressed because it was testimonial—that is, it was incriminating not just because of its slurred delivery but also because its *content* revealed his disoriented mental state. A majority of the Court agreed and ordered that the answer be suppressed because the Fifth Amendment

---

4. The refusal to submit to a blood-alcohol test has been similarly held outside the protection of the Fifth Amendment, and thus evidence of the refusal is admissible at trial. See *South Dakota v. Neville*, 459 U.S. 553 (1983).

applied and *Miranda* had not been complied with (that is, no warnings had been administered). Four Justices concluded, however, that the suspect's response to the sixth birthday question was *non*testimonial:

> If the police may require Muniz to use his body in order to demonstrate the level of his physical coordination, there is no reason why they should not be able to require him to speak or write in order to determine his mental coordination. That was all that was sought here. Since it was permissible for the police to extract and examine a sample of Schmerber's blood to determine how much that part of the system had been affected by alcohol, I see no reason why they may not examine the functioning of Muniz's mental processes for the same purpose.

496 U.S. at 607 (Rehnquist, C.J., concurring in part and dissenting in part, joined by White, Blackmun, and Stevens, JJ.). In sum, the line of demarcation between testimonial and physical evidence is not always bright and clear.

The reasonableness clause has also been utilized to monitor police actions that may not reach the level of egregiousness of *Rochin v. California*. When the police use excessive force or effectuate an arrest or search in an overly zealous manner, this may violate the Fourth Amendment. In *Tennessee v. Garner*, 471 U.S. 1 (1985), a case in which deadly force was used to apprehend a fleeing suspect, the Court held that the use of deadly force is sometimes unreasonable under the Fourth Amendment, as where the suspect does not appear to be armed or dangerous. Also in *Graham v. Connor*, 490 U.S. 386 (1989), a civil case seeking damages for the use of excessive force, the Court subjected such police conduct to a reasonableness clause analysis. The test is whether the officer's conduct was objectively reasonable, without regard to the officer's subjective motivation.

EXAMPLES

1. Dizzy was observed driving erratically by officers on highway patrol. She was pulled over and required to perform several sobriety tests, including balance and coordination tasks as well as a recitation of the alphabet. Dizzy's unimpressive performance was videotaped by one of the officers and is now offered against her at trial. Would admission of the evidence violate Dizzy's Fifth Amendment right against compelled self-incrimination?

2. On November 5 the First Savings Bank was robbed. The bank teller described the perpetrator as a man six feet tall, 175 pounds, with jet black hair, wearing a green nylon jacket, red running shoes, and a blue woolen hat. A man was arrested on the other side of town 40 minutes after the robbery who met the description perfectly, except that he had gray (not black) hair. The arresting officer noted in his report that the suspect's hair was wet and sticky, "as if he had just shampooed it."

    A lineup was conducted in which the suspect and five others were displayed to the bank teller. The detective in charge of the case required the suspect (over his and his counsel's objection) to apply black dye to his hair before appearing in the lineup, and he was positively identified. If you were representing this suspect, what constitutional objections would you raise to this procedure?

3. Armed with a valid warrant to search Ann Arbour's apartment for controlled substances, police arrived at the location and conducted an extensive search. After finding nothing, they took Arbour to City Hospital where, over her strong objection, she was subjected to a body cavity examination by a staff doctor. Unlawful drugs were removed and turned over to the police. May this evidence be offered against Arbour at trial?

4. Dizzy (from example 1) was stopped by officers because of her erratic driving, and observations of her slurred speech and alcohol breath confirmed their suspicions that she was under the influence. Even though Dizzy requested and consented to a Breathalyzer test, which was available at the station, she was required to submit to a blood test drawn by a technician. She now seeks to suppress the results. How should the court rule?

5. While driving home from soccer practice, Sarah Soccermom was stopped by Officer Brute for failing to secure her young children in seatbelts. Brute yelled at Sarah, jabbed his finger at her, and accused her of being a neglectful mom. When she was unable to produce her license and registration, explaining that her wallet had just been stolen, Brute called her a liar. He proceeded to place her under arrest in handcuffs. Fortunately a friend drove by and took charge of the children. Sarah was taken to the station, booked, and placed in a cell for an hour. Assuming there is statutory authorization for the arrest on the traffic violation, is the Fourth Amendment implicated by Brute's conduct?

EXPLANATIONS

1. The Fifth Amendment privilege applies only to evidence of a testimonial nature. A suspect may be compelled to display himself (as in a lineup) or display his coordination (as in a walk-a-straight-line sobriety test) without triggering the Fifth Amendment. Because the recitation of the alphabet compelled Dizzy to communicate in an incriminatory manner, that question is closer. While the Supreme Court has explicitly left the question open (see *Pennsylvania v. Muniz*, 496 U.S. 582, 603 n.17 (1990), and *Pennsylvania v. Bruder*, 488 U.S. 9, 11 n.3 (1988)), the import of its decisions suggests that the alphabet sobriety test is nontestimonial and thus does not implicate the Fifth Amendment. Several courts have so held. See *Stange v. Worden*, 756 F. Supp. 508 (D. Kan. 1991); *People v. Bugbee*, 201 Ill. App. 3d 952, 559 N.E.2d 554 (1990); *Jacquin v. Stenzil*, 886 F.2d 506 (2d Cir. 1989). But compare *Allred v. State*, 622 So. 2d 984 (Fla. 1993) (recitation of alphabet is a testimonial response within the protection of the self-incrimination clause of the Florida constitution).

2. Requiring a suspect to alter his appearance for purposes of identification arguably violates his right against compelled self-incrimination. The courts, however, have held otherwise. Reasoning that the Fifth Amendment applies only to testimonial and not physical evidence, it has been held that, for purposes of identification, suspects can be required to dye their hair, see *United States v. Brown*, 920 F.2d 1212 (5th Cir. 1991); shave, see *United States v. Valenzuela*, 722 F.2d 1431 (9th Cir. 1983); wear a wig, see *United States v. Murray*, 523 F.2d 489 (8th Cir. 1975); and wear a false goatee, see *United States v. Hammond*, 419 F.2d 166 (4th Cir. 1969). In none of these situations, the courts ruled, was the defendant compelled to testify against himself.

   It could be argued that the police action here "shocks the conscience" and thus violated the suspect's rights under the due process clause. See *Rochin v. California*, 342 U.S. 165 (1952). Such claims have not succeeded in similar cases. See *United States v. Brown*, supra, in which the court observed that requiring the suspect to dye his hair "reduce[d] the chance of misidentification" and, further, that "the defendant has no right to disguise himself at the time of the crime, then refuse to do so again to confound identification." 920 F.2d at 1215.

3. *Rochin v. California*, supra, *Schmerber v. California*, 384 U.S. 757 (1966), and *Winston v. Lee*, 470 U.S. 753 (1985), all underscore the special protection afforded to the body under the Fourth and Fourteenth Amendments. While searches of the type conducted in example 3 are not *always* unconstitutional, they require substantially more justification than simply a demonstration of probable cause to believe evidence of criminal activity will be found. In *Winston v. Lee*, supra, for example, the surgical procedure contemplated was deemed a substantial intrusion requiring a demonstration of special need for the evidence as well as particularized probable cause. Compare *United States v. Adekunle*, 980 F.2d 985 (5th Cir. 1992) (border search involving stomach x-rays of drug smuggler suspect and forced ingestion of laxative held not violative of Fourth Amendment because laxatives were found to be given for reasonable medical purposes; defendant was at significant risk of death if the drugs leaked from swallowed balloons; the court also noted that the laxatives, unlike the emetic in *Rochin*, did not cause the expulsion from the body of something that would not normally and routinely be expelled).

A Massachusetts case illustrates this approach weighing the magnitude of the bodily intrusion to determine an appropriate level of justification. In *Rodreques v. Furtado*, 410 Mass. 878 (1991), the police secured a warrant to search the subject's vagina for narcotics, the procedure to be conducted by a licensed physician at a designated hospital. The procedure was performed, and the subject subsequently brought a civil action alleging a violation of her state constitutional rights. In a decision applying the qualified immunity doctrine (a civil analogue to the good faith exception, see §7.3.3) to the police officer defendants, the Supreme Judicial Court took the opportunity to suggest special requirements for such searches in the future:

> It is difficult to imagine a more intrusive, humiliating, and demeaning search than the one conducted inside the plaintiff's body. In cases such as the present one, where the police seek to conduct a search inside the body of an individual, it may be appropriate to require a higher level of certainty than "mere" probable cause. If less than probable cause is required in cases where the level of intrusion is relatively low [citing *Terry v. Ohio*], it may be appropriate to require a higher level of certainty in cases involving extremely intrusive searches. Additionally, we think it sound

policy to require that, in the future, such a warrant be issued only by a person legally trained, i.e., a judge. . . . [W]e shall deem a warrant authorizing the search of a body cavity to be invalid unless issued by the authority of a judge, on a strong showing of particularized need supported by a high degree of probable cause.

410 Mass. at 888.

4. Where there are alternative methods available to determine the percentage of alcohol in the blood, the *Schmerber* justification for an immediate warrantless entry into the body disappears. Given the value placed upon one's bodily integrity, the insistence upon the intrusive blood test was unreasonable. See *Nelson v. City of Irvine*, 143 F.3d 1196 (9th Cir. 1998).

5. Even when there is probable cause for an arrest or search, it is now established that the manner in which the police conduct themselves may implicate the reasonableness clause of the Fourth Amendment. See *Tennessee v. Garner*, supra above. The extreme conduct of Brute here may fit that description. See also *Atwater v. City of Lago Vista*, 165 F3d 380 (5th Cir. 1999).

§11.3 Entrapment

Certain crimes such as drug offenses, prostitution, and bribery involve willing participants. In order to control these so-called victimless crimes where witnesses are unlikely to come forward, the government must resort to unusual means, sometimes even encouraging the commission of the offense itself. The use of undercover officers to engage prostitutes or purchase narcotics are examples of this approach. When the government crosses the line between investigating crime and creating it, however, the entrapment defense comes into play.

There are two basic sources of law for the entrapment defense. One is a traditional common-law defense that has been recognized by the Supreme Court in federal criminal cases (and by some state courts under their own common law); the other, which has not been explicitly adopted by the Supreme Court, is premised on the due process clause of the U.S. Constitution. Unlike the exclusionary remedy, which suppresses a particular item of evidence, the entrapment defense acts as a complete bar to the prosecution.

§11.3.1   The Common Law Defense

The entrapment defense can be traced back to *Sorrells v. United States*, 287 U.S. 435, 454 (1932), in which the defendant was indicted for possessing and selling whiskey in violation of the National Prohibition Act. An undercover federal agent, having gained the trust of the defendant, enticed Sorrells to provide him with liquor. Sorrells had initially resisted, but after several requests he sold liquor to the agent and was arrested. The Court, concluding that the evidence warranted a finding that the agent had instigated the offense, which Sorrells had no previous disposition to commit, held that the defense of entrapment should have been available to the defendant.

Elaborating on the defense in subsequent cases (see *Sherman v. United States*, 356 U.S. 369 (1958) and *United States v. Russell*, 411 U.S. 423 (1973)), the Court has emphasized that the key question is distinguishing "between the trap for the unwary innocent and the trap for the unwary criminal." The thrust of the defense is a focus on the predisposition of the defendant to commit a crime. The defense is available only where an agent of law enforcement procures the commission of a crime by an individual not otherwise predisposed to commit it. This "subjective" approach contrasts with an alternative that looks not at the propensities of the particular defendant but rather at the conduct of the government: Where law enforcement officers act in a manner likely to instigate a criminal offense, the defense would apply. This so-called objective approach, originally proposed by Justice Roberts in his concurring opinion in *Sorrells*, has never commanded a majority of the Court but is followed by several states and the American Law Institute (ALI) Model Penal Code.

In raising the entrapment defense, the defendant has the initial burden of showing government inducement. The burden then shifts to the government to show the defendant was ready and willing—predisposed—to commit the offense. Entrapment is generally a jury question, although on occasion judges have found entrapment as a matter of law.

In a refinement of the entrapment defense, the Court held in *Jacobson v. United States*, 503 U.S. 540 (1992), that the government must not only prove predisposition to defeat an entrapment defense, but must also demonstrate that the predisposition was not itself the product of government action. Jacobson claimed that his prosecution for receiving child pornography through the mail should be barred because the crime resulted from a 2 1/2-year campaign of correspondence by the government acting through fictitious organizations and a bogus pen pal. The Court agreed: "Where the Government has induced an individual to break the law and the defense of entrapment is at issue, . . . the prosecution must prove beyond reasonable doubt that the defendant was disposed to commit the criminal act *prior to* first being approached by Government agents" (emphasis added). To the four dissenters, the Court had in effect added a new requirement that the government must have a reasonable suspicion of illegal activity before engaging in a sting operation.

Remember that because the entrapment defense is based on common law and not constitutional grounds, the states are not compelled to adopt it.

§11.3.2   Due Process

In *United States v. Russell*, 411 U.S. 423, 431 (1973), the Court, while acknowledging that the entrapment defense was not based on the Constitution, nonetheless left open the possibility that "we may some day be presented with a situation in which the conduct of law enforcement agents is so outrageous that due process principles would absolutely bar the government from invoking judicial processes to obtain a conviction." The Court confronted the issue again in *Hampton v. United States*, 425 U.S. 484, 495 (1976). Defendant, convicted of distributing heroin, claimed that the narcotics he sold to undercover agents had been supplied to him by a government informant and thus argued, based on the statement in *Russell*, that he should be acquitted as a matter of law regardless of his predisposition to commit the crime. The Supreme Court disagreed. Writing for the plurality, Justice Rehnquist held that predisposition precluded *any* defense of entrapment. Five Justices kept alive the notion that under appropriate circumstances government conduct amounting to a violation of due process might preclude a prosecution even where predisposition had been shown.

Although the Supreme Court has yet to allow a due process defense in any case before it, some circuit court rulings have done so when the government conduct has been found outrageous. In *United States v. Twigg*, 588 F.2d 373 (3d Cir. 1978), one of the leading cases, a government informant proposed to the defendant that a laboratory to manufacture "speed" be set up and then supplied the equipment, raw materials, and laboratory site to accomplish that purpose. The informant maintained exclusive control over the manufacturing process because he was the only one who had the expertise to manufacture the drug. The court held that the government involvement reached "a demonstrable level of outrageousness" and thus the prosecution was barred.[5] In *United States v. Lard*, 734 F.2d 1290 (8th Cir. 1984), the court overturned the conviction based on entrapment as a matter of law, finding the defendant to be not predisposed. The court went on to state, however, that "apart from the entrapment defense, [the agent's] over-involvement in conceiving and contriving the crimes here approached being 'so outrageous that due process principles should bar the government from invoking judicial processes to obtain a conviction.' "

EXAMPLES

1. FBI agents posed as employees of Sheik Abdul, a fictional Mid-eastern oil billionaire, and spread the word that the sheik was interested in building a convention center complex in South Philadelphia but wanted to avoid problems with city approval and building regulations. The plan was designed to catch public officials inclined toward taking bribes. Several private meetings were arranged between the agents and two members of the city council whom the agents were informed by a well-connected local lawyer were "open to discussion on these kind of issues." At the meetings, held in the penthouse suite at a posh downtown hotel, the councillors were wined and dined while the agents described the convention center project, repeatedly emphasizing the sheik's insistence on expediting the project and avoiding red tape. The councillors remained silent until the third such meeting, at which they were asked, "So, can you guys grease this project along?" They then assured the agents that the city council would quickly approve the project and that the building inspectors "ain't gonna monkey with your project because they're gonna get the word from us to lay off." The agents asked, "What's this special consideration gonna cost the sheik?" and one city councillor responded, "30K." Thirty-thousand dollars was paid to each councillor, and one responded, "Gentlemen, you just bought yourself some true friendship." The entire transaction was videotaped.

---

5. Other circuit courts have disagreed. See *United States v. Santana*, 6 F.3d 1, 3–4 (1st Cir. 1993); *United States v. Milam*, 817 F.2d 1113, 1115 n.2 (4th Cir. 1987); *United States v. Beverly*, 723 F.2d 11, 12 (3d Cir. 1983).

The city councillors have been indicted by federal authorities for bribery. What are their chances of successfully raising the defenses of entrapment and violation of due process?

2. DEA agent Sam Stud, posing as an importer of illegal drugs, makes contact with Sarah Susceptible, an owner of several airplanes. Sarah is suspected of working for a Colombian drug organization. Sam proposes that she allow him to use her planes for purposes of drug smuggling. She initially refuses despite the offer of substantial money. Undaunted, Sam sends Sarah various gifts and gradually develops a sexual relationship with her. Ultimately Sarah allows her planes to be used for drug smuggling. The government has uncovered other evidence indicating Sarah was indeed a drug smuggler. This evidence would make it difficult for Sarah to use a common-law entrapment defense because the government could readily demonstrate that she was predisposed to commit the offense. Could Sarah claim that Sam's sexual advances constituted outrageous conduct violating due process?

EXPLANATIONS

1. To make out an entrapment defense, the councillors must show both that the crime was instigated by the government and that they were not predisposed to accepting bribes. Entrapment occurs only when the criminal conduct is the product of government activity, and when the defendant would not otherwise have engaged in the prohibited act. Where government agents merely afford opportunities for the commission of the offense, prosecution is not barred. In other words, the councillors must show that they were the victims of a trap for the unwary innocent. See *Sorrells v. United States*, 287 U.S. 435, 454 (1932); *Sherman v. United States*, 356 U.S. 369 (1958); *United States v. Russell*, 411 U.S. 423 (1973).

The initial burden is on the defendants to show that their act was induced by the government. More would need to be known about the nature of the conversations at the various meetings, but it appears at least arguable that there is sufficient evidence of inducement to submit the issue to the jury.

As in most entrapment cases, the crux of the matter is predisposition, an issue upon which the prosecution bears the burden of proof. *Jacobson v. United States*, 503 U.S. 540 (1992), mandates that, in order to defeat an entrapment defense, the government must not only prove predisposition but must also demonstrate that the predisposition was not itself the product of government action. At issue is the defendant's subjective state of mind. Factors relevant to the predisposition issue include the defendant's past involvement in similar criminal activity, the reasons law enforcement focused their attentions on him, the nature of the enticements offered, and the extent to which the defendant indicated reluctance and resisted efforts to engage him in criminal activity. Again, more information would be needed to analyze the prospects for an entrapment defense.

In the case on which this example is loosely based, *United States v. Jannotti*, 673 F.2d 578 (3d Cir. 1982) (the leading ABSCAM case), the trial judge granted defendants' motions for acquittal following their convictions by the jury, concluding there was entrapment as a matter of law because the large size of the bribes created too great a temptation even for an innocent suspect. The Court of Appeals reversed and ordered the jury's verdict reinstated. The Third Circuit observed: "Even if the dollar amount offered were relevant to disprove predisposition, a question which we do not decide, we find nothing in the record to support the district court's conclusion that in today's inflationary times, city councilmen would view sums of $30,000 as so large or generous as to overcome an official's natural reluctance to accept a bribe." 673 F.2d at 599.

Regarding the due process defense, defendants must demonstrate that the extent of government overreaching was so outrageous as to amount to a constitutional deprivation. In the view of five Justices in *Hampton v. United States*, 425 U.S. 484, 495 (1976) (two concurring with and three dissenting from the plurality's opinion), this defense is available even to predisposed defendants. Given the rare successful invocation of this defense, however, defendants will very likely fail, as they did in *Jannotti*. Police involvement in the crime would have to reach what Justice Powell described as "a demonstrable level of outrageousness before it could bar conviction." Unlike *United States v. Twigg*, 588 F.2d 373 (3d Cir. 1978), where prosecution was barred because the government initiated and actively participated in the establishment of a laboratory to produce an unlawful drug, the government in our example merely created a fictional set of circumstances, providing an opportunity for the defendants to agree to be bribed. See also *United States v. Mosley*, 965 F.2d 906, 909–910 (10th

Cir. 1992) (finding lack of outrageous government conduct where defendant approached agent for purpose of buying marijuana, and agent sold cocaine to defendant at allegedly low price); *United States v. Payne*, 962 F.2d 1228, 1231–1232 (6th Cir. 1992) (finding lack of outrageous government conduct where undercover agent posed as drug dealer trying to launder money, even though defendants were unknown when undercover operation commenced and government provided money to be laundered); *United States v. Tobias*, 662 F.2d 381, 386–387 (5th Cir. 1981) (finding lack of outrageous government conduct where DEA provided formula and some chemicals for manufacture of PCP, chemicals were not difficult to obtain, and DEA provided no financial aid for defendant's operation).

Predisposed defendants appear to be more successful in raising the due process defense in state court proceedings. In *People v. Isaacson*, 378 N.E.2d 78 (N.Y. 1978), the court dismissed the case based on a violation of due process where the police engaged in misconduct and trickery to secure a drug sale by a predisposed defendant. *Isaacson* introduces four factors to be considered when determining due process violations: 1) whether the police manufactured the crime that otherwise would not have occurred, or merely involved themselves in an ongoing criminal activity; 2) whether the police engaged in criminal or improper conduct repugnant to a sense of justice; 3) whether the defendant's reluctance to commit the crime is overcome by appeals to humanitarian instincts such as sympathy or past friendship, by temptation of exorbitant gain, or by persistent solicitation in the face of unwillingness; and 4) whether the record reveals simply a desire to obtain a conviction and not to prevent further crime or protect the populace. 378 N.E.2d at 83. In *State v. Hohensee*, 650 S.W.2d 268 (Mo. Ct. App. 1982), the court reversed a conviction based on a violation of due process where a predisposed defendant acted as a lookout during a burglary sponsored and operated by the police. See also *State v. Glosson*, 462 So. 2d 1082, 1085 (Fla. 1985) (finding violation of due process where informant was paid contingent fee conditioned on cooperation and testimony in criminal prosecutions against defendants); *Commonwealth v. Mathews*, 500 A.2d 853, 857 (Pa. Super. Ct. 1985) (finding violation of due process where police assisted in physically bringing property from out of town to manufacture methamphetamine in police vehicle, supplied money to purchase food and other supplies for defendants, supplied manual with proper formula to manufacture drug, and supplied governmental chemist to instruct defendants on detailed steps through formula); *Metcalf v. Florida*, 614 So. 2d 548 (Fla. Dist. Ct. App. 1993) (finding illegal manufacture of crack by law enforcement for reverse sting operation constituted violation of due process right of the Florida constitution).

Alternatively, in *Mondello v. State*, 843 P.2d 1152, 1160 (Wyo. 1992), the court denied the due process defense where the defendant, planning to buy only one ounce of cocaine for his personal use, was tricked by the government through continuous pursuance into buying two for the purpose of reselling the second. The court distinguished "the police conduct in tricking and cajoling" the defendant from *Twigg* on the basis that the defendant had already sought out the government informant to purchase cocaine; the defendant was not solicited. Id. In *Rivera v. State*, 846 P.2d 1, 3 (Wyo. 1993), the court denied the due process defense where the undercover officer not only fronted a portion of the purchase price the defendant paid for marijuana, but also offered the marijuana for lower than the going rate. In *State v. Pleasant*, 684 P.2d 761, 762–763 (Wash. Ct. App. 1984), the court, despite recognizing the enforcement techniques as "personally abhorrent," denied the due process defense where the officer and informant instigated the crime by posing as a construction company, reviewing the defendant's application, and, after writing "possible employment" on the application, asking the defendant if he could procure marijuana.

2. In seeking dismissal of the indictment, Sarah must establish that the government engaged in outrageous behavior in connection with the criminal act and that due process considerations bar a government prosecution. In *United States v. Cuervelo*, 949 F.2d 559 (2d Cir. 1991), the court addressed the question of outrageous government conduct in the context of a sexual relationship. The court suggested that the defendant must show that the government "consciously set out to use sex as a weapon in its investigatory arsenal," that the sexual relationship was initiated by the agent or allowed to continue to exist to achieve the government objective, and that the sexual activity occurred during the same period and was intertwined with the criminal activity. From the facts it appears that Sarah would have at least a chance of meeting the above criteria.

12

Technology and the Fourth Amendment

The courts have long struggled with issues concerning the application of the Fourth Amendment, adopted in 1791, to new technologies such as electronic surveillance. See *Katz v. United States* 389 U.S. 347 (1967), discussed in §3.2. This chapter touches on some of the emerging problems raised by ever-more sophisticated law enforcement at the start of the new millennium. How does the doctrine relating to an individual's privacy interest discussed in the previous chapters apply to the interception of wireless communications, to searches of computers, and to scientific techniques like thermal imaging and DNA testing?

Cordless and cellular phones are well on the way to replacing the phone booth used by Mr. Katz for his fateful conversation. Initially, because of the ease with which the radio waves emitted by cordless phones could be overheard or intercepted, it was held that there was no expectation of privacy and thus no Fourth Amendment applicability. See, e.g., *United States v. Smith*, 978 F.2d 171 (5th Cir. 1992). But courts like the Fifth Circuit recognized that evolution of the technology making cordless communications more private would render the caller's expectation of privacy more reasonable. Congress addressed the issue in 1994 by encompassing cordless phones in the provisions of the Electronic Communications Privacy Act, 18 U.S.C. §2510, which requires detailed warrants prior to interception and contains an exclusionary rule provision. (Cellular phones were covered by the Act.)

With the ubiquitous presence of computers and the movement of documents through cyberspace, what constraints apply when law enforcement officials seek to search someone's computer files or email?

We know that the Fourth Amendment generally requires a search warrant issued upon probable cause and describing with particularity the place to be searched and the items to be seized. (See Chapter 4.) But what does this mean when the search is of a computer's hard drive and files? How specific does the warrant have to be in describing the items to be seized from a computer? Does the plain view doctrine permit investigators to seize computer files relating to crimes other than those described in the warrant if they come across them in their search? Are deleted files entitled to any protection under the Fourth Amendment, or are they regarded as discarded trash outside the purview of the amendment? In executing a search warrant for a computer, what reasonableness requirements apply: How long may police hold a computer? Who has standing to challenge a computer search? What is the scope of a consensual search regarding a computer?

Consider the following scenario. Federal customs agents engaged in an investigation of child pornography are monitoring a "chat room" on the Internet. They view a number of images depicting children engaged in sexual activities and discover from the Internet service provider that the computer from which the images had been sent is owned by Sally Sleaze at an address in Brooklyn, New York. The agents submit this information on an affidavit for a search warrant, which the magistrate issues. The warrant authorizes a search for 1) any and all computer software and hardware, computer disks, and disk drives; and 2) any and all visual depictions, in any format or media, of all minors engaging in sexually explicit conduct.

Pursuant to the warrant the agents enter Sleaze's apartment and seize the computer together with dozens of floppy disks. Using a specialized utilities program that has an "undelete" function, the agents are able to recover hundreds of previously deleted images of child pornography, including the images the agents had originally viewed on the website. What issues would be raised when the prosecution offers these images into evidence at the trial of Sleaze for possession of child pornography?

Assuming that the agents' information constituted probable cause to search, the most likely strategy for the defense would be to focus on the particularity requirement. In the case upon which this scenario is based, *United States v. Upham*, 168 F.3d 532 (1st Cir. 1999), the defendant's argument that the authorization to search all computer hardware, software, disks, and disk drives was overly broad was rejected by the court, which concluded that it was the narrowest definable search reasonably likely to turn up the pornographic images sought.

But what if the defendant had *several* computers in his home or office, some of which had no connection to the alleged crime? And even if there is only one computer, investigators will not know what a file on it contains until they open it, which is likely to reveal documents beyond those particularly described in the warrant.

The First Circuit in *Upham* found solice in its observation that a "sufficient chance of finding some needles in the computer haystack was established by the probable-cause showing in the warrant application," and that "a search of a computer and co-located disks is not inherently more intrusive that the physical search of an entire house for a weapon or drugs." 168 F.3d at 535. But what about the files that had been deliberately deleted that the investigator is now able to recover and undelete? *Upham* rejected the government's analogy of deleted files to abandoned trash, à la *California v. Greenwood* 486 U.S. 35 (1988) (discussed in §3.2), in finding an expectation of privacy. Nonetheless the court upheld the search of trashed files as within the purview of the warrant and no different than a detective pasting together scraps of a torn-up ransom note when the warrant authorizes seizure of such note.

Given the storage capabilities of computers, they provide a tempting opportunity for exploratory rummaging, an evil that the Constitution's framers sought to address in the particularity clause of the Fourth Amendment. If the files on the disk are labeled with sufficient specificity so that there is a good likelihood that the evidence enumerated in the warrant will be found within those files, the search must be so confined, and extension *beyond* would violate the Fourth Amendment. See *United States v. Carey*, 172 F.3d 1268 (10th Cir. 1999). If, however, the files are not clearly labeled, the officer may open them as part of the search for items authorized by the warrant. In the process, he may come upon matters immediately apparent as evidence of other crimes. Since the officer is in a lawful vantage point, this extension of the search may be justified by the plain view doctrine. See §6.8.

To return to our hypothetical scenario, the scope of the investigators' search of Sleaze's computer for pornography is dependent upon the extent to which the contents of the files are readily apparent from their titles. If they cannot reasonably ascertain fom the labels what is contained inside, they may be permitted to "rummage" through the files and "seize" matters relating to other crimes that they come across inadvertently.

Another interesting problem arises with regard to "consensual" searches (discussed in §6.7). Such searches are often used by police to avoid the requirements of the Fourth Amendment. Does a consensual search of a residence include a search of the contents of computers found there? The scope of such searches is limited to what a reasonable police officer would understand from the conversation with the consenter. Oftentimes the officer states an objective for the search when asking for consent. If, for example, an officer asks for permission to search for an intruder or evidence of an entry, a search of a computer would clearly be beyond the permissible scope. See *United States v. Turner,* 169 F.3d 84 (1st Cir. 1999).

Perhaps the most serious threat to personal privacy arises from law enforcement's use of advanced technologies. Thermal imaging (discussed in §3.2) and gas chromotography can open an individual's home, and all the activities therein, to the prying eyes of the government. DNA testing can reveal the most intimate details about the subject—indeed, her very genetic makeup. A strand of hair or a discarded cigarette butt can be the source of information about an individual's medical condition, life expectancy, and family history. While these techniques may optimize the ability of police to solve crimes, they clearly come at the expense of the privacy rights that lie at the core of the Fourth Amendment. Drawing a balance here will be an early challenge for the courts in the twenty-first century.

APPENDIX

Checklist and Review Problems

Material in the previous chapters has of necessity been presented in a segmented fashion to permit the reader to explore the discrete issues involved in constitutional criminal procedure. Actual encounters between police and the citizen often raise a whole series of issues and may implicate more than one constitutional provision. It is the purpose of this appendix to "pull it all together" and demonstrate the interrelation between matters discussed in the text. We begin with a checklist, which is helpful in analyzing complex criminal procedure problems, and then return to our examples and explanations for a final review.

Checklist

I. **Search & Seizure and Arrest**
  A. Does the Fourth Amendment apply?
    1. Is the conduct governmental (as opposed to private)?
    2. Has a reasonable expectation of privacy been violated? [If "Yes" on both, move ahead.]
  B. Was the conduct justified?
    1. Identify the type of intrusion (for example, stop, arrest, frisk).
    2. Identify the level of justification required (for example, probable cause, reasonable suspicion, administrative).

C. Was a warrant required?
   1. For a search, did the conduct fall within an established exception to the warrant requirement? [See E, below.] If not, a warrant is required.
   2. For an arrest, did the arrest occur in a home or a public place? If the former, a warrant is required.
D. If a warrant was required, were the prerequisites for a valid warrant complied with?
   1. Was it issued by a neutral and detached magistrate?
   2. Was there probable cause supported by oath or affirmation?
   3. Did the warrant particularly describe the place to be searched and items to be seized?
E. If a warrant was not required, were the prerequisites for warrantless search and seizure complied with?
   1. Emergency exception
      a. Exigency
      b. Probable cause
   2. Search incident to arrest
      a. Lawful arrest (probable cause)
      b. Limited to grabbable space
   3. Automobile exception
      a. Mobile vehicle
      b. Probable cause
   4. Stop and frisk
      a. Reasonable suspicion to believe criminal activity is afoot
      b. Reasonable suspicion to believe subject is armed and dangerous
   5. Administrative and inventory searches
      a. Noncriminal purpose
      b. Limits on police discretion
   6. Consent
      a. Voluntary
      b. Third-party authority (actual or apparent)
   7. Plain view doctrine
      a. Lawful intrusion
      b. Item immediately apparent as contraband or evidence
F. If a violation occurred, does the exclusionary rule apply?
   1. Does the subject have standing?

      2. Is the proceeding a criminal trial or other proceeding in which the rule applies?

      3. Did the officers act in reasonable reliance upon a warrant (or otherwise act in good faith)?

      4. Is the evidence offered solely for impeachment?

  G. Does the derivative evidence doctrine apply?

      1. Is the item the fruit of the poisonous tree (but-for causation)?

      2. If so, does one of the exceptions apply?

         a. Did the taint become attenuated?

         b. Was there an independent source?

         c. Would the item have been discovered inevitably?

II. Interrogation and Confessions

  A. Was the confession obtained in violation of the due process clause?

      1. Was the confession involuntary under the totality-of-the-circumstances analysis?

      2. Was the confession the product of coercive police conduct?

  B. Was the confession obtained in violation of the *Miranda* doctrine?

      1. Was it obtained during custodial interrogation?

         a. Custody

         b. Interrogation (or its functional equivalent) [If "Yes" on both, go ahead.]

      2. Were adequate warnings provided?

      3. Was there a valid waiver?

         a. Knowing and intelligent

         b. Voluntary

      4. Did suspect invoke right to silence or to counsel?

         a. If right to silence, was right scrupulously honored?

         b. If right to counsel, did suspect initiate further communication?

      5. Do any of the exceptions apply?

         a. Public safety

         b. Impeachment

      6. Does the derivative evidence doctrine apply?

  C. Was the confession obtained in violation of the Sixth Amendment *Massiah* doctrine?

      1. Deliberate elicitation

2. Following the initiation of adversary criminal proceedings
3. Waiver

EXAMPLES
Search & Seizure

1. Sarge's Sporting Goods, concerned about shoplifting, has hired security guards to patrol the store and has also installed video cameras in areas not open to public view, including the three small dressing rooms in which customers can try on clothes. Signs in the store advise customers: "Shoplifters are prosecuted to the full extent of the law."

   While monitoring the video, security guard Karp observed a male customer enter a dressing room, shut the curtain, and begin pouring a white powder into a rolled dollar bill. Karp immediately telephoned the state police headquarters and reported her observations. Captain Trout advised her: "It sounds like coke. You keep watching him until we can get there. Don't let him go!" Karp continued to monitor the dressing room area and saw the customer sniffing the white powder.

   When the state police arrived moments later, the customer was just leaving the dressing room. Captain Trout grabbed the suspect, Drew, and proceeded to search his pockets, finding a vial of white powder (which was later determined to be cocaine). Trout took Drew's closed backpack and informed him that he was under arrest. The suspect was then taken to police headquarters and booked. Captain Trout opened the backpack and found a notebook that contained a list of names, addresses, amounts of "product," and dates of delivery.

   Trout reviewed the list and recognized the name of Kevin Crack, who had been previously identified by a reliable informant as involved in a narcotics ring in the area. Relating all this information in a sworn affidavit, the captain applied for a warrant to search Crack's home. The magistrate issued a warrant to search the home "for any and all items related to narcotics."

   State police officers executed the warrant four days after it was issued and discovered large amounts of cocaine, as well as scales and packaging materials used to distribute the substance. They also seized several weapons found in a closet in the basement. As the officers were leaving Crack's home, Crack pulled up in his jeep. When he saw the police, he gunned the vehicle in reverse and attempted to flee. The officers gave chase and pulled him over. Upon approaching the vehicle the officers smelled marijuana. Crack was placed under arrest. The officers then searched the jeep and found a large quantity of marijuana in the glove compartment.

At the upcoming trial of Drew and Crack for conspiracy to distribute narcotics, the prosecution proposes to use all the items seized, as well as the testimony of the security guard, against the defendants. Based on your Fourth Amendment analysis, what evidence is admissible against each defendant?

Interrogation and Confessions

2. Junior, a 17-year-old high school dropout, is a suspect in a series of burglaries in the Oak Square area. Uniformed officers Mutt and Jeff proceeded to his home, where they found him alone. The officers stated that they wanted to ask him some questions, and Junior responded that his parents were not at home and he did not want to talk to the officers until they returned. The officers asked if they could wait inside, and Junior agreed.

   While the three were seated in the living room, Mutt said to Jeff: "Somebody is going to do some jail time for these break-ins, and I'd hate to see this poor kid take the fall." Junior's face dropped, and he began to sweat profusely. He agonized for several moments with a pained expression on his face, and then stated: "I guess I've got no choice. Let me tell you about these jobs." Junior proceeded to implicate himself in the burglary ring.

   Will Junior's statement be admissible against him at trial?

3. Assume the same facts as in example 2, except that immediately after Junior's face dropped and he began sweating, Officer Mutt advised him of his *Miranda* rights. Junior responded that he wanted to talk to his parents before he said anything. Officer Jeff stated: "Look kid, we don't have to involve your folks in this mess. Just tell us about these jobs and we'll see to it that you get off as easily as possible."

   Junior then made the confession set out in example 2. Will it be admissible against him at trial?

The Whole Nine Yards

4. Nell Nigel parked her Saab Turbo in front of the bank and left her infant child, Charlie, in the backseat while she quickly ran in to cash a check. When she returned, the car was gone. She frantically asked a teenaged boy standing nearby if he had seen who

had driven away in the car, and the boy responded that "an old guy in red suspenders was hanging around the car, but I didn't see him get in." Nell telephoned the police and reported the boy's statement. Officers arrived on the scene but were unable to determine the whereabouts of the Saab or infant.

Six hours later, an anonymous caller told the desk sergeant at police headquarters that an old man sitting on a park bench near Duck Pond had just "ripped off a neat car but found a real surprise inside." Officers proceeded immediately to the pond and found an elderly man on the bench. As they approached him, the officers noticed he was wearing red suspenders. While his partner pointed his revolver at the man, Officer Booth asked him to identify himself, and he responded that he was Sam Soap. "OK, Soap, you better tell us where the baby is before you get into some real trouble," yelled Officer Booth. And Sam responded: "How was I supposed to know the kid was in the car when I took it?" Booth asked: "Where's the boy now?" Soap answered that the baby was at his apartment on Elm Street, but that he didn't know if he was still alive.

The officers grabbed Soap and sped in their cruiser to the apartment on Elm Street. When Soap refused to open the door for them, the officers broke it down. Inside they found Charlie, who was very cranky but otherwise okay. The officers took the baby and Soap back to the police station, where Soap was advised of his *Miranda* rights (and Charlie was reunited with his mother). Officer Booth learned that two other patrol officers had just been sent to Soap's apartment in response to a neighbor's call that an infant had been crying loudly all day.

Soap was taken into an interrogation room by Officer Booth and asked if he was ready to "tell the whole story." Soap responded that he wanted to talk to a lawyer first. Booth stated: "That's your business, but it's going to really slow things down." Soap was taken to a cell. An hour later Soap asked the guard whether they had found an attorney for him yet. The guard summoned Booth and when he arrived at Soap's cell, the suspect stated: "How long is it going to take to get me a lawyer?" Booth responded: "Why don't we just talk this thing through?" Appearing dejected and distraught, Soap said, "Yeah, alright," and proceeded to confess to the theft of the Saab and the taking of the infant. Based on the statement, the officers located the car on the outskirts of town; Soap's fingerprints were found on the steering wheel.

Which if any would be admissible against Soap at trial: His statement at Duck Pond; his statement in the jail cell; the discovery of Charlie in Soap's apartment; the discovery of the Saab and Soap's fingerprints?

EXPLANATIONS
Search & Seizure

1. The threshold question with regard to Drew is whether the Fourth Amendment is applicable at all. This depends upon whether there is both a) governmental action (see §3.2); and b) violation of the suspect's reasonable expectation of privacy (see §3.3).

   In the case of the encounter with Drew, it was a private security guard who made the initial observations on the video monitor. Private security personnel are generally not regarded as governmental actors for purposes of the Fourth Amendment. See example 1 in §3.1. Had there been no governmental involvement at all, the Fourth Amendment would not be implicated. The state police, however, did enter into the picture. Captain Trout advised (indeed ordered) the security guard to continue monitoring Drew and to hold him until the police arrived. Given this governmental encouragement and involvement, the requirement for public action is met. See §3.1.

   The amendment applies to the monitoring of the dressing room after the captain's order, however, only if that action constitutes a search. Did Drew have a "reasonable expectation of privacy" when he closed the curtain of the dressing room? Although there were signs warning customers of the strict enforcement of shoplifting laws, in all likelihood a court would rule that society recognizes a legitimate expectation of privacy in a closed dressing room. See §3.2. That would mean that the Fourth Amendment was applicable to the monitoring.

   What does the amendment require in this context? The crux of the protection against unreasonable search and seizure is the requirement for justification before a search is conducted. See Chapter 4. The observations occurring before the conduct became "governmental" might provide the justification for the monitoring that followed after the conversation with the captain. (Given the nature of the circumstances, the exigency exception would probably apply to excuse the absence of a warrant. See §6.2.) If there was not sufficient justification for the continued monitoring, however, that search would be in violation of the Fourth Amendment and the direct result, that is, the observations of the guard, would be subject to suppression.

The indirect results of the search would have to be analyzed under the derivative evidence doctrine. See §7.2. It would have to be determined, for example, if the notebook found in Drew's backpack was sufficiently attenuated from the monitoring so that the taint has dissipated. With regard to the search of Crack's home, which could be causally traced back to the initial encounter with Drew, we would have to determine whether the evidence was obtained from an independent source (that is, the information from the reliable informant) or would have inevitably been discovered in the usual course of events (as a result of the informant's tip). (For each subsequent unlawful action that occurs in our example, the derivative evidence "ripple effect" consequences must be similarly explored.)

Assuming Karp's initial observations provided sufficient justification for the continued monitoring, then the additional observations of Drew using the drug would probably constitute probable cause for arrest. See §4.1. A lawful arrest in a public place may be effected without a warrant if the officers have probable cause to believe the subject has committed or is committing a crime. See §5.5. The search of Drew's pockets (yielding the vial of cocaine) was within the proper scope of a search incident to an arrest. Note that although the search preceded announcement of the formal arrest, the existence of probable cause prior to the grabbing and search makes the latter lawful. See *Rawlings v. Kentucky*, 448 U.S. 98 (1980). The opening of Drew's backpack at the police station could not be justified as a search incident because it was not contemporaneous with the arrest. See §6.3.

The warrantless search of the backpack may be justified as an inventory search if it was conducted pursuant to established procedures for all suspects in custody. See §6.6. A suspicionless inspection of this kind is permitted because its purpose is administrative and not the collecting of evidence. See §4.5. Assuming that there was no provision for an inventory search, then search of this container would likely require a warrant. See discussion of *United States v. Chadwick* in §6.3.

This takes us to the warrant to search Crack's home. Drew could argue that the events leading up to the application for the warrant violated his Fourth Amendment rights, and that because information so obtained had been used to secure the warrant, it is tainted, and the items seized pursuant to it could not be used in evidence against him. (Crack would have no standing to complain about these actions against Drew and thus could not challenge the warrant on those grounds. See §7.3.1.) The derivative evidence question is complicated by the fact that in obtaining the warrant the police also relied on information from an independent source, the informant. If this other information was itself sufficient to constitute probable cause, then the warrant would be valid and the evidence seized could be used at trial.

In any event, the warrant could be lawfully issued only if the information contained in the affidavit established probable cause to believe seizeable items would be found at Crack's home. See §§4.1, 5.2. This requires us to analyze the reliability of the informant's tip that Crack was involved in a narcotics ring. Was there sufficient information set out from which the magistrate could reasonably conclude that 1) the informant was credible; and 2) that his conclusions had a solid basis in fact? On the first point we would need to know what the informant's prior track record has been; and on the second point we need to know on what his conclusions were based. In the absence of specifics, probable cause might be lacking even under the flexible *Illinois v. Gates* totality-of-the-circumstances standard: whether there is a "fair probability" that contraband or evidence of crime will be found in the place to be searched. The tip would have to be weighed together with the corroborating information developed by the police.

A "staleness" issue is also raised because the warrant was not executed until four days after its issuance. See §4.1, example 13. Given that the information known to the police is of an ongoing narcotics operation, however, this short delay is likely not to affect the existence of probable cause.

In addition to the probable cause requirement, a warrant must particularly describe the place to be searched and the items to be seized. See §5.2.3. An issue is raised here as to whether "any and all items related to narcotics" satisfies the latter requirement. The goal of limiting police discretion at the scene of the search was certainly jeopardized by the open-ended nature of this description.

Even if there were problems with the warrant either as to probable cause or particularity, the evidence seized may nonetheless be admissible because of the good faith exception to the exclusionary rule. We would have to address the issue of whether the officers acted reasonably in relying on the warrant. See §7.3.3.

While the seizure of scales and packaging materials together with the narcotics was authorized by the warrant, weapons found in the closet were also seized. The lawfulness of this seizure would depend upon the applicability of the plain view doctrine. See §6.8. Because the items were found while the officers were lawfully on the premises and searching within the proper confines of a search for narcotics, and the items were immediately apparent as either contraband or evidence of crime, they could lawfully be seized.

Finally, the stop of Crack's car as he was fleeing was probably justified by reasonable suspicion given all the information known to the officers at the time. See §§4.2–4.4. The detection of the odor of marijuana likely provided the police with probable cause both to arrest him and to search his jeep for items related to narcotics activity under the automobile exception. See §6.4. Because the search was limited to the interior of the vehicle, it could also be justified under the search incident to the arrest exception. See §6.3.

Interrogation and Confessions

2. In answering this question, we must keep in mind the three overlapping constitutional approaches to interrogation and confessions: due process voluntariness, *Miranda*, and *Massiah*.

First, a statement that is the product of coercive police action and not the voluntary choice of the suspect is inadmissible for all purposes under the due process clause of the Fifth and Fourteenth Amendments. See Chapter 8. The officers' conduct with regard to Junior was arguably coercive, but probably not sufficiently so to satisfy the threshold coercion requirement of *Colorado v. Connelly*. If it is determined that he was subjected to coercion, we would have to determine whether the conduct overcame Junior's free will sufficiently to compel the statement. The structure of this inquiry would be the totality-of-the-circumstances approach weighing Junior's particular vulnerabilities (for example, lack of education, age) and the circumstances of the interrogation (for example, absence of parents, two police officers).

Second, if Junior was subjected to custodial interrogation then he was entitled to the *Miranda* protections, most notably the warnings. Because he received no warnings, the statement would be inadmissible (except to impeach his testimony if he took the stand, see §9.3.2). See Chapter 9.

Was Junior in custody? Even though he was not under arrest or in the police station, he may nonetheless be deemed in custody if a reasonable person in his situation would have believed himself not free to leave. See §9.2.1. Was Junior subjected to interrogation? Even though there was no formal questioning, if the conduct of the officers was the functional equivalent of interrogation, then the *Miranda* doctrine is applicable. See §9.2.2. The inquiry is whether the words or actions of the police were such that they should have reasonably foreseen the likelihood of eliciting an incriminating response. Here we must take into account the limitations and susceptibilities of Junior that were known to the officers at the time.

Third, the *Massiah* doctrine renders statements inadmissible when they are deliberately elicited from the suspect in the absence of counsel, provided that the Sixth Amendment right to counsel is triggered. This occurs only when adversary judicial proceedings have been initiated. See Chapter 10. Thus, even if Junior could establish that the police set out to evoke his statement, he could not take advantage of *Massiah*. If this encounter had occurred subsequent to a grand jury indictment or an arraignment following arrest, then the actions of the police would be scrutinized under *Massiah*.

3. Assuming that Junior was subjected to custodial interrogation here (the custody question involves the same analysis as example 2, but the direct question asked here clearly constitutes interrogation), the issue becomes one of waiver. We must begin the analysis, however, with the question of whether Junior invoked either his right to silence or to counsel when he responded that he wanted to talk to his parents before saying anything. See §9.2.5. If this amounted to an exercise of the right to silence, then interrogation should have been terminated and resumed only after Junior's right had been scrupulously honored. If it was a request for counsel, then interrogation should have been terminated until Junior was either provided counsel or initiated further conversation.

In addition to these requirements, Junior's confession could be admitted only after the prosecution establishes that he made a knowing, intelligent, and voluntary waiver. See §9.2.4. This showing would be problematic because of Junior's age and lack of education. Moreover, the officer's inducement ("we'll go easier on you") may undercut the voluntariness of the waiver and even may constitute sufficient coercion to implicate due process concerns. See Chapter 8.

The Whole Nine Yards

4. We must identify the possible violations of constitutional rights and then trace the exclusionary rule ripple effects of each.

   Beginning with the initial encounter at Duck Pond, did a seizure occur that would implicate the Fourth Amendment and thus require a level of justification? While not all street encounters constitute seizures, Soap arguably was subjected to one when the officers asked him to identify himself at gunpoint. The test for seizure is whether a reasonable person under the circumstances would have believed himself free to leave. See §4.3. If this confrontation amounted to a stop, then it had to be justified by reasonable suspicion that Soap was involved in criminal activity. While this requires a particularized and reliable basis in fact, the statement of the teenager at the crime scene together with the anonymous call probably suffice to justify the brief detention. See §4.2. If not, however, the stop was unlawful, and the statement made by Soap would be inadmissible as its direct result.

   It should also be noted that the confrontation with Soap in which the officer pointed his revolver at him arguably constituted an intrusion equivalent to a full arrest. See §4.3. If this were the case, probable cause would be required. See §4.1. Although *Illinois v. Gates* has established a flexible standard, on the facts here it is unlikely that probable cause to arrest existed.

   How far would the taint of the unlawful stop (or arrest) travel? Arguably the discovery of the baby should be suppressed because it was achieved by exploiting Soap's statement directing the officers to his apartment. See §7.2. On the other hand, the entry into the apartment was somewhat removed from the initial stop (separated by time and by Soap's statement), so it could be said that the taint had dissipated. Moreover, there is an argument that the infant would have inevitably been discovered anyway by the officers sent in response to the neighbor's call about the crying infant.

   In addition, if the encounter at Duck Pond amounted to custodial interrogation, then Soap's statement (and to a limited extent, the fruits of that statement, see §9.3.3) would be subject to suppression on *Miranda* grounds. There was interrogation when Officer Booth directed at Soap two questions that did not constitute general, on-the-scene fact gathering. See §9.2.2. Moreover, the simultaneous pointing of the gun at the suspect may have put him in custody. See §9.2.1. In the absence of the warnings, his statement may be inadmissible. Even if *Miranda* is applicable here, it is arguable that the public safety exception should apply because of the compelling need to find the missing infant as quickly as possible. See §9.3.1.

When the officers sped off in the cruiser with Soap, he was clearly under arrest, requiring probable cause. See §4.1. Given all the information known to them at that time (including Soap's incriminatory statement), that standard appears to have been met. It would also appear that the police had probable cause to search his home for the missing boy. Entry into a home (without consent) generally requires a warrant, but these circumstances are an excellent candidate for application of the emergency exception. See §6.2. The discovery of Charlie thus does not appear to have been the direct result of an unlawful search. Note that it may have been the indirect result of an earlier illegality (that is, the stop) and thus subject to suppression under the derivative evidence doctrine.

At the station house, Soap clearly invoked his right to counsel following the *Miranda* warnings. The question thus becomes whether the subsequent questioning in the jail cell was proper. Once the right to counsel is invoked, the suspect may not be interrogated until counsel is provided or the suspect himself initiates further communication. See §9.2.5. Did Soap initiate further communication when he inquired as to the appointment of counsel? Although the Court has adopted a broad definition of "initiation" (including *Bradshaw*'s "What is going to happen to me now?"), Soap's inquiry here underscored his desire to have the advice of counsel and should not be deemed as license to resume questioning. His confession should therefore be suppressed (although it may be introduced for impeachment if he takes the stand, see §9.3.2).

The discovery of the Saab resulted from the information provided in the confession, raising the issue as to whether it must be suppressed together with the fingerprint evidence. Even if his statement is found to be a violation of *Miranda*, the indirect fruits of that statement are not necessarily inadmissible. See §9.3.3. The situation would be different, however, if it were determined that Soap's jail cell confession was the involuntary product of police coercion. It is arguable that Officer Booth's treatment of the elderly suspect constituted coercive conduct that played upon his vulnerable condition, in which case his confession (and its fruits) would be inadmissible for all purposes. See Chapter 8. A finding of a due process violation in these circumstances, however, is unlikely.

If there was further information indicating that the Saab would have been discovered eventually (for example, it was abandoned in an illegal parking space), the inevitable discovery exception to the derivative evidence doctrine might apply.

Assuming that the Saab is not deemed the fruit of the poisonous tree, then the search of the Saab and the discovery of the fingerprints would likely be lawful because the officers had sufficient information to constitute probable cause to search the vehicle. The automobile exception to the warrant requirement would thus apply. See §6.4.

Table of Supreme Court Cases

Index